Studies in British Art

The Romantic Interior

THE BRITISH COLLECTOR AT HOME
1750–1850

Clive Wainwright

Published for the
Paul Mellon Centre for Studies in British Art by
Yale University Press
New Haven and London · 1989

FOR MY PARENTS

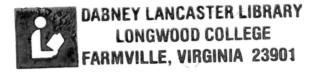
Designed by Faith Brabenec Hart
Filmset in Linotron Bembo by Best-set Typesetter Ltd, Hong Kong
Printed in Hong Kong by South Sea International Press Ltd

Library of Congress Cataloging-in-Publication Data

Wainwright, Clive.
    The romantic interior: the British collector at home, 1750–1850/
by Clive Wainwright.
        p.   cm.
    Includes index.
    ISBN 0-300-04225-6
    1. Interior decoration—England—History—18th century.
2. Interior decoration—England—History—19th century.   3. Art,
Medieval.   4. Art, Renaissance.   5. Art—Collectors and collecting—
England.   I. Title.
NK2043.A1W35   1990
747′.888′094109033—dc20   89-33705
                                                                      CIP

ACKNOWLEDGEMENTS

During the twenty years of research that preceded the completion of this book I have been fortunate to have been given unstinting help and advice by a very wide range of librarians, archivists, curators, antiquaries and other scholars. It is thus likely, I am afraid, that some of these will by accident be left out of the list that follows, and to them I apologize.

At Abbotsford Patricia Maxwell-Scott and the late Dr James Corson gave me every help and encouragement. At the National Library of Scotland my research on the Scott papers was made a pleasure by the help given by Alan Bell, Iain Gordon Brown and James Ritchie. In Scotland Anthony Dixon, Ian Gow, David Learmont, James Macaulay, Avril Osborn, Bob Peacock and the late John Pinkerton have all contributed in different ways.

At Charlecote Lady Alice and Sir Edmund Fairfax Lucy, C. Routh, Mr and Mrs Pattison, Anthony Mitchell and Geoffrey Haworth have all helped me in my investigation of that fascinating house.

I have gained more help than I can describe from the daily contact over many years with my colleagues past and present at the Victoria & Albert Museum. They by the standards of scholarship they set and by their knowledge of the objects they look after — some few of which I will illustrate — have been an unfailing inspiration and source of expertise for me.

I must particularly single out Michael Archer, Malcolm Baker, Claude Blair, Anthony Burton, Shirley Bury, Stephen Calloway, Marian Campbell, Frances Collard, Joe Earle, Phillipa Glanville, John Hardy, John Harthan, Michael Holmes, Simon Jervis, Len Joyce, Rose Kerr, Lionel Lambourne, Ronald Lightbown, Tom Macrobert, John Murdoch, Anthony North, Ron Parkinson, Sir John Pope-Hennessy, Anthony Radcliffe, Charles Saumarez-Smith, Robert Skelton, Anna Somers-Cocks, Michael Snodin, Sir Roy Strong, Sue Stronge, Peter Thornton, Charles Truman, Rowan Watson, Lisa White and Paul Williamson, and for help and advice with photography, Isobel Sinden and Ken Jackson.

I was particularly fortunate to have the criticism and advice of Professors Joseph Mordaunt Crook, John Wilton-Ely and William Vaughan in the writing of the Ph.D. thesis which formed the basis of this book.

Others from this country and abroad who have helped me are Megan Aldrich, William Allan, Patricia Astley Cooper, Clive Aslet, Reinier Baarsen, Sir Henry Bedingfeld, David Beevers, Sir Geoffrey de Bellaigue, Marcus Binney, Frances Carey, John Cherry, Hermine Chivian Cobb, John Cornforth, Camilla Costello, Stephen Croad, William Duck, Michael Farr, Charlotte Gere, Georg Himmelheber, John Hopkins, William Johnston, Jill Lever, George and Martin Levy, Jules Lubbock, Anne Lyles, Arthur Magregor, Michael McCarthy, John McKee, the Duke of Norfolk, David Parker, Margaret Richardson, Jane and Hugh Roberts, Sarah Rodger, Tim Rogers, John Martin Robinson, Andrew Saint, Rosalind Savill,

Timothy Stevens, Sheena Stoddard, Hugh Thompson, Robert Thorne, Sir Francis Watson, Sir George White, Stephen Wildman, Tim Wilson, Lucy Wood and Pamela Wood.

Nina James gave invaluable help in preparing the manuscript for publication. The Landmark Trust kindly provided a suitably antiquarian tower in which to write the concluding chapter.

My thanks also go to John Nicoll of Yale University Press for encouraging me over the years to turn my research into a book and to Faith Hart for her sensitive editing of the manuscript.

Finally, but most important of all, without the constant advice, support and encouragement of Jane my wife this work would never have been begun let alone completed.

CONTENTS

INTRODUCTION

The 'Romantic Interior' is not a stylistic term, but one that is defined in part by the character of the objects it contains and in part by the motives of those who create these interiors. These interiors could in theory contain either classical, mediaeval or Renaissance works of art and antiquities. Their creators need only acquire a range of objects that date from an earlier period. As I shall confine myself to the eighteenth and nineteenth centuries, the objects with which I shall be concerned will mainly date from before 1700. A Romantic Interior created today could well contain Georgian, Victorian and early twentieth-century objects — all would seem suitably ancient to our late twentieth-century eyes. It is crucial for such interiors that the objects they contain are ancient, but these need not go together either stylistically, or in terms of date or indeed nationality.

Before the 1830s Romantic Interiors were the exception rather than the rule, but as the nineteenth century progressed they became more and more common. Today many people prefer not to furnish their interiors with contemporary objects, choosing instead either to collect antiques themselves or to employ an interior decorator to do so on their behalf. In the eighteenth century, however, it was usual in grand houses to have interiors, fittings and furnishings designed by an architect or upholsterer so that there was a coherent style throughout.

Of course, in the case of a particularly interested and imaginative patron who was already a collector — or who had inherited ancient family objects — and a sensitive architect, works of art and antiquities were often incorporated into interiors that were filled largely with modern objects. Even in these cases the overwhelming character would still have been one of modernity, with new carpets, curtains, wallpapers, light fittings and furniture. In 1750, for instance, the style of these furnishings could have been neo-classical, Rococo, Chinese or Gothic, but all newly manufactured and thus new in appearance.

As early as the 1750s when one has classified interiors into one or another of these stylistic categories there are a few examples that fall outside them. These are the Romantic Interiors, which I shall examine in detail. By 1850 so numerous are they that they have become almost commonplace and indeed form a significant minority set to grow to outnumber all other types of interiors by the late twentieth century. I have therefore chosen to examine the century 1750 to 1850 to chart and explain the rise in popularity of this mode of furnishing interiors in Britain.

I shall not, except in passing, deal with the paintings that in many cases formed such a prominent part in these interiors or in the collecting of paintings by the collectors under scrutiny. The role of paintings in such interiors will be clearly seen in many of my illustrations; also, the history of the collecting of Old Master paintings has been reasonably well covered in print.

Having stressed that the term 'Romantic Interior' is not a stylistic one, I have largely confined myself to those that contained mediaeval and Renaissance objects. It would be possible to carry out a study for a similar period of time concentrating only on interiors furnished with classical objects, though for such interiors there would be no classical furniture available: none survives.

The general stylistic character of the interiors I shall study was described by Richard Norman Shaw and his generation as 'Old English', though who coined the term is unknown. Its use here would seem to preclude Welsh and Scottish interiors. But, as we shall see, Sir Walter Scott considered that Abbotsford was in the 'Old Scotch' style, and certainly many of the more minor antiquarian interiors were very local in character. I consider that most of the interiors I shall discuss are manifestations of the Gothic Revival and form a vital element in that international enthusiasm for the mediaeval world which was such an important part of the Romantic Movement in art and literature.

The Department of Furniture and Woodwork at the Victoria & Albert Museum was given responsibility for the museum's collections of Victorian furniture in 1968, the year in which I joined the department. In the decade that followed, the wide stylistic range of Victorian furniture and the interiors created for it were subjected to careful scrutiny and research, as were those of the period around 1800 which immediately preceded them. The museum took the lead in this research, its collections and archives becoming the focus for others working in the field. It was also deeply involved in the research leading up to and following from the seminal Council of Europe exhibition of 1972 devoted to neo-classicism, which examined anew eighteenth-century interiors in this style.

Then the research for the exhibition devoted to the Rococo style planned for the mid-1970s — finally staged in 1985 — subjected interiors in that style to new scrutiny. In 1974 the epoch-making exhibition 'The Destruction of the English Country House', besides arousing public anger at such wanton destruction, focussed attention upon the history and the surviving documentation of both destroyed and surviving houses.

During the 1970s the whole field of British architecture and interiors was transformed by the research and publications of the pioneering scholars of that decade — Marcus Binney, Howard Colvin, John Cornforth, J. Mordaunt Crook, Mark Girouard, John Harris, Peter Thornton and Roy Strong. Thus by the later 1970s the stylistic classification of interiors of the eighteenth and nineteenth centuries had reached a new level of sophistication. It was, however, obvious that, as is so often the case in other disciplines, when one has classified and then sub-divided a subject into neat categories, some few examples remain outside one's system. These examples, I suggest, form a class of 'Romantic Interiors'.

It is arguable that, because by their very nature such interiors are each so singular and indeed unique, they should each be in a class of one, their own. They do, however, have some common characteristics that may outweigh their differences. Whilst they may contain some modern objects, they take their especial character from the ancient objects brought together from different periods, countries and stylistic traditions to furnish them out. The overwhelming stylistic impression gained by the visitor to any such interior might be of Britain in the Middle Ages or of France in the reign of Louis XIV — or, indeed, as at Goodrich, of ancient Asia in the 'Asiatic Armoury' or of ancient Greece in the 'Greek Room'.

Such interiors are in marked contrast to a neo-classical room by Adam, a Gothic Revival room by Pugin or a neo-Norman room by Hopper, all of which, though in an ancient style, are furnished with modern objects designed in the ancient style, not with objects in themselves ancient. As we shall see in the following chapters, the furnishings of many Romantic Interiors span a far wider gamut of period and style than those furnished with modern objects merely in one *historical style*.

It is interesting that once one has become familiar with the concept and the characteristics of Romantic Interiors one's view of other interiors changes. The number of interiors furnished exclusively with modern objects at the time of their creation is smaller than one may think. Whereas an Adam interior is usually stylistically pure, in that the objects within it are classical, they may not all be neo-classical; often an ancient Etruscan vase or an ancient Roman torso helps to adorn the room. At Hopper's Penrhyn Castle, which was totally modern and which has modern Norman-style furniture, Willement was employed to glaze several windows with ancient stained glass.

The issue is, of course, further complicated by the passage of time, for even if an interior was furnished in the eighteenth century totally with modern objects in only one style, if it has been continuously lived in until today the 'accretion syndrome' — as it has been called — will often have transformed it into something approaching a Romantic Interior in appearance. It may well be that if one studied and classified only interiors created in the past, but presently lived in, they would all to some degree fall into this category. I have, however, chosen to discuss interiors as they were during the lifetime of their creators.

I will frequently stress the importance of the antiquarian motives of the collectors who were the impresarios who created these interiors. Their individual views of the past and the character of the interiors which they created to house its artefacts are very diverse. I have selected five houses which contain sets of Romantic Interiors suitable for close analysis: Strawberry Hill (1747–96), Horace Walpole's suburban retreat on the western outskirts of London; Fonthill Abbey (1796–1822) in Wiltshire, built for William Beckford; Abbotsford enlarged (1816–26) for Sir Walter Scott; Charlecote Park re-edified (1828–57) by George and Mary Elizabeth Lucy; Goodrich Court (1829–35) in Herefordshire, built for Sir Samuel Rush Meyrick. These interiors are singled out for full analysis for particular reasons.

First, I wished to cover thoroughly the years 1750–1850 and not have one example following after the other, but to overlap them and thus allow direct comparison. Scott started collecting before Walpole died and before Beckford had started to build Fonthill, and the Lucys had begun to re-edify Charlecote several years before Meyrick started to build Goodrich.

Second, these case studies also represent a wide range of possibilities. Fonthill and Goodrich were completely new buildings. Strawberry Hill and Abbotsford began as modest houses which were added to and extended to such a degree that the original structures were completely subsumed into the new. Charlecote was a large, ancient and architecturally important building which, though added to externally and altered internally, retained its original character. Dozens of buildings large and small of the eighteenth and nineteenth centuries which contain — or contained — Romantic Interiors fall into one or other of these three groups.

Third, to allow a full discussion of their creation, full documentation in the form of contemporary sources and extensive illustrations of the interiors and the objects which they contained had to exist. Luckily with Abbotsford and Charlecote not only do they exist intact, but the very extensive surviving documentation allows their present state to be very closely compared with their state when originally created.

The interiors were chosen first. Thus their creators were not selected to represent a specific social class who were particularly active in the creation of Romantic Interiors. None was, as it happens, from an ancient aristocratic family. Walpole, though he inherited the title of Lord Orford late in life, was the son of a Whig Prime Minister. Beckford was a colonial; he would probably have been granted a peerage were it not for his social indiscretions. Scott and Meyrick were practicing lawyers from middle-class families who both earned their baronetcies. Lucy was county, his family having been long established in Warwickshire. Only Beckford of them all was truly wealthy.

There were, however, many fabulously wealthy aristocrats who created important Romantic Interiors: for instance, the Duke of Northumberland at Alnwick, the Earl of Shrewsbury at Alton Towers, the Duke of Norfolk at Arundel, the Earl of

Cholmondeley at Cholmondeley Castle, Lord Stuart de Rothesay at Highcliffe and the Earl of Stafford at Costessy. The Romantic Interiors in such grand seats tend to be well documented and represented by surviving illustrations. Many more modest rooms in town houses of middle-class collectors are not documented and were not photographed or painted. Sometimes a sale catalogue of the collection that once adorned them survives as partial evidence, several of the collectors in both these categories make brief appearances in later chapters.

I first became deeply interested in this subject when I spent a week in the icy December of 1969 searching through the muniments at Charlecote for evidence of which objects the Lucys had purchased from the Fonthill sale. During the following two decades the research for publications including those on Fonthill, Charlecote and Abbotsford has proceeded and this book has grown from this research.

The subject of the Romantic Interior is a complex one and the range of relevant manuscript and printed sources is very large. So extensive are these sources that I have not included a bibliography, but my footnotes will I hope provide the grist for several mills. I intend to publish more on this subject in the future and would therefore welcome information correcting any errors and suggesting new avenues for investigation. I would also be grateful to be informed of the present whereabouts of the objects I have illustrated but whose locations are unknown to me.

1

PRECEDENTS

He doth not so adore the Ancients as to despise the Modern.
Grant them but dwarfs, yet stand they on giants shoulders, and
may see the further.   Thomas Fuller

Although it is possible to imagine a Romantic or Antiquarian Interior filled with classical objects, the terms 'antiquary' and 'antiquarian' have, since the seventeenth century, been more often associated with an interest in mediaeval or at least British antiquities than with those of ancient Greece and Rome. In the eighteenth century the terms 'virtuoso' and 'connoisseur', whilst in some ways synonymous with the term 'antiquary', were most often used to describe a person interested in classical antiquities.

The Society of Antiquaries of London was the focus for those with antiquarian interests from its foundation in 1717, as it had in fact been since it began informal meetings in 1707. The Society published in 1717 a broadside: 'The Society of Antiquaries, London, January the first 1717. Agreed to meet one evening every week to cultivate the knowledge of ANTIQUITIES OF ENGLAND.'[1] Thus, the prime interest of the Society and its fellows was British antiquities, though by 1783 Horace Walpole had resigned as a fellow to join the newly formed Society of Antiquaries of Scotland,[2] partly in protest at the English society's concerning itself with Roman remains, rather than concentrating on the study of British antiquities. Walpole wrote on 12 May 1783 to the Earl of Buchan, the prime mover of the Scottish society, that

> The pursuit of national antiquities has rarely been an object, I believe, with any university . . . I have often thought the English Society of Antiquaries have gone out of their way when they meddled with Roman remains, especially not discovered within our island. Were I to speak out, I should own that I hold most relics of the Romans, that have been found in Britain, of little consequence, unless relating to such Emperors as visited us. Provincial armies stationed in so remote and barbarous a quarter as we were then, acted little, produced little worth being remembered.[3]

Yet even Walpole was to mix Roman antiquities with his British antiquities in the Romantic Interiors he created at Strawberry Hill.

The antiquary, as a character in the literature of the seventeenth and eighteenth centuries, was often portrayed as an eccentric lover and collector of objects rather for their age and historical associations than for any aesthetic merit. This is in marked contrast to the gentlemanly connoisseur who after returning from the Grand Tour loaded with classical antiquities joined the Society of Dilettanti rather than the Society of Antiquaries. John Earle, Bishop of Salisbury, as early as 1628 published his oft-quoted description of an antiquary.

> He is one that hath that unnatural disease to be enamoured of old age and wrinkles, and loves all things — as a Dutchman do cheese, — the better for being mouldy and worm-eaten . . . A great admirer he is of the rust of old monuments . . . He will go you for forty miles to see a saint's well or a ruined abbey . . . His

estate consists much in shekels, and Roman coins ... He loves no library, but where there are more spiders volumes than authors ... His very attire is that which is the eldest out of fashion and his hat is as antient as the tower of Babel.[4]

Salisbury Cathedral seems to have been a hotbed of antiquarian thought at this time, for in 1648 Thomas Fuller, Prebendary of the Cathedral and himself a prominent antiquary and scholar, took a more charitable view of the characteristics of an antiquary: 'Others, for fear travellers should take no notice that that skill in Antiquity dwells in such an head, hang out an ancient hat for the sign, or use some obsolete garb in their garments, gestures, or discourse. He doth not so adore the Ancients as to despise the Modern. Grant them but dwarfs, yet stand they on giants shoulders, and may see the further. Sure champions of Truth followed in the rere, as ever march'd in the front.'[5]

Though intended as a caricature, this view of the antiquary as eccentric can only have been reinforced by the appearance and life-style of certain of the early members of the Society of Antiquaries. Browne Willis, the celebrated topographer who died in 1760, was described by his fellow antiquary William Cole: 'he had more the appearance of a mumping beggar than a gentleman ... dressed in an old slouched hat, more brown than black, a weather-beaten large wig, three or four old fashioned coats, all tied round by a leathern belt, and over all an old blue cloak ... he had new made when he was elected member for the town of Buckingham, about 1707'.[6]

Sadly we have no record of the interiors Willis created for his collection in his house at Whaddon in Buckinghamshire.[7] Later we will encounter Jonathan Oldbuck, a Scottish antiquary very much in the mould of Earle's. Of the five creators of the antiquarian interiors which together make up this study — namely, Walpole, Beckford, Scott, Meyrick and Lucy — Walpole and Meyrick were members of the Society of Antiquaries of London whilst Walpole and Scott were members of the Scottish Society. None of them remotely resembled the caricature antiquary described.

The crucial figure in the creation of these Romantic Interiors is the patron, the collector of the multifarious objects which go to clothe the walls and fill or indeed overfill his rooms. Over and over again in this study it will be the patron rather than his architects or upholsterers who will be the impresario responsible for organizing the complex process of creating such interiors. The term 'creator' is appropriate in connection with these interiors, for they were often created over many years by the slow accretion of objects rather than designed on a drawing board in an architect's office. The more usual Georgian and Victorian interiors designed down to the last door knob in the office of Kent, Adam, Holland, Pugin or Burges could be completed in a matter of months, the time taken depending upon the efficiency of the firms and craftsmen manufacturing and installing the furniture, textiles, metal-work and so on.

In these cases it is wholly appropriate that the architects should be given the credit, but in the houses with which I shall deal a succession of architects, professional and amateur, antiquarian friends of the patron, and antique dealers were all manipulated and in some cases played off one against the other by collectors of strong character like Scott or Beckford. Only these patrons had the time, the motivation and the energy to see the whole process through the long years required to create their ideal environment.

In some cases the patrons had a vision of the completed interiors, but in others, their evolution was more *ad hoc*. Indeed, though several of the most celebrated names in British architecture will make their appearance, the auctioneers and the antiquities brokers play a more crucial role, for they sought out and sold to the patron the objects and architectural fragments used to create these singular interiors.

The central role of the patron as the person who chose the architects, and the brokers, and decided which antiquities to use can be illustrated by two quotations.

In 1634 Peacham in *The Compleat Gentleman* laid down the various accomplishments required of a gentleman, including such diverse talents as Cosmography, Drawing, Painting, Exercise of the Body, Fishing, and Antiquities. Antiquities, he said, should be the pursuit of 'all ingenious Gentlemen, who are the onely men that imploy Poets, Painters and Architects, if they be not all these themselves. And if they be not able to judge of their workes, they well deserve to be couzened.'[8]

In 1731 Pope in his 'Moral Epistle' to the Earl of Burlington described Burlington's role as patron and arbiter of taste. Plate 1, which shows Burlington[9] taking his ease while dealers and artists crowd at his feet jostling his architect out of the way, illustrates Pope's verse:

> Is it less strange, the Prodigal should wast
> His wealth, to purchases what he ne'er can taste?
> Nor for himself he sees, or hears, or eats;
> Artists must chuse his Pictures, Music, Meats:
> He buys for Topham, Drawings and Designs,
> For Pembroke Statues, dirty Gods, and Coins;
> Rare Monkish manuscripts for Hearne alone,
> And Books for Mead, and Butterflies for Sloane.[10]

I shall confine myself to Britain to keep this study within reasonable bounds, though the same process of creating Romantic Interiors furnished with mediaeval and Renaissance objects was taking place on the Continent. But, like the Gothic Revival itself, the Romantic Interior evolved later on the Continent than in Britain.[11] The creation, however, of interiors furnished with classical objects mixed with modern curiosities has a far longer history in continental Europe, and these interiors of the period before the mid-eighteenth century are far better documented than their British counterparts. A little needs to be said about the Continent to set Britain in context in 1750, for it was what they had seen in Europe that inspired Walpole, Beckford, Meyrick, Lucy and to a lesser extent Scott. They and their contemporaries were also very dependent upon the Continent for the supply of antiquities, whether they where purchased there or through the British antique trade.

The celebrated mediaeval church treasuries, which survived on the Continent into the eighteenth century, must have had very much the appearance of Romantic Interiors. Indeed the activities of their mediaeval and Renaissance creators closely resemble those of their secular contemporaries purchasing from dealers and accepting gifts of antiquities both ancient and modern. One of the most famous treasuries, St Denis on the outskirts of Paris, is of particular relevance to us. In this case the celebrated Abbot Suger (1081–1151) founded the collection by gathering together a truly staggering collection of objects: 'another most precious vessel of prase, carved into the form of a boat, which king Louis, son of Philip, had left in pawn for ten years; we had purchased it with the King's permission for sixty marks of silver when it had been offered to us for inspection.'[12]

Various publications and guide books describe, illustrate and discusss the abbey and the treasury during the seventeenth and early eighteenth centuries.[13] Translations were published for the use of the many English visitors. Several visitors described what they saw, including John Evelyn, who noted the visit in his diary. The collection was dispersed during the French Revolution. This gave Beckford and his contemporaries who had seen the collection *in situ* the chance to acquire some rich pickings. Fortunately a number of major objects were retained by the Louvre where they are still on display. Other less famous ecclesiastical treasuries were also dispersed at the same time.

On the Continent the whole methodology of secular collecting and the creation of suites of interiors devoted to specific classes of objects was codified, and elaborate theoretical principles relating to their planning and interpretation were established and published as early as the sixteenth century. The subtle distinctions between

Plate XV.   Vol. III, facing p. 262.

N. Blakey inv. et del.   Ravenet Sculp.

What brought S.ʳ Visto's ill-got Wealth to waste?
Some Dæmon whisper'd Visto! have a Taste.—
Epis: on Taste.

1. Lord Burlington as collector (*The Works of Alexander Pope Esq.*, 1751, III)

Curiositatenkabinetts, Rariotatenkabinetts, Kunstkammers, Wunderkammers, Armamentariums, Cimelothecas, Studiolos and *Thaumathecas* were either unappreciated or ignored by British collectors and therefore need not detain us here. Full and scholarly studies of this whole subject as far as continental Europe is concerned exist[14] which demonstrate clearly how provincial British collectors were before the mid-eighteenth century. But interestingly, for political and economic reasons I shall discuss later, the Beckford and Meyrick generation of the early nineteenth century were able to form collections of European significance.

Despite the theoretical principles underlying the formation and arrangement of many continental collections, visitors often came away with an impression of a chaotic assemblage of disparate objects, very similar to the impression one gains today at Abbotsford or which is apparent from the contemporary illustrations of Strawberry Hill. Elaborate printed catalogues designed for visiting tourists or scholars existed for many continental collections. These catalogues were frequently laid out in a logical way, but often enough the objects themselves were simply arranged with an eye to aesthetic impact, rather than according to any theoretical or educational principles.

The result was a situation all too familiar to modern exhibition visitors: the objects were not shown in the same order as in the catalogue, the only difference being that in the past it was the taste of the collector that determined this order whereas today it is the taste — or lack of it — of the exhibition designer. If one accompanied the collector himself through the rooms furnished with his collection while he described what one was seeing, all became clear. For each object fitted into the collector's mental model of his collection, which may or may not have been based upon intellectually sound principles. His brain alone stored the invisible yet vital cross-references that linked one object or group of objects with another. Their disappearance on the death of the collector frequently meant that what to him was a supremely logical assemblage of objects seemed to the next generation a chaotic jumble of curiosities.

Some continental collections of which illustrations survive give the impression of clarity and order, others seem to be in a state of chaos. In both cases their relevance as the ancestors of the British Romantic Interiors is obvious. Surviving illustrations are crucial to any real examination of historical interiors. Published descriptions give little clue to the actual appearance of collections and such descriptions by visitors have to be read with caution if we are seeking an accurate impression of what was actually seen. In cases where a published description or catalogue, contemporary illustrations and visitors' manuscript descriptions all survive, it is often obvious when these sources are collated that the visitor wrote up his impressions afterwards using the published description as an *aide-mémoire*. This is even more likely to be the case when the visitor later prepared his impressions for publication.

Paintings, drawings and prints can, however, sometimes be misleading in not actually showing the interior as it was. Sometimes the artist, sometimes the collector himself, chose not to show the interior and the collection which furnished it as it actually appeared. For instance, the celebrated Zoffany painting of Townley surrounded by his collection of classical sculpture had since the eighteenth century been thought to be an accurate representation of the collection, but has recently been shown to include objects known never to have been displayed together in the room portrayed.[15] It is, however, impossible to generalize. One must in each case minutely examine all the evidence.

Plate 2 is a case-study for the comparison of a clear contemporary illustration with the surviving remains of the collection, which can be used to demonstrate the accuracy of the illustration. We have a view which, though possibly somewhat idealized, would seem to be largely an accurate one of the rooms that housed the Duke of Brandenburg's collection in Berlin. It dates from 1696[16] and shows a room devoted to the display of a range of antiquities including medals and coins. One

measure of the accuracy of this illustration is gained by comparing its representation of the four splendid coin and medal cabinets shown standing against the walls with the surviving cabinet in Schloss Kopenick in East Berlin.[17] As can be seen in Plate 2, these were elaborate lacquer cabinets with rich pseudo-oriental mounts, lock-plates and hinges. The surviving cabinet is identical to those illustrated and is known to be by Gerard Dagly. Further indication of the accuracy of the illustration is provided by the survival of other objects depicted. For instance, the the lay figure dating from the 1520s shown on the desk on the right is still in Berlin.[18]

The Brandenburg collection and, for instance, the Dresden collections[19] had by 1700 already been divided into distinct and separate sections. Thus 'Naturalia' — that is the animals, vegetables and minerals — were shown separately from works of art and antiquities. The concept of separation had spread to Britain by the time Walpole began to collect and, as we shall see later, Walpole was to deplore the all-embracing character of Sir Hans Sloane's collection. But naturally, both in Britain and on the Continent, alongside the sophisticated, classified collections occupying interconnecting, but separate rooms or galleries, the mixed collections survived and indeed still survive today. Small local museums and country house museums throughout both Europe and Britain still contain marvellously varied collections. They display such items as birds, stuffed animals, fossils, paintings, armour, local bygones and archaeological specimens which follow no apparent intellectual programme. It may well be, however, that the original plan died with the original founder or indeed curator.

One of the best-known and documented continental collections of the old all-embracing variety is shown in Plate 3. This illustration dates from 1655[20] making it contemporary with the Tradescant collection, and depicts the collection of Ole Worm (1588–1654), the Danish antiquary, scholar, doctor and teacher. Here as with the Brandenburg collection it is possible to compare the objects, which fortunately survive, with the actual engravings in Worm's own published catalogue.[21] Worm's museum represents a type which had by the date of his death in 1654 existed for well over a century.

I shall only briefly mention the very similar Italian museums for which splendid illustrations also survive. Three examples are those of Ferrante Imperato, illustrated in 1599;[22] Museum Calceolarianum, illustrated in 1622;[23] and Museum Cospiano, illustrated in 1677.[24]

4. The cabinet of curiosities at the Bibliothèque Sainte Geneviève, Paris (C. Du Molinet, *Le Cabinet de la Bibliothèque de Sainte Geneviève . . .*, 1692)

5. The cabinet of curiosities at the Bibliothèque Sainte Geneviève (Du Molinet, *Le Cabinet*)

One French example of a very mixed collection of the late seventeenth century is marvellously captured in a series of views (Plates 4 and 5) published in 1692.[25] This collection was housed in the rooms adjacent to the library of the Abbey of St Geneviève in Paris. These various illustrations from Germany, France and Scandinavia occurring as they did in published catalogues were of course known to English antiquaries and collectors who naturally used them as models for the display of their collections.

Horace Walpole and his friend the antiquary William Cole on the evidence of the published book went in search of the St Geneviève collection while in Paris in 1765. But Cole reported that in the abbey church was 'a small altar, on which is a curious Cross & an *Ecce Homo* made out of a single Peice of Coral & given to this Altar by Father Claud Molinet, a Canon Regular of this House & Author of the beautiful Book, called, *Le Cabinet* . . ., printed at Paris in 1692, in Folio, with his own Print, & several Views of the fine Library in this Abbey & Plates of all the Curiosities & Medals then contained in it'.[26]

They found that the collection had been reorganized and the interiors altered. At the Revolution the collection was largely dispersed, and the building itself was to be demolished in 1807. The engraved views were, however, sufficient to give Walpole and his friends a very clear idea of continental precedents, which they could easily follow when the time came to furnish Strawberry Hill.

But Romantic Interiors containing mediaeval antiquities were, along with the Gothic Revival itself, late in emerging on the Continent by comparison with Britain. In France, for example, little seems to have happened before 1800 to inspire the creation of such interiors. But a powerful incentive was provided by the creation of the Musée des Monumens Français by Alexandre Lenoir.[27] In the old Couvent des Petits Augustins, Lenoir gathered together a wide range of mediaeval and Renaissance antiquities displaced from chiurches and other buildings by the Revolution; it was opened to the public in 1791. A whole generation of French antiquaries and collectors had their eyes opened to the picturesque effect that could be created by displaying mediaeval antiquities together. Guidebooks were written for visitors, including one in English.[28] Indeed many English visitors were impressed and influenced by the museum. The Reverend William Shepherd wrote on 2 July 1802:

This morning we spent three or four delightful hours in the Musée National des Monumens François organized by Citizen Lenoir. This enlightened artist, scandalized by the destruction of the monuments of ancient art, which modern barbarism had proscribed in all the provinces of the republic, requested permission from the Convention to collect and combine their scattered fragments . . .

the windows and the cloisters are ornamented with pained glass, transported from the glowing windows of a thousand churches, which the bigotted intolerance of modern philosophy had doomed to devastation and pillage.[29]

As we shall see later, after the defeat of Napoleon the museum was broken up and some of its antiquities, such as the glass, were purchased by English dealers. Others were returned to the buildings from which they had been removed and yet others were purchased by French dealers and collectors.

One of the first French collectors to create an extensive series of domestic Romantic Interiors seems to have been Alexandre Du Sommerard (1779–1842),[30] the creator of the Musée de Cluny. He had begun to collect mediaeval antiquities early by French standards and used them to create a series of Romantic Interiors in his house in the rue de Menars. He is shown (Plate 6) in 1825 in one of these interiors describing an object from the collection to a friend. His collection grew to such a size

6. Du Sommerard in his study with a fellow collector in the early 1830s, rue de Menars, Paris (A. Du Sommerard, *Les Arts au Moyen Age . . .*, 1838–46)

7. An interior at the Hôtel de Cluny, Paris (Du Sommerard, *Les Arts*)

8. The Chapel at the Hôtel de Cluny (Du Sommerard, *Les Arts*)

that he rented the decaying mediaeval Hôtel de Cluny in 1832. The Hôtel was conveniently situated in the centre of Paris and while he lived there Du Sommerard opened the rooms furnished with his collection to the public. As Plates 7 and 8 show, 'his romantic taste dictated the way the objects were arranged, and he was more concerned with evoking historical associations than with presenting the pieces for their artistic value . . . His exhibition soon became one of the attractions of Paris, and the Hôtel de Cluny was for ten years the haunt of litterateurs, artists and patrons; it became one of the acknowledged centres of a new cult of the Middle Ages among the Romantics.'[31]

Not every visitor, however, was impressed, and an Englishman, Thomas Raikes, described his visit in 1834:

We had now a ticket of admission . . . Every broker's shop in Paris seems to have been ransacked for remnants of worm-eaten furniture, to complete the collection with which this old Gothic building is literally stuffed . . . a chessboard and men in cristal de roche, at which two men in armour seem to have been puzzling themselves for the last four centuries; the chapel as it then existed with a mannequin priest in chasuble et etole . . . this burlesque exhibition, which the worms and moths hold in disputed possession with him [Du Sommerard].[32]

The dummy figure of the monk can be seen in Plate 8.

Du Sommerard even found his way into one of the best French novels on the theme of collecting, Balzac's *Cousin Pons*. Balzac tells us that Pons 'possessed three elements of a collector's success, the legs of a deer, the time of an idler, and the patience of a Jew . . . Du Sommerard . . . endeavoured at one time to establish relations with the old musician [Pons], but that prince of bric-à-brac died without ever penetrating behind the veil of the Pons collection.'[33]

The influence of Du Sommerard's Cluny interiors was probably not particularly strong in England, for by the time he created them such interiors were not unusual there. Indeed French artists of the stature of Delacroix were coming to study English Romantic Interiors as early as the 1820s. The influence of the Cluny in France and elsewhere on the Continent was, however, considerable, especially when the French government acquired the Cluny and the collection as a museum after Du Sommerard's death. Appropriately, his son Edmond became the first curator. Du Sommerard's international influence was reinforced by the publication from 1838 to 1846 of five magisterial folios devoted to his collection, *Les Arts au Moyen Age*, and from which Plates 6 through 8 are taken. But even here Du Sommerard and his French fellow-antiquaries had such pioneering books to build on as Shaw's *Specimens of Ancient Furniture* of 1836 and Meyrick's *A Critical Enquiry into Ancient Armour* of 1824. The whole story of continental Romantic Interiors is a fascinating one deserving a book in its own right.

Something needs to be said concerning the history of the display of collections in England before 1750. No modern history of museums, public and private, in this country has been published,[34] quite apart from any major study of the display of collections in domestic interiors. The study of both these groups for the period before 1750 is gravely hampered by the paucity of illustrations, whereas for the Continent a considerable number of illustrations exist, several of which I have reproduced here.

The most celebrated English seventeenth-century collection is the Tradescant collection, which formed the basis of the Ashmolean Museum. I need not discuss it at length, as it was minutely examined in print in the year of the tercentenary of its transfer to Oxford.[35] The collection was housed for some years in Tradescant's house in London, but sadly we have no illustrations of the interiors and very few descriptions of how it was displayed.[36] Neither do illustrations survive of how it was displayed in 1683 when it was transferred to the purpose-built Ashmolean Museum in Oxford. But from the descriptions we do have and from Tradescant's own published catalogue[37] it is obvious that it followed the pattern of Worm's collection, mixing together antiquities and naturalia.

It is important to consider whether there is any real distinction between Romantic Interiors of the domestic variety, to which I have devoted this study, and private museums. Numbers of the continental examples were museums or collections open to scholars, like the Brandenburg collection. In other cases, as with the Cluny, scholars and indeed ticket-holders were admitted, but Du Sommerard actually inhabited the interiors that housed the collection. Of course, the scale of the collection and the interiors that house it are also relevant, for in a domestic house the owner has perforce to co-exist with the collection in his daily life. The Elector of Brandenburg, however, occupied a substantial Palace and could furnish his antiquities rooms as formal museum galleries and his living quarters in a more domestic manner.

The Ashmolean Museum itself falls into a new category as the first public museum in England and, though the collection was no more rationally arranged than that of most private collectors, it was a purpose-built public museum and not a dwelling. I feel that the key test is whether the owner actually dwelt in the interiors he had created. Whether the public on occasion had access is irrelevant, for many country houses were open to the public on set days from the early eighteenth century. This did not alter their status as domestic houses and, as we shall see, Horace Walpole issued tickets in advance to parties wishing to visit Strawberry Hill. Sometimes private collections and the houses created for them became public museums, as is the case of the Sir John Soane Museum. Today's visitor to this museum is, however, left in no doubt that Soane actually lived in the house — the domestic furniture is still *in situ*.

The most important seventeenth-century collection of antiquities in England in art-historical terms was that of Thomas Howard, Earl of Arundel, who died in 1646. Walpole stated that Arundel's 'chief amusement was his collection, the very ruins of which are ornaments now to several principal cabinets. He was the first who professedly began to collect in this country and led the way to prince Henry, king Charles and the duke of Buckingham.'[38] Henry Peacham remarked of Arundel, 'To whose liberall charges and magnificence, this angle of the World oweth the first sight of Greek and Romane Statues, with whose admired presence he began to honour the Gardens and galleries at Arundel-House about twenty years ago and hath ever since continued to transplant old Greece into England.'[39]

Though his collection consisted largely of classical and Renaissance objects, Walpole owned one of the Earl's mediaeval objects and the Duchess of Portland another. Beyond the two splendid Daniel Mytens portraits of the Earl and Alethia his wife[40] we have no clue as to how the bulk of the Earl's collection was displayed. The Earl is depicted in his sculpture gallery at Arundel House and his wife in the picture gallery. Despite our ignorance about its arrangement, the collection had, as Walpole pointed out, a great impact upon all subsequent collecting in Britain.[41]

But to move into the eighteenth century, several British collections are mentioned in the following chapters. The Bateman, Portland and Oxford collections were all sold at auction in Walpole's lifetime, and he acquired objects from them. We shall meet William Stukeley (1687–1765)[42] as a collector of mediaeval antiquities in Chapter 2. He was, as its first secretary, a very active member of the Society of Antiquaries of London and he was also a member of its provincial fellow society, the Gentlemen's Society of Spalding in Lincolnshire, which was founded in 1712.

Stukeley's book *Itinerarium Curiosum* of 1725 was illustrated from his own drawings and based upon his extensive travels in search of ancient buildings and antiquities undertaken since 1710. This book became the vade-mecum for all who travelled in search of the British past and its surviving artefacts. Stukeley represents the beginning of a widespread change in the attitudes of many collectors and antiquaries as their interests moved away from classical antiquities towards native British ones. As we have seen, the very foundation of the Society of Antiquaries of London came about as a manifestation of this growing interest. Stukeley wrote that when at Cambridge from 1703 to 1708 he 'had now begun to conceive a passionate love for [classical] Antiquities, but I saw that my Affairs would not indulge in foreign speculations of that sort, and so I turned my thoughts for a leisure Amusement to those of my own Country. I frequently took a walk to sigh over the Ruins of Barnwell Abbey, and made a Draught of it.'[43]

For someone not wealthy enough to travel frequently to the Continent or who had a profession that precluded time to travel abroad, the study and by analogy the collecting of British antiquities was a very attractive alternative to the study of classical ones. Stukeley was a doctor and later a clergyman, William Cole a clergyman, Thomas Gray a Fellow of a Cambridge College, and James Essex an architect. Many of the antiquaries and collectors interested in British antiquities at this period were by no means rich.

Stukeley created Romantic Interiors in several of his houses; he wrote on 25 October 1727 to his friend the antiquary Samuel Gale describing his house at Grantham to which he had moved in 1726: 'I have done buying books. I have now fitted up my library (& 'tis just full), so that I may properly say I begin to live. There are two windows ... The prospect from it is very noble & delightful ... I have adorn'd my study with heads, bas reliefs, bustos, urns ... I look upon myself as dead to London, & what passes in the learned world. My study is my elysium.'[44]

In 1748 he moved back to London with his collection and settled in Bloomsbury, where he had taken the living at the Church of St George the Martyr in Queen Square. Stukeley's rectory was in Gloucester Street, which ran south from Queen Square and was two minutes' walk from the Great Ormond Street house of his old friend Dr Mead, the celebrated collector. Stukeley set about the creation of a set of appropriately Romantic Interiors to house his by now much larger collection. He wrote in his diary on 28 August 1751:

We celebrated the dedication of my library. Present . . . Mr Folks, Mr Fleetwood, Dr Parsons, Mr Pond, Mr de la Costa, Mr Baker, Mr Sherwood, senr and junr. . . . The great window was spread o'er intirely with fossils of all kinds, which were extremely admired; the great lump of *corallium tubulatum* found in the river Ribel . . . another filled full with juice of black flint, which I picked up from the pavement of pebbles before neighbour Curtis's door, Stamford . . . the bone I took out of the stratum of brickearth in digging at Blomesbury . . . a model of Stonehenge, as in its present state, some of the stone, the common sort, polished, the granite of the lesser obeliscs; a busto which I cut of Julius Caesar's head in clunch; an orrery which I made at Stamford; a Roman cup and saucer intire, in fine red earth dug up at Trumpington; Bishop Cumberland's clock the first long pendulum . . . lastly to render it a compleat rout, I produced a pack of cards made in Richard II. time.[45]

Stukeley's guests are of interest. Martin Folkes, the celebrated numismatist, was president of the Royal Society and vice-president of the Society of Antiquaries and he like Stukeley was a Freemason. He lived in Queen Square and was thus a near neighbour to both Stukeley and Mead. He was also a collector, and after his death in 1754 his immense library was sold as was' his considerable collection.[46] Sadly there is no record of how he housed the collection. Mendes da Costa, F.S.A. and F.R.S., was clerk and librarian to the Royal Society until his imprisonment in 1767 for appropriating their funds. He was also the author of *A Natural History of Fossils*. His considerable collection was seized and sold after his imprisonment. Henry Baker and James Parsons were both also F.S.A. and F.R.S. Arthur Pond, F.S.A., was a collector, artist and dealer.[47]

The other interiors in Stukeley's house must also have been packed with antiquities, but sadly no descriptions or illustrations of them exist. However, the scope of Stukeley's collection can be seen from the catalogue of the sale held after his death.[48] Lot 61 was Bishop Cumberland's clock and lot 74 the model of Stonehenge. Lot 85 was 'An antique enamell'd shrine, with the print v. philos Transact No. 490'; the print had been published in *Philosophical Transactions of The Royal Society* in 1748. This mediaeval enamel chasse depicting the martyrdom of Becket was probably the most important object in Stukeley's collection; it has been described in a fascinating article about the collectors of such pieces in Stukeley's day.[49] After being lost for fifty years this chasse was sold at Sotheby's on 13 December 1979 for £420,000 (Plate 9)[50] and is now on loan to the British Museum.

9. William Stukeley's mediaeval enamel chasse (Sotheby's, London)

The breadth of Stukeley's scholarship and interests is further attested by the contents of his library,[51] which included 1,121 lots, amongst which were lot 461, Da Costa's book on fossils, and lots 1034 and 1035, two numismatical books by Folkes. Stukeley is, I feel, a good representative example of a whole group of eighteenth-century antiquaries who were also collectors and whose social and scholarly life focussed upon the Society of Antiquaries and the Royal Society. Many of them were clergymen, doctors and lawyers; they were not wealthy and most of them are completely forgotten today, and little documentation survives to inform us about their lives, their collections or the rooms they furnished with them.

Those crucial sources for any study of the eighteenth century, Nichols's *Anecdotes* and his *Illustrations*, furnish brief details of the lives of some of these men. In his section 'Memoirs of Eminent Antiquaries'[52] Nichols discusses no fewer than forty-one of them including Stukeley himself and his friends Parsons and Baker. But even the brief details given by Nichols show that they were all part of a close-knit group of friends, often meeting and corresponding about both the study and the collecting of antiquities. It would be fascinating to know more about so many of them, for instance Robert Ainsworth, F.S.A. (1660–1743), schoolmaster, scholar, author and collector, who in 'the latter part of his life . . . used to employ himself in very much rummaging the shops of obscure brokers in every quarter of the town; by which

Remains of Aldgate, Bethnal Green

View of Mr Greene's Museum at Lichfield

10. Ebenezer Mussell's house at Bethnal Green (J.P. Malcolm, *Views within twelve miles round London ...*, 1800)

11. View of Mr Greene's Museum at Lichfield (*Gentleman's Magazine*, 1788)

12. Mr Greene's clock (Victoria Art Gallery, Bath)

means he often picked up old coins and other valuable curiosities at a small expense'.[53]

I have been unable to discover any clue to the appearance of the interiors that housed the extensive collection of Ebenezer Mussell, F.S.A. He had the distinction, however, of creating a remarkable 'antiquarian exterior' in London.

> Mr Mussell was a skilful collector of books and other curiosities. He was in 1721 a considerable purchaser at the sale of John Kemp's famous Museum of Antiquities; and added largely to his collection from the sales of the Earl of Oxford and Dr Mead. He resided near Aldgate, and had also a house on Bethnal Green. On the demolition of the old City Gates, having purchased the material of Aldgate, he removed them to his residence at Bethnal Green, and placed them in the front of a building adjacent to his house.[54]

The building in 1800[55] is shown in Plate 10, and we shall meet Mussell again in Chapter 2.

To move out of London and to the later part of the century, Richard Greene of Lichfield dwelt in the museum he created. He died in his seventy-eighth year in 1793[56] having spent more than forty-five years amassing his considerable collection. It included antiquities, ethnographical specimens, minerals, stuffed animals and mediaeval manuscripts.[57] In some ways the collection was in the tradition of Worm and Tradescant, for Greene, like them, hung animals from his ceilings. 'On the ceiling. Tortoise, Seale, or Sea Dog ... crocodile, four, feet three inches long. Three Saws of the Saw Fish.'[58] In other ways his museum looked forward to the modern museum. James Boswell, who visited it in 1776 with Dr Johnson — also a native of Lichfield — noted that

> It was truly a wonderful collection both of antiquities and natural curiosities, and ingenious works of art. He [Greene] had all the articles accurately arranged, with the names of the contributors upon labels, printed at his own press, and on the stair-case leading to it was a board, with the names of the contributors marked in gold letters ... Mr Green told me that Johnson said to him 'Sir, I should as soon have thought of building a man of war, as collecting such a museum.'[59]

A view of one of Greene's interiors was published and described in 1788 (Plate 11). 'A collection of South-Sea rarities, brought over by Capt. Cook and other navigators, fills the glass-case on the left-hand. The opposite or on the right-hand, contains a collection of fire arms ... In the centre of the inner room appears an uncommon musical altar-clock, whose outer case ... represents a Gothic church tower.'[60] The clock and its case still exist in the Victoria Art Gallery in Bath (Plate 12).

By the 1790s there were a number of similar house museums throughout the country, which, as one moves into the nineteenth century, form the prototype for small local public museums. But, whereas in the 1750s the interiors at Strawberry Hill bore a recognizable resemblance to Stukeley's interiors, by the 1790s the richness and scale of the Fonthill interiors place it in a different world from that of Greene's museum.

Even in Beckford's day there was a place for the professional man with modest means who had the imagination to compensate for the lack of real wealth. Sir John Soane was just such a man, but I will not in this study deal with Soane and his remarkable museum for three reasons. First, it has been very well documented by Soane and others[61] and of course still exists for all to visit. Second, it overlaps in time so precisely with Abbotsford and Fonthill that I have more than enough illustrations of Romantic Interiors of this period. Third, the overpowering impression gained by visitors to the museum is of an assembly of classical antiquities (Plate 13), though in fact mediaeval and later antiquities are mixed with classical ones.

The only interiors that are not predominantly classical are the Monk's Parlour (Plate 14) and the Shakespeare Recess (Plate 15). The very concept of the monk is mediaeval and indeed the interior of the room is decorated with mediaeval fragments, though the furniture and the stove are far from Gothic in style. The adoption of the Immortal Bard as an ancient hero ties in with the use of the same cast of his tomb at Charlecote (Chapter 8) and Abbotsford (Chapter 6). The very existence of Soane's house as the public museum it became after his death made it a useful prototype for the furnishing of Romantic Interiors in Britain during the rest of the nineteenth century.

Having briefly sketched in the British and continental background before 1780, one further aspect of my subject needs to be mentioned. I shall touch from time to

13. The central space in Sir John Soane's Museum, London (Sir John Soane, *Description of the House and Museum ...*, 1835)

14. The Monk's Parlour in Sir John Soane's Museum (Soane, *Description*)

15. The Shakespeare Recess in Sir John Soane's Museum (Soane, *Description*)

VIEW IN THE MUSEUM.
LOOKING DOWN TO THE BELZONI SARCOPHAGUS, AND TOWARDS THE PICTURE ROOM

VIEW IN THE MONK'S PARLOUR.

VIEW IN THE SHAKESPEARE RECESS.

time upon that nostalgia for 'Old England' which is so powerful a part of the Romantic Movement in this country, paralleling as it does the adoration of the classical world by the neo-classicists at this time. I am thinking of those aspects of our past that relate to life in and around the domestic no use. It was the concept of ancient hospitality that appealed to the imagination of many antiquaries, artists, authors, architects and indeed country gentlemen.

The neo-classicists had always had a problem in 'selling' the architecture of ancient Greece and Rome, which was so obviously conceived for the Mediterranean climate, to any patron who was less than besotted by the classical world. Our inclement weather decreed that many neo-classical buildings were inappropriate for England, as Pope recognized in his famous line that those in Burlington's circle were 'Proud to catch cold at a Venetian door'.[62]

But, by contrast, what could be more inviting than the blazing log fire and a jolly banquet in a mediaeval great hall! This vision of the glorious and hospitable past started long before the eighteenth century. There was indeed some basis in fact, the revels connected with the mediaeval Christmas being particularly well recorded: one fifteenth-century manuscript describes the bringing in of the traditional Christmas boar's head after which the throng assembled in the great hall sat down to

> Good brewed ale and wine, I dare well say,
> The boars head with mustard armed so gay,
> Furmity for pottage, and venison fine,
> And the umbles of the doe and all that
> ever comes in.[63]

Not only did the Georgians and Victorians look nostalgically back to the festivities and the copious eating and drinking, but they also admired the concept of all the social classes eating together in the great hall. Indeed this way of life was not long past when the nostalgia for it set in. John Selden wrote as early as the 1650s: 'The Hall was the place where the great Lord did us'd to eat, (wherefore else were the Halls made so big?) Where he saw all his Servants and Tenants about him. He eat not in private . . . except in times of sickness; when once he became a thing coopt up, all his greatness was spoil'd. Nay the king himself used to eat in the Hall, and his Lords sate with him, and then he understood men.'[64]

In 1689 Thomas Shadwell, 'Poet Laureat and Historiographer Royal to their Majesties', also deplored the passing of ancient hospitality in one of his plays:

> But our new-fashioned Gentry love the French too well to fight against 'em; they are bred abroad without knowing anything of our Constitution, and come home tainted with Foppery, slavish Principles and Popish Religion. They bring home Arts of Building from hot countries to serve our cold one . . . For my part, I think 'twas never good days, but when great Tables were kept in large Halls, the buttery-Hatch always open, Black Jacks and a good smell of Meat and March-Bear, with Dogs Turds and Marrow-bones as Ornaments in the Hall: These were signs of good House-keeping, I hate to see Italian fine Buildings with no Meat or Drinks in 'em.[65]

An anonymous writer voiced his criticism of the continuing rage for neo-classicism in 1739, the very year Walpole left for the Continent with his head full of thoughts of the classical splendour of Italy:

> There is surely nothing more absurd than to see, as one often does, a *Venetian* Window and a *Grecian* Portico stuck on to an old decaying Mansion Seat . . . I own I am always griev'd to see the venerable Paternal Castle of a Gentleman of an ancient Family, and a competent Fortune, *tasted* and dwindled down into an imperfect Imitation of an *Italian Villa*, and the good old profitable Orchard laid out into a Waste of Green, bounded by fruitless Trees. Methinks there was

16. The Great Hall at Cothele (N. Condy, *Cothele* . . . , *c*.1840)

17. The Dining Room at Cothele (Condy, *Cothele*)

something respectable in those old hospitable *Gothick* Halls, hung round with the Helmets, Breast-Plates and Swords of our Ancestors; I entered them with a Constitutional Sort of Reverence, and look'd upon those Arms with Gratitude, as the Terror of former Ministers, and the Check of Kings. Nay, I even imagin'd that I saw some of those good Swords, that had procur'd the Confirmation of *Magna Carta*, and humbled *Spencers* and *Gavestons*. And when I see these thrown by, to make Way for some tawdry Gilding and Carving, I can't help considering such an Alteration as ominous even to our Constitution.[66]

The mediaeval code of chivalry was also increasingly admired. Voltaire, whom one does not normally associate with such matters, described its manifestations in his *General History of Europe*. A reviewer of the book commented in 1755 on the vow-taking ceremony of a mediaeval knight, who, 'After having fasted from sun-rise, confessed himself . . . [and was] placed by himself at a side table, where he was neither to speak, smile, nor to eat, while the knights and ladies who were to perform the principal parts of the ceremony, were eating, drinking, and making merry at the great table.'[67]

The concept of mediaeval hospitality grew rapidly in the eighteenth century. Horace Walpole, for instance, wrote from Strawberry Hill to his friend Horance Mann in distant Italy on 26 December 1748: 'Did you ever know a more absolute country gentleman? Here am I come down to what you call keep my Christmas! Indeed it is not in all its forms; I have stuck no laurel and holly in my windows, I eat no turkey and chine, I have no tenants to invite, I have not brought a single soul with me.'[68]

The idea of having tenantry in at Christmas had, because of its supposed mediaeval connections, become a feature of country house life by the mid-nineteenth century. Indeed, many new Gothic Revival houses were provided with

Great Halls for just such events. William Burges, at his celebrated country house Knightshayes of 1869–73, created for his client 'The great feature of the interior . . . a large Hall to be used for the reception of the owner's tenantry. This is fitted up with a gallery and rostrum at one end.'[69]

Those who were lucky enough to own an ancient house already could use it for such events as they imagined had been the practice of their mediaeval ancestors in days of yore. Cothele, the late mediaeval house in Cornwall, was one of these. Plate 17 shows the family dining room, but for appropriately feudal events the Great Hall (Plate 16) saw 'that refreshing sight of the good old domestics of the present noble possessor of Cothele, in full activity of preparation for the annual banquet to all the tenantry. Which will be soon most the great objects of attraction? The knight's armour, and the corslets, and the matchlocks, and the enormous antlers, or the beef and the pudding, and the punchbowl?'[70]

Predictably, the owner of Cothele who had re-edified the interiors was George Edgcumbe, 1st Earl of Mount Edgcumbe, F.S.A., a close friend of Walpole's. In 1789 he had proudly entertained King George III at Cothele and the King had sat on a suitably splendid ebony sofa (Plate 18) almost certainly newly acquired following Walpole's example at Strawberry Hill. It immediately became a relic and it and 'The chairs in the best parlour were, until very lately, charged with brass plates, which imported that on the 25th August, 1789 the King and Queen with three princesses royal . . . condescended to take breakfast with the late earl and countess of Mount Edgcumbe. The effect of the inscription was such, that most of those who afterwards visited the house were anxious to sit in the same chairs . . . it was found necessary to take away the plates, in order to preserve the chairs.'[71] Cothele survives much as in Plates 16 and 17 and now belongs to the National Trust.

Not everyone involved in the antiquarian movement believed that early nineteenth-century hospitality did indeed revive that of the Middle Ages. Pugin in his book *Contrasts* recognized that both the mediaeval country house and the monastery had dispensed charity and depicted the mediaeval poor being fed beef, mutton, bacon, ale, cider, milk, porridge, bread and cheese while the denizens of the "modern poor house" eat gruel, oatmeal and potatoes.[72]

18. A seventeenth-century Indo-Portuguese ebony sofa at Cothele (National Trust)

Other aspects of feudal festivities besides eating and drinking, such as the musicians, jesters and tournaments, held a powerful appeal for the antiquaries, artists, authors and collectors involved in the Romantic Movement. In some cases such mediaeval customs survived and indeed overlapped with their revival. In northern England and Scotland during the later Middle Ages pipers were part of grand households; indeed they survived in some few families right through to the eighteenth century, and to this day the Duke of Northumberland has his own personal piper. But by the seventeenth century pipers and other entertainers, rather than being permanent members of the household, were paid to come in at Christmas and other festivals only. At Naworth Castle, for instance, the Howards paid for such entertainments at Christmas and New Year in 1633: 'To the fellow with the hobbie horse, by my Ladie's command ii.s. vid.d. . . . To John Mulcaster the Piper for playing here all Christmas and New Year xx.s.'[73] The standards seem, however, to have declined, for at New Year 1648 at Naworth, 'Paid the piper which could not play well 2.6. Paid the piper came with the mummers 2.6.'[74] The idea of mummers, hobby-horse men and pipers performing at Christmas was to become the very stuff of Victorian historical novels and paintings.

Mummers were still a feature of village life when Thomas Hardy was growing up, and in one of his best novels he tellingly defined the nature of folk revivals. His modern heroine Eustacia Vye would not have regretted their passing, but the mummers emerge as they always had from the gloom of Egdon Heath one night before Christmas;

Of mummers and mumming Eustacia had the greatest contempt. The mummers themselves were not afflicted with any such feeling for their art, though at the same time they were not enthusiastic. A traditional pastime is to be distinguished from a mere revival in no more striking feature than in this, that while in the revival all is excitement and fervour, the survival is carried on with a stolidity and absence of stir which sets one wondering why a thing that is done so perfunctorily should be kept up at all. Like Balaam and other unwilling prophets, the agents seem moved by an inner compulsion to say and do their alloted parts whether they will or no. This unweeting manner of performance is the true ring by which, in this refurbishing age, a fossilized survival may be known from a spurious reproduction.[75]

In the nineteenth century the whole tradition of piping was preserved by Walter Scott and his fellow antiquaries just before it finally died out. Scott lured a piper into his household at Abbotsford, and in October 1818 Lockhart saw 'A tall and stalwart bagpiper in complete Highland costume ... Scott took occasion to explain that *John of Skye* was a recent acquisition ... when the cloth was drawn the never failing salver of *quaighs* introduced, John of Skye, upon some well known signal entered the room, but *en militaire* without removing his bonnet and taking his station behind the landlord, received from his hand the largest of the celtic bickers brimful of Glenlivet.'[76] It was thus only natural that Queen Victoria should appoint her own piper at Balmoral, where a piper pipes at meals to this day.

At least as widespread as pipers in Scotland were harpers in Wales, about whom clung the same memories of ancient festivals and hospitality. As early as the 1740s harpers were being associated with the survival of ancient British customs and culture. John Parry (1710–1782), the 'Blind Harpist' of Ruabon in North Wales, came to London in 1746 and performed at Ranelagh Gardens.[77] He was the harper in the household of Sir William Watkins Wynn of Wynnstay in Denbighshire and made the English aware for the first time of ancient Welsh music by publishing in 1742 *Antient British Music*. Thomas Gray heard him play at Cambridge in May 1757 and wrote to William Mason: 'Mr Parry has been here & scratched out such ravishing blind Harmony, such tunes of a thousand year old with names enough to choak you, as have set all this learned body a'dancing.'[78] Gray, inspired by Parry and his other studies of Welsh history, composed his Welsh poem *The Bard*.

Despite the 'taking up' of Welsh music, eighteenth-century travellers in Wales felt that harpers and bards were a dying race. Edward Byng, for instance, comments upon them frequently while travelling in Wales in the 1780s and 1790s. He felt sad at what he saw as their certain demise and wrote while at Carnarvon in July 1784. 'I pity my grandchildren who will hear its [the harp's] merits and fame, in their grandfathers and other pages; wishing in vain, for that retrospective delight which I am now enjoying ... the tunes of greatest antiquity such as might formerly have gladden'd the breast of Llewellyn and urged Glendowr to face the field at Shrewsbury.'[79]

In Llangollen in July 1793 Byng encountered two harpers: one in each inn both blind! (I suppose that they put out their eyes when young, as they do those of bullfinches who are taught to pipe) ... were I a Scotch or Welsh resident, I certainly would retain a piper of harper depend upon it, that hilarity would accompany him: he would lead the dance: and to the bowling green, and to the dairy in the Summer; and in Winter he would enliven the hall and make merry in the laundry.[80]

Help was, however, at hand and, though Byng never employed a harper, others did, and from 1790 Edward Jones (1752–1824) was 'Bard to His Majesty Prince of Wales'. After the coronation of George IV, Jones became King's Bard' and from 1805 actually lived in St James's Palace.[81] By the 1820s when Jones died enthusiasts for Welsh culture like the celebrated Ladies of Llangollen were encouraging the bards, the harpers and their Eisteddfods just as Scott and his friends were encouraging pipers and Scottish culture.

Thus harpers in Wales, pipers in Scotland, hobby-horses, mummers and morris dancers in England all survived just long enough to become part of the Gothic Revival as applied to folk culture. Fools and jesters did not survive quite long enough to be taken up and preserved, but they frequently figure in Romantic literature and painting. The subject of fools and jesters is a fascinating one which was well covered in print as early as 1807 by the antiquary and scholar Francis Douce, Walter Scott's friend.[82] Fools were quite common until the early seventeenth century. Alethia, Countess of Arundel, was even painted with her dwarf, her dog and her fool by Rubens in 1620.[83] It is interesting to find mediaeval traditions surviving — or had they been revived? — in a family so modern as to collect classical antiquities.

A mid-seventeenth-century painting shows Thomas Skelton, the fool, who was a member of the household of the Pennington family of Muncaster Castle in Cumberland.[84] He is depicted in his chequered blue, yellow and white fool's gown holding his last will and testament in his hand.

But in the later seventeenth century the decline of fools was rapid; in 1680 Shadwell in his play *The Woman Captain* states that it was 'Out of fashion for great men to keep fools'.[85] The last recorded fool in England seems to have been Dicky Pearce, the Earl of Suffolk's fool, who died — of what I cannot discover — during the revels at Berkley Castle in 1728. His epitaph was composed by none other than Dean Swift and is still visible on his tomb in Berkley churchyard.

> Here lies the Earl of Suffolk's fool
> men call'd him Dicky Pearce;
> His folly served to make folks laugh
> When wit and mirth were scarce.
>
> Poor Dick, alas! is dead and gone,
> What signifies to cry?
> Dickies enough are still behind
> To laugh at by and by.[86]

In Scotland the tradition lingered on a while longer, for Scott wrote to Douce on 9 February 1808: 'it might be interesting to you to know that fifty years ago there was . . . not an *all-licensed* fool — half crazy and knavish — many of whose *bon mots* are still recited and preserved. The late Duke of Argyle had a jester of this description, who stood at the sideboard among the servants and was a great favourite.'[87] I can find no record of later examples in Britain and no rich mediaevalist saw fit to revive the tradition in the nineteenth century. The fool, however, appears frequently in paintings, novels and plays and, as one might expect, the most sympathetic and lifelike portrayal is in the person of Davie Gellatley, the fool to the Bradwardine family of Tully-Veolan, in Scott's first 'Waverley' novel, *Waverley*.

It was by no means beyond the imagination or financial resources of mediaevalizing gentlemen of the nineteenth century to revive any ancient custom, and, although fools did not catch their fancy, tournaments did. By the 1820s tournaments had been revived much on the lines described by Scott in *Ivanhoe*, the most celebrated being the Eglinton Tournament of 1839 (Plate 19), the story of which has been fully told elsewhere.[88] Less well known are the 'Old English Games' held in August 1827 at Firle, the seat of the Gage family in Sussex. The local newspaper described how 'The sports commenced by Gentlemen riding with light spiked staves at rings and apples suspended by a string after which they changed their weapons for stout poles, and attacked two Quintayns'.[89] A painting of the event survives at Firle, as does the suit of armour which the Hon. Henry Gage purchased from Pratt and wore at the Eglinton Tournament itself.

19. *The Eglinton Tournament* by E.H. Corbould, 1842 (Victoria Albert Museum, London)

Anthony Trollope in *Barchester Towers*, published in 1857, describes such an event in his famous 'Ullathorne Sports' where 'Riding at Quintain' featured. Such mediaeval-style events found their way into a whole range of sporting activities, and archery and hawking very much came back into fashion.

In 1850 Dr W.P. Brookes held his Much Wenlock Olympian Games, thus paving the way for the modern Olympic Games. Though the precedents were wholly classical, along with such Grecian events as the Pentathlon, Brookes included 'Tilting at the ring; a dramatic and exciting contest between mounted competitors, each trying to spear a small ring hanging from a bar ... a sport practised in the middle ages as a preparation for jousting ... Brookes possibly drew the idea from Strutt's *Sports and pastimes of the English People* published in 1801.'[90] A herald and a page presided dressed in Tudor-style costumes, which are preserved in Much Wenlock Museum.

I have introduced these various ancient customs in an attempt to recapture the rich and complex sources available to those people in the later eighteenth and nineteenth centuries who sought to re-create their own microcosm of 'Old England' in their own home or on their country estate. If you did not own an ancient country seat, you could create one from scratch using the means and the materials which I shall describe in this study. If you did, however, own an ancient house you could cherish it as it was or 'early it up', as the modern American interior decorators picturesquely describe the process. Charlecote Park is the latter type of house.

The introduction of imaginative additions pervades that book which found its way into so many country house libraries and which helped to form a whole generation's attitude to the British past, namely, Joseph Nash's *The Mansions of England in the Olden Time*. Nash stated that he wished to present houses such as Hatfield, Penshurst, Knole or Charlecote,

> in a new and attractive light; not as many of them now appear, gloomy, desolate, and neglected, but furnished with the rude comfort of the early times ... with the family and household of the 'old English gentleman' surrounded by their everyday comforts, sharing the more rare and bounteous hospitalities offered to guests, or partaking of the boisterous merriment of Christmas gambols.[91]

Haddon Hall (Plate 20) is shown at Christmas with mummers, morris dancers, a hobby-horse man and numerous merry revellers. Nash provided what I suspect is a reasonably accurate picture of what those Christmas revels at Naworth in the middle of the seventeenth century must have been like. No new Gothic Revival house was

20. Christmas festivities at Haddon Hall (J. Nash, *The Mansions of England ...*, 1839–49)

21. The Great Hall at Adare Manor in the 1880s

complete without its Great Hall built to house the revived mediaeval-style revels at festivals such as Christmas. Plate 21 shows the Great Hall at Adare Manor in Ireland.

One of earliest and most spectacular of the large-scale Gothic Revival banquets which were to become such a feature of Victorian life was that held by the 12th Duke of Norfolk in the newly complete Baron's Hall at Arundel Castle on 15 June 1815. Unusually for a Goth the Duke was a republican who had supported both the French and American Revolutions[92] and therefore determined to celebrate the six hundredth anniversary of the signing of the Magna Carta in appropriate style. Eighteen turtles had already arrived at the castle by 14 June when

> dinner was in preparation for eight hundred persons; twenty five cooks had been engaged for several days; three calves had already been used in the kitchen . . . two chests containing parts of twenty suits of armour had been received from the marquess of Townsend, and several armourers from Birmingham were engaged . . . It was first intended that the duke and barons should equip themselves in those awful habilments of war; but on examing them they were found in so delapidated a state that the idea was abandoned. Two suits, however were scoured and placed on wooden dummies to guard the baron of beef; which, on a silver dish, was destined to be elevated on a cushion covered with velvet.[93]

The powerful appeal of the life that was once lived — or thought to have been lived — and which could be revived in our ancient mansions was not only confined to Romantic novelists, artists and antiquaries. Three of our most rigorously intellectual philosophers fell under its spell in one such house. From 1814 to 1817, Jeremy Bentham, the celebrated utilitarian, rented and lived six months of the year at Forde Abbey, an outstandingly beautiful mediaeval house in Dorset. Bentham often remarked that 'Nobody who could stay here would ever go from hence . . . Nobody is so well anywhere else as everbody is here.[94] James Mill and his son John Stuart Mill often came to stay. John later wrote:

> This sojurn was, I think, an important circumstance in my education. Nothing contributes more to nourish elevation of the sentiments in a people than the large and free character of their habitations. The middle-age architecture, the baronial hall, and the spacious and lofty rooms of this fine old place, so unlike the mean and cramped externals of English middle class life, gave sentiment of a larger and freer existence and were to me a sort of poetic cultivation, aided also by the character of the grounds in which the Abbey stood.[95]

Having sketched out the pre-history of the Romantic Interior both in Europe and Britain, I shall by the analysis of five case-studies follow their development from 1750 to 1850. In 1780 they were unusual and by 1850 so many existed that they constituted a major strand of taste in interior decoration. The case-studies are Strawberry Hill, Fonthill Abbey, Abbotsford, Charlecote Park and Goodrich Court. They are carefully chosen to cover the period from 1750 onwards, but, because the creation of each often stretched over decades, they overlap one another. They differ not only in date, but also in type: Fonthill and Goodrich were newly built; Strawberry Hill and Abbotsford were modest, older structures dramatically expanded whilst Charlecote was a substantial, ancient house added to and re-edified. They were all, however, conceived or adapted to house remarkable collections of ancient objects. They all exemplify those fundamental changes in public taste taking place in the later eighteenth and early nineteenth centuries as it moved away from its admiration of the classical world to that of the Middle Ages. As early as 1762 Richard Hurd saw this movement developing : 'The ages, we call barbarous, present us with many a subject of curious speculation. What for instance is more remarkable than the Gothic CHIVALRY? or than the spirit of ROMANCE which took its rise from that singular institution?'[96] All the interiors I shall describe were created by individuals who were imbued with this 'Spirit of Romance'.

2

THE TRADE

He generally managed to bring over many interesting carvings
and other antiquities purchased in the old stores of Holland and
Flanders.   Benjamin Ferrey

The acquisition of the appropriate furnishings for a Romatic Interior
was far more complicated and time-consuming than would have been the furnishing
of an interior in the modern style. Antiquities and architectural fragments could be
purchased from shops or auctions or acquired as presents from friends. At
Strawberry Hill and Abbotsford, antiquities presented to Walpole and Scott by their
friends played an important part in the creation of their interiors. Also, once
Walpole's guidebook to Strawberry Hill had been published with his generous
acknowledgements of these gifts, those other friends who followed their example
knew that they would be similarly commemorated in future editions of the
guidebook.

Scott's friends felt that his house would become — as it indeed did — a Scottish
national monument to which patriotic Scots should present relics. Meyrick
benefited to a lesser extent from gifts. Although Scott presented him with a Scottish
sword and was appropriately thanked in the catalogue, his collection was greatly
enriched by only one celebrated gift — the Douce collection. George Hammond
Lucy seems to have received few gifts, though he had a wide circle of friends.
William Beckford, perhaps because of his peculiar social position, received few gifts.

This analysis of collections in terms of the sources of supply could be applied to
many other collections contemporary to those mentioned here. It is thus important
to realize that some of the most important objects acquired by these collectors
whether by gift or purchase had not been through the trade.

Collectors have always been particularly keen to acquire objects directly from
private sources and in such cases it is often far easier to establish fully their
provenance. These objects were usually in their original condition, not having been
'improved' by an unscrupulous dealer. The trade itself consists of two parts, the
auctioneers and the dealers, both being dependent one upon the other in that most
buyers and sellers at auctions have also been dealers.

But for collectors the opportunity to buy untouched objects with secure
provenances does occur when the auction of a long-established private collection
takes place. It is even better when the sale takes place at the collector's house, as with
the celebrated sales at Stowe, Fonthill Abbey and Strawberry Hill. In such cases the
buyer who actually travels to the sale can see the objects *in situ* in the interiors which
they furnished. It is not unknown for auctioneers to insert objects from other
sources in such sales, but the experienced collector can usually spot these. In most
cases collectors merely view the sale, leaving the bidding to a dealer whom they
commission.

Only the most intrepid actually bid for themselves. George Hammond Lucy bid
at the Fonthill sale against the agents of George IV and the Duke of Westminster,
and William Beckford bid at the La Vallière sale in Paris against the agents of Louis
XVI, the Holy Roman Emperor and Horace Walpole. Walpole's mania for ebony

furniture drove him to travel to the depths of the country to view and leave bids at the Conyers sale, though he did remark that it was unusual for a gentleman to travel into the country for such a purpose.

The history of British auction sales has been well covered in print as has that of picture dealing, but the history of the trade in antiquities has yet to be written. The whole question of when and where the antique shop made its first appearance in Britain has not been explored. The antique shop is such a common feature of life today that many people imagine that they always existed. Many of the collectors dealt with here visited shops and auction rooms throughout Europe during the second half of the eighteenth century. Indeed, it may be that the increase in the number of antique shops in this country in the first two decades of the nineteenth century was in part due to British collectors being unable to travel abroad. No sooner had Napoleon been defeated, than British collectors rushed to Paris in search of antiquities only to find the city full of other British collectors.

In the earlier eighteenth century, when classical antiquities and Old Master paintings were the main preoccupation of collectors, a trip to the Continent was the most obvious way to acquire such objects. But as more professional people began to collect — as with Stukeley and his friends — and also to turn their attention to mediaeval antiquities it became convenient for dealers to have shops in this country. There were many mediaeval and Renaissance objects for dealers and collectors alike to purchase in Britain, though, of course, supplies also came from the Continent.

The three major firms of auctioneers in Britain today, Sotheby's[1] Christie's,[2] and Phillips, existed during most of the period under consideration. Sotheby's, founded in 1744, tended before the 1850s to concentrate on selling books. Christie's, founded in 1766, had always sold the whole range of paintings and antiquities. The history of Phillips has not been written, but they only came to prominence when they persuaded William Beckford and Mr Farquahar to allow them to sell the contents of Fonthill Abbey in 1823. Christie's had been retained by Beckford in 1822 to sell the contents of the Abbey, but the sale was cancelled. Phillips, naturally, lifted many of the catalogue entries from Christie's catalogue.

However, during the period 1750–1850 many other auctioneers were active — some for a considerable time, others for only a matter of months — and some totally forgotten firms conducted sales of celebrated collections. Auctioneers had existed long before the foundation of Sotheby's. The first surviving book auction catalogue in Europe is of a sale held in Leiden in 1593 and that for the first English book sale dates from 1676.[3] The first recorded sale of paintings in this country was held at Somerset House in 1674,[4] and the first armour sale in March 1691.[5]

Large numbers of auction catalogues exist from which fascinating information can be gleaned concerning every aspect of the collecting of works of art and antiquities in Britain. In some cases copies annotated by someone who actually attended the sale survive and these often provide fascinating information about the prices and the buyers. Many of these have been listed in various publications and most importantly in Lugt's magisterial volumes; but many remain inadequately listed (for instance, in the Victoria & Albert Museum Library and the British Library) and appear in no published source. I have examined every British sale catalogue dating from before 1850 that is in the Victoria & Albert Museum Library and I quote from several here. Most scholars have concentrated upon picture sales, but have neglected those of carved woodwork, furniture, stained glass and the other antiquities so necessary for anyone furnishing a Romantic Interior.

We shall see in the following chapters how important the provenance of objects was to the collectors who used them to adorn their houses. Walpole said in 1784 when describing his collection: 'the following account of pictures and rarities is given with a view to their future dispersion. The several purchasers will find a history of their purchases . . . Such well-attested descent is the genealogy of objects of the virtu.'[6] It is, of course, the case that objects have a continuous life of their own

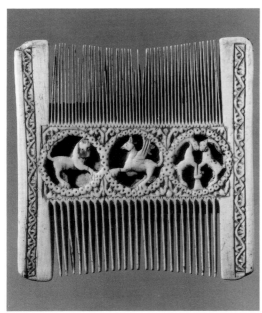

22. Queen Bertha's Comb (British Museum, London)

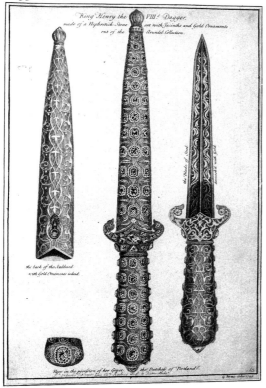

23. George Vertue's engraving of Henry VIII's Dagger, 1749

and are merely the temporary property of collector after collector, each cherishing the object for a short time only, his or her name being in due course added to the ever-growing 'attested descent'. I shall discuss the St Denis–Beckford–Newburgh–Zouche–Morgan–Metropolitan Museum chasse, which is an excellent example of this.

The first great British collector in the modern sense was, as we saw, Thomas Howard, Earl of Arundel, and his old-established collection when dispersed provided objects for several of the most celebrated eighteenth-century collections including Walpole's. Arundel at his death in 1646 bequeathed his collection to his wife Alethia who on her death in 1654 left a large part of the collection to her son William Viscount Stafford. Stafford was attainted in 1678 and beheaded in 1680; his title was to be reclaimed by his descendants in the 1820s. Stafford's part of the Arundel collection remained in Tart Hall, his house in Westminster. It was here — now re-named Stafford House — that the collection was auctioned in 1720.

The collection contained a remarkable range of objects, and the sale included sections devoted to 'The Japan', 'The Silver and Gilt Plate', 'The Crystal Vases', 'The Agat Cups' and 'Cabinets, Stone Tables, Indian Chests Peer-Glasses and China'.[7] In the section 'Several Sorts of Things' along with lot 1, 'Two Cups of Unicorn's Horn', and lot 4, 'A Morter of Serpentine Stone', was lot 6, '2 parcels of Combs of great Antiquity'. This lot probably included one of Arundel's most interesting mediaeval objects, Queen Bertha's Comb (Plate 22).[8]

Humphrey Wanley, the celebrated Saxonist and librarian to the Earl of Oxford, organized the purchase of the comb by the Earl. In an early documented instance of 'squaring the opposition' at a sale, Wanley recorded in his diary: '14 May 1720 . . . Mr Howard said that a certain Gentleman of a considerable Estate had read the Inscription upon Queen Bertha's Comb & that he would bid for it, as would several others, and among them his own Lady. Upon this, I prevailed with him to take-off Mrs Howard; & went after Mr Pownhall to see if he was come to Town, & to direct him a little; which I did accordingly.'[9]

In the event it was successfully purchased for the Earl. It was not in the sale of his collection in 1741, but passed on the death of his son to his kinswoman the Duchess of Portland. At the sale of her collection on 8 June 1786, Horace Walpole purchased the comb for 18s. It was lot 12 on the twenty-third day of the Strawberry Hill sale of 1842 when it sold for £3.13.6 and is now in the British Museum. Thus the study of this one object throws light upon the character, the formation and the dispersal of several famous collections, and demonstrates that auction room psychology has changed little since 1720.

The inscription upon the comb referred to by Wanley roughly translated reads: 'This comb was sent from Pope Gregory to Queen Bertha'. Bertha was the wife of Ethelbert, King of Kent in the early seventh century; Pope Gregory died in 604. The history of the comb before it was acquired by Arundel in the early seventeenth century is unknown. It certainly does not date from the seventh century, but its true date is still being debated, as is the date when the inscription was added; though the latter must surely have been there when Arundel acquired the comb early in the seventeenth century.

Another fascinating object from the Arundel collection was a dagger, which was probably part of lot 92 of the Jewels section of the Stafford House sale, 'A dagger of Jacynths, very rich in gold'. It was bought by the Earl of Oxford and, like the comb, passed on his death into the Portland collection. In 1749 it was engraved by Vertue (Plate 23), who noted on the plate 'King Henry the VIII's Dagger made of a Nephretick Stone set with Jacinths and Gold Ornaments out of the Arundel Collection'. This provenance was not, I am sure, invented by Vertue, who knew Harley and the Arundel collection well. Walpole, who owned the actual copy of the engraving in Plate 23, certainly believed the Henry VIII provenance and used it to date a simpler version of the dagger that he owned.

Had it been included in the Portland sale, Walpole with his mania for Tudor objects would certainly have attempted to buy it, and he describes the dagger in his notes on the sale.[10] It remained in the Portland family until well into the nineteenth century, but its location today is not known. It has been thought that the Henry VIII provenance was fanciful and that the dagger was seventeenth-century Turkish. It seems, however, likely to be Iranian and to date from the mid-sixteenth century.[11] Henry certainly owned similar objects and Arundel certainly acquired objects from the Tudor royal collections probably through his friendship with James I and Charles I.

Edward Harley, Earl of Oxford, added to his father's library, which on his death in 1741 consisted of almost 8,000 manuscripts, 50,000 printed books and about 400,000 pamphlets.[12] The manuscripts were purchased in 1753 by the British Museum for £10,000. Dr Johnson helped to catalogue the books and commented upon their auction: 'It excels any library that was ever yet offered to sale in the value as well as in the number of the volumes which it contains.'[13] This auction was one of the great bibliographical events of the eighteenth century.

The auctions of those antiquities from the Harley collection which did not pass to the Duchess of Portland, though on a lesser scale than that of the library, provided great opportunities for a new generation of collectors to plunder an ancient collection. Walpole purchased a number of coins at the coin sale.[14] The main sale commenced on 8 March 1742 and included a 'great variety of Greek and Roman antiquities ... Busto's, and Bronzes ... scarce books of Prints and Drawings ... collected by the late Mr TALMAN ... divers other valuable curiosities out of the ARUNDEL collection'. Walpole was again a buyer. This sale was at Mr Cocks's house in the Great Piazza, Covent Garden, and Vertue's splendid frontispiece to the catalogue is Plate 24.

Christopher Cocks had been an auctioneer since before 1720 and on his death in 1748 his business was taken over by Abraham Langford (1711–1774). Langford was in 1754 and 1755 to auction Dr Mead's famous collection of works of art and antiquities from which Walpole again bought a number of lots. Indeed by the mid-eighteenth century auction sales were very much part of the social round. Lady Mary Coke in her diary amongst the record of her gossip and social life includes auctions as normal everyday events. On 7 April 1769 'Ly Litchfield & Ly Betty Mackenzie made me a visit. I proposed their going with me to the Auction. They consented, & we went; bought several things. Dined at home, & went to the Duchess of Ancaster's in the evening.'[15]

Throughout the 1760s and the 1770s the numbers of auctions increased as did the proportion that included mediaeval and Renaissance objects rather than classical ones alone. Some of the sales were of anonymous collections whilst others were advertised as being the property of celebrated antiquaries and collectors. For instance on 5 March 1764 was sold the *Musaeum Thorsbeyanum ... collection of the late Ralph Thoresby Gent F.R.S. ... coins and medals in Gold, Silver &c, Manuscripts, Curiosities ... auction by Whiston Bristow, Sworn Broker. At the Exhibition Room, Spring Gardens, Charing Cross.* Thoresby (1658–1725) was the great topographer from Leeds who published in 1715 *the Ducatus Leodinensis*, which includes in an appendix a comprehensive list of his collection. Collections of such importance often did not come on to the market immediately after their collector died; in Thoresby's case the auction took place after the death of his son.

Collectors of Thoresby's generation with an interest in mediaeval antiquities had benefitted from the lack of interest in them by most collectors and were also able to take advantage of the diverse range of British antiquities thrown on to the market during the Civil Wars. Thus, when the collectors of Walpole's generation heard of the sale of such collections, they knew that there was the chance of making important acquisitions.

In February 1777 Langford sold the *A Catalogue of ... Collection of coins, medals*

24. George Vertue's frontispiece to the catalogue of the 1742 sale of the Harleian Collection

... beautiful Painted Glass of John Ives Esq, F.R.S., F.S.A., and Suffolk Herald Extraordinary. Ives had acquired much of his collection privately from the estate of Thomas Martin, the Norfolk antiquary, who had, by marrying the widow of the seventeenth-century herald and antiquary Peter Le Neve (1662–1729), acquired the collection formed after the Civil Wars by Le Neve's father and added to by Le Neve himself.

Thus Walpole was able to purchase lot 75 in the Ives sale: 'Two ancient pictures on boards, being the shutters to the altar of the Abbey of St Edmund's Bury'. Walpole used these fine, late fifteenth-century Flemish panels to decorate the Chapel in the Woods at Strawberry Hill. The Bury St Edmunds provenance is probably wrong, but these panels almost certainly came out of an English church either at the Reformation or during the Civil Wars and were probably acquired by the Le Neve family in Norfolk where they lived. Such opportunities to purchase ecclesiastical fragments did not exist in Walpole's day except when an old-established collection was sold. The panels were sold once again at the Strawberry Hill sale in 1842 and they are now on display in the Church of All Hallows by the Tower in London.

As we saw in the last chapter with Stukeley's circle, not all collectors were aristocrats or even gentlemen. In 1790, for instance, was sold in three sales the collection of William Rawle, 'Accoutrement Maker'; we shall meet him again when we discuss the trade in ancient armour. On 10 March 1794 Sotheby's sold the collection of another tradesman collector, though in this case the collection seems to have been closely related to his business: *The property of the late Barak Longmate, Engraver of Noel Street, Soho: comprehending a curious collection of books on Heraldry, County History, Antiquities. &c with a great number of M.S correction, additions, and notes by Longmate. Likewise a large collection of Heraldic manuscripts.*

By the early nineteenth century many sale catalogues exist which give evidence of the large numbers of collections that had been formed by scholars and antiquaries of quite modest means. Such collections are often known only through these sale catalogues and many are, of course, anonymous. Fortunately, someone who attended the sale may have noted the name of the collector and, if one is very lucky, the buyers and prices in his copy of the catalogue. For this reason it is important to collate as many copies of any one catalogue as possible. So random are the survivals of catalogues and so numerous were the auctioneers at this date it has proved impossible for me to form any clear idea of the extent of the collecting of antiquities of the type with which I am concerned.

Most aristocratic collectors added their collection to those of their ancestors already housed at their seat, thus their collections are often well documented. The collections formed by middle-class collectors present far more of a problem, as these were usually dispersed at their death. Even when a sale catalogue exists it is usually impossible to establish how they displayed their collection and whether it was used to create a Romantic Interior or was just kept locked away in cupboards. Such collections were housed in perfectly commonplace rented houses in London and were rarely described and even more rarely illustrated *in situ*.

One such which is documented to a limited extent may be used to represent many others that certainly existed. This was the important collection formed by the scholar and antiquary Francis Douce (1757–1834). Douce bequeathed his collection of antiquities to Sir Samuel Rush Meyrick, and his books and manuscripts he left to the Bodleian Library.[16] He was for a while Keeper of Manuscripts at the British Museum and was not a wealthy man, though late in life he inherited money. 'Upon his marriage [in 1799] he purchased a house in Gower-street, and though his means were slender, he was enabled by economy to live in a genteel style, and to indulge his love for books, prints, and coins ... He at length found a house in Charlotte-street ... he then moved to Kensington-square.'[17] None of these houses was large or especially adapted for his collection and 'his houses in Upper Gower Street and later in Charlotte Street must have been quite inadequate. It is not as though Douce stopped short at acquiring 13,000 printed books and 400 manuscripts; his diary of accessions reveals a stream of antiquarian objects of all kinds.'[18]

Fortunately, Douce's friend the eccentric bibliographer Thomas Frognall Dibdin left us this description of Douce's study at Charlotte Street in 1817:

> His maple-wooded bookcases rejoice the eye by the peculiar harmony of the tint with the rich furniture which they enclose. Here a bit of old, bright stained glass, exhibiting the true long-lost *ruby tint*; there, an inkstand, adorned in high cameo-relief, by the skill of *John of Bologna*; a little regiment, pyramidically piled, of the rarest China cups, out of which seven successive Emperors of China quaffed the essence of bohea. Persian boxes, Raffael-ware, diptychs, and chessmen — the latter used by Charles V. and Francis I., on their dining together, *tête à tête*, not long after the battle of Pavia, Korans, missals, precious manuscripts . . . and the parchment roll which Handel wielded in beating time on the first representation of his Messiah.[19]

Douce, however, commented when this description was first published in 1832 by Dibdin: 'What can this flighty Mercury mean by "inkstand of John of Bologna, Persian boxes, Chessmen of Charles V & Francis, Korans, Regiomontanus' staff, madrigals & Handels parchm. roll?" All absolute *Bedlam*, for not one of these articles do I possess or know anything about them.'[20] These remarks by the collector himself demonstrate how careful one must be about contemporary descriptions, but when these are the only surviving evidence they have to be seriously considered. There is, however, no doubt that Dibdin certainly captured something of the character of his friend's collection as it was displayed in his house, and it is of interest for this reason.

Two literary figures of the generation before Douce were also antiquaries and collectors. Samuel Ireland was a celebrated Shakespearean scholar, and Richard Gough a topographer of genius. Ireland's collection was sold by Sotheby's on 7 May 1801: *Books, Paintings, Miniatures, Drawings, Prints and various Curiosities*. The first day's sale included a wide range of historical relics — lot 36 was a 'part of Wickliff's Vestment' — but a number naturally related to Ireland's interest in Shakespeare. Lot 19 was 'A purse made of glass beads, given by Shakespeare to his eldest daughter' and lot 29 'A silver box, gilt, with the Scene of the ghosts first appearance to Hamlet, in that play, embossed upon the lid; belonged to Joseph Addison Esq., bought at his sale by Mr Ireland'.

Richard Gough's collection was also sold by Sotheby's starting on 10 July 1810: *Museum Goughianum . . . Prints, Drawings, Coins, Medals, Seals, Painted Glass, Paintings, Pottery, Brass Monuments*. This collection covered both ancient Roman and mediaeval antiquities. Lot 282 'A collection of ancient tiles, and a few fragments of tesselated pavements' and lot 303 'A Sconce inlaid with enamel, an ancient candlestick, and three pairs of ancient snuffers' are typical.

The sale catalogues that survive from the year of the Gough sale indicate that other collectors, about whom we know very little, had also put together collections much the same in range and content as his. For instance, in 1810 and 1811 King & Lochee of London sold *The valuable cabinet of Gold, Silver and other coins . . . collected at a very considerable expence . . . By the late Joseph White Esq of Islington . . . Aug 2 1810*. The rest of this collection was sold by the same auctioneers on 1 May 1811: *A Catalogue of . . . Shells, Minerals, Fossils, Polished Stones together with several miscellaneous articles*. Lot 15 on the third day was 'A carving in stone, from Glastonbury Abbey' and lot 18 'Head of an ancient British adze, formed of flint. How White housed and displayed his collection we will probably never know, but anyone furnishing a Romantic interior at this period could have obtained first-rate material at King & Lochee's Great Room, No. 38 King Street, Covent Garden. Indeed they sold on 22 May 1811 an anonymous collection including *A Catalogue of . . . stuffed birds in fine preservation, a few shells, ancient armour, bronzes, carvings in ivory, missals*

. . . and other miscellaneous articles. Lot 1 on the first day, 'Skins of serpents', represented a specialist taste, but many including Scott and Meyrick would have been attracted to lot 51 on the second day, 'Highland sword and target, left by the army of the Pretender, at Ashburn, in Derbyshire in 1745'.

I have chosen a few sales to give some indication of both the richness of the collections constantly being offered for sale and the opportunities they gave for new collectors, antiquaries and scholars to build up large and varied collections with which to furnish their houses, though, of course, then as now, most of the buyers at these sales were dealers, some acting on their own behalf and others as agents for collectors. It is unfortunately impossible to tell from the lists of buyers — when these happen to exist — for whom a dealer was buying.

It would be tedious to describe many of the sales of the 1820s and 1830s, though several important ones are dealt with later in this chapter and in subsequent chapters. There was a continuous and indeed growing stream of auctions of antiquities during these decades and the survival of greater numbers of catalogues makes the study of their content easier than for the earlier period.

Not all the objects used to furnish Romantic Interiors came through auctions or the trade. Objects were constantly being excavated whether by accident or by archaeologists. Many collectors were amateur archaeologists who added the objects excavated to their collections; others appropriated objects turned up by the plough on their own land. Scott owned several excavated antiquities, which he displayed in his interiors at Abbotsford, and he also initiated at least one excavation himself. Farmers, engineers, architects and builders frequently discovered antiquities during their day to day work.

For instance, Sotheby's sold on December 1832: *Catalogue of the Architectural, Historical and Miscellaneous Library of the late Mr William Knight F.S.A. Assistant architect and President Superintendent to the New London Bridge Also his very interesting collection of Antiquities and other curiosities found on removing the old London Bridge.* Lot 442 was 'Four very Ancient Dirks, a piece of Chain Armour, two Ancient Spurs &c found in making the foundation . . . of the New Bridge'. Rather more bizarre was lot 443, 'The Lower Jaw, and three other bones of Peter of Cole Church the original architect of London Bridge found on removing the foundation of the Ancient Chapel'.

Some archaeolgists created interiors totally furnished with their excavations: one well-documented example is the Moss House which William Cunnington, the famous Wiltshire archaeologist and collaborator of Sir Richard Colt Hoare of Stourhead, created in his garden at Heytesbury in Wiltshire. Its appearance in about 1810 was described by Cunnington's daughter:

> At the end of the lawn was a large Summer or Moss House . . . The walls were constructed of sturdy limbs of trees ranged side by side, and covered on the outside with dry heather, while the inside was lined with moss. Shelves fixed around . . . on these appropriate supports were arranged the numerous urns and larger objects found in the barrows. On either side were smaller cells . . . in these were many of the larger fossils . . . On the floor of the centre compartment was a plan of the temple of Avebury, formed of large pebbles.[21]

Auction catalogues sometimes throw light upon the nature of the stock of antique dealers and a few catalogues exist of sales of their stock. One very early example is for a very large sale of 1,265 lots, quite apart from the paintings: *A Catalogue of all the Curiosities And Stock in Trade of that late ingenious Mr Peter Parquot, Toy Men and Vertoso deceased . . . Oriental and other Agats . . . fine Canes and all sorts of Curiosities, in Gold, Silver, Amber, Ivory and fine wood . . . sold by Auction for the Benefit of his Widow and Children, on Monday the 5th of February 1727–8 at the first house with Iron Rails on the Left Hand, in Bow-Street.*

Mr Isaacs supplied the Lucys at Charlecote, but on 14 February 1844 Messrs

Foster sold *The capital collection of pictures of the Dutch, Flemish and French schools, the entire property of Mr Samuel Isaacs of regent Street ... to be sold in consequence of the Proprietor retiring from business.* What happened to Isaacs' stock of furniture and other antiquities is not recorded.

On 2, 3 and 5 June 1807 Christie's sold the stock of a Mr Innocent. This was 'Robert Innocent, goldsmith, toyman and dealer in natural curiosities 15 Little Newport Street, Leicester Square.'[22] The sale catalogue stated that Mr Innocent was 'retiring from the business and removed from his house ... the stock comprised a great assortment of stones, agates, crystals, miniatures, shells, minerals, carvings in ivory, eight small stained glass windows and ... the cap in which King Charles I was beheaded.'[23]

In the following chapters we shall come across the names and the activities of numerous dealers, or brokers as they were more usually called. Dr Johnson defines a broker as '1. A factor; one that does business for another ... 2. One who deals in old household goods.'[24] The *Oxford English Dictionary* gives several definitions including 'A second hand dealer' and quotes from several literary sources dating back to the fourteenth century. Ben Jonson referred in 1598 to 'a Houndsditch man, sir. One of the deiul's own neere kinsmen, a broker'.[25]

Another term used until the early nineteenth century was 'nicknackitarian'. An interesting law case concerning a widow who claimed she had been swindled took place in 1802. 'The plaintiff was a *nicknackitarian*, that is a dealer in curiosities, such as Egyptian mummies, Indian implements of war, arrows dipped in the poison of the upas-tree, bows, antique shields ... in short, almost every rarity that the most ardent virtuoso would wish to possess.'[26] By extension both a broker's shop and a Romantic Interior were often referred to as a 'nicknackitory', and the term 'knick-knack' survives today.

Despite the existence of the term 'nicknackitarian', the use of the word 'broker' was much more usual. Sir Walter Scott wrote to his friend Daniel Terry on 10 November 1822: 'I would to Heaven I could take a cruize with you through the brokers, which would be the pleasantest affair.'[27] On 18 June 1823 Scott wrote again to Terry: 'next spring, perhaps, we may go prowling together through the brokers' purlieus'.[28]

We have few references to the activites of brokers in the early eighteenth century, but the German traveller Uffenbach visited two in London in 1710:

> In the afternoon we were at Herr Campe's, who lives at Charing Cross in the house of a 'Thincker' or tinman. He is really a sword-cutler by trade, though he shows no signs of it. For he has taken to dealing in ancient coins, in which he has done so well that he now has set up for himself alone and has two fairly large rooms full of antiques ... Campe has so many elegant things that I think it would not be easy to find as many in any private collection; but I doubt that they are all genuine ... I believe that there were as many as two hundred to two hundred and fifty of all kinds of things ... In the second room, which was smaller, there were only large statues.[29]

Later in 1710 Uffenbach reported that he:

> Called on an Italian ... His name is Francesco Beneditti of Lucca, and he is well known everywhere as a antiquarian and an artful fellow who has lived for many years in France and nearly ten years here. He is a Mass priest and secretly, says Mass every day at the Venetian Ambassadors. He does a lively trade in antiques, and manages to swindle the English shockingly, palming off on them for prodigious sums articles which he gets from France and Italy for nothing. He is not only well known to all who have collections but is also their prime counsellor in all matters concerning their medals and antiques.[30]

There is no indication where this Italian lived. In fact very little is known about where brokers lived and traded at this period or whether they had shops or dealt from home.

A considerable number were certainly trading from Moorfields in the City. It was an area also favoured by second-hand booksellers; the collector Ralph Thoresby, whose sale I mentioned above, wrote in his diary on 29 January 1709: 'In Moorfields bought very rare edition of the New Testament.'[31] On 21 he may again wrote: 'Took a walk into Moorfields, picked up a few old books.'[32] In 1761 this description was published: 'Lower Moorfields ... the east side of this part of Moorfields is taken up by shops, where old books are sold at the south east corner, and second-hand goods of all sorts along that side.'[33]

By the 1760s enough dealers had congregated together in Moorfields to give their name to a street. Lady Mary Coke, whom we met earlier attending auctions, wrote on 18 April 1768: 'went by the new road to Moor Fields to the carpet manufactory ... we went from the carpet mamufactory to a place called Broker's row, where I bought several things; my Coach was almost filled'.[34] Broker's Row does not appear on maps of the 1770s and 1780s, but it was appropriately situated near the mythical Grub Street, both being nicknames for streets with far less exciting real names.

However, by 1799 the northern half of Little Moorfields is marked on maps as 'Broker Row'. In *Johnstone's Directory* for 1817 Broker's Row Moorfields is listed and had twenty-eight premises which housed ten 'Brokers and Appraisers', two 'Furniture Brokers' and six 'Upholders' or 'Cabinet Makers'. By the late 1820s the name no longer appears in directories as in Moorfields, but two more streets of this name appear in the 1838 directory. This lists Broker's Row, Redcross Street, Southwark, with its nine premises, seven occupied by furniture brokers, and Broker's Alley off Drury Lane with twelve premises housing three furniture brokers and one fur broker. Both are still listed in the 1850 directory, but Moorfields never appears again up to 1850.

One useful source of information concerning brokers is the insurance records. In 1775 Samuel Swain, 'Upholder and Broker' who was trading 'At the Woolpack, & near Belland Walk in Broker Row Moorfields', insured his house and its contents for the not inconsiderable sum of £800.[35] Whether or not Swain dealt in antiquities is not recorded. In 1780 Joseph Wilkinson, 'Broker and Cabinetmaker' of Broker Row, Moorfield, insured his utensils and stock for £500.[36]

These records show that other areas contained groups of brokers; there were, for instance, several in Ratcliffe Highway in the East End in the 1780s. they also show the start of the other two brokers' enclaves mentioned above. In 1777 John Draper, cabinet-maker and broker, insured his premises at the corner of Queen Street in Redcross Street, Southwark,[37] whilst between 1775 and 1783 four cabinet-makers and brokers insured premises in Drury Lane near to Broker's Alley.

A cabinet-maker and broker might only have dealt in relatively new second-hand furniture, but even if not primarily interested in ancient furniture he would certainly have traded in it if he came across it; and with his workshop he was in a perfect position to 'improve' ancient pieces that came his way.

The Moorfields area certainly still contained brokers as late as the 1820s, for a commentator writing of that period stated:

> When I remember Moorfields first, it was a large, open, quadrangular space, shut in by the Pavement to the west, the hospital, and its outbuildings to the south, and lines of shops without fronts, occupied chiefly by dealers in old furniture, to the east and north. Most of these shops were covered in by screens of canvas or rough boards, so as to form an apology for a piazza ... a broken-down four-poster or a rickety tent bedstead might be secured at almost any price ... a tall, stiff, upright easy chair, without a bottom; a cupboard, with one shelf left of three, and with half a door; here a black oak chest, groaning to be screaped, so thick with ancient dust that it might have been the den of some unclean animal in

Noah's Ark . . . These miscellaneous treasures were guarded by swarthy men and women of Israel.[38]

By the 1820s, however, one area was beginning to take over as the main centre of ther antiquities trade. In keeping with the growth of London beyond the bounds of the old city this area was in the West End and conveniently placed for the collectors who were tending by this date to live in areas like Westminster and Mayfair. The area in question was Soho and the streets immediately to the north such as Berners Street and Mortimer Street. Between Mortimer Street and Oxford Street was Hanway Yard,

> now widened, improved, and called Hanway Street. It was extremely narrow and dirty at the time referred to [1820s], but it possessed several attractions. At one corner (and it is still there) was Baldock's old china shop, a sort of museum for Chinese horses and dragons, queer-looking green vases . . . At the end nearest to Oxford street therer was something still more fascinating, in the shape of a muffin and crumpet shop . . . The rest of the yard was tenanted by Jew dealers in curiosities, or, indeed, in anything that turned up.[39]

The 1842 Post Office Directory lists twenty-eight buildings: those occupied by brokers were, number No. 1, 'E.H. Baldock Antique Furniture dr'; No.4, 'Newton Mr R. Curiosity dealer'; No. 6, 'Moses Benjamin Curiosity dealer'; No. 7, 'Rees Soloman Jeweller'; No. 17, 'Hitchcock Chas glass & chinaman'; No. 26, 'Unsworth Geo glass & china warehouse'; and, of course, at No. 28 was 'Gast Mrs Eliza, Muffin Baker'.

In 1833 J.C. London, in discussing the trade in ancient furniture and woodwork, singles out 'Wilkinson of Oxford Street, Hanson of John Street . . . Kensett of Mortimer Street . . .'[40] John Street was just off Hanway Yard. By 1858 one of the celebrated features of Soho was

> the display of manufacturers of antique furniture and curiosity shops. It is a fact worthy of notice, that old furniture can be manufactured in this locality of any age and all manner of styles from clumsy dutch of the 15th century to the elaborate workmanship and beautiful design of the reign of Louis the 14th . . . many have added to their archaeological stores from this antiquarian warehouse of articles that have been manufactured with the stamp of hoary age.[41]

The census returns for 1831 do not differentiate between brokers of furniture and antiquities and all other types of brokers. But in the 1841 census, furniture borkers are specifically listed. For the country as a whole, 437 furniture brokers are listed of whom 285 are in London and Middlesex. It is, however, particularly instructive to examine the distribution within London, 132 are in Middlesex and 153 in the metropolis itself. For some unaccountable reason the 1841 Post Office Directory lists 217 furniture brokers. The census shows 3 in the City, 3 in Kensington, 5 in Clerkenwell, 12 in the East End 12, 31 in Holborn, 13 in Finsbury, 28 in Westminster and 49 the area around the Tower. The 28 in Westminster, which took in Soho and Bond Street, is no surprise, but the 49 near the Tower is odd. These latter must, I feel, be mainly dealers in cheap second-hand furniture, as there is no evidence of dealers in antique furniture or curiosities being denizens of this area. The 1842 Post Office Directory lists 10 antique furniture dealers, 9 of whom were in or near Soho. This same directory lists 46 curiosity dealers, 37 of whom were in Soho or the West End.

By 1850 Wardour Street in Soho was, above all others, associated with the antiquities and furniture trade. Its rise to fame was swift, as can be documented by the directories. In 1817 there were no brokers in Wardour Street, though there were 13 cabinet-makers and carvers. By 1838 there were 9 brokers and 12 cabinet-makers, by 1850 there were 23 brokers and 24 cabinet-makers. But by 1860 the numbers were 16 brokers and 21 cabinet-makers and, despite this decline after 1850, the area had become associated in the public mind with the antiquities trade.

These businesses thrived in what were domestic houses 'rebuilt in the first quarter of the eighteenth century ... most of these ... buildings probably remained standing until the second half of the nineteenth century by which date many were occupied by antique dealers, furniture makers and brokers, through whose activites the term "Wardour Street" came to denote ... furniture of questionable antiquity'.[42]

This image of Wardour Street as the home of spurious antiquity is further confirmed by the *Oxford English Dictionary*, which defines the term 'Wardour Street English' as 'Applied to the pseudo-archaic diction affected by some modern writers especially of historical novels' and quotes from an article of 1888 entitled 'Wardour Street English' which stated that 'This is not literary English of any date, this is Wardour Street Early English — a perfectly modern article with a sham appearance of the real antique about it'.

From the evidence I have given it would seem that the Mortimer Street, Hanway Yard area north of Oxford Street was by the 1820s popular with brokers, who gradually spread southwards into Soho during the 1830s. There is no doubt that the centre of gravity of the broking trade moved west from the City to Soho between the mid-eighteenth and mid-nineteenth centuries. Curiously, the auctioneers had been centred on St James's and Covent Garden since the late seventeenth century. Thus the move of the brokers to the west brought them closer to the auction rooms.

The fact that so many cabinet-makers and carvers operated in Soho, as well as silversmiths and goldsmiths, was of great importance to the antique brokers in that it made their access to restorers, improvers and outright fakers very easy. As we saw above, the geographical proximity of the broking trade to the cabinet-making trade was as much the case in the mid-eighteenth century in Moorfields as it was later to be in Soho. Far more research needs to be done on the geographical distribution of the antiquities brokers and indeed on how the trade operated, I have here only given a few pointers to the situation in the decades before and after 1800.

Before describing several of the prominent brokers, a little must be said about the appearance of their shops. I have already described a shop in 1710, but few such descriptions survive. Richard Gough, the antiquary mentioned above, left a rare description of the shop of John Millan. Millan, who died in 1784 aged more than eighty-one traded as a book and curiosity dealer for more than fifty years from a shop in Charing Cross. Gough visited his shop on 5 March 1772:

> last night, I penetrated the utmost recesses of Millan's shop; which, if I may borrow an idea from Natural History, is incrusted with Literature and Curiosities like so many stalactitical exhudations. Through a narrow alley, between piles of books, I reached a cell, or *adytum*, whose sides were so completely cased with the same *supellex*, that the Fire-place was literally *enchasse dans la muraille*. In this cell sat the Deity of the place, at the head of a Whist party, which was interupted by my inquiries ... I emerged from this shop, which I consider as a future herculaneum, where we shall hereafter root out many scarce things now rotting on the floor, considerably sunk below the level of the new pavement.'[43]

In 1827 Sir Walter Scott, who by that date had very wide experience of broker's shops, described how 'No shop is so easily set up as an antiquary's. Like those of the lowest order of pawnbrokers, a commodity of rusty iron, a bag or two of hobnails, a few odd shoebuckles, cashiered kail-pots, and fire irons declared incapable of service, are quite sufficient to set him up. If he add a sheaf or two of penny ballads and broadsides, he is a great man — an extensive trader.'[44]

Even in the late 1840s there seem not to have been large numbers of shops selling antiquities, but there is a description of a group in Monmouth and St Andrew Streets, both in the notorious area of Seven Dials:

Old furniture, or curiosity shops, such as we find in Wardour Street, are a new species — and amongst the most interesting. Humbler collections of curiosities are to be found in Monmouth Street, St Andrew's Street, and the New Cut . . . In no other part of London is the use of cellar-shops so conspicuous as in Monmouth Street. Every house has a cellar, to which acess is gained by a flight of steps from the open street; and every cellar is a shop, mostly for the sale of second hand boots and shoes, which are ranged round the margin of the entrance; while countless children — noisy dirt happy brats — are loitering within and without.[45]

The only other adequate description of a broker's shop of before 1850, though in a novel, is very well observed. In *The Old Curiosity Shop* Dickens describes the shop in which Little Nell dwells with her grandfather, who was an antiquities broker. It was first published in 1840 as a part of *Master Humphrey's Clock*, later appearing as a distinct novel. Dickens sadly does not indicate which area the shop was supposed to be in, but he certainly had visited such shops, for by the time he was furnishing his house in Doughty Street, Bloomsbury, in 1837 he had purchased several pieces of second-hand furniture.

Dickens scholars have spent a great deal of time attempting to establish which shop Dickens had in mind: evidence was produced that it was 10 Green Street just off Leicester Square.[46] This cannot, however, have been the shop, for the Post Office Directories show that it was occupied by a currier in 1837 and a baker from 1839 to 1850. The other firm candidate was 24 Fetter Lane,[47] but sadly this was occupied by a circulating library in 1838 and was unoccupied from 1842 to 1845. Perhaps some modern Dickens scholar will take the matter further.

Little Nell in the company of the novel's narrator returns to the shop at night and sees through the glass panel in the front door:

at length a faint light appeared through the glass which, as it approached very slowly, the bearer having to make his through a great many scattered articles . . . It was a little old man with long grey hair . . . The place through which he had made his way at leisure was one of those receptacles for old and curious things which seem to crouch in odd corners of this town and to hide their musty treasures from the public eye in jealousy and distrust. There were suits of mail standing like ghosts in armour here and there, fantastic carvings brought from monkish cloisters, rusty weapons of various kinds, distorted figures in china and wood and iron and ivory: tapestry and strange furniture which might have been designed in dreams. The haggard aspect of the old man was wonderfully suited to the place; he might have groped among old churches and tombs and deserted houses and gathered all the spoils with his own hands.[48]

25. *The Old Curiosity Shop* by George Cattermole, 1842 (The Dickens House, Doughty Street, London)

Several of the illustrations in this novel are by George Cattermole, a close friend of Dickens, who took great interest in their subjects. Dickens wrote to Cattermole on 13 January 1840 about the first illustration, which depicted Master Humphrey's room: 'make me a little sketch for a wood-cut . . . the subject an old quaint room, with antique Elizabethan furniture, and in the chimney-corner an extra-ordinary old clock'.[49] Shortly after this, Cattermole drew his highly atmospheric illustration of the old curiosity shop by candlelight which appeared in the fourth published part of *Master Humphrey's Clock*. Late in 1842 Cattermole painted two finished water-colours after his illustrations and these he gave to Dickens, who wrote to thank him on 20 December: 'It is impossible for me to tell you how greatly I am charmed with those beautiful pictures, in which the whole feeling and thought and expression of the little story is rendered to the gratification of my inmost heart.[50] One of these watercolours (Plate 25) is of the interior of the Old Curiosity Shop and is still in Dickens's house in Doughty Street. Several artists were inspired by this novel, as R.B. Martineau's painting of Little Nell giving Kit his writing lesson in the midst of the antiquities (Plate 26) shows, but it was Cattermole, specializing as he did in

26. *Kit's Writing Lesson* by R.B. Martineau, 1852 (Tate Gallery, London)

27. *Don Quixote in his Study* by George Cattermole (Victoria & Albert Museum, London)

28. *Don Quixote in his Study* 'composed and photographed from the life' by William Lake Price, 1856 (Victoria & Albert Museum, London)

watercolours and paintings on antiquarian and historical subjects, who most brilliantly captured the scene described in the novel. He followed in the tradition of so many earlier artists and had a collection of antiquities with which he furnished his house and which he used as historical props in his paintings. Rubens and Cosway had such collections, and we know that Cattermole used his collection to create a series of splendid Romantic Interiors in his own house in Clapham Rise. It was here that he entertained friends like Dickens, Macready, Thackeray, Maclise, Bulwer-Lytton, Forster and Landseer.

> His son Leonardo recalled that the drawing room was: as unlike a modern drawing-room as possible, but very 'George Cattermolean' in its sombre picturesqueness; a large, long room ... a dark flock paper relieved by gold bars (designed by my father) ... furnished almost entirely with the heavy carved furniture which had belonged to Lord Byron, and which my father bought on taking his chambers in the Albany ... Here was a large carved oak and satin-wood cabinet, with exquisitely carved figures in *alto-relievo* ... The studio was under the drawing room ... Here again was old carved furniture, an escritoire with hideous, gaping, 'Old Curiosity Shop' faces on it. A 'Girgione' life-size knight in armour frowned from above a bookcase ... Armour and tapestry hung the walls. The room was lighted by a large old-fashioned pedestal brass oil-lamp, the light from which glinted upon various antique swords, cross-bows, firelocks and romantic appurtenances of ancient warfare.[51]

Part of Cattermole's collection was sold after his death in 1868 *Catalogue of the remaining works of the late G. Cattermole ... old carved cabinets and tables and the contents of the studio ... Messrs Christie ... March 8 1869* the rest being retained by his son. Cattermole certainly used his antiquities to advantage in a host of paintings on historical and literary subjects such as *The Murder of the Bishop of Liège (Scene from Quentin Durward)* of 1836 and *After the Battle of Newbury* of 1843. Plate 27 is his painting *Don Quixote in his Study* which includes a whole range of antiquarian impedimenta probably from Cattermole's collection. Here he was following in an established tradition, for Delacriox had painted this subject in 1824 and Bonington a year or two later. It was, of course, possible for an artist to invent on the canvas props that did not exist, though even before the Pre-Raphaelites and their generation placed such a high premium on actual observation many artists worked from real objects.

It is interesting that with the emergence of photography the old artisitic tradition of using antiquities as props continued, though in this case they had to be available at the moment the photograph was taken. This can be very aptly demonstrated by a photograph of Don Quixote in his study (Plate 28) very similar in composition to the Cattermole painting. Who sat for the 'Don' is not known; the print dates from 1855 and is inscribed 'Composed and Photographed from the life by Lake Price'.

William Lake Price (1810–1891) was trained as a watercolourist and architectural draughtsman in the studio of A.C. Pugin, but became a pioneer early photographer, publishing *A Manual of Photographic Manipulation* in 1858. The existence of the antiquities used as props in photographs such as this, like their existence in paintings, had a powerful influence upon collectors furnishing their houses in a style similar to that depicted by the artists or photographers. Such props were, of course, usually purchased from brokers and often became part of the artist's own collection.

There is one particularly well-documented example of an artist specially buying antiquities to illustrate in a picture. The picture in question is *The Antiquary's Cell* (Plate 31), which is closely based upon the description of the study of the hero of Scott's novel *the Antiquary* discussed later. It was painted in 1836 by E.W. Cooke (1811–1880), later celebrated as a marine painter. Cooke had trained with Lake Price in the studio of A.C. Pugin, and during the 1830s Price was painting mainly watercolours of antiquarian subjects very similar to *The Antiquary's Cell*. Cookes's diary for 1835 tells the story of the creation of the picture over four months:

> March 13 ... to a great many furniture and armour dealers I bought a pair of Gauntletts ... April 2 ... to Wardour Street looked at old furniture most splendid ... bought a fine carved chair. Also looked at china ... my fine chair came home from Hull's ... Thurs 14 ... went to several jews shops and bought silk for my old chair ... All day arranging an antiquaries room with armour and curiosities &c in my study. Made a sketch in colour in evening by candlelight ... completed the arrangement of my room and commenced the outline of a picture of it in evening Miss Waring came to see it ... they lent me china jars to group with rest ... went to town ... I took up, old pictures & old clothes made exchanges with Jews in Princes Street for china jar carvings helmet &c ... June 15

29. A study of armour by E.W. Cooke of 1835 for *The Antiquary's Cell* (Victoria & Albert Museum, London)

30. A study by candlelight by E.W. Cooke for *The Antiquary's Cell*, 1835 (Victoria & Albert Museum, London)

31. *The Antiquary's Cell* by E.W. Cooke, 1835
(Victoria & Albert Museum, London)

very busy all day clearing out study of the curiosities, antiquities &c . . . Friday July 10 sent my picture of 'Olla podrida' to Mr Sheepshanks.[52]

Two studies by Cooke for the painting survive: one is of armour (Plate 29); the other is clearly the colour sketch made by candlelight (Plate 30).

The use of the picturesque term 'Olla podrida' is amusing, but appropriate, for a picture depicting such a singular assemblage of antiquities. the term is a Spanish one that describes a stew containing a wide range of ingredients. Sheepshank bequeathed the picture and the two studies along with his remarkable collection of modern pictures to the Victoria & Albert Museum.

Cooke's description of the creation of the picture amply demonstrates how he set about creating the effect he needed for the picture, going to the lengths of sketching by candlelight. It is also obvious how dependent he was on the stock in the broker's shops. He also specifically mentions Wardour Street and the name of Hull who traded from a shop in Wardour Street. Cooke as a fellow pupil of Pugin in his father's — A.C. Pugin's — studio may well have met Hull through A.W.N. Pugin. Princes Street, mentioned by Cooke, was a street known for its brokers and was off Leicester Square.

Once Scott's novel *The Antiquary* had been published in 1816, artists throughout Europe depicted the subject, and in 1829, several years before Cooke's picture, Bonington had painted *The Antiquary* (Plate 32).

We have few representations of the interiors of broker's shops, but even more rare are exterior views. I have found no watercolours of British shops before 1850. There is a photograph from about 1900 of the shop of the brokers called Hardingham, which was at 32 York Street, Westminster (Plate 33). When the premises were demolished the shop-front went to the Victoria & Albert Museum. I suspect that the photographs show the shop window filled with much the range of objects one would have seen in a broker's shop in the 1840s except that the style of the furniture would have been different. The seventeenth-century armchair and the oak chest might have been in a shop in the 1840s, but the Georgian mahogany chairs, desk and tripod table become saleable items only after the rise of neo-Georgianism in the 1860s.

A commentator writing in 1898 of the Wardour Street firm of Edwards & Roberts noted that 'Old oak though it still fetches a good price, is not so much in demand as it was, and the "rage" during the last twelve years has been for furniture of "Chippendale", "Sheraton", "Hepplewhite" and "Adams" ... The old French styles of the period Louis XIV, XV, XVI, and the "Empire" are much in request.'[53]

One of the earliest brokers about whom there is information is John Murray (1670–1748). He was variously referred to as 'The Houndsditch Broker' or 'Murray of Sacomb' and seems to be the only eighteenth-century broker of whom we have a portrait. George Vertue painted a watercolour of him in 1738, which is in the Victoria & Albert Museum. The Vertue engraving of him (Plate 34) dates from 1752. Vertue knew Murray and wrote in November 1733 to the great collector the Earl of Oxford: 'at my earnest request and Mr Murray's favour we went straight to Ware and he excused me from returning back to his house at Sacombe where I should have rested the night as your Lordship appointed.'[54]

It seems that 'Murray has immortalized himself, however in the annals of

32. *The Antiquary* by R.P. Bonington, 1829 (Wallace Collection, London)

33. Hardingham's shop, London, *c.*1900

penes R.Rawlinson.LLD.R.et AT.SS.S.

G.Vertue ad vivum delin.1738. et fculp.1752.

Natr.Jan.24.1670. Ob.13 Sep.1748.

Hon.! Maister John Murray of Sacomb;
The Works of Old Time to collect was his Pride,
Till Oblivion dreaded his Care;
Regardless of Friends intestate he dy'd,
So the Rooks & the Crons were his Heir. GN.

34. John Murray of Sacomb by George Vertue,
1752 (Victoria & Albert Museum, London)

book-purchasers by having procured for lord Oxford the first edition of *Tindal's New Testament*.'[55] Indeed 'Lord Oxford thought himself under such obligations to his "jackall" that he settled upon him 20L. a year for life,'[56] The term 'jackall' is particularly apt for the scavenging character of the early brokers. Murray also appears in the diary of Humfrey Wanley, the Earl of Oxford's librarian, in 1721 and 1724 as a 'Dealer in books.'[57]

But he dealt in far more than books. On 15 March 1762 Horace Walpole's friend Henry Zouch wrote to him, 'I have an oval medal in silver of Cha[rles] I . . . I bought this medal some years ago of one Murray, an old man near Hertford, who had been a collector for Lord Oxford, and had several curiosities himself. He told me he was a domestic for Lord Russell and attended him upon the fatal scaffold when he fell.'[58] Russell was executed in July 1683 for his involvement in the Rye House Plot.

Little more seems to be known about Murray. An enquirer wrote in 1785 to the *Gentleman's Magazine*: 'Can any of your correspondents give some anecdotes of Murray of Sacombe, the antiquary, once Hearne's correspondent? He was, I am told, a very singular character.'[59] No anecdotes were forthcoming, but the engraving (Plate 34) was described. Obviously Murray was no ordinary broker — having known Oxford, Hearne and Vertue — despite his lowly origins.

A large correspondence between Hearne and Murray survives, though not all Hearne's friends thought well of him. Rawlinson, the antiquary, wrote to Hearne in 1729: 'between us two, my Brother . . . seems to think the Houndsditch Broker not a little vainglorious; *Proletarius non generosus* were the terms he used.'[60] Hearne, however, wrote in his diary on 22 May 1733: 'I used to desire Mr Murray to have a Catalogue drawn of all his books . . . Mr Murray's collection must be very old, and in many respects very extraordinary.'[61] One longs to know more about this singular character.

Only one antiquities broker of the generation following Murray seems to be at all documented and then only in a fragmentary way. The broker was Angel Carmey, described in 1817 as 'A foreigner long residing here and a great dealer in coins, medals, antiquities &c, between sixty and seventy years ago.'[62] We hear of him first when Stukeley mentions him: 'In 1750 Dr Mead bought the coin of ORVINA, gave it to the K. of France . . . I got a poor drawing of the coin . . . a better from Mr Carmy.'[63] Carmey not only dealt in coins, for Dr Ducarel wrote to Horace Walpole on 9 September 1762: 'Though it seems almost impossible to make any additions to your immense Treasure of Antiquities, yet I cannot help acquainting you that the two following curiosities are to be disposed of — 1. an antient beautiful Candlestick (from some church in Kent), inlaid with gold and silver, with several inscriptions in characters of the XI century; 2. an antient Pix Box . . . finely enamelled and quite perfect. They belong to Mr Carmey who lives near Ranelagh House at Chelsea.'[64] Carmey wrote to Ducarel from Chelsea on 22 September 1762: 'Sir, The trifle of present of the Corinthian Brass Candlesticks I sent you yesterday, I am extremely glad to hear you are well pleased with them.'[65]

Carmey does seem to have climbed a little further up the scholarly and social scale than Murray, for he was elected to the Society of Antiquaries on 23 January 1752, a week before Arthur Pond. Stukeley, Ducarel and Walpole were fellows, but brokers were not usually accepted in their social circle. Carmey was apparently in poor health by 1762, for he wrote to the secretary of the Society of Antiquaries: 'Chelsea July 1762. Sir, The bearer will pay you the 3 guineas arrear I am indebted to the Society and as my indifferent state of health has prevented my coming to the society these three years last past . . . An Carmey.'[66] This is the last mention of Carmey; when and where he died I cannot discover.

I have found no well-documented brokers of the late eighteenth century, but by the early nineteenth century we are on much safer ground. Edward Holmes Baldock (1777–1845), one of the most important, will appear at Fonthill, Abbotsford and

Charlecote, and I have quoted a description of his shop above. He was for instance listed in the 1824 directory as 'E.H. Baldock Antique Furniture & ornamental china dealer 7 Hanway Street, Oxford Street'. He had been in that street since 1808 and retired from business in 1843 a rich man, but he has been so well dealt with in print that I will not discuss him at length.[67]

Baldock, like so many brokers before and since, was involved in 'improving' or 'sophisticating' and in some instances totally fabricating objects from old fragments. He certainly 'improved' the Sèvres porcelain that he sold; Frederick Litchfield, whose father had worked for Baldock, tells us of 'Baldock Sèvres ... sold by Baldock, a well known dealer whose place of business was in Hanway Yard as the fashionable resort of the collector of those times was called. he dealt in what were then known as fine goods, but in his desire to supply clients with more Sèvres china than he could procure, he employed a clever artist a Quaker named Randall, to redecorate the white or very sparsley decorated pieces.'[68]

To judge from the quantities of loose carvings and other fragments sold in his retirement sales — *A Catalogue of the Extensive and Beautiful stock ... of Mr Baldock who has retired from business ... Florentine mosaïc cabinets ... Ancient carvings ... Sèvres, Dresden, Chelsea & ornamental china ... Messrs Foster and Son on the Premises Hanway Street ... 25th , 26th & 27th may 1843* (a second sale was held late in July 1843 also at Hanway Street) — Baldock had the stock to manufacture a whole range of furniture, metalwork and mounted ceramics.

We shall see in the Drawing Room at Charlecote (Plate 202) two dwarf ebony cabinets created from the doors of a seventeenth-century ebony cabinet. These cabinets came from Fonthill and may well have been supplied to Fonthill by Baldock who certainly made up ebony furniture. Lot 146 in the May 1843 Baldock sale was 'A pair of ebony cabinet doors, richly engraved, the centres boldly carved in subjects Mutius Scaevola and Quintus Curtius'. These are just the type of doors on the Charlecote cabinet; these doors were bought by Hull the Wardour Street dealer for £2.12.6. Indeed the list of buyers at these sales reads like a roll call of the London antiquities brokers.

By the 1830s so famous was Baldock that his name had become synonymous with the display of ancient objects, and Benjamin Disraeli wrote to his sister Sarah on 31 March 1832 concerning a dinner party given at his Pimlico house by Nathaniel Smith Machin, the senior partner in a Covent Garden firm of auctioneers:

he [Machin] is a merchant, and has a mania *for distinguished men* at his table and all that ... a most good natured, vulgar, servile braggadicio ... we dined in a sort of Gallery with a skylight, the walls covered with splendid pictures, Italian and Spanish — the table and sideboard groaned with silver waiters and massy flagons, the drawing rooms for china, bijouterie, and indian screens like Baldock's shop. The dinner very good.[69]

After Baldock's retirement in 1843 'Mr Samuel Litchfield, [who] was at one time buyer to the famous Mr Baldock ... succeeded to his business and connection ... when Mr Frederick Litchfield [son of Samuel] purchased the Sinclair Galleries [in 1895] he transferred his business from his old established premises in Hanway Street to Shaftesbury Avenue.'[70]

Only three other brokers have been studied to any extent: first, Kensington Lewis (1790–1854) who, though he mainly dealt in modern silver, handled important antique pieces such as the celebrated Aldobrandini Tazze and was involved in the Fonthill sale;[71] second, the picture dealer William Buchanan, who as we shall see in Chapter 8 sometimes dealt in antiquities and about whom an excellent scholarly study has recently and, finally, John Coleman Isaac, about whom more information exists than for any other broker.[73]

Isaac played an important role in supplying armour to Goodrich Court. He started out in business before 1815 in partnership wth Gabriel Davies and they advertised in February 1826; 'Ancient Armour and Arms — Davies and Isaac of 41 Craven street, Strand, beg most respectfully to inform the connoisseur that they have just imported several cap-a-pie suits of fluted and plate polished steel armour . . . Dresden and Sevre Porcelaine, Cabinets, Mosaic Tables.'[74] By 1829 Davies had retired and Isaac had removed to 12 Wardour Street where he remained until 1864. He not only dealt from this address but, like most of the other brokers in the street, lived on the premises. The 1851 census lists the household as Isaac himself, his wife Sarah, his mother Mary and one servant and states that Sarah had been born in Germany and Isaac himself in St Martin's Lane.

Isaac spent a great deal of time travelling, especially in Germany where his wife's family may well have helped him. He certainly had modern furniture in the Gothic Revival style made in Germany, for he wrote to his wife in November 1836: 'Before I left Furth I ordered one of those large Gothic Arm Chairs out of Pugin's book, it is to cost £2 7s.'[75] The book was A.W.N. Pugin's *Gothic Furniture* published in 1835; to whom the chair was sold is unknown, though Charles Scarisbrick is a possibility.[76]

John Coleman Isaac should not be confused with his near neighbour Samuel Isaacs of 131 Regent Street who traded in the 1830s as an 'Importer of Paintings China and Curiosities' and whose sale I have already noted.

Of the multitude of brokers who have not been studied, several are particularly relevant to my theme. Of Edward Hull, Pugin's biographer Ferrey tells us: 'It was in the summer of 1832 when calling at the well known furniture dealers, Messrs Hull, In Wardour street that the Earl of Shrewsbury first became acquainted with Pugin's great talent for design. Observing some drawings upon a table executed in a beautiful manner he enquired the name of the artist.'[77]

35. John Swaby's table (H. Shaw *Specimens of Ancient Furniture* ..., 1836)

Ferrey was wrong about the date: 1834 just after Hull's move to Wardour Street is more likely. The Victoria & Albert Museum has a volume of drawings of Gothic Revival furniture by Pugin inscribed Edward Hull and dated 1834 and this may well be the volume referred to. In 1835 Hull had chairs made to Pugin's design for the new house Pugin was building for himself in Wiltshire.[78]

In 1834 Hull handled one of the largest and most important pieces of mediaeval church metalwork to pass through the English market during the whole nineteenth century. It was illustrated and described by Henry Shaw: 'Brass Reading-Desk of the latter part of the fifteenth century. This specimen, which is in height 6th. 7in., was brought from Brussels, and is now in the possession of Mr Hull, of Wardour Street.'[79] It is probable that this object had actually been imported by Pugin himself, for he frequently brought antiquities from the Continent in his own ship and sold them to dealers or his clients. Lord Shrewsbury bought the lectern and presented it to Oscott College chapel, then being decorated by Pugin. Sadly the lectern was sold from Oscott in the 1960s and is now in the Metropolitan Museum in New York.

In 1834 Hull had only just taken over the premises of the broker John Swaby at 109 Wardour Street and in the directory for 1835 he is still listed as 'Curiosity dealer 55 St Martin's lane & 109 Wardour Street'. He had been at the St Martin's Lane address since about 1828. By 1838 he was calling his premises an 'Ancient Furniture Warehouse' and was buying very actively at sales to furnish it with stock. He supplied quantities of furniture and carvings to Charles Scarisbrick to furnish Scarisbrick Hall, which was being built to Pugin's designs from the mid-1830s on.

But by 1844 Hull was dead, for the Scarisbrick papers record a payment to 'the estate of the late ed Hull Dec.d.'[80] The directories up to 1848 continue to list Edward Hull at 109 Wardour Street but in that year the entry changes to George Hull, 'Curiosity Dealer'. The 1851 census gives George Hull, born in Bisley in Bedfordshire, upholsterer, aged forty-three, his wife and servant, as living at 109 Wardour Street. Thus if, as seems probable, George was Edward's son and was born in 1808, Edward must have been at least in his mid-fifties when he died.

Also of importance was John Swaby, who was involved at Charlecote and Abbotsford. As we shall see in Chapter 7, he certainly had a shop in Wardour Street by 1822. The first directory to list him is that of 1823, where he is listed as a curiosity dealer of 109 Wardour Street. He remained at this address until the premises were acquired by Hull in 1834. He had been in the trade since at least 1819 when he was employed by the Crown: 'Mr Swaby has been employed under Bantings to value the china and glass of everyday description.'[81]

Swaby was actively buying at sales from just before 1820. In 1822 he bought at the celebrated Wanstead sale, and in 1823 he was an active buyer at the Fonthill Abbey sale. Unlike many of his fellow brokers he did not sell all his purchases immediately, but was a collector himself. He is listed by Shaw as owning the 'Table of the time of Henry 8th from Hill Hall, Essex. In the possession of Mr Swaby' (Plate 35)[82] This was still in his collection when he died nearly thirty years later.

After he gave up his shop in Wardour Street in 1834 he still bid at sales, though perhaps only for his own collection. He bought at the Stowe sale in 1848, but was called 'Esq.' in the buyers list, whereas the dealers were the usual 'Mr', and is listed as of Muswell Hill. He lent furniture to the Gore House Exhibition of 1853, being listed as 'John Swaby Esq, Torriano Place, Kentish Town'.[83] His precise date of death is unknown, but his extensive collection was sold in March 1860. This consisted of 972 lots: *A Catalogue of the rare and beautiful works of art and valuable collection of pictures of the late John Swaby Esq.... majolica ... enamels ... carvings in ivory and boxwood ... silver and bijouterie, agate, crystal and jade ... arms and armour ... carved oak and marguetrie furniture ... auction by Mr Phillips ... 5 March 1860.*

On reading the catalogue it becomes obvious that Swaby had continued to purchase throughout his retirement, for the collection sold in 1860 included lots bought as long ago as the Fonthill sale of 1823 and as recently as the Strawberry Hill sale of 1844 and the Bernal sale of 1855. Lot 587 was the very table illustrated by Shaw. The essentially incestuous character of the closely interdependent worlds of dealing and collecting is made clear by a sale such as Swaby's. Bernal, for instance, purchased from John Coleman Isaac, Beckford from Baldock. When the Swaby collection was sold, the next generation had an opportunity to buy. At the Swaby sale prominent dealers of the 1860s such as Webb, Pratt and Durlacher were purchasers in some cases for stock and in others on commission for other collectors.

Another major broker was John Webb, who by 1825 was established as an upholsterer and cabinet-maker at 8 Old Bond Street, where he remained until the 1850s. As well as carrying on the business usually associated with these trades, he also dealt in antiquities; two of the pieces illustrated in Shaw's *Specimens* were owned by Webb. One was an 'Ebony chair formerly belonging to Horace Walpole at Strawberry Hill. Now in the possession of Mr Webb of Old Bond Street' (Plate 36).

He also owned a 'Cabinet of the time of Elizabeth or James 1st' (Plate 37). Webb's firm, however, also made a wide range of modern furniture ranging from the royal throne and other pieces to Pugin's design for the House of Lords[84] to elaborate reproductions of continental eighteenth-century pieces for the Marquess of Hertford and the Duke of Northumberland.[85]

In 1848 he helped to furnish an interesting Romantic Interior for Isambard Kingdom Brunel, who collected mediaeval and Renaissance antiquities and modern historical paintings. In March 1849 Webb exhibited at the Society of Arts a silk fabric. 'This revival of a good Elizabethan example is executed in rich crimson and gold colours, and is a perfect specimen of hand-loom sumptuousness ... in the first instance, applied to an Elizabethan room in the house of Mr Brunel.'[86] the room in question was 'a fine dining room ... for which he [Brunel] ordered Shakespearean scenes by living artists, Landseer, Cope, Horsley, etc. the "Shakespeare Room" was panelled in plaster grained to imitate oak and had a plaster pendent ceiling, Venetian mirrors, red velvet curtains and was considered the last word in sumptuous good taste.';[87] Brunel and his father were friends of Pugin and his father and could well have met Webb through them.

By the later 1840s Webb was dealing in antiquities and paintings of the highest

36. John Webb's ebony chair (Shaw, *Specimens*)

37. John Webb's oak cabinet (Shaw, *Specimens*)

quality and was a buyer at the Strawberry Hill sale of 1844 and the Stowe sale of 1848. By the 1860s he had retired from business and spent much of his time until his death in the 1870s at his Villa Hollandia near Cannes. He became a friend of Henry Cole, the director of the South Kensington Museum, to which institution he sold a wide range of objects and left £10,000 to establish the John Webb Trust Fund for the purchase of objects. Webb would seem to have been the most important all-round broker in antiquities and pictures of the mid-century and seems to have conducted his business more like his Bond Street successors of this century than the denizens of Houndsditch, Moorfields, Hanway Yard and Wardour Street.

The several dealers singled out seem to be particulary important, but little work has been done on this subject and the sources are very dispersed. With more research, others will certainly emerge from obscurity, but before we leave the world of the brokers I must consider the opportunities which existed on the Continent for both dealers and collectors. The whole trade in antiquities was far more highly developed on the Continent during the sixteenth, seventeenth and eighteenth centuries than it was in Britain.

One early example of collecting abroad is provided by John Evelyn, who on 3 February 1644 visited a shop in Paris:

> neere the *Pont Neufe* the Street is taken up with Montebanks, Operators, Puppet players, & a little farther is the *Vale de Misere* . . . among the Houses is a shop called *Noah's Arke,* where are to be sold all sorts of Curiositys, naturall & Artificial, for the furniture of Cabinets, Pictures & Collections, as of Purcelane, China . . . Shells, Ivory, Ebony: Birds, dryed *Fishes, Insects:* &c of more Luxury than Use.[88]

British collectors and brokers continued to buy from continental shops and auctions throughout the eighteenth century, though they bought late Renaissance and classical objects rather than mediaeval ones. However, the general fashion for the type of collecting with which I am concerned here coincides with the French Revolution and the upheavals of the Napoleonic Wars.

In 1791 the European Museum in London exhibited for sale pictures, stained glass and other objects, the catalogue stating that:

> Wars and Commotions are seldom favourable to the fine Arts, the late Revolutions in France and Flanders have deprived these Countries of many inestimable Productions which otherwise, could never have been removed; many of the valuable Pictures now consigned to the European Museum, but for this reason, would have always remained inalienable. The Demolition of the Convents and Religious Houses has also contributed towards the Enriching of this Collection, the curious painted Glass, several Pictures in the highest Preservation, and other Curiosities decorated for Ages the venerable Monastery of Carthusians at Louvaine.[89]

The celebrated German art historian Gustav Waagen commented in 1838, after carefully examining collections of works of art and antiquities in this England: 'when the storm of the French Revolution burst over the different countries of Europe . . . scarcely was a country overrun by the French, when Englishmen skilled in the arts were at hand with their guineas.'[90] During the Peace of Amiens large numbers of dealers, collectors and tourists flocked to Paris, and one anonymous tourist reported from Paris in August 1802 that he went in search of

> old ornamental furniture, which had been taken out of the various palaces and Noble's houses, by the patriots in the days of plunder. Of this there are many choice specimens in the old brokers' shops, but they are not exposed to public view, and it is necessary to inquire for them . . . In one place to which we went, up three pair of stairs, in a dirty paved court, where there was a depot of both old

and new furniture, the men were, as usual, very dirty without coats and, like other workmen, but were taking snuff out of rich gold boxes.[91]

Some collectors like Beckford and Meyrick went to Europe themselves, but most preferred to stay in England and buy the importations of brokers.

Brokers with the nerve and capital could make a fortune, but the game was fraught with pitfalls. One example is William Buchanan, the celebrated picture dealer, who also dealt in antiquities. 'By the end of 1803 Buchanan, with £30,000 tied up in pictures, many of which were held up in Italy by the British naval blockade, was running into serious difficulties.'[92] Buchanan had written on 9 February 1803 to his associate: 'Irvine knows every picture of any note which can be sold in Italy, and will sweep that quarter pretty thoroughly; and should the offer be refused, the leading people may look long before such may occur again — indeed without another Revolution in Italy the opportunity may never occur again.[93] But, despite the risks of purchasing and transporting objects in time of war, the high financial rewards drove the dealers on. Buchanan wrote to Irvine on 3 June 1803: 'I observe that war, which has now taken place, ... makes Selection more necessary than ever, as Speculators will now come forward, and we must be prepared from superior merit in works we bring foreward, to throw others in the back ground.'[94]

The activites of both brokers and collectors were considerably helped by the existence of a variety of continental brokers and middlemen. One of the most important was the Abbé Luigi Celotti (c.1765–c.1846), who was by 1801 the secretary and librarian to Count Giovanni Barbarigo in Venice. Celotti will appear in Chapter 7 as the supplier of Venetian chairs to Abbotsford and in Chapters 5 and 8 for his involvement in the importation of the *pietre dure* table once at Fonthill and now at Charlecote. Though Celotti was involved in the importation into this country during and after the Napoleonic Wars of a wide range of works of art and antiquities, it is for his involvement in the importation of paintings and manuscripts that he is best known.

Irvine, the Scottish picture dealer and an associate of Buchanan, wrote on 26 July 1828 to his client Sir William Forbes of Pitsligo: 'I have just received a letter from an Abbé Celotti of Venice, written from Milan ... he wished to propose to me a picture by Giorgione and several others which he possesses.'[95] He also dealt extensively in manuscripts; in 1816 he acquired the greater part of the library of Don Tomaso da Lucca and in February 1821 he sold the Saibanti and Canonici manuscripts at Sotheby's.[96] Celotti manuscripts from this and other sales found their way into British collections; for instance, Sir Thomas Phillips, the famous manuscript collector, owned a considerable number.[97]

On 11 June 1816 Sir Walter Scott wrote to his friend Mathew Weld Hartstonge who wrote to him from Brussels: 'books and paintings are here wonderfully cheap, & with the latter I have nearly broke myself — I think it would be a good speculation for any person who was a competent judge to purchase paintings here & at Antwerp & freight a vessel with them & dispose of them in London the duty on importation into England is I understand an English pound for every square foot of canvas ...'[98] Several years later in November 1823 another of Scott's friends, the great collector J.B.S. Morritt of Rokeby, wrote to him from Florence: 'How I wish you would come here, for I have been rummaging old stores ... old cabinets, carved work by Benvenuto Cellini and gimcracks of various sorts as wd have been meat and drink to you for at least a twelve month.'[99]

Although Scott never did freight a ship, others did and it is totally in character that Pugin even used his own ship. His friend and biographer Benjamin Ferrey relates of Pugin:

First, owner of a small boat which he kept for his own pleasure, he successively commanded a smack, and afterwards a schooner, in which amongst other merchandise he generally managed to bring over many interesting carvings and other antiquities purchased in the old stores of Holland and Flanders. Thus he used these excursions as subservient to the object of forming a museum ... one of the chief attractions in his residence at Ramsgate. During one of these voyages he was wrecked on the Scotch coast ... where he and his men all but perished.[100]

The extent of Pugin's collection formed in this way can be judged from the sales held after his death in 1852.[101] Pugin's involvement in the antiquities trade and his friendship with Hull and Webb led to him to incorporate ancient objects and woodwork into his buildings. I have already mentioned the Oscott Lectern in this context. One of his most important houses — Scarisbrick Hall in Lancashire — is filled with ancient wood carvings introduced by Pugin, many of which were purchased from Hull.

In some cases dealers themselves freighted ships with antiquities. In the Stowe sale of 1848 the furniture of the State Drawing Room included:

several very superb specimens from the Doge's Palace at Venice ... about the latter end of the eighteenth century, the once celebrated Marina Palace became untenanted, and gradually fell into decay ... about fourteen years ago, when one Gasparoni, a clever Italian dealer in curiosities, resident at that time in Milan prevailed upon the then possessors of the palace to dispose of the whole contents

38. The Grand Drawing Room at Stowe by Joseph Nash, 1845 (Windsor Castle, Royal Collection, Her Majesty the Queen)

to himself. Some idea of the quantity of furniture he thus possessed himself of, may be gathered from the fact, that Gasparoni chartered a vessel expressly to convey the same to England ... upon his arriving in the Thames, he offered the whole to Mr Colnaghi for £700.[102]

39. An eighteenth-century Italian chair from Stowe (Wallace Collection, London)

It is explained that the furniture was offered to several brokers, namely Colnaghi, Baldock, and Town & Emanuel. The last firm bought the whole shipment and sold several pieces to the Duke of Buckingham for Stowe, but pieces also went to Wilton, Burghley and Narford. However, in 1848 'The state bed and some other valuable articles, still remain in the possession of Messrs Town and Emanuel, who have already netted £6,000 by that portion of furniture disposed of'.[103]

The pieces at Stowe are described in the sale catalogue, but Queen Victoria visited the house in 1845 and decided that the drawing room containing this furniture was 'one of the most perfect interiors ever witnessed ... [and] upon the return of the court to Windsor, Mr Joseph Nash was sent down to Stowe, by Her Majesty, to make a drawing of the apartment ... being the only record in existence of the room as it then appeared'.[104] Fortunately the Nash watercolour still exists (Plate 38) and shows the elaborate carved and gilded Baroque chairs, sofas, side tables and picture frames from the suite. The table in the apse is now in the Wallace Collection as are two of the chairs (Plate 39). Gasparoni's imagination in importing a whole shipload of furniture could doubtless be compared with the activities of other continental dealers, but ironically Town & Emanuel without stirring themselves from their Bond Street premises seem to have made far more profit than Gasparoni.

As we shall see when we consider the trade in ancient woodwork, the importation of shiploads of works of fine and decorative art was so widespread by the 1820s that the term 'Importation Sale' became commonplace on the title-pages of auction catalogues. The temptation to offload dubious or inferior objects on to English collectors and dealers was often too great to resist. The Liverpool art dealer Thomas Winstanley observed as early as 1828:

> since the termination of the late continental war, every corner of Europe has been searched ... Even when the importation duty was considerable, the facilities of smuggling gave opportunities of importation to hundreds, I may say of thousands of inferior Pictures, the only recommendation of which — that *'they came from the Continent'*. Since duty was reduced, I have been informed that small vessels have been wholly freighted with Pictures, many of which have already sold in London.[105]

Winstanley refers only to paintings, but the situation was the same with antiquities. Indeed several of the more audacious English collectors actually went to continental auctions and bid against both continental dealers and collectors and English dealers. The 'Vellumane' Sir Thomas Phillips bought no fewer than 650 manuscripts at the sale of the Meerman library in The Hague in June and July 1824. He wrote to his wife from Holland on 4 July: 'The MSS sold uncommonly dear, owing to two or three villainous booksellers who came over from England ... I shall not bring my books over with me but take a house somewhere in Holland & put them in it, or else a room or chambers I cannot afford to pay the duties.'[106]

Phillips in fact attempted to circumvent the customs regulations. On 1 October 1824 he wrote to the Chancellor of the Exchequer: 'I take the liberty of begging to know if ... I could not have the duties upon some valuable MSS (which I bought at Meerman's sale) removed ... I am anxious to bring them over to England, but the duty of 1/- per lb weight is so enormous, particularly when bound in wooden covers that it deters me from bringing them over.'[107] In the event Phillips failed to alter the rate of duty on manuscripts, but this, like that on pictures and antiquities, did little to deter the English from purchasing and importing them.

It was not even necessary to penetrate deep into continental Europe in search of

40. *Street Scene in Alençon* by J.S. Cotman, 1828 (Museum & Art Gallery, Birmingham)

objects, for broker's shops abounded in northern France. John Sell Cotman, between the end of the the war in 1815 and 1820, made three sketching trips to Normandy which resulted in his celebrated publication *The Architectural Antiquities of Normandy* of 1822. He visited Alençon in August 1820 and made several drawings.[108] One of these he worked up into a watercolour in 1828: *Street Scene in Alençon* (Plate 40) depicts a view down the main street with the ruined church of Notre Dame on the left.[109]

But of far more relevance is the curiosity shop on the right (Plate 42) with its wares spilling out into the street. This is a rare illustration of such a French shop of this date. One must assume that Cotman included it merely because it happened to be there opposite the church, which was the main subject of the picture. Cotman only commented: 'Sketched Church though bad at Alençon — & Castle odd.'[110]

No armour or other metalwork is apparent in Cotman's watercolour, but paintings, sculpture, a large ceramic pot and an elaborate chest are visible. The delights of the interior of the shop can only be guessed at. Cotman himself certainly collected both antiquities and armour, some of which may well have been bought in Normandy. In 1834 when he moved from East Anglia to London some of his collection was sold; lot 147, for instance, was 'A complete suit of bright steel armour' and lot 149, 'A pikemans suit of armour ... temp Charles I'.[111]

I have found another much later illustration of the interior of a French broker's shop. This was painted by Bernard Sickert in about 1895 and is of a shop in Dieppe (Plate 41).

There had, of course, been continental auctions since the sixteenth century, which were sometimes attended by English dealers and collectors. But by the 1850s the distribution of continental sale catalogues was highly organized. The auctioneer J.M. Heberlé of Cologne sold a wide range of antiquities in his rooms during the 1850s. By 1859 he was distributing his catalogues through a network of bookshops and broker's shops in such far-flung places as Amsterdam, Augsburg, Berlin,

41. *A Curiosity Shop in Dieppe* by Bernard Sickert, *c*.1895 (Tate Gallery, London)

42. (facing page) A detail from *Street Scene in Alençon* (Museum & Art Gallery, Birmingham)

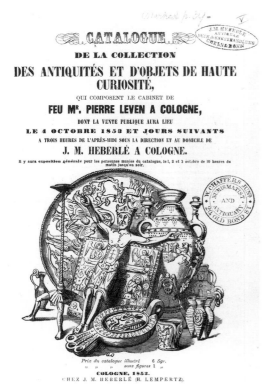

43. The title-page of the catalogue of an auction
held in Cologne in 1853

Copenhagen, Leipzig, London, Paris, St Petersburg, Rome and Vienna.[112] The sale 'conditions' include specific instructions on how to bid by post, and the catalogues were also illustrated. Amongst the four shops listed in London from which catalogues could be bought was 'Chaffers Jun Numismatist and Antiquary 66 Jermyn St'. In 1853 Chaffers was operating from 20 Old Bond Street, and was it he or perhaps his father who was listed in the 1846 Post Office Directory as 'Pawnbroker 42 Watling Str'?

A copy of an 1853 Heberlé catalogue survives. The title-page (Plate 43) is stamped 'W. Chaffers Junr, 20, Old Bond St, Numismatist and Antiquary' and 'J.M. Heberlé Antiquar, Buch & Kunsthandlung, Coeln & Bonn'.[113] The sale included furniture, manuscripts, ceramics, metalwork, ivories and enamels. The stamp might indicate that this copy was purchased from Chaffers, but it might actually have been Chaffers own copy of the catalogue, for his name is written against several lots though there is no indication whether he attended the sale in person.

Another London shop that sold Heberlé catalogues was Davis Nutt, 'Foreign and Classical Bookseller 270 Strand'. His label appears on the title-page of another surviving sale catalogue, that of the library of Sulpiz Boisserée, which took place in Bonn in 1854.[114] The Bonn end of Heberlé's business was run by H. Lempertz, and the catalogues were distributed in the same way as those of the Cologne sales. The sale of the Boisserée library would have been of great interest to English architects and antiquaries. It is ironic that as early as 1818 Sulpiz was complaining about English collectors 'despoiling Germany of its early treasures'.[115]

Sulpiz and his brother Melchior had been responsible for building up a celebrated collection of mediaeval paintings and antiquities, which had been greatly admired by Goethe. The collection was largely formed during the Napoleonic Wars. The paintings went mainly to the Alte Pinakothek in Munich.[116] The brothers were also closely involved in the completion of Cologne Cathedral, and their many interests are represented in the 5,985 lots in their library sale.

One anecdote illustrates the opportunities that existed on the Continent for alert and wily dealers. The dealer in question was the younger Samuel Pratt listed in the 1847 Post Office Directory as 'Cabinet maker, upholsterer & importer of Ancient Furniture & Armour &c. 47 New Bond Street and 3 Grosvenor St'. There were three Pratts, Samuel senior having started out at the Bond Street address as early as 1817 as a 'Trunk Maker'. Henry was in partnership with the two Samuels. The son of the famous collector Ralph Bernal told how, while he and his father sat at breakfast one day,

> a well-known Bond Street dealer was announced, who said that he had brought a curious crystal which he had bought on the continent, and for which he wanted 10L. Mr Bernal drew from his pocket a magnifying glass ... and carefully examined the curiosity. He then said 'I'll take it' and gave the money. When the dealer had left Mr Bernal ... said 'I gave what he asked because I saw what was engraved in the corner'. The purchase ... proved to be a unique gem made to the order of Lothair, King of France between 954 and 986 A.D. ... the possession of which at his death [Bernal's] was competed for by England and France and is now in the treasure room of the British Museum.[117]

The crystal is one of the most important Carolingian works of art to survive, and the inscription Bernal deciphered reads 'Lotharius Rex Francorvm Fieri Ivssit'. It spent most of its existence in the Abbey of Waulsort on the Meuse and 'After remaining undisturbed in that abbey for more than eight hundred years, it was lost at the period of the French Revolution ... Possibly it was thrown into the Meuse on the occasion of the French advance; for about the middle of the last century it reappeared in the shop of a Belgian dealer who said that it had been recovered from the bed of that River.'[118]

The crystal was offered for sale but 'attracted no notice in the "old curiosity shop" in the Place Musée, Brussels, till the more practised eye of Pratt of Bond Street discovered its latent antique charms and obtained it from Barthélemy the dealer for the price asked — ten francs, but Mr Bernal became the purchaser for ten pounds. Mr Didron subsequently sought its possession by offering the latter one hundred pounds.'[119] Alphonse Napoleon Didron was the great French mediaevalist and friend of Viollet-le-Duc. At the Bernal sale the crystal sold for £267 and was purchased by John Webb acting on behalf of the British Museum. This anecdote illustrates the unique opportunities that existed on the Continent after the Napoleonic Wars when Britain was the wealthiest nation in the world and English dealers and collectors could outbid all others.

Naturally the activities of those dealers and collectors soon began to have the obvious effect upon both the price and the supply of objects. As early as 1821, quite soon after the wars had ended, William Bullock, the owner of the Egyptian Hall, wrote to Sir Walter Scott: '28 October . . . I promised you when in London that I would endeavour to procure you from Denmark and Sweden such military and other antiquities as might be suitable for your collection, but I did not meet with one article worthy of your notice on sale there is not a suit of armour in Denmark and Germany, France and Italy has been drained to supply English collectors and it will shortly bear a higher price on the continent then here.'[120]

Several years later, in 1829, Lord Braybrooke of Audley End wrote while in Antwerp: 'Steencering's collection of curiosities for sale were very odd and not uninteresting, but he was hardly civil & quite indifferent as to disposing of them . . . I offered him 20 francs for 2 little articles which I bought since for fr 12 thinking myself bound to purchase something but he refused it with disdain at another place I bought two armoires which will turn out well . . . in no other town have I seen carved oak for sale the uniform answer to all enquiries being "the Jews collect it all & send it to England.'[121]

The same situation seems to have prevailled well into the 1830s, for Coleman Isaac wrote to Ralph Bernal from Paris in October 1835: 'As I know *almost all* the quarters of this city, where dealers in such matters are found . . . They complain of good things being scarce in Paris, yet they complain of the *prices* wch are asked in London for such matters; they say curious glass is dearer in London.'[122]

Despite these complaints such immense quantities of works of art and antiquities existed on the Continent that these shortages were only temporary, and prices remained low, compared with Britain, well into the second half of the century.

3

THE FURNISHINGS

Walking past Exton the glaziers door, I saw a cart load of
painted glass, just taken from S. George's church windows to
put clear glass in ... I used my influence with Mr Exton, and
got the glass.   William Stukeley

The creation of Romantic Interiors involved the thoughtful
accumulation of various decorative elements, namely, woodwork, stained glass and
armour. Ancient woodwork was used both in the creation of rooms and in the
manufacture of furniture. The habit of incorporating ancient classical fragments into
interiors was well established by 1700. William Stukeley, the antiquary, did just this
in his library at Grantham. It is possible that some of these fragments were
mediaeval, though most were probably classical. By December 1737, however,
Stukeley was certainly buying mediaeval carvings of stone: 'got an elegant piece of
religious sculpture, on alabaster, being St. Audry in her habit ... Mr Samuel Gale,
gave me another like carving on alabaster of S. John Baptists head.'[1] By 1746 he was
certainly acquiring wooden carvings, for he wrote on 1 August 1746: 'I lately rec'd a
waggon load of curious antique wooden figures from Croyland. There are
Cherubims of oak as big as life which supported the principles of the roof ... I have
got likewise two of S Guthlakes devils in stone.'[2] Croyland was the ruined Abbey
not far from Stukeley's home in Grantham.

Such ruins were vandalized by collectors throughout the eighteenth century. On
2 July 1790, long after Stukeley's death, the ubiquitous John Byng visited Croyland:

Nothing can be more noble, more Gothic, or more elegantly carved than the
front (now tottering) ... not the smallest remain of stain'd glass, monuments; or
anything antient ... The front is so seam'd by rents, that down it must soon
come; the finest monument in the kingdom: and wou'd that I were near it then
(not too near) to save, and carry off some of the carved figures.[3]

Horace Walpole and his circle were deeply involved in collecting ancient
woodwork. Walpole's close friend the antiquary William Cole wrote to Walpole on
14 May 1768: 'I have fixed on a most deplorable downfall[en] old cottage or small
farm-house ... I shall be obliged totally to make it a new house in every respect
except pulling it down, I would fain, especially for my own room or two below
stairs, make it as Gothic as I can. If you have any offcast old casements, any old
Gothic ornaments that would do for a chimney, or old wainscot that would work up
into a Gothic sort of furniture.'[4]

In 1774, while staying in Gloucestershire with his friend George Selwyn, Walpole
went in search of antiquities. On 15 August he 'found in a wretched cottage a child
in an ancient oaken cradle, exactly in the form of that published from the cradle of
Edward II — I purchased it for five shillings, but don't know whether I shall have
fortitude enough to transport it to Strawberry Hill — people would conclude me in
my second childhood.'[5] In the event Walpole never claimed the cradle, thus leaving
the simple cottar with five shillings and an antique to sell to the next collector to
happen by. Edward II's cradle had only been published a few months before

Walpole discovered this second example.[6] Edward's cradle is now in the Museum of London, though how long before 1774 it was made is open to question.

Fragments of ancient carved wood could, of course, be used and re-used in all manner of ways. Sir Richard Colt Hoare, the Wiltshire antiquary, noted in 1826: 'We were shown in the house of Mr Scammell some very ancient carved work in wood representing St George and the Dragon &c which was once used as a bacon box, but now converted into a bureau.'[7]

As the nineteenth century wore on collectors from London were forced farther and farther afield in their search for antiquities. One suitably distant area was the Lake District. 'The district of Wyresdale is perhaps more deserving the attention of the moral philosopher and antiquary, than any other part of the country. Amid the seclusion of the Wyredale hills ... the humble remains of the Sistanti, are labouring to preserve and improve their little patrimonies, the thatched cot, and the oaken furniture of their forefathers are still dear to them.'[8]

Though this cherished furniture was probably for sale to the London collector, even here he had to compete with the local antiquaries who were busy buying up furniture and carvings to furnish houses new and old. One such new house was that of a Mr Cawthorne who 'created a very neat building in the Gothic style which he has called Wyresdale Tower ... The whole interior strongly reminds one of Di Vernon in *Rob Roy*. The oak parlour ... is fitted out in the style of Henry eight's time. The dark oak panels have a sombre appearance.'[9]

By the mid-1820s the major London auction houses were holding auctions of ancient woodwork. For instance, on 10 November 1825 Christie's sold *Catalogue of ... a large collection of ancient and very curious carvings in wood many of which may be found suitable for the fitting up of private chapels, and many of them applicable for the furniture in gothic mansions ... the whole of which have lately been imported from the continent*. It is obvious from the auctioneer's copy of the catalogue, which survives, that the carvings came from several sources, some being consigned by Edward Baldock. The buyers were mainly dealers, including such celebrated figures as Swaby and Webb. Such sales continued throughout the 1830s and 1840s.

The 6th Duke of Devonshire was 'One day walking with a friend in Berners Street [when] we were tempted into an auction-room, and found carved oak being knocked down. I bought to right and left, and became possessed of almost all that you see here the fittings of some German monastery and the woodwork of an old fashioned pew.'[10] Though published anonymously, the author is known to have been the 6th Duke himself. This woodwork was described after it had been installed at Chatsworth in what was called the Oak Room and which still survives. The date of this sale is unknown, but it might possibly have been that of 15 June 1836: *Importation sale — 2 Berners Street ... Sale of Gothic and other oak carvings just landed comprising fine specimens of the XU & XVI centuries ... about 10,000 pieces; The whole well worthy the attention of the Nobility, Gentry, Architects and collectors ... by Mr C Deacon at his spacious rooms*. On 31 January Foster, the auctioneer of Pall Mall, had sold 'Some ancient carved fittings suited to a Library or Chapel' Lot 135 was 'a noble organ case in solid oak ... 14 ft wide by 16 ft height'. Many other similar sales could be cited from the 1830s and 1840s.

Ancient woodwork could also be purchased from specialist dealers. In 1835 Mr T. Fairs had for sale 'A fine specimen of the manner of fitting up a room with Elizabethan fragments [which] may be seen in Mortimer Street, at the office of Mr Fairs a London house-painter of the very first taste.'[11] Fairs is listed in the 1827 directory as 'Painter to His majesty, 23 Mortimer Street'.

One particularly well-documented dealer in ancient furniture and carvings was Horatio Rodd, who had a shop in Great Newport Street near Leicester Square from the 1820s to the 1840s. Rodd is unique amongst the dealers of this period in that he issued catalogues of his stock. That of 1824 is *A Catalogue of Authentic portraits ... marble busts ... a few carvings in wood, carved frames &c*. The catalogue of 1842 was

44. The title-page of Horatio Rodd's 1842 catalogue

even illustrated and included 'carvings in Oak, Ivory, & Boxwood, Antique Furniture & Plate'. There was also 'An Elizabethan chimney-piece. From an old house at Bow, Middlesex, said to have been the residence of Sir Francis Drake'. This piece is illustrated on the title-page (Plate 44).

These dealers, like so many of the antiquities brokers, had their shops in Soho and its immediate neighbourhood. There were, for instance, the Wrights: 'Messrs W & J Wright 144 Wardour Street. At the end of last century Mr W. Thrale Wright carver and gilder to H.R.H. Princess Sophia Matilda, occupied the present premises and began to import oak panelling, carving and marquetry . . . For more than a century the business has been carried on . . . and "Old Curiosity Shop" is still the most appropriate description of the business.'[12] In the 1850 Ratebook the Wrights are listed as occupying three premises, the house at No. 27 Wardour Street, the house, yard and workshops at No. 22 and the house and warehouses at No. 20.[13] In the directories of this period they are listed as antique furniture dealers, but had they merely dealt they would not have needed workshops and they, like most such dealers, probably 'improved' the objects in which they dealt.

It was, as we have seen with Stukeley and his contemporaries, and with Scott and his, possible to obtain carved woodwork without tapping continental sources of supply. The main sources both here and abroad were the churches, but by the 1840s due to the rising interest in ecclesiology in Britain this source began to dry up. The ecclesiologists naturally admired the ancient woodwork *in situ* in the churches for which it had been made and fought any attempt by dealers or collectors to remove it. At this period a host of archaeological societies were springing up to keep an eye on these matters. One reported in 1843:

> The possessor of lands belonging to a despoiled abbey in Somersetshire is said to have in his drawing-room an entire rood screen, stolen from a neighbouring church . . . Again seven old seats, bearing the donors name and humble prayer, have been torn from a church near Bridgewater and deposited among the curiosities of an amateur collector. Richly carved seat ends are vanishing year by year from churches . . . some are taken by the rich and wealthy and used for dining room panels and bookcase doors.[14]

There are many examples of the importation from the Continent of woodwork for the embellishment of both the interiors and the exteriors of buildings in Britain. Though more expensive and difficult to transport, it was also possible to import carved stonework. The most dramatic example of this was the purchase and importation in the late 1820s of both carved woodwork and carved stonework from Rouen in specially built barges for the embellishment of Highcliffe Castle in Hampshire. These purchases were made by Lord Stuart de Rothesay, the British Ambassador in Paris for two periods between 1815 and 1830.

Carved woodwork and stonework and stained glass from several sources including the great Norman abbey of Jumièges were incorporated into the interiors at Highcliffe.[15] The most dramatic feature of the exterior is a spectacular late Gothic oriel window, which Rothesay purchased from a mediaeval house visited by him in the course of the demolition he may well have encouraged. This was La Grande Maison at Les Andelys in Normandy, the demolition of which is shown in Plate 45, and the oriel can be clearly seen on the right. This illustration and others of the interiors and carved details were published in 1825.[16]

The house in its complete state had been drawn and etched by Cotman and published with a description by Dawson Turner in their *Antiquities of Normandy* in 1822.[17] The furniture was largely eighteenth century rather than mediaeval, and a number of the important pieces of French Empire furniture, which Rothesay purchased in Paris to furnish Highcliffe Castle, were recently bequeathed to the Victoria & Albert Museum, where they are on display.

The French antiquities brokers and demolition contractors were naturally delighted to help British collectors like Rothesay in every way, but French scholars and literary figures became increasingly enraged at the despoilation of their heritage. Victor Hugo spoke for them all in his splendid article 'Guerre aux Demolisseurs!' published in 1825, prompted by purchases such as Rothesay's from Jumièges: 'On nous a dit que des anglais avaient acheté *trois cents francs* le droit d'emballer tout ce qui leur plairait dans le débris de l'admirable abbaye de Jumièges. Ansi les profanations de lord Elgin se renouvellent chez nous, et nous en tirons profit.'[18]

His pleas did not fall upon deaf ears, and pressure from Hugo and other like-minded conservationists led to the creation by the French Government in 1830 of the post of Inspecteur des Monuments. In 1834 Hugo's friend the author Prosper Mérimée was appointed to the post, and it was he who employed the celebrated architect and scholar Viollet-le-Duc to restore so many of France's historic buildings. Hugo had even in 1831 cast a mediaeval building as the hero of *Notre Dame de Paris*, his most celebrated novel.

Closely related to the trade in ancient carvings was that in furniture itself. There were, as we have seen, a few collectors who in the eighteenth and early nineteenth centuries furnished their houses with ancient furniture, but it was not until the 1830s that this practice became widespread. Shaw's seminal book *Specimens of Ancient Furniture*, with Meyrick's text, was published to meet the demand for a work of reference; 'The painter, the sculptor, and the architect, when called upon to portray or imitate any article of early domestic furniture have been obliged to trust to imperfect descriptions or to their own imaginations.'[19]

Scott bemoaned the lack of such a book when furnishing Abbotsford, and Meyrick recognized this need when he wrote in his introduction: 'A feeling has now arisen for the ancient decorative style, which it is hoped the present work will materially assist; for however beautiful the elegant simplicity of Grecian forms, these are not of themselves sufficient to produce that effect that should be given to an English residence.'[20]

Furniture brokers naturally used this book, and, as we saw, several of the pieces illustrated belonged to well-known brokers like Webb and Swaby. So new was the

45. Demolition of La Grande Maison at Les Andelys (C. Nodier & J. Taylor, *Voyages Pittoresques et Romantiques . . .*, 1835)

study of such ancient furniture that the question of genuineness was viewed very differently from today. If genuine pieces could be found, they were of course avidly bought and sold, but even these were frequently altered to suit dealers or collectors. If genuine pieces were not available, pieces were made up from the ancient wood carvings of which as we have seen there was no shortage. In 1835 J.C. Loudon wrote:

> No one ought to attempt it who is not a master of composition on abstract principles; but, indeed (in London, at least) the attempt is scarcely necessary; since there are abundant remains of every kind of Elizabethan furniture to be purchased of collectors. These, when in fragments, are put together, and, made up into every article of furniture now in use; and, as London has a direct and cheap communication with every part of the world by sea, the American citizen or the Australian merchant, who wishes to indulge in this taste, may do it.[21]

Loudon goes on to name a number of furniture brokers including Nixon & Son of Great Portland Street. By the early 1840s there were a

> multitude of warehouses which now display their attractive stores, not merely in Wardour Street, but in almost every quarter of the metropolis. Of course these numerous dealers must be maintained by a certain number of customers and there is no doubt that many of them reaped a lucrative harvest. The stock of old furniture remaining in the obscure and poorer habitations of this country was soon exhausted: large importations have in consequence been made from the continent particularly from Germany ... great quantities of detached and fragmentary portions of architectural carvings have been collected and worked up into forms now required by modern convenience, but which were perhaps unknown at the time when the materials thus employed were originally designed.[22]

46. Ancient woodwork from Rodd's 1842 catalogue

Various methods were employed to age artificially 'made-up' furniture, but the most widespread was to stain the whole piece to a dark and plausibly ancient colour to mask the differing colours of old and new wood. The Bristol antiquary and collector George Weare Braikenridge recorded in his recipe book:

> To darken new oak to look like old. Two recipes given to me by Mr Swaby dealer in old carved wood London 1½ Pint of water & ½ lb of shag Tobacco, the liquor to be boiled away one third. Logwood & water with coperas-Alum to fasten the color. Add Alum for a green cast. pearl Ash for a brown cast. Umber & Soaper's Lees mixed — sufficient of the latter to dissolve the umber suffered to remain on for three weeks before the polish is given with oiling.[23]

Almost all ancient furniture known to us today, quite apart from the fakes and made-up pieces, is coated with such stains applied during the nineteenth century. When made, mediaeval and Renaissance oak furniture if not painted was not stained or polished in any way but, left as natural white oak or walnut. The few genuine pieces that happened to survive into the nineteenth century would have darkened somewhat through age and use, but they, like the made-up pieces, were stained when they passed through the trade.

One of the best-organized brokers was, as we have seen, Horatio Rodd, who dealt in pictures, furniture and other objects. His illustrated catalogue (Plate 44) included 'Elizabethan Bedstead, carved in oak ... 25 gs' (Plate 46). He had published a catalogue as early as 1824, but this was not illustrated. Though it consisted largely of paintings, it did include some furniture and carved woodwork, including 'Six high backed chairs, very finely carved in walnut-tree ... £7.7s.'[24]

Two types of turned chairs seem to have had a particular fascination for the creators of Romantic Interiors; one group were triangular and the other of ebony. Walpole acquired triangular chairs at the auction in 1775 of the collection of his friend Richard Bateman. Bateman had acquired his chairs from farmhouses in the Welsh Marches near his country seat at Shobdon in Herefordshire. Following Bateman's example Walpole attempted to acquire similar chairs from this same area. He wrote to his friend Cole who was staying in Cheshire on 9 March 1765:

> Mr Bateman has a cloister at Old Windsor furnished with ancient wooden chairs, most of them are triangular ... turned in the most uncouth and whimsical forms. He picked them up one by one, for two, three, five or six shillings apiece from different farmhouses in Herefordshire. I have long envied and coveted them. There may be such in poor cottages in so neighbouring a county as Cheshire ... When you are copying inscriptions in a churchyard in any village, think of me, and step into the first cottage you see.[25]

In the event, Cole did not acquire any chairs for Walpole, who eventually purchased several at the sale of Bateman's collection. He and Bateman called them 'Ancient Welch' chairs, which gave them connotations of an ancient British and Druidic nature. Such chairs had been made throughout Britain, though at quite what date is a matter of debate. I would suggest that they are no earlier than the second half of the seventeenth century and may indeed have still been in production in remote areas such as Wales almost up to the time Batemen purchased his examples They were never designed for grand houses and would have been made for the very farmhouses where Bateman found them.

Many examples could be found of the discovery of ancient furniture by eighteenth-century collectors and also of the manufacture of fakes to deceive the less astute collectors. In some cases, celebrated pieces were reproduced, these reproductions eventually passing as genuine pieces. For instance, in 1826 a particularly famous turned chair was published.[26] This was reputed to be the very chair in which Abbot Whiting of Glastonbury sat at his trial after his abbey had been dissolved by Henry VIII. The chair still exists in the Bishop's Palace at Wells in Somerset, though it is not Tudor, but coeval with Bateman's chairs. By 1835 the broker Kensett of Mortimer Street was selling 'a correct fac-simile of a chair taken from Tintern Abbey ... and two other chairs from Glastonbury; one of which, called the abbot's chair, is of very elaborate workmanship, and the other no less remarkable for the simplicity of its construction, Correct copies of these celebrated chairs are manufactured by Mr Kensett for sale.'[27]

The 'abbot's' chair is the triangular turned one and the other the so-called Glastonbury Chair, the latter being identical to that owned by Walpole (Plate 77). The ease with which these old reproductions can pass as originals is demonstrated by the chair (Plate 47), identical to that at Wells, which was acquired by the Victoria & Albert Museum in 1916 as a genuine ancient chair and which was on display as such until recently. It was then discovered to be a later reproduction of the one at Wells, and may indeed be one of Mr Kensett's 'fac-similes'.

Turned ebony chairs were even more widely used to furnish antiquarian interiors than triangular chairs. One of the Strawberry Hill chairs was published by Shaw (Plate 36). These low ebony chairs with their barley-sugar twist turning were thought to be of Tudor date, as I have discussed elsewhere,[28] and there is also an ebony sofa of this type at Cothele (Plate 18).

Besides these ebony chairs, which were collected by Walpole, Scott and Beckford, there were the tall-backed ebony chairs as at Charlecote. These latter chairs were also thought to be of sixteenth-century date, though Elizabethan rather than Tudor. Both these types of ebony chairs are oriental and of seventeenth rather than sixteenth-century date, though more research is needed to establish their precise date and country of origin. To the antiquaries and collectors of the eighteenth and nineteenth centuries their exotic black appearance and their supposed Tudor connections were quite sufficient to commend their use in Romantic Interiors.

There exists a considerable body of documentation of the trade in and taste for

47. A turned triangular chair of the mid-nineteenth century (Victoria & Albert Museum, London)

ancient furniture in the period with which I am concerned. I have chosen a few examples to demonstrate how both the collectors and the brokers from whom they purchased the furniture viewed this vital and highly visible element in the furnishing of these interiors. One letter written by an architect to a client for whom he was undertaking the refurbishment of an ancient house gives the flavour of one of these enterprises towards the middle of the nineteenth century. The architect was William Burn, the house Falkland House in Fife and the client Onesophorous Tyndall Bruce. Work had started in 1839 on this large Jacobean house on which Bruce was to spend £30,000 over the next five years.[29] Burn wrote to Bruce on 4 May 1842 giving a fascinating run-down on where to go in London to acquire the raw material for the creation of his Romantic Interiors:

> For old oak carvings go to messrs Pratt No. 47 New Bond Street, Webb and Cragg No. 8 Old Bond Street, Messrs Street & Son Brewer St Golden Square & J. Nixon & Co 123 Great Portland Street — and for the most splendid carvings of every description to W.G Rogers No. 18 Church Street Soho where you will be charmed ... for Tukey carpet I beg you will call for Mr Cardinal, Levant Warehouse Gt St Helens Bishopsgate ... for Cabinets and China do not omit going to Baldocks Hanway Street ... which is the best place in London.[30]

Pratt, Baldock, Webb and Nixon we have already encountered, Street is listed as a curiosity broker in a number of directories and William Cardinal is listed as an importer of Turkey carpets. William Gibbs Rogers was the celebrated woodcarver who also dealt in ancient carvings. Thus we see that a collector from the provinces could by this date come to London and purchase all the furnishings needed to create a Romantic Interior. Had Bruce wanted armour, Pratt could also have provided that.

It is interesting that all the above brokers had shops within less than a mile of each other except William Cardinal, and even he, according to the directories, had a second shop in Prince's Street near Leicester Square very close to the others. This letter also underlines the fact that in so many Romantic Interiors it was the patron who collected the required furnishings rather than the architect, probably on just such a trip to London as that projected by Bruce.

The collecting of armour for display in Romantic Interiors in the mediaeval and Old English style is a complex and interesting subject that is discussed in more detail in connection with Goodrich Court, when I deal with the interiors created by Sir Samuel Rush Meyrick, the greatest armour collector this country has produced. Walpole collected armour avidly to embellish the interiors at Strawberry Hill. Sir Walter Scott collected the armour which still survives at Abbotsford.

Certainly the presence of armour in any plausibly ancient house was regarded as essential by the late eighteenth century. Thus the urge to re-create this ambience in ancient buildings that had lost their furnishings or to create it in new ones in the ancient style by introducing arms and armour was perfectly natural. Though it soon became *de rigueur* for any ancient family to own and display its armour, some were still modernizing their houses, and in a poem published in 1783 entitled 'Of an Old Courtier and a New' the house of the old courtier:

> With an old hall, hung about with guns, pikes, and bows,
> With old swords, and bucklers, which hath born many shrewd blows,

is contrasted with that built to replace it after his death by his son:

> With a new hall, built where the old one stood,
> Wherein is burned neither coal nor wood,
> And a new shovel-board table whereon never meat stood;
> Hung round with pictures which doth the poor little good.[31]

However, Walpole's desire to decorate Strawberry Hill with armour was wholly

60

in keeping with the views of some of his contemporaries. The long-established continental precedents for the display of armour will be dealt with when I describe Goodrich. But the whole question of the collecting and the collectors of armour in both Britain and Europe from the Middle Ages on has been so thoroughly discussed in print that I need not deal with it at length here.[32]

By the 1760s both European and oriental arms and armour were available at auction in London. In June 1765 there was sold at auction '98 ... sword of James IV of Scotland taken at Floddenfield. 99 A Scymitar taken from the Bashaw of Damascus at the siege of Vienna ... 100 A Chinese dagger ... 101 Indian arms, viz 2 targets, bow and arrows and pikes.'[33]

As in other fields of collecting, by the end of the eighteenth century, specialist brokers and collectors had begun to emerge while general antiquities brokers and auctioneers continued to sell arms and armour along with their general stock in trade.

Some dealers became collectors in their own right, as did William Rawle, whom we have met already and who was in business as a 'Military accoutrement Maker' from premises in the Strand. His profession brought him into close contact with military men from whom it was often possible to purchase ancient arms and armour. He died in 1789. 'After a lingering illness, Mr Wm Rawle, accoutrement-maker, in the Strand, well known to the gentlemen of the army for his improvements in that branch, and equally well known to the lovers of virtu for his valuable collection of medals, bronzes, arms, and other curiosities — He was actually possessed of the sword with which Oliver Cromwell turned out the long parliament. Major Grose notices this circumstance in his *History of English Armour*.'[34] Rawle's collection was sold in 1790: ... *the valuable collection of Antiquities and curiosities ... of Mr William Rawle ... sold by auction ... By Mr Hutchins ... March the 10th 1790*, the celebrated sword fetching £9.15.0. One of the buyers at the sale was Horace Walpole.

Meyrick's publications of armour superseded all previous ones. However the vade-mecum of armour collectors in the late eighteenth century was the book mentioned in Rawle's obituary, namely, Francis Grose's *A Treatise on Ancient Armour and Weapons* published in 1786. Grose (1731–1791), soldier, antiquary, artist and topographer, was a fascinating character whose writings and cartoons give a clear and witty picture of the antiquarian world of his day. Though a prominent antiquary himself, he satirized antiquaries and collectors in just the way Scott was to do a decade or so later in *The Antiquary*. Grose wrote in his essay 'On the Irrational Pursuits of Virtu' that: 'Among the numerous purchasers of coins, marbles, bronzes, antiquities and natural history, how few of them have their pursuits directed to any rational object ... I fear the majority of our present collectors ... rather hope that being possessed of rare and costly articles will serve for their passport to fame, be admitted as as proof of their learning and love of the sciences, and at the same time obliquely insinuating some idea of their riches.'[35]

As with the other antiquities, much of the armour came from the Continent during and after the Napoleonic Wars via the brokers. Some came as loot, for in 1815 the allied armies, after taking Paris, divided between them Napoleon's superb collection of armour. Some of the British share was displayed at Woolwich Arsenal, where it was seen by the Duke of Wellington and Mrs Arbuthnot on August 1822: 'to the Repository where we saw all the models & all the armour etc. taken at Paris, amongst the rest the armour of Barnard & the famous *masque de fer,* Madame de Levien showed it to M. de Chateaubriant who cld not conceal his fury at the sight.'[36]

The display of arms and armour imparted a suitably ancient appearance to an interior, which fitted in with the late Georgian concept of ancient hospitality. One interior arranged in this way in the later eighteenth century was the mediaeval Great Hall at Cothele. Nicholas Condy published the Great Hall as it was in the 1830s (Plate 16) and he singled out for notice 'The knight's armour, and the corslets, and the matchlocks'.[37]

48. The Great Hall at Parham in the 1890s

In some cases the embellishment of ancient Great Halls with armour reached almost lunatic proportions, as at Parham in Sussex (Plate 48). This large collection of armour and particularly helmets was amassed by Robert Curzon (1810–1873), later the 14th Baron Zouche. Curzon was a prominent antiquary and palaeographer and author of that classic of book collecting *Visits to Monasteries of the Levant*.[38] As early as 1835 he wrote of 'how nice it must have been in the 15th century to wear a murrey coloured gown read Sir Tristan de Leonois seated in a carved throne in an old Gothic room with the sun streaming on the illuminated pages of the book through the rare ymagerie of the mullioned window.'[39]

It was in the Great Hall at Parham in 1871 that a young lady visitor found the spirit of olden times still alive: 'One of the things I liked best at Parham were the prayers that Lord Zouche read before we went to bed. He read them in the great hall: the servants stood in a long row at the other end, & from a very dim lamp & from the wood fire, so our end of the hall was all dim & ghost-like, fot the fire flickered and the Knights came to life again, & moved their helmets.'[40]

Much of the armour at Parham was in fact fake, having been purchased by Curzon from Pratt, the celebrated broker,[41] the discoverer of Lothair's crystal. He had come to prominence as an armour dealer in 1839 when he had provided the ancient armour for the Eglinton Tournament. From 1839 his firm was listed in the directories as 'Importers of Antique Furniture &c 47 New Bond Street'. The Eglinton Tournament and the way in which the idea of armour-clad knights jousting (Plate 19) caught the public imagination has been well described.[42] Pratt not only provided the armour but even arranged for two 'Bow Street Runners' to attend the event to look after security.[43]

In April 1838 Pratt had organized an exhibition of ancient armour, much of which was later to be used at Eglinton. The press were enthusiastic in their praise of both the armour and the way in which it was displayed: 'An exhibition of Gothic and other armour . . . is one of the most brilliant and interesting ever seen in London. The principal portion of it consists of the collection of the illustrious House of Ferrara.'[44] *The Times* commented: 'A very interesting exhibition of ancient armour has been opened at No. 3 Lower Grosvenor Street and the room in which it is exhibited has been appropriately fitted up from a design of Mr Cottingham the architect . . . at a table in this truly Gothic apartment are seated six grim figures in full armour, apparently in debate.'[45]

L.N. Cottingham, the prominent Gothic Revival architect, antiquary and collector, can be relied upon to have designed a dramatic and archaeologically correct setting for this armour. Cottingham was also to design the stands at the Eglinton Tournament the next year. This was not the first such exhibition in London,[46] but coming just before the Tournament it was admirably calculated to catch the public's attention. Pratt had purchased the bulk of this armour from Count Oddi of Padua and after the Tournament he offered the whole collection to the Tower of London.[47]

It should not be thought, however, that the use of arms and armour to embellish interiors was a peculiarly British fashion. Cripps-Day discusses continental collecting, and in 1811 it was noted that

A whim is lately prevalent among the young fellows of the *better classes*, in Paris, which shews itself in ornamenting their bed-chambers, and particularly their bed's head, with arms and armour of all kinds: insomuch, that the famous armour of Don Quixote is completely outdone. Arms offensive and defensive of every country display themselves with the most grotesque effect . . . This eccentricity has been of the greatest benefit to the dealers in battered antiquities.[48]

Later in the century the arrangement of the elaborate and splendid armour collection of Napoleon III as part of Viollet-le-Duc's reconstruction of the Château de Pierrefonds was to upstage every British armoury.

In some interiors fake armour made from papier mâché was used for decoration. Indeed when hung high in a baronial hall unless one climbed a ladder and closely examined it, it easily passed for the real thing. It was easy to make:

The helmets shields, heads of banners . . . formed with paper which is much lighter but more durable than composition. Ornaments in this material are produced by the following method . . . by placing the object face downwards in a shallow vessel filled with liquid plaster of Paris; the subject should be oiled before the plaster is poured upon it: when the plaster is set and become quite hard, upon

49. The Great Hall at Cholmondeley Castle in the 1890s (Walker Art Gallery, Liverpool)

50. The imitation armour made by George Bullock in 1805 (Walker Art Gallery, Liverpool)

removing the model a mould will remain in the plaster, with ever part perfectly formed. This is quite sufficientley hard to form paper ornaments.[49]

How early this practice of manufacturing such fake decorative armour started I cannot discover, for without documentary evidence it is impossible to say whether armour shown in interiors in watercolours and engravings was genuine or of papier mâché. A form of fired ceramic was also used, for it has recently been discovered[50] that in 1805 George Bullock — whom we shall meet at Abbotsford — provided a wide range of arms and armour in this material to decorate the Great Hall at Cholmondeley Castle in Cheshire. The convincing and misleading appearance of this armour can be seen in the photograph of it *in situ* at Cholmondeley (Plate 49). In Plate 50 the helmet top left was copied from a plate in Grose's *Treatise* and that on the bottom right from a piece in Green's Museum.

One last aspect of armour collecting is of interest: its use as props and studio furnishings by artists. As we have seen, Cooke, Cotman and Cattermole all owned armour in the opening decades of the nineteenth century. In the late eighteenth century Richard Cosway furnished his house at 20 Stratford Place, Oxford Street, with a quite significant collection, which was sold after his death: *Catalogue of & very curious and valuable Assemblage of miscellaneous Articles of Taste and Virtu, The Property of that distinguished artist and virtuoso Richard Cosway R.A. consisting of Ancient Armour, Buhl and India Cabinets ... By Mr Stanley ... May 22 1821.*

One well-documented collection of arms and armour was just beginning to be built up in the 1840s by the famous Scottish painter Sir Joseph Noel Paton.[51] Paton can be seen in his studio surrounded by his collection in Plate 51. Paton had by the 1870s put together an important collection, buying in 1872 several celebrated pieces from the Meyrick collection including the Pembridge Helm and the Battle Abbey Sword now both in the Royal Scottish Museum. By the mid-nineteenth century it was *de rigueur* for any artist painting historical pictures to have some armour at least. The patrons who bought the pictures that illustrated the armour often in turn integrated the paintings into their own Romantic Interiors; in some cases they even collected armour similar to that depicted in the paintings.

By the 1850s armour had become, to photographers (Plate 28) as to painters, and indeed to anyone involved in the creation of Romantic Interiors, an essential element in the whole richly romantic mix of ancient objects that went into their furnishing.

The last of the elements that went to make up the Romantic Interior to be considered is ancient stained glass. At Abbotsford and Goodrich all the glass was modern, but at Strawberry Hill and Fonthill there was a mixture of modern and acquired ancient glass. At Charlecote, an ancient house, there was already Elizabethan glass *in situ*, though this was supplemented by new glass in the same style.

The ancient glass at Fonthill and Strawberry Hill came, like so much during the later eighteenth and early nineteenth centuries, from the Continent.[52] Even before large quantities of continental glass began to arrive late in the century, collectors were able to ancient glass buy in England. On 28 November 1736 William Stukeley wrote from his home in Stamford: 'It was observed with great regret what miserable havoc is made daily in the painted glass of the churches of the town ... At St George's they have destroyed wholly several entire windows within three years last past.'[53] Stukeley soon began to acquire such glass to save it from destruction:

> This year, 1737, the churchwardens of *S. Martin's* took away all the painted glass of that church, and put up plain glass in the stead. This was by order of the minister to prevent his wearing spectacles ... after it was done he complained of too much light ... Thus these incurious and thoughtless people demolish these most admirable ornaments ... glaziers commonly broke it all in pieces and sold it for old glass. Sometimes I heard of it before execution done, and purchased the pieces; sometimes a large light for the worth of the broken glass, and put up great quantitys at my house on Barnwell.[54]

To Stukeley's anguish this removal of large quantities of glass continued and even more was removed from St George's Stamford, for he noted on 19 December 1739:

51. Sir Joseph Noel Paton in his studio by John Ballantyne, 1867 (National Galleries of Scotland, Edinburgh)

'Walking past Exton the glazier's door, I saw a cart load of painted glass, just taken from S. George's church windows to put clear glass in the room. Birdmore rectore ibidem. I used my influence with Mr Exton, and got the glass.'[55]

This situation prevailed throughout the country and Thomas Gray, who as we shall see was closely involved with Walpole in the furnishing of Strawberry Hill, wrote to the poet Wharton on 9 May 1761: 'you can pick up some remnants of old painted glass, wch are sometimes met with in farm-house, little out-of-the-way churches & vestries, and even at country-glasiers shops, &c.'[56] As late as the 1790s Lincolnshire, the very area of Stukeley's operations half a century before, was still a happy hunting ground for collectors.

The Hon. John Byng recorded in his diary on 20 June 1791 that in Ramsey in Lincolnshire: 'I entered a glaziers shop, in the hope of finding stain'd glass (part of my pursuit) and was lucky enough to fill one pocket with fragments from Upwood Church (of which the glazier is repairer) offering them so high a price, as to confound, the shop-boy viz six pence.'[57] But, despite the demand from collectors, glass was being destroyed through ignorance even while Byng and his contemporaries were searching for it. Byng wrote on 8 July 1797 that, while at Spilsbury in Lincolnshire, 'I enquired at an old glazier's shop, for stain'd glass'; he said, "That they made no account of it, for that month since, they took down a painted window from Bolingbroke Church, which was all thrown away or broken by the boys'.[58]

At this time glass was being removed from mediaeval churches not only by ignorant church wardens and incumbents, but also by architects carrying out 'destructive' restorations. As has often been told in print, James Wyatt removed mediaeval glass from Salisbury Cathedral and this was then smashed by the glaziers for the scrap lead. In 1788 a Salisbury glazier wrote to a Mr Lloyd of Conduit Street in London: 'Sir, This day I have sent you a Box full of old stained and painted glass, as you desired me to doe, which I hope will suite your Purpos, it is the best that I can get at Present: But I expect to Beate to Peceais a great deal very sune, as it his of now use to me, and we do it for the lead.'[59]

For those who did not relish the thrill of the chase from one country glazier to another by the 1750s, ancient glass was readily available in London. In 1761 Samuel Paterson of Essex House in the Strand had on offer a . . . *collection of Rare Old Stained or painted Glass . . . of the German and Flemish Schools . . . in fancy Frames of Colour'd Glass, composed of such sizes as may be conveniently hung up against the squares of common windows and adapted to the Private Chapels, Saloons, Summerhouses, Grottoes &c.* Walpole was involved in the importation of continental glass as early as 1743, but he noted that 'In 1761 Paterson an auctioneer at Essex House in the Strand opened his first exhibition of painted glass, imported in like manner from Flanders'.[60]

However, as with the importation and trade in ancient armour and woodwork, it was the French Revolution and the outbreak of the Napoleonic Wars that lead to the wholesale export of continental glass. Included amongst the several types of antiquities dispersed by the European Museum in London was glass. In 1791 it advertised for sale 'a Grand Scarce and Curious Assortment of Painted Glass, not to be equalled in this Kingdom; collected from the Convents and religious Houses during the late Commotions and Revolutions in France and Flanders'.[61]

Luckily, this whole trade in glass is far better documented than that in the other antiquities I have described. The activities of one particular broker are well recorded; he was John Christopher Hampp (1750–1825) who, though born in Germany, settled in Norwich in 1782 as a master weaver, only later dealing in glass.[62] One of his account books records his activities from 1802 to 1804, when he joined the many English collectors rushing to France during the Peace of Amiens to purchase antiquities.[63]

In 1804 Hampp held an exhibition of imported glass in both Norwich and London and issued *A catalogue of the ancient stained glass for sale at the warehouse in Norwich and No. 97 Pall Mall London.* The catalogue listed 284 items,[64] and this glass found its way into buildings both ecclesiastical and secular.[65] Hampp purchased at least some of his glass from other brokers, as he recorded in his account book: '1802 Feb 12 of Tailleur St Paul at Malta £9.15.'[66] Tailleur was the glazier who worked for Alexandre Lenoir at the Musée des Monumens Français in Paris, and Hampp also bought from Lenoir himself.[67]

Hampp has become infamous, however, because he purchased directly from the churches themselves, especially in Rouen. In 1821 the Rouennais historian Eustâche de la Queriere noted that 'The beautiful stained glass windows of St Jean were all carried off in 1802 during the Peace of Amiens by an Englishman named Hampp the only condition being that he filled the empty spaces which he did with plain glass. At the same time he acquired all the stained glass of St Nicholas, St Caude-le-Vieux, the Châtreuse, and part of that of St Herbland. These filled 17 great boxes.'[68] In Hampp's defence it must be said that the ecclesiastical authorities were only too keen to sell to him.

Lenoir was no less rapacious, though of course he was preserving the glass in France and at times actually competed with Hampp. The antiquary E.H. Langlois in 1823 told how Lenoir was also after glass in Rouen, and Lenoir said in 1802: 'Yes, the windows of the Châtreuse de Rouen ... I made friendly overtures with the object of obtaining the acquisition for the Museum, but to my regret I did not succeed. I believe they passed into that absorbing gulf called England to which today all our art treasures are going.'[69]

Hampp and his partner Stevenson sent a considerable quantity of glass to auction in 1808: *catalogue of a most valuable and unique collection of Ancient Stained Glass ... for Churches, Collegiate Buildings and Gothic Country Residences ... Mr Christie ... June 16 1808*. Lot 62 on the second day was some of the Rouen glass: 'The Presentation in the Temple, 8 feet 4 by 4 feet 9. This Fine picture once ornamented the Church of St Nicholas Rouen'; it sold for £152.5.0. Also lots 43–55 on the first day were the very glass from the Châtreuse at Rouen that Lenoir had also attempted to acquire.

One interesting case of the incorporation of ancient glass into the private chapel of one of those 'Gothic Country Residences' mentioned in so many of the auction catalogues was Ashridge in Hertfordshire (Plate 52). This vast and elaborate Gothic Revival house — which still survives — is almost on the scale of Fonthill and was indeed, like Fonthill, largely designed by James Wyatt. Also like Fonthill it was completed after Wyatt's death by Sir Jeffry Wyatville.[70] The history of this glass from its manufacture in Renaissance Germany through its remarkable survival during several continental wars has been fully told.[71] All the glass from the Ashridge chapel was removed in 1928 and is now in the Victoria & Albert Museum (Plate 53). How Lord Brownlow acquired the glass is unknown, but Hampp would seem to be the most likely broker to have imported it.[72] Though Wyatville completed the chapel in the early 1820s, we know that the glass was not fully installed by then, for the glass included the charming inscription: 'An humble individual of the same name as the Prophet Amos, the top Figure in the Head of this Window, first commenced fixing these Windows in the year 1811 & finished the Windows in the year 1831.'[73]

The Ashridge glass stayed in place for almost a century, but glass is very easily portable and some of what exists in Romantic Interiors today may have been used successively in several places. When Walpole's friend William Cole died he bequeathed his papers to the British Museum, but he directed to be removed 'the stained glass, which Mr Cole ordered in his will to be sold, and plain glass put in its place'.[74] This glass had been built into the old house at Milton near Cambridge which the celebrated Gothic Revival architect James Essex had extended and gothicized for Cole.

Essex in fact acted at the auction of Cole's collection for the antiquary Richard Gough and wrote to Gough from Cambridge on 18 March 1783: 'I endeavoured to execute your commissions at the auction; but, notwithstanding the severity of the weather, it is amazing how many people attended the sale ... the two bow-

52. The Chapel at Ashridge (H.J. Todd, *The History of . . . Ashridge*, 1823)

53. A panel of mediaeval German stained glass from Ashridge (Victoria & Albert Museum, London)

windows of the study, I bought for you, but could get no more . . . lot 3, which altogether were not worth 5s sold for nearly £6 to a person who came more than thirty miles in the snow and rain to buy them.'[75] The glass bought for Gough was almost certainly incorporated by Essex into the house that he extended for Gough at Enfield. Essex designed a new library the window of which included ancient stained glass.[76]

A good example of the survival *in situ* of ancient glass incorporated into an antiquarian interior is at Plas Newydd. I shall describe the woodwork elsewhere, but it also contains both British and continental stained glass.[77] The house overlooks the ruins of the mediaeval monastery of Valle Crucis, in the ruins of which the celebrated Ladies of Llangollen actually excavated remains of ancient glass which they incorporated into their windows.[78] It is not possible to say exactly when between the late 1770s and the 1820s they discovered and installed the glass, and, indeed they mixed it with glass from other sources. But according to Dr Johnson's friend Mrs Thrale, some ancient glass was in place by March 1796.[79] As with ancient woodwork, there must be many cases of ancient glass being incorporated into ancient buildings and now passing as original to those buildings.

In dealing with the sources of supply from which antiquaries, architects, collectors and brokers of the eighteenth and early nineteenth centuries selected the ancient objects to furnish their Romantic Interiors, I have covered several aspects of the decorative arts. The whole subject of this chapter is, as far as Britain is concerned, largely uncharted territory; for instance, the activities of the brokers with whom I have dealt are shrouded in mystery. The role of the sale rooms is clearer and has to some extent been dealt with in print, but the way in which the brokers operated at auction sales is complex. Sometimes one can gain an insight into their activities, as at the celebrated Stowe sale described above:

> During the sale scarcely any respectable persons could enter the mansion without being importuned to entrust their commission to persons of this class [brokers]: you were told that the applicant belonged to the 'London Society of Brokers' ... that it was no use to offer personal biddings as the brokers attended for the purpose of buying and would outbid any private individual ... The villany of the system will be judged when we add that four or five of these men generally work together.[80]

As I have pointed out, some of the more celebrated individuals, like Scott and Walpole, were presented with numerous objects which helped them to clothe their walls and furnish their cabinets with much less recourse to brokers than Beckford, Meyrick or Lucy. The friends who presented the objects had sometimes owned them for some while but in other cases had recently purchased them from brokers themselves and were thus in effect acting as middlemen between the trade and the celebrated collector. By the 1850s, when this study ends, the antique trade as we know it today had become established. The 'Houndsditch Brokers' doubtless still existed alongside the denizens of Wardour Street. But the centre of gravity of the trade had moved to Bond Street and the West End; the brokers had become antique dealers and their curiosity shops art galleries.

By 1850 the whole range of objects and materials whose sources I have described were being combined together in Romantic Interiors both urban and rural, real and fictional. When in 1850 Thackeray — that pioneer of the Georgian Revival — sends his hero Pendennis to dinner with Lady Clavering in fashionable Grosvenor Place the character of her interiors should come as no surprise:

> they admired the dining-room with fitting compliments and pronounced it very 'chaste' that being the proper phrase. There were indeed, high-backed Dutch chairs of the seventeenth century; there was a carved buffet of the sixteenth; there was a sideboard robbed out of the carved work of a church in the Low Countries, and a large brass cathedral lamp over the round oak table; there were family portraits from Wardour Street, and tapestry from France, bits of armour, double-handed swords and battle axes made of carton-pierre, looking-glasses, statuets of saints, and Dresden china — nothing, in a word, could be chaster.[81]

54. Strawberry Hill from the garden by William Pars, *c.*1780 (Victoria & Albert Museum, London)

4

STRAWBERRY HILL

> The following collection is made out of the spoils of many
> renowned cabinets; as Dr Meade's, lady Elizabeth Germaine's,
> lord Oxford's, the duchess of Portland's, and of about forty
> others more of celebrity.   Horace Walpole

Horace Walpole purchased Strawberry Hill in 1747 and from that time until his death in 1797 he was continuously extending the house as well as adding to his collection. Fortunately both the interiors and the exterior were comprehensively recorded in a wide range of prints, drawings, watercolours and paintings, most of which were commissioned by Walpole himself. He also chronicled the progress of the building and the aquisitions for his collection in hundreds of letters.[1]

The date 1784 is of particular relevance to the study of Strawberry Hill and its collections, for in that year Walpole published the second edition of his *Description*;[2] this replaced the first unillustrated edition of 1774. The second edition was extensively illustrated with plans, elevations and perspective illustrations of both the exterior and the interiors. The 1774 edition had been used by visitors to the house from its publication until 1784, and most copies of the 1774 edition have several pages of 'additions' which list objects added to the collection since 1774. Walpole, it would seem, was continually rebinding the copies of the book to include the additions.

The year 1784 is a very good date at which to examine the interiors of Strawberry Hill, for, although Walpole had more than a decade to live, the furnishing of the interiors had reached a reasonably steady state. The active stage of his collecting career was over, although a steady trickle of objects arrived year by year well into the 1790s. The last page of 'additions', which appears in many copies of the 1784 edition, was printed in 1791 and includes objects acquired up to June of that year.

The collections at Strawberry Hill were not broken up until 1842, the sale being well documented in contemporary newspapers and periodicals. Most important of all is the long and detailed sale catalogue, which exists in seven editions.[3]

The study of Walpole's life, house and collections has been greatly extended and deepened by the efforts of the late W.S. Lewis whose numerous Walpolean publications will be referred to where relevant; the 1934 article appearing in the *Metropolitan Museum Studies* must, however, be singled out as particularly appropriate to this chapter.[4] Strawberry Hill in the 1920s is shown in two articles in *Country Life*,[5] and more recently in the same periodical there appeared the best modern analysis of the building.[6] The most complete chronology of the growth of the building was published in the catalogue of the first exhibition in England to be devoted to Walpole and his house.[7]

Before discussing in detail the interiors at Strawberry Hill in 1784, Walpole's early collecting activities and those of his contemporaries must be considered. He was not unique or even avant-garde in building a Gothic Revival house in the late 1740s, and he seems to have had scant regard for the style much before the mid–1740s. He often visited his father's great Palladian house at Houghton in Norfolk. His father, Sir Robert Walpole, the Prime Minister, was at the height of his powers and, until

55. The front of Strawberry Hill (H. Walpole, *Description of Strawberry Hill* ..., 1784)
56. The south front of Strawberry Hill by E. Edwards, 1784

his departure on the Grand Tour of the Continent in 1739, Walpole seems to have been more interested in Palladianism than in any earlier style. Immediately upon his arrival in Italy he threw himself into the task of collecting the very Greek and Roman antiquities that were appropriate furnishings for a Palladian house. It was not until his purchase of Strawberry Hill in 1747 that he came round to appreciating Gothic architecture.

Walpole returned to England in 1741, after spending almost two and a half years abroad. While there, he had purchased both the standard modern Grand Tour souvenirs and classical antiquities. Horace Mann, the British Minister at the Court of Tuscany, had become Walpole's close friend during the latter's stay in Florence. Mann wrote to Walpole concerning a new table top on 14 May 1740: 'Hugford has not begun your scagliola, but will soon. I'll haunt him till 'tis done. Send me a thousand commissions; I am happy whilst I am employed for you.'[8] Walpole accumulated a collection of interesting modern objects which were later assimilated into the collections at Strawberry Hill. Mann wrote on 24 June 1741 concerning Walpole's purchases of Venetian glass: 'Cecco tells me you have bought such loads of glass; you was in the right to buy a good deal as much I fear will be broke in its way home.'[9]

Walpole also shipped back an interesting collection of classical antiquities, which he described in a letter of 9 April 1743 to his friend the classical scholar and Cambridge University librarian Conyers Middleton: 'On opening my boxes, I find what I suspected, that there is little new, or curious enough to deserve your notice; my chief purchases having lain in medals, and pictures. I must mention to you, though I don't know whether that sort of antiquity comes under your description, a bust of Vespasian in the finest black marble. I bought it at Cardinal Ottoboni's sale, and it was allowed in Rome inferior to nothing but the Caracalla. I have a dozen smaller busts.'[10] The bust can be seen *in situ* at Strawberry Hill in Plate 85. It was bought at the Strawberry Hill sale by William Beckford for £220.10.0; Walpole had paid £23 for it in Rome[11] and it was sold in 1978 for £16,000.[12]

Middleton replied to Walpole on 15 April 1743:

> You have many curiosities, I see of singular rarity, and your collection if you should ever be disposed to publish it would made a reputable volume of itself, so it would be a pity to injure any design of that sort by a prior and separate edition of any part. I now have almost finished what I think sufficient to be said on each particular of my little stock ... but if you are inclined rather to strengthen your own collection, as I hinted above, to publish it, I shall be very willing to give up all my stock to you for a reasonable consideration, and to publish all together under the title of your museum, which has often been done by the noble and curious abroad, but never yet by anyone in England.[13]

Walpole displayed a greed for ownership that he shared with all collectors and wrote to Middleton on 21 April 1743:

> But can you believe I would let the world think I had the vanity to employ Dr Middleton in describing — whose museum? Mine! I stop here for my own sake, for the prosecution of this thought might be somewhat mortifying to me. For your other offer of letting me have your antiquities, as great an obligation as it is, I am hardy enough to accept it, I mean when you have published them. I am not virtuoso enough to buy Charles the Fifths helmet or Queen Elizabeth's one spur, but I should have a satisfaction in showing any one this piece of painting was brought from Rome by Dr Middleton; this is the urn that he describes in such a page.[14]

Middleton's catalogue was published in November 1744[15] and not surprisingly he praised Walpole's collection and alluded to a catalogue of it: 'Ex his autem agri Romani divitiis, neminem profecto de peregrinatoribus nostris thesaurum inde

57. An ancient Roman bronze bust of Caligula by G.D. Harding, 1801

58. The Walpole Cabinet (Victoria & Albert Museum, London)

deportasse credo et rerum delectu et pretio magis aestimabilem ac quem amicus meus nobilis, Horace Walpole in Angliam nuper adexit.'[16]

Walpole certainly was not attracted to the idea of publishing his collection either alone or in conjunction with Middleton; he wrote to Mann on 18 June 1744: 'I have lately made a great antique purchase of all Dr Middleton's collection which he brought from Italy, and which he is now publishing. I will send you the book as soon as it comes out. I would not buy the things till the book was half printed, for fear of an *e museo Walpoliano*. Those honours are mighty well for such known and learned men as Mr Smith the Merchant of Venice.'[17]

Thus Walpole's purchases on the Continent when combined with the Middleton collection formed a respectable and interesting group of classical antiquities. Middleton had, however, somewhat exaggerated the importance of Walpole's collection, there being a number of far more extensive collections of such objects in this country by 1744.

Walpole did add classical antiquities to his collection from time to time for the rest of his life. In 1767 Horace Mann gave him a 'small bust of Caligula with silver eyes . . . It was found with some other small busts at the first discovery of Herculaneum, which happened by digging a well for the prince d'Elboeuf, who resided many years afterwards in Florence, where it was sold on his return to France.'[18] Mann wrote to Walpole on 28 June 1767: 'The Caligula was indeed always admired by everyone who saw it and the great antiquarian [Prince d'Elboeuf] of whom I bought it always carried it about in his pocket wrapped up in cotton.'[19] It (Plate 57) was housed in the Tribune at Strawberry Hill and was lot 68 on the fifteenth day of the Strawberry Hill sale and sold for £48.6.0. It was bought for Beckford by Hume and was immediately displayed at Lansdown Tower.

Many of these classical objects were incorporated into the interior decoration at Strawberry Hill, but for a long while Walpole kept certain of the classical antiquities in his family house in Arlington Street off Piccadilly. This is demonstrated by his comments when the house was burgled in 1771; he wrote to Mann on 22 March: 'I found in three different chambers, three cabinets, a large chest, and a glass case of china wide open, the locks not picked but forced . . . Not a single piece removed. Just so in the Roman and Greek cabinet.'[20] One of the newspapers reported that he had in the house 'large sums of money and a number of antique coins, medals, medallions, etc., to the value of near £3,000'.[21]

His growing collection perhaps combined with the impending purchase of the Middleton collection prompted Walpole to commission the first piece of furniture to relate specifically to his collection. The piece was, however, uncompromisingly classical (Plate 58), a style appropriate to his classical antiquities, whereas many of the pieces made for him after the purchase of Strawberry Hill in 1747 were to be Gothic in style. Walpole wrote to Mann on 19 July 1743: 'I have a new cabinet for my enamels and miniatures just come home, which I am sure you would like.'[22] The cabinet was conceived for the classical interiors of the Arlington Street house, but was eventually to be given pride of place in the Tribune at Strawberry Hill (Plate 82) and is described thus: 'A cabinet of rose-wood, designed by Mr. Walpole; on the pediment, statues in ivory of Fiamingo, Inigo Jones and Palladio, by Verskovis, after the models by Rysbrack. In the pediment, Mr. Walpole's arms, a cupid and a lion, by the same: on the doors bas-reliefs in ivory, Herodias with the head of the Baptist, by Gibbons . . . Within the cabinet of enamels and miniatures.'[23]

By the expedient of hanging the enamels and miniatures on both the back of the cabinet and the backs of the doors Walpole packed a remarkable number of these small objects into it. The overall design of the cabinet was uncompromisingly Palladian in conception — indeed one of the ivory statues is of Palladio himself — and is thus somewhat old-fashioned for 1743. To what extent did Walpole actually design it?

The triangular pediment bears a close resemblance to one of the door-cases at

75

Houghton, but whether this was in Walpole's mind when he designed the cabinet we can only surmise. As we saw above, Walpole attributed one of the ivories to Grinling Gibbons, a carver whom he much admired, and one feature of the cabinet is the close relationship of the swags at the base of the cabinet to Gibbons' work. Is this a coincidence? Or was Walpole combining together Palladian classicism and Gibbons' brand of Baroque naturalism to create what is certainly one of the most singular and interesting pieces of cabinet furniture of the mid-eighteenth century? It is these two elements in combination with the ancient and modern classical ivories and the statues which make this such a fascinating object.

Which cabinet-maker constructed it is unknown, though Hallet is the most likely candidate, in that he was working for Walpole shortly after this date. We do, however, know that Verskovis, carved the modern ivory work and possibly the wooden swags, both these parts differing in style and detail from the cabinet work. Walpole described him thus: 'James Francis Verskovis, an excellent carver in ivory, born in Flanders, but settled in Rome, where he was much employed by English travellers, that he concluded he should make a fortune in England: he came over — and starved . . . carved also in wood.'[24]

In the early 1740s, while Walpole was contemplating the direction his collecting activities might take, the Harleian collection came up for auction following the death of Edward Harley, Earl of Oxford. Interestingly, Harley's collection also included a group of objects from the Arundelian collection[25] and Vertue's splendid frontispiece (Plate 24) shows a group of objects from the auction. Walpole bought several lots, including 'A Curious Vase . . . with a *Bacchanalian* of Boys, by *Fiamingo*'[26] for 16 guineas.

The collection was, as we have seen, not just devoted to classical objects, but it also included mediaeval and later pieces. At the Harleian coin sale Walpole demonstrated that interest in the Elizabethan period which was to influence so much the interiors at Strawberry Hill; he bought four Elizabethan coins including 'a piece of one of her last sovereigns on which her face is most admirably expressed'.[27]

That Walpole was unsure which collecting tradition to follow, even after the acquisition of the Middleton collection and the experience of examining the great Harleian collection in the sale room, was demonstrated in April 1746, when he wrote an essay in the form of a pseudonymous letter to a periodical entitled the *Museum*. This essay had the rather unlikely title of 'A scheme for raising a large sum of money for the use of the Government by laying a tax on message cards and notes'. The letter ends: 'I am, Sir, your humble Servant Descartes'. Though at first sight this subject seems totally irrelevant to Walpole's collecting activities it includes a very clear exposition of what he thought a museum might contain:

> To the Keeper of the MUSEUM. Sir . . . The notion I have of a *Museum*, is an Hospital for every Thing that is *singular*; whether the Thing have acquired Singularity, from having escaped the Rage of Time; from any natural Oddness in itself, or from being so insignificant, that nobody ever thought it worth their while to produce any more of the same Sort. Intrinsic Value has little or no Property in the Merit of *Curiosities* . . . To instance in two sorts of Things, which I said had Pretensions to places in a *Museum*. If the Learned World could be so happy as to discover a Roman's old Shoe (provided the Literati were agreed it were a shoe, and not a leathern Casque, a drinking vessel, a Balloting box, or an Empress's Head-Attire), such a Shoe would immediately have the *Entrée* into any Collection in Europe; even tho' it appeared to be the Shoe of the most vulgar Artizan in Rome, and not to have belong'd to any beau of Classic Memory. And the Reason is plain; not that there is any intrinsic Value in an old Shoe, but because an old Roman Shoe would be a *Unique*; a Term which you, who have erected a *Museum*, know perfectly well is a Patent of *Antiquity*. Natural Oddity is another kind of Merit which I mention'd. Monstrous Births, Hermaphrodites,

Petrifactions, &c are all true Members of a Collection. A Man perfectly virtuous might be laid up in a *Museum* not for any intrinsic value but for being a *Rarity*; and a Dealer might honestly demand five Hundred pounds for such a man of Sir H[ans] S[loane] or Dr M[ead]. A third sort (and I won't run into and more Descriptions) are Things become *Rare* from their Insignificance.[28]

I have found no evidence as to why Walpole did *not*, like so many of his friends and contemporaries, collect natural and animal specimens as described in his essay. It may well be that the satirical vein in which the essay is written indicates that he was never drawn to such objects. There is certainly another reason why he may have been diverted from collecting such things. Even though he had been living at Strawberry Hill for several years, his collecting was still rather random when, following the death of Sir Hans Sloane on 11 January 1753, Walpole was made a trustee of his collection. In 1753 he wrote to Mann:

> You will scarce guess how I employ my time, chiefly at present in the guardianship of embryos and cockleshells. Sir Hans Sloane is dead, and has made me one of the trustees to his museum, which is to be offered for twenty thousand pounds to the King ... He valued it at fourscore thousand, and so would anybody who loves hippopotamuses, sharks with one ear, and spiders as big as geese! It is a rent charge to keep the foetuses in spirits![29]

The Sloane collection was naturally of great importance to the development both of the history of collecting and of museums in England in the early eighteenth century. Despite the impression Walpole gave, many of the objects were not in fact natural or ethnographical; there were, for instance, 700 cameos, 23,000 coins and medals and 50,000 printed books. But there is no doubt that the prime interest in the collection lay in the groups like the 12,500 vegetables and vegetable substances and the 5,843 shells.[30]

In fact, Walpole did own a collection of shells, which he kept at Arlington Street, though he may, of course, have inherited these from his father. He certainly still owned them when he wrote to Mann on 22 March 1771 in connection with the burglary at Arlington Street: 'All was turned topsy-turvy and nothing stolen. The glass case and cabinet of shells had been handled as roughly by these impotent gallants.'[31] This collection apart, Walpole did not on the evidence of the letters or the accounts of Strawberry Hill collect 'Monstrous births, hermaphrodites, petrefactions'; rather, he followed the Harleian and Arundelian style of collecting.

It is perhaps appropriate here to examine further Walpole's attitude to collecting and to his own collection. He wrote to Mann on 29 August 1772 of acquiring 'a sumptuous state bedchamber, which was finished but today, and which completes my house. It must terminate it, for I have at last exhausted all my hoards and collections and such a quantity of things were scarce ever amassed together!'[32] He again wrote to Mann on 17 February 1773: 'I not only cannot accept more presents from you, but I would be heaping them on my tomb. My health is gone; pain is my lot; and what are the fair things of this world to me any longer? I leave off making purchases and put a stop to my collection: it were the hoarding of a miser, to pile my house with curiosities, when I shall enjoy them so little; and extravagance to buy when, my lease of life is running out very fast.'[33]

He was still writing to Mann in the same vein eight years later: 'There is no end of your gifts — but there must be! Remember, reflect, how little time I may have to enjoy them — they will only figure in my inventory at my death ... Oh! how sad is the thought that you are *never* to see your presents arranged and displayed *here* with all the little honour I can confer on them — but they are all recorded in my catalogue — and whosoever reads it, will think I had no shame or gratitude.'[34] Mann died in 1786, ten years before Walpole.

By 1784 Walpole was declaring even more strenuously that he had lost interest in collecting when he wrote to Lady Ossory on 12 November: 'I have seen Mr Duane, who is feeble indeed; but his head is clear, and his appetite for buying curiosities still alert — consequently — I am much more superannuated for I find that passion has taken flight too!'[35]

His passion was soon aroused anew when an exciting auction sale was in prospect. The Duchess of Portland died on 17 July 1785 and before a week had elapsed Walpole was writing to Lady Ossory, on 23 July: 'the Duke will reserve the principal curiosities — I hope so, for I should long for some of them, and am become too poor to afford them — besides that it is ridiculous to treat one's self to playthings when one's eyes are closing.'[36]

The next year he seemed to lose interest again and he wrote to Lord Buchan on 17 June 1786: 'I am so old and infirm, that it would be idle in me to think of increasing my collection. I have no pursuits left nor activity enough to meddle either with virtu or letters.'[37] He was, however, rejoicing in a letter to Lady Ossory only three weeks later about having spent the not inconsiderable sum of £359.3.6 at the Portland sale on 5 July 1786: 'I asked why they were so long mowing one of my meadows? they said it was so thick they could not cut it. I have really double the quantity of any other year — yet doubt these riches will not indemnify me for the Portland Sale! — however, here my collection closes.'[38]

It does seem the case that, while protesting both age and poverty, Walpole was quite unable to stop himself collecting. Perhaps he best summed up the problem when he wrote to Cole on 7 August 1781: 'I have too often been guilty myself of giving ridiculous prices for rarities, though of no intrinisic value, that I must not condemn the same folly in others. Everything tells me how silly I am! — I pretend to reason, and yet am a virtuoso!'[39] Many collectors, both before and after Walpole, have wrestled with the illogical nature of the collecting passion, though he seems to have written more about his feelings than most. It does seem from reading his letters and from a comparison of the 1784 *Description* and its pages of 'additions' with the new edition of the *Description* in the Works of 1798 that after 1791 his collecting activities almost ceased. It is worth pointing out that in 1791 he was seventy-four years old!

As stated above, the 1784 *Description* is the single most important source for the study of Strawberry Hill and its contents. Walpole refers in letters to both the 1784 and the earlier edition of 1774; he wrote to Lady Ossory on 14 November 1774: 'I grow so old, that I find the quiet composed life I lead here more agreeable than the ways of London, and the same eternal round of the very same things. I am making catalogues of my collection, building a hot-house, ranging my medals which I have brought hither, sorting and burning papers.'[40] Six years later he was deeply involved in planning a new edition of the *Description*; he wrote to Cole on 19 December 1780: 'but to finish my Catalogue — and that will be awkwardly enough, for so many articles have been added to my collection since the *Description* was made, that I must add them in the appendix, or reprint it — and what is more inconvenient, the positions of many of the pictures have been changed; so it will be a lame piece of work.'[41]

The first edition was mainly for the use of visitors, but eventually it was not shown even to them. Walpole wrote to Lady Ossory on 15 September 1787:

> the *Description* of this place; now, though printed, I have entirely kept up, and mean to do so while I live for very sound reasons, Madam, as you will allow. I am so tormented by visitors to my house, that two or three rooms are not shown to abridge their stay. In the *Description* are specified all the enamels and miniatures, etc., which I keep under lock and key. If the visitors got the book into their hands, I should never get them out of the house, and they would want to see fifty articles which I do not choose they should handle and paw.[42]

Visitors had in fact been a problem for years. Walpole had written to Cole on 14

June 1769: 'I am now so tired of it, that I shudder when the bell rings at the gate. It is as bad as keeping an inn, and I am often tempted to deny its being shown, if it would not be ill-natured to those that come, and to my housekeeper.'[43] The housekeeper, of course, received money for dealing with the parties of visitors. At first, Walpole wrote a note to give permission to visit, but in 1774 he had printed at the Strawberry Hill press a special ticket,[44] which he sent to visitors. In 1784 he had printed a set of Rules which gave details of the opening times and rules for conduct and ended by stating 'They who have Tickets are desired not to bring Children'.[45]

I have not the space to give a full bibliographical analysis of the 1784 *Description*,[46] but several points must be noted. Walpole, as described, continued to add objects to his collection right up to the early 1790s, and this is nowhere better demonstrated than in the additions of the 1784 *Description*. The additions (pp. 89–92), which form signature 'N', include objects bought at the Duchess of Portland's sale in July 1786 and are said to have been printed in the summer of that year;[47] they lists 44 objects. The section 'Curiosities added since this book was compleated' is pp. 93–4 and forms signature 'O', which was probably printed in 1789,[48] for it includes the 'Hair of King Edward IV cut from his corpse when discovered in St George's Chapel at Windsor 1789; given by Sir Joseph Banks'. This section includes 34 items. The last section, 'More additions', forms signature 'O2' and was probably printed in 1791[49] and includes 41 items. The edition of the *Description* in the *Works* of 1798 does not include any further additions beyond those of 1791, nor does any copy of the *Description* itself that I have examined.

Walpole gained the experience required to publish and write the *Description* even before he bought Strawberry Hill, for as early as 1736 he had compiled a list of his father's pictures at Houghton.[50] He continued to work on this collection and he completed this work in August 1743. Although Sir Robert Walpole died in March 1745 and the book was not published until 1747, the dedication is dated 24 August 1743. The book was entitled *Aedes Walpolianae; or, a Description of the Collection of Pictures at Houghton Hall in Norfolk The Seat of the Right Honourable Sir Robert Walpole Earl of Orford* and it went through two further editions in 1752 and 1767.[51] The introduction runs thus:

> The following account of Lord Orford's collection of pictures is rather intended as a catalogue than a description of them. The mention of cabinets in which they have formerly been, with the addition of the measures, will contribute to ascertain their originality, and be a kind of pedigree to them. In Italy, their native soil is almost all *Virtu*, descriptions of great collections are much more common and much more ample. The princes and noblemen there who loved and countenanced the ARTS, were fond of letting the world know the curiosities in their possession. There is scarce a large collection of medals but is in print. Their gems, their statues, and antiquities are all published. But the most pompous of this sort are the Aedes Barbarinae[52] and Giustinianae[53] the latter of which are now extremely scarce and dear. Commerce which carries along with it the curiosities and arts of countries as well as the riches, daily brings us something from Italy. How many valuable collections of pictures are there established in England on the frequent ruins and dispersions of the finest galleries in Rome and other cities! . . . There are not a great many collections left in Italy more worth seeing than this at Houghton.[54]

Here we see Walpole putting forward several ideas he was to develop further in the 1784 *Description*, namely, the importance of the 'pedigree', the rarity of published catalogues of English collections and the international movement of works of art from one country and collection to another. The 1774 *Description* had no preface; the 1784 edition did. It, taken with the preface to *Aedes*, reveals so much that is germane both to Walpole's attitude to collecting and to the creation of Strawberry Hill and indeed to that of later Romantic Interiors that it must be quoted at some length.

It will look, I fear, a little like arrogance in a private Man to give a printed Description of his Villa and Collection, in which almost every thing is diminutive. It is not however intended for public sale, and originally was meant only to assist those who should visit the place. A farther view succeeded; that of exhibiting specimens of Gothic architecture, as collected from standards in cathedrals and chapel-tombs, and showing how they may be applied to chimney-pieces, cielings, windows, ballustrades, loggias &c ... Catalogues raisonnes of collections are very frequent in France and Holland; and it is no high degree of vanity to assume for an existing collection an illustration that is allowed to many a temporary auction — an existing collection — even that phrase is void of vanity. Having lived unhappily to see the noblest school of painting that this kingdom beheld, transported almost out of the sight of Europe, it would be strange fascination, nay, a total insensibility to pride of family, and to the moral reflections that wounded pride commonly feels, to expect that a paper Fabric and an assemblage of curious Trifles made by an insignificant Man, should last ... Far from such visions of self-love the following account of pictures and rarities is given with a veiw to their future dispersion. The several purchasers will find a history of their purchases; nor do virtuosos dislike to refer to such a catalogue for an authentic certificate of their curiosities. The following collection is made out of the spoils of many renowned cabinets; as Dr Meade's, lady Elizabeth Germaine's, lord Oxford's, the duchess of Portland's, and of about forty more of celebrity. Such well-attested descent is the genealogy of the objects of virtu — not so noble as those of the peerage, but on a par with those of race-horses. In all three, especially the pedigrees of peers and rarities, the line is often continued by many insignificant names ... In a house affecting not only obsolete architecture, but pretending to an observance of the costume even in the furniture, the mixture of modern portraits, and French porcelaine, and Greek and Roman sculpture, may seem heterogeneous. In truth, I did not mean to make my house so Gothic as to exclude convenience, and modern refinements in luxury. The designs of the inside and outside are strictly ancient, but the decorations are modern. Would our ancestors, before the reformation of architecture, not have deposited in their gloomy castles antique statues and fine pictures, beautiful vases and ornamented china, it they had possessed them?[55]

The reference to paintings leaving Europe refers to the sale in 1779 of the Houghton pictures to Catherine the Great of Russia by Walpole's nephew George, 3rd Earl of Orford. The breaking up of the Houghton collection made Walpole more than ever aware of the transitory character of a collection of objects brought together by an individual collector. He indicates, however, that some solace can be gained from the fact that by publishing a catalogue of the collection some record at least survives. He also realized that to be even one link in the pedigree, even an 'insignificant' one, gives a collector a measure of immortality. As we saw, there was no introduction to the 1774 *Description*, but even by this date he was preoccupied with the eventual dispersal of his cherished collection and even the disfigurement of his beloved house.

On 9 May 1772 he wrote to William Mason: 'In short, this *old, old, very old castle*, as his prints called old Parr, is so near to being perfect, that it will certainly be ready by the time I die, to be improved by Indian paper; or to have the windows cut down to the ground by some travelled lady.'[56] On 6 March 1780 he wrote to Cole of 'all my favourite, brittle transitory relics, which will soon vanish with their founder — and with no great unwillingness for himself'. But it was certainly the break up of the collection of his old friend Dicky Bateman of Old Windsor that shook him most of all.

Bateman had a singular collection, but his house and its contents had more direct effect on the shaping of Walpole's taste and more influence on his interiors at

Strawberry Hill than any other. Walpole wrote to Lady Ossory on 26 July 1775: 'went to Old Windsor to see poor Mr Bateman's auction. It was a melancholy sight to me in more lights than one. I have passed many pleasing days there with him and Lady Hervey, and felt additional pain by reflections on my child Strawberry! All pulled to pieces.'[57] He had also written to Cole: 'Consider Strawberry is almost the last monastery left, at least in England. Poor Mr. Bateman's is despoiled: Lord Bateman has stripped and plundered it . . . I was hurt to see half the ornaments of the chapel, and the *reliquaires*, and in short a thousand trifles exposed to sneers. I am buying a few to keep for the founder's sake . . . I suppose Strawberry Hill will have the same fate! It has already happened to two of my friends.'[58] Indeed, Bateman's name duly appears in the pedigrees of several of the objects described in the 1784 *Description*.

In describing the creation of the interiors at Strawberry Hill itself I will follow the dating evolved recently,[59] which is close to that published by W.S. Lewis.[60] I cannot deal with all the interiors, but have chosen for detailed treatment those that best exemplify the innovatory nature of Walpole's schemes of interior decoration. I shall discuss at some length the Great Parlour or Refectory (1754), the Library (1754), the Holbein Chamber (1759) and the Armoury (1753). The Gallery (1763) and the Tribune (1763) I shall illustrate and only mention briefly.

It should be stressed that, though the complex process of furnishing each of these rooms started as soon as each was complete in the architectural sense, I shall be discussing them as they had become by 1784. The illustrations, other than those from the 1784 *Description*, mainly date from the 1780s. In some cases it has been possible to ascertain the date of acquisition of objects in a particular room. The *Accounts* are mainly concerned with the cost of building and decorating works: not many purchases for Walpole's collection are specified.

The best source for this information is the letters, which sometimes disclose that Walpole had just bought an object; in other cases he happens to mention an object he might already have owned for years. In this latter case, we at least know a latest date for its entry into his collection. Given the space and the years of research necessary, it would be possible to establish how the whole collection and the way in which it was used to furnish the rooms changed over the fifty years after Walpole purchased Strawberry Hill in 1747. The exterior of the house in 1784 appears in Plates 54 through 56 and the plans in Plates 66 and 67.

The Great Parlour is not illustrated in the *Description*, though a watercolour exists (Plate 60). The chimney-piece is, however, engraved in the *Description* (Plate 59). 'It [the Great Parlour] is thirty feet long, twenty wide and twelve high; hung with paper in imitation of stucco. The chimney-piece was designed by Mr. Bentley: upon it stands a fine Etruscan vase, between two bottles of black and gold porcelaine.'[61] The vase and bottles (Plate 60) are a singular combination of objects and the bottles, though described as 'black', are probably 'Two Oriental blue and gold China long neck bottles and two brackets.'[62]

The mention of paper in imitation of stucco is interesting, it being at this period a new innovation. Lady Luxborough, for instance, had written to william Shenstone from her house at Barrells in Warwickshire on 13 February 1751:

Moore (who has lately been at London) talks to me of a sort of stucco-paper, which I never heard of; and says Lord Foley has done his Chapel in Worcester-shire with it (the ceiling at least). By his description, the paper is stamped so deep as to project considerably, and is very thick and strong and the ornaments are all detached, and put on separately. As suppose for example it were the pattern of a common stucco-paper, which is generally a mosaic formed by a rose in a kind of octagon, it seems in this new way one of the roses is to be bought singly; so you have as many in number as the place requires, which are pasted up separately, and then gilt.[63]

CHIMNEY IN THE GREAT PARLOUR.

59. The chimney-piece in the Great Parlour at Strawberry Hill (Walpole, *Description*)

60. The Great Parlour in 1788 by John Carter

Thomas Gray wrote to Thomas Wharton on 8 September 1761: 'you seem to suppose, that they do Gothic papers in colours, but I never saw any but such as were to look like Stucco'.[64] It would have been much more mediaeval for Walpole to have hung the walls at Strawberry Hill with tapestry, and indeed many neo-classical houses of this period were hung with modern neo-classical tapestry. Walpole, however, preferred the newly fashionable wallpaper.

Gray wrote to Wharton on 18 September 1759, five years after the completion of the Refectory: 'Yet I allow tapestry (if at all tolerable) to be of a proper furniture for your sort of house; but doubt if any bargain of that kind is to be met with, except at some old mansion-sale in the country, where People will disdain tapestry, because they hear that Paper is all the fashion'.[65]

Wallpapers were used in other rooms at Strawberry Hill, but they were not described as being in imitation of stucco. Plate 60 shows no pattern on the wall or ceiling, and the word 'hung' could relate to either. If, however, Walpole was referring to flat paper, it is possible that it was the monochrome variety described by Gray and the pattern was not pronounced enough to show up in the watercolour. Another possibility is that Walpole was referring to the enriched cornice as being in stucco paper, meaning papier mâché; that there was confusion between the two is obvious from the letters quoted.

Papier mâché was extensively used elsewhere at Strawberry Hill for ceilings. If this were the case, it would explain Walpole's odd statement to Chute in a letter of 30 April 1754: 'The last time I went to Strawberry, I found the stucco men as busy as so many Irish bees, plastering up eggs and anchors for the frieze of the eating room, but I soon made them destroy all they had done.'[66] As Plate 60 shows, the frieze — it was still *in situ* — did not consist of classical eggs and anchors. A plaster frieze would have been cast and nailed up in the usual way, so would Walpole have spoken of plastering up? Lady Luxborough talked of paper ornaments being 'pasted up separately'. I would suggest that is what Walpole meant and that the frieze is papier mâché plastered up by the stucco men.

The chimney-piece is one of Bentley's most original creations (Plate 59) and, unlike most of the others at Strawberry Hill, it was not based upon a tomb. Another important feature of the room was the stained glass, confined here, as in several other rooms, to the upper lights of the window to allow Walpole an unimpeded view of the landscape he had helped to create. Later Gothic Revivalists were to disapprove of this non-mediaeval practice, but Walpole did not wish Strawberry Hill to be 'so Gothic as to exclude convenience'.

The window is described thus: 'On each side of the window, the top of which has some fine painted glass, and one ridiculous Dutch piece representing the triumph of Fame, who is accompanied by Cato, Cicero, and other great men in square caps and gowns of masters of arts.'[67] A footnote states: 'there is another Dutch emblematic pane ... Another pane is painted with a cobbler whistling to a bird in a cage by Pearson, scholar of Price, This window was altered and enlarged in 1774.' The bill for the alteration survives: '1774. Nov. for new window in the great parlour'.[68] James Pearson was born in Dublin but spent some years at least working in London.[69] The pane with the cobbler is still in place in this window at Strawberry Hill.

Walpole thought highly of Pearson but certainly had problems with him prompting his complaint to Cole on 20 November 1770: 'I am enraged and almost to despair, at Pearson the glass-painter, he is so idle and dissolute — he has done very little of the window, though what he has done is glorious, and approaches very nearly to Price.'[70] The description given above of the Great Parlour window is not at all full, but a more complete one exists in the Strawberry Hill sale catalogue.[71] From this it is clear that all of the glass was ancient except for the Pearson piece. It may well have been that these ancient fragments were repaired and leaded up by Pearson: 'the new window' mentioned in the *Accounts* surely does not refer to the one pane that Walpole mentions as being by Pearson.

Walpole incorporated a wide range of ancient glass into the windows throughout

61. An English fifteenth-century stained glass panel depicting the arms of John of Gaunt (Victoria & Albert Museum, London)

62. A German fifteenth-century stained glass panel depicting the arms of the Counts of Virneburg (Victoria & Albert Museum, London)

Strawberry Hill and in this he was one of the group of people involved in creating the market for ancient glass. As early as 13 February 1750 he was writing to Mann: 'I am going to build a little Gothic castle at Strawberry Hill. If you can pick me up any fragments of old painted glass, arms or anything, I shall be excessively obliged to you. I can't say I remember any such thing in Italy, but out of old chateaus I imagine one might get it cheap, if there is any.'[72]

Mann apparently did not discover any, but Walpole could write to him by 16 April 1753: 'I have amassed such quantities of painted glass, that every window in my castle will be illuminated with it, the adjusting and disposing it is vast amusement.'[73] This large quantity of glass had been purchased through the good offices of Walpole's friend Dicky Bateman. Walpole described how this occurred: 'about the year 1753, one Asciotti an Italian, who had married a Flemish woman, brought a parcel of painted glass from Flanders, and sold it for a very few guineas to the honourable Mr Bateman of Old Windsor. Upon that I sent Asciotti again to Flanders, who brought me 450 pieces, for which, including the expense of his journey, I paid him thirty-six guineas.'[74] This glass lasted Walpole for some while, but, as we shall see later, he was always on the look-out for more ancient glass for Strawberry Hill. The source of the two pieces in Plates 61 and 62 is unknown.

The Great Parlour contained both fashionable modern furniture and specially designed Gothic Revival pieces (Plates 60 and 63 through 65). The *Description* lists 'a Bureau of black Japan; on it a clock, supported by a bronze figure of a woman reading . . . card tables of rose-wood carved in china . . . a fire screen of admirable needle work representing a vase of flowers . . . mounted in mahogany, carved and inlaid with ivory . . . a fire screen embroidered with knotting'. The sale catalogue adds very little more information, except as far as the clock is concerned: 'A magnificent or-molu 14–day clock, of large size, by Julien le Roy, with finely formed bronze figure of a Female reading.'[75] Le Roy was a well-known Parisian clockmaker and, when one compares Walpole's clock with others known to be by him, it would seem to date from about 1758. When Walpole purchased it is unknown, but it does appear in the main text of the 1774 *Description*, which gives a latest date for its purchase. It still survives at Waddesdon.[76]

Two sofas are clearly seen in Plate 60; they are standard 1750s mahogany sofas. It is interesting that they are shown with their red gingham covers, which would have been taken off on special occasions to reveal some more exotic upholstery material. They were in fact supplied specially for the room: '1755 Sep. 20. pd Hallet . . . for 2 Sophas for eating room 20–12–0.'[77] This quite substantial price might point to an expensive upholstery material such as silk damask, though Hallet was one of the most celebrated cabinet-makers of his day[78] and his furniture was by no means cheap. The two chairs on either side of the window are again standard products, but they are unlikely to date from the 1750s. They do not appear in Hallet's bill and would seem likely on stylistic grounds to date from the later 1760s.

The Gothic furniture designed specially for the room is, none the less, quite remarkably advanced for 1754. According to the *Description*, 'The chairs are black, of a gothic pattern, designed by Mr Bentley and Mr Walpole. The Table of Sicilian jasper on a black frame designed by Mr Bentley . . . over each a looking glass in a gothic frame of black and gold, designed by Mr Walpole. Inclosed in the tops of the frames, with their arms and coronets, are the portraits of George Walpole third Earl of Orford, and of George Cholmondeley Viscount Malpas.' One of the glasses is shown in Plate 63.

The descriptions in the sale catalogue do not add any facts concerning the chairs or mirrors, but of the table it says: 'the top of Sicilian jasper, of the rarest kind, on a black frame, with 8 twisted legs, the top 6 feet long and 3 feet wide'.[79] A watercolour of the table survives (Plate 64) and shows what a singular object it was; its style with its barley-sugar twist legs was Tudor or Elizabethan rather than Gothic and, as we shall see, related closely to the ancient ebony furniture in the Holbein

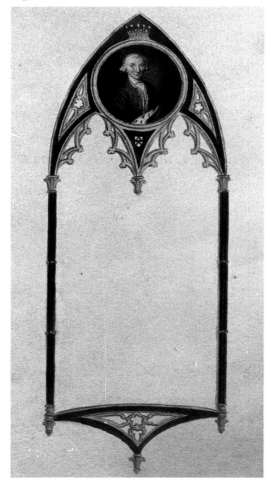

63. A mirror in the Great Parlour by G.D. Harding, 1801

64. The table in the Great Parlour by G.D. Harding, 1801

65. One of the dining chairs from the Great Parlour (Victoria & Albert Museum, London)

Chamber. The maker of the table is unknown, though it may be that listed in the *Accounts* — '1756 . . . Nov 1. pd for large marble table &c. 23.2.0.'[80] — which was designed by Bentley, who was soon to be dropped as one of Walpole's designers, but who without doubt had a very imaginative grasp of Gothic forms, the chimney-piece (Plate 59) being one of the most inventive of his Gothic designs.[81]

The Gothic chairs and the mirrors (Plates 60, 63 and 65) were supplied by Hallet: '1755 Sept 20. pd Hallet . . . for 8 black gothic chairs at 3–15–0; 30–00–0. for black frames to Gothic glasses 13–00–0.'[82] Several of the chairs and one of the mirrors still survive.[83] Walpole wrote to Bentley on 27 July 1754:

> In the first palce, my chairs! if you had taken a quarter of the time to draw what they might be, that you have employed to describe what they must not be, I might possibly have had some begun by this time. Would one not think it was I who made charming drawings and designs and not you? I shall have very little satisfaction in them, if I am to invent them! My idea is a black back higher, but not much higher than common chairs, and extremely light, with matted bottoms. As I found yours came not, I have been trying to make out something like windows — for example [here is a drawing of chair with a back resembling a three-light ecclesiastical window] I would have only a sort of black sticks, pierced through: you must hatch this egg soon, for I want chairs in the room extremely[84]

Bentley must have supplied the designs eventually, for he and Walpole were jointly credited with the design and Hallet presumably supplied the finished chairs before his bill was paid in September 1755. The chairs are of the greatest importance to the history of eighteenth-century Gothic Revival furniture, for, until they were designed, Gothic style chairs followed a very different pattern. The backs were, as Walpole states, inspired by mediaeval lancet windows, whereas the usual Gothic chairs of this date either follow the conventional chair form for the period with Gothic details added or are so bizarre as to bear no resemblance to mediaeval prototypes whatsoever.

Thus Walpole and Bentley together, though from the letter quoted it would seem that the idea was actually Walpole's own, were amongst the first and perhaps *the* first to base chair backs upon Gothic window tracery. This form of chair back rapidly became commonplace, but in 1755 it was highly original.

The mirrors did not and indeed could not follow any mediaeval precedent, for glass mirrors of this size did not exist at that period. They were 'designed' by Walpole perhaps after he had experienced Bentley's inefficiency over the chair designs. In character, though not in deatil, the mirrors owe a great deal to the lunatic Chinoiserie mirrors of the 1730s and 1740s. Walpole might almost have been criticizing the chairs and mirrors when he complained to Bentley on 5 July 1755 of the 'Batty Langley-discipline: half the ornaments are of his bastard Gothic and half of Hallet's mongrel Chinese. I want to write over the doors of most modern edifices, *Repaired and beautified, Langley and Hallet Churchwardens.*'[85]

In fact the columnar supports of the chair back bear an uncomfortably close resemblance to some of the Gothic orders illustrated in Langley's book of 1747.[86] Also a motif similar, but not identical to the eight floriated cusps on the two roundels in the back of the chair, appears in plate XXXIV of the Langley's book. It is also interesting to note that the enriched cornice of the Great Parlour is quite similar

66. Plan of the ground floor at Strawberry Hill (Walpole, *Description*)

67. Plan of the principal floor (Walpole, *Description*)

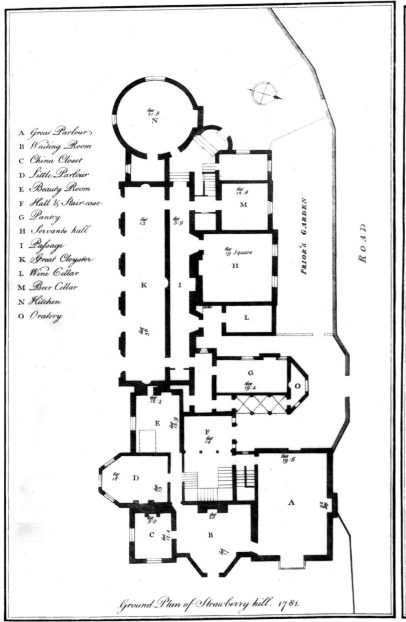

A. Great Parlour
B. Waiting Room
C. China Closet
D. Little Parlour
E. Beauty Room
F. Hall & Stair-case
G. Pantry
H. Servants hall
I. Passage
K. Great Cloyster
L. Wine Cellar
M. Beer Cellar
N. Kitchen
O. Oratory

Ground Plan of Strawberry hill. 1781.

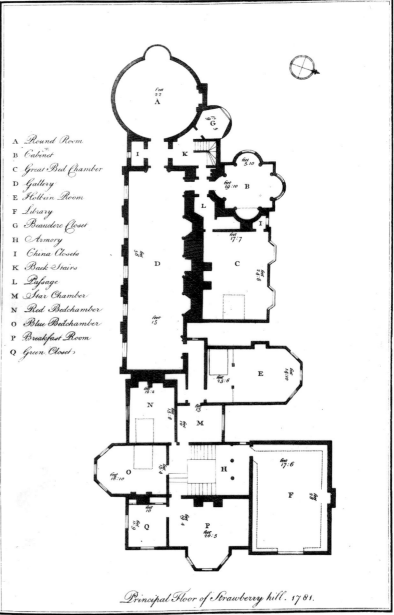

A. Round Room
B. Cabinet
C. Great Bed Chamber
D. Gallery
E. Holbein Room
F. Library
G. Beauclerc Closet
H. Armory
I. China Closets
K. Back Stairs
L. Passage
M. Star Chamber
N. Red Bedchamber
O. Blue Bedchamber
P. Breakfast Room
Q. Green Closet

Principal Floor of Strawberry hill. 1781.

to that in plate LI of Langley's book; thus, despite the fact that Walpole so scorned Langley's attempt to apply rules to Gothic design, unintentionally or not the Gothic detail at Strawberry Hill, whether designed by Walpole or Bentley, owed something to Langley's publications.

The furnishings of this room were, as we can see, a mixture of standard Georgian furniture and specially designed pieces in the Tudor or Gothic style, but no attempt was made to arrange the furniture in anything other than the modern manner. In fact, Plate 60 shows the room arranged in precisely the way that every grand dining room in England was arranged at this date except when set for dinner. It was usual to keep the chairs against the walls of the room to leave the centre clear of furniture so that visitors could promenade around the room to admire the pictures and the decoration.

When such a room was set for dinner, a dining table or more probably several tables which fixed together were brought into the room or possibly pulled out from the walls. The Gothic chairs at Strawberry Hill would then be moved away from the walls and placed around the table. No complete inventory for Strawberry Hill survives, and there is no reason why Walpole should have mentioned plain dining tables in the *Description*.

These tables could have stood against the wall in the Great Parlour, but if one compares the plan (Plate 66) with the watercolour view (Plate 60) it will be seen that two chairs and the 6 foot Gothic table with twisted legs had to be accommodated on the 19 foot 6 inch wall opposite the window, this not being visible in Plate 60. Two 4 foot dining tables could in practice just have fitted on the wall, but inventories of this period usually demonstrate that these tables were kept in the passage outside the dining room. To take an example local to Strawberry Hill, at Osterley Park, which Walpole visited several times, the inventories show that the two dining tables were kept where they still stand today in the passage outside the dining room. The Osterley tables are each 4 feet 5 inches wide, 5 feet 8 inches long when extended but only 1 foot 11 inches wide with the flaps down.

The tables at Strawberry Hill could well have stood in the Entrance Hall or in the Waiting Room. At the time of the Strawberry Hill sale the Hall contained 'A pair of beautifully carved mahogany card tables, oblong shape, with rising flaps, carved legs'.[87] Could these be the dining tables? By 1842 eighteenth-century dining habits had been forgotten and dining tables to the uninitiated could easily have been mistaken for card tables. Moreover, Georgian card tables usually have baize tops and those mentioned here do not appear to have them.

The last object I must mention from this room is a splendid horn which was hung over the ebony table, 'a hunting–horn, finely enamelled on one side in colours, on the other in chiaro scuro, with the history of saint Hubert'.[88] In the sale it was said to be 'rare Limoges enamel and perfectly unique. It is undoubtedly one of the most remarkable gems of this rare collection.'[89] It was sold for the enormous sum of £141.15.0 to John Webb, the Bond Street dealer, and is now in the Louvre.

The Library (Plates 68–70), which is directly above the Great Parlour, as the plan (Plate 67) shows, was also completed in 1754: 'July 2d. pd Clermont for painting the library ceiling 73–10–0.'[90] Adrien de Clermont (1716?–1783) is mentioned in Walpole's *Anecdotes of Painting*: 'a Frenchman, for many years in England, painted in grotesque, foliages with birds and monkeys, and executed several ceilings and ornaments of buildings . . . particularly a gallery for Frederic prince of Wales, at Kew . . . a ceiling for lord Northumberland at Sion. Clermont returned to his own country in 1754.'[91]

Walpole and Bentley collaborated in the design of this ceiling. Walpole wrote to Bentley on 17 March 1754: 'I must apply you to my library ceiling; of which I sent you some rudiments. I propose to have it all painted by Clermont; the principal part is chiaroscuro, on the design which you drew for the Paraclete [the Hall]: but as that pattern would be surfeiting so often repeated in an extension of 20 feet by 30, I propose to break and enliven it by compartments in colours, according to the enclosed sketch, which you must adjust and dimension.'[92]

The completed ceiling (Plates 68 and 69) Walpole described thus: 'The ceiling was painted by Clermont, from Mr Walpole's design drawn out by Mr Bentley. In the middle is the shield of Walpole surrounded with the quarters borne by the family. At each end in a round is a knight on horseback, in the manner of ancient seals, that next to the window bears the arms of Fitz Osbert, the other of Robsart ... On either side is the motto of the family. *Fari quae sentiat*; and at the ends, MD.CC.LIV, the year in which this room was finished, expressed in Gothic letters: the whole on a mosaic ground.'[93] This elaborate ceiling still exists, and is one of the most complex and interesting painted schemes of the eighteenth-century Gothic Revival.

The rest of the Library was described thus: 'The books are ranged within Gothic arches of pierced work, taken from a side-door case to the choir in Dugdale's St Paul's. The doors themselves were designed by Mr Chute. The chimney-piece is imitated from the tomb of John of Eltham earl of Cornwall, in Westminster-abbey; the stone-work from that of Thomas duke of Clarence, at Canterbury.'[94] The design of the bookcases was not without its problems, once again caused by Bentley, who produced a design which still exists.[95] Walpole wrote to him on 19 December 1753: 'For the library, it cannot have the Strawberry imprimatur: the double arches and double pinnacles are most ungraceful; and the doors below the book-cases in Mr Chute's design had a conventual look, which yours totally wants.'[96]

The Chute designs were executed, but not until some months had passed, for Walpole wrote again to Bentley on 2 March 1754: 'Mr Chute was here yesterday ... We have determined upon the plan for the library, which we find will fall in exactly with the proportions of the room, with no variations from the little door-case of St Pauls, but widening the longer arches. I believe I shall beg your assistance again about the chimney-piece and ceiling.'[97] The room is 28 feet long, 17½ feet wide, and 13 feet high,[98] and all the architectural details mentioned above were taken from books housed in the very room, mainly in Press E, which housed the topographical books. The shelving of these, like all the other books at Strawberry Hill, has been carefully established by Professor Hazen.[99]

It was, of course, impossible for Walpole and his 'Committee of Taste' actually to visit Old St Paul's, which was destroyed in the Great Fire of 1666, but Wenzel Hollar's engravings in Sir William Dugdale's *The History of St Paul's* of 1658 gave them all the material they needed. Its pressmark in the Strawberry Hill Library was E.2.27.[100] Walpole and his friends could easily have visited Westminster Abbey to see the tomb of John of Eltham. They seem, however, to have stayed at Strawberry Hill and chosen the motifs for the Library chimney-piece from Walpole's copy of John Dart's *Westmonasterium* (1742), pressmark E.1.12.[101] Similarly, the stonework of the fireplace was copied from the plate on page 67 of Dart's *The History and Antiquities of the Cathedral Church of Canterbury* (1726), pressmark B.1.3.[102]

The room seems to have been almost completed by early 1755, for the *Accounts* record: '1755 Feb. 8. pd for the 2 great Rooms 1019–8–11'.[103] The other room mentioned is the Great Parlour. The finishing touches to the Library were carried out when the artist John Henry Muntz appears in the *Accounts*: '1756 June 24. pd Mr Muntz for painting the ... gothic letters in library.'[104]–these were presumably the date 1754 in Roman numerals mentioned above.

One large and two small quatrefoil windows in the Library provided the only opportunity for the display of stained glass; this can clearly be seen in Plate 70. Walpole described the glass: 'The large window and two rose windows have a great deal of fine painted glass, particularly, Faith, Hope, and Charity, whole figures in colours; a large shield with the arms of England, and heads of Charles 1st. and Charles 2nd.'[105] All these pieces can be discerned in Plate 70. A much fuller description of these windows is given in the sale catalogue.[106] It is not clear where Walpole obtained this glass. Some may have been part of the shipment from

68. The Library at Strawberry Hill by John Carter, 1788
69. The Library (Walpole, *Description*)

Flanders that Asciotti had obtained for him in 1753, but surely this would not have included the arms of England and the heads of Charles I and II?

Oddly, no furniture is listed for the Library in the *Description* and none is shown in Plate 69. Walpole is depicted sitting in a mid-eighteenth-century chair in Plate 70, and Plate 68 shows a pedestal desk in the middle of the room only. The desk, of a totally mundane character, appears to have been of mahogany,[107] but cannot be traced at the sale anywhere in the house. The chair, equally mundane, is impossible to identify as part of any of the suites that appear in the illustrations of other rooms. Perhaps it was Muntz's? It certainly resembles the standard artist's sitter's chair of this date.

The sale catalogue lists in this room, besides small items such as screens, 'Lot 53. A handsome Ecritoire of Finest marquetry richly worked with the arms of the House of Waldegrave, enclosing compartments for letters, mounted with chased or-molu, of Louis Quatorze style. Lot 54. A pair of beautiful old carved solid ebony chairs, of the Elizabethan period, pierced backs, richly decorated with Birds, Flowers and Figures, twisted rails the frames finely carved with scrolls, and cane seats. Lot 55. A pair of Ditto ... Lot 56. Ditto.'[108] The 'Ecritoire' still survives in an English private collection.

The chairs, however, sound very similar to those in the Holbein Chamber (Plate 72) and would thus be part of the large group which were at Strawberry Hill as early as 1759. During the 1750s Walpole had corresponded with various friends about ebony chairs and on the basis of his research became the first person to associate these pieces with the Tudor period. This association was to survive well into the nineteenth century and we will encounter many similar chairs in other Romantic Interiors.

The crucial chairs were those at Esher Place, which Gray mentioned in a letter to Walpole in August 1752:

> The true original chairs were all sold ... there are nothing now but Halsey-chairs, not adapted to the squareness of a Gothic dowager's rump. And by the way I do not see how the uneasiness and uncomfortableness of a coronation-chair can be any objection with you: every chair that is easy is modern, and unknown to our ancestors. As I remember, there were certain low chairs, that looked like ebony, at Esher, and were old and pretty. Why should not Mr Bentley improve upon them?[109]

This letter had been prompted by a discussion concerning ebony furniture. Walpole was interested in Esher Place for two reasons, namely, that Cardinal Wolsey had lived there and that it had been extended in the Gothic style by William Kent. Walpole wrote to Montagu on 11 August 1748: 'Esher I have seen again twice and prefer it to all villas ... Kent is Kentissime there.'[110] Gray wrote to Thomas Wharton on 13 August 1754: 'you do not say enough of Esher. It is my favourite place. It was a Villa of Cardinal Wolsey's of which nothing but a part of the Gate-way remain'd, Mr Kent supplied the rest, but I think with you, that he had not read the Gothic classicks with taste or attention. He introduced a mix'd Style, wch now goes by the name of the *Batty Langley* Manner.'[111] Esher was a fascinating building of which only the centre part survives.[112]

By at least 1759, Walpole was collecting chairs of this type. Gray wrote to Wharton on 18 September 1759 concerning the furnishing of the Holbein Chamber: 'the chairs & dressing table are real carved Ebony picked up at auctions'.[113] Walpole bought most of his ebony pieces at one particular sale. He wrote to Montagu from Huntingdon on 30 May 1763:

> I believe I am the first man that ever went sixty miles to an auction. As I came for ebony, I have been up to my chin in ebony; there is literally nothing but *ebony* in the house; all the other goods, if there were any, and I trust my Lady Conyers did

70. Walpole seated in his Library by J.H. Muntz, late 1750s (P. Toynbee, *Strawberry Hill Accounts*, 1927)

not sleep upon ebony matresses, are taken away. There are two tables and eighteen chairs, all made by the Hallet of two hundred years ago. These I intend to have; for mind, the auction does not begin till Thursday. There are more plebeian chairs of the same materials, but I have left commission for only the true black blood.[114]

The reference to Hallet is interesting, for it was he who supplied the Gothic chairs for the Great Parlour which, in that they were *ebonized*, were to some extent inspired by the ebony chairs discussed here, Gray shared Walpole's passion for ebony and wrote to Wharton on 5 August 1763 concerning Walpole: 'he has purchased at an auction in Suffolk ebony-chairs & old moveables enough to load a waggon'.[115] The purchase appears in the *Accounts* under December 1763: '18 ebony chairs and two tables 45−0−0.'[116] Gray was wrong in stating that the auction was in Suffolk; as we saw, Walpole wrong in stating that the auction was in Suffolk; as we saw, Walpole wrote from Huntingdon.

In fact the Conyers seat, Staughton House, was in the village of Great Staughton, three miles from Kimbolton in Huntingdonshire. The Lady Conyers referred to was Jane, wife of Sir Ralph Conyers (1697−1767), the 5th Baronet.[117] The Conyers had possessed Staughton House since 1675 when Sir John Conyers married Mary Newman, heiress to the Baldwyns estate, which had included the Great Staughton property. The baronetcy became extinct in 1810.[118] What prompted the 1763 sale, I have been unable to discover, but even more puzzling is why this small manor house in the depths of the country contained such a remarkable hoard of ebony. Could it be that one of the Conyers family had been in the East India trade?

There seems to have been no more major pieces of furniture in the Library at Strawberry Hill, but there were a large number of objects of virtu housed in the room. There was also one curious brass object (Plate 71) shown in Plate 68 in front of the fireplace — 'An ancient curfeu, or couvre-feu; from Mr Gostling's collection.'[119] Gostling was a minor canon at Canterbury.[120] Brass curfeus such as this date from the seventeenth century and were used to cover a fire at night, but they were intended for fires in open hearths, it being impossible to use them in conjunction with a fire basket like that in the Library. Evidently Walpole's anti-quarianism did not extend far enough for him to forego the modern convenience of a basket grate for an open fire with which the curfeu could actually be used.

A prominent feature in the Library was six Roman ossuaria (Plates 68 and 70), two of which Walpole had bought from Dr Mead's collection in 1755 during the first phase of furnishing the room. The catalogues of the sales of Mead's collections of prints, gems, bronzes, busts and drawings were housed in Library press Q.[121] One of the Mead pieces was described as 'A square ossuarium; heads of rams, a festoon and birds, the inscription',[122] and may be that seen on the left in Plate 70.

One of the most singular objects in the room was

A clock of silver gilt, richly chased, engraved, and ornamented ... This was a present from Henry 8th. to Anne Boleyn; and since, from lady Elizabeth Germaine to Mr Walpole. On the weights are the initial letters of Henry and Anne, within true lovers knote; at top, *Dieu et mon Droit*; at bottom, *The most happy* — One of the weights, agreeably to the indelicacy of that monarch's gallantry, is in a shape very conformable to the last motto. The pedestal is adorned with small heads of bronze gilt of the age of Henry 8th, but which did not belong to the clock.[123]

Walpole's coy allusion to the model for the weight doubtless amused the visitors to Strawberry Hill when they read the *Description*. The clock and the bracket are now in the Royal Collection. The actual date of the clock is at present in dispute, but the bracket was probably made for Walpole.

As far as Strawberry Hill was concerned, the clock joined a large collection of

71. The curfeu from the Library

other Tudor relics. Lady Betty Germaine seems to have given it to Walpole in 1760.[124] She had a predilection for Tudor and Elizabethan relics, as the sale catalogue of her collection demonstrates.[125] This included the 'curious clock that Sir Francis Drake had with him on his voyage round the world'[126] and the 'Dagger of Henry VIII designed by Holbein and most magnificently ornamented with diamonds and rubies.'[127] This dagger was closely related to one in the Portland collection (Plate 23), and Walpole purchased Lady Betty's for 50 guineas and housed it in the Tribune at Strawberry Hill.[128]

Besides his books, Walpole housed in his Library rare manuscripts and other precious objects. He noted in the *Description*: 'Catalogue of the 25 most precious coins and medals in rosewood case.'[129] He referred to part of the Library as his 'sanctum sanctorum', a term later used frequently by other collectors including Walter Scott, as we shall see in Chapter 6. On 14 October 1760 he wrote to George Montagu concerning a visit of the Duke of York to Strawberry Hill: 'I showed him all my castle ... But observe my luck; he would have the sanctum sanctorum in the library opened; about a month ago I removed the MSS to another place ... what was I to do next?'[130] Walpole used the term again in relation to a visit of the King and Queen to see George Selwyn. Walpole wrote to Lady Ossory on 16 August 1788: 'I am curious to know what relics he has gleaned from the royal visit that he can *bottle* and place in his *sanctum sanctorum*.'[131] This quotation is particularly interesting because it shows that Walpole believed that relics were being continuously created so that they could be collected and displayed with more ancient examples in collections such as his or George Selwyn's.

The most prominent object (Plate 68) in the Library after its acquisition in 1787 was the glass case containing 'The fishing eagle, modelled in terra-cotta, the size of life. This bird was taken in lord Melbourn's park at Brocket-hall, and in taking it one of the wings was almost cut off, and Mrs Damer saw it in that momentary rage, which she remembered, and has executed exactly. She has written her own name in Greek on the base, and Mr W added this line, *Non me Praxiteles finxit at Anna Damer 1787*.'[132] Mrs Anne Seymour Damer (1749–1828), the daughter of Field Marshall Conway, Walpole's friend, exhibited a number of works at the Royal Academy between 1784 and 1818. Walpole bequeathed Strawberry Hill to her for life and she lived there until 1810 when she made over the estate to Lord Waldegrave.

The Holbein Chamber (Plates 72 through 74) was completed in 1759, although by May of that year the room had not been given a name: 'May. pd Price for fitting up three windows for the new Bedchamber towards the road 15–15–0.'[133] By September, besides having a name, it was structurally complete: 'Sept 27. pd for the Holbein Chamber.'[134] Walpole described the main features: 'The ceiling is taken from the queen's dressing-room at Windsor. The chimney-piece, designed by Mr Bentley, is chiefly taken from the tomb of archbishop Warham at Canterbury ... The pierced arches of the acreen from the gates of the choir of Choir of Rouen; the rest of the screen was designed by Mr Bentley.'[135] Gray wrote to Wharton on 18 September 1759:

Mr W: has lately made a new Bed-chamber, wch as it is in the best taste of any thing he has yet done, & in your own Gothic way, I must describe a little. You enter by a peaked door at one corner of the room (out of a narrow winding passage you may be sure) into an Alcove in wch the bed is to stand, formed by a screen of pierced work opening by one large arch in the middle to the rest of the chamber, wch is lighted at the other end by a bow-window of three days, whose tops are of rich painted glass in mosaic. The ceiling is coved & fretted in star & quatrefoil compartments with roses at the intersections, all in papier-mache the chimney on your left is the high-altar in the Cathedral of Rouen (from whence the Screen also is taken) consisting of a low surbased Arch between two octagon Towers, whose pinnacles almost reach the ceiling, all of Nich-work.[136]

72. The Holbein Chamber at Strawberry Hill by
John Carter, 1788

Gray incorrectly gives the source of the chimney-piece as Rouen, but, as we saw,
Walpole took it from Warham's tomb at Canterbury, as depicted in Dart's *Canterbury*, a book he had in his library. Bentley altered the design somewhat in execution,
as a comparison of the actual chimney-piece with the engraving on page 489 of
Dart's book demonstrates. The screen (Plate 73) was, as Gray states, taken from the
choir doors at Rouen Cathedral, but it is likely that the standard published source
provided the illustration that was used rather than a motif-mongering trip to Rouen
itself. Oddly, Walpole did not have this book in his library,[137] though Beckford did
(Plate 119).

The ceiling was 'Taken from the queen's dressing room at Windsor'. No
illustration of this ceiling seems to exist and a description of the room in Walpole's
day[138] does not mention the ceiling. The room at Windsor was considerably altered
in the early nineteenth century. 'In the Autumn of 1804 a number of important
changes were made in King Henry VII's building. Since the destruction of its eastern
division in the seventeenth century, the upper floor had contained the "Queen's

94

SCREEN OF THE HOLBEIN CHAMBER.

Dressing Room" and an ante-chamber ... The two rooms were now thrown into one.'[139]

Nothing recognizably the model for the Holbein Chamber ceiling now survives at Windsor,[140] thus it is impossible to know how close the two were. The manufacturer of this papier mâché is not recorded and neither do we know whether the ceiling at Windsor was especially copied for Walpole or whether it was a standard one available to all. As no other identical one is known I suspect that it was produced for Walpole only. The most likely manufacturer would have been Mr Bromwich of the leading manufacturer of papier mâché, who supplied other ceilings for Walpole.

Gray commented further on the furnishings: 'The hangings uniform purple paper, hung all over with the Court of Henry, ye 8th, copied after the Holbein's in the Queen's Closet at Kensington, in black & gold frames.'[141] These pictures after the Holbein's dictated the name of the room. Walpole said they 'were taken off on oil-paper by Vertue from the original drawings of Holbein in queen Caroline's closet at Kensington.'[142] The effect of the black and gold frames on the purple paper must have been dramatic. Hanging in the room were also a number of drawings and paintings attributed to Holbein, as well as 'Henry, 8th fine whole figure in terra cota, by Holbein; from lady Elizabeth Germaine's collection.'[143] This interesting object was only a few inches high, but had an impeccable provenance. Walpole bought it from the Germaine sale of 1770 in which, as we saw, there were a number of interesting Tudor relics, and previously it had been in the Arundel collection and Charles I's collection.[144]

The Tudor connections extended even further when one examines the other objects in the room, for hanging on the wall 'By the bed, [was] The red hat of cardinal Wolsey'.[145] Walpole's own label read: 'found in the great Wardrobe by Bishop Burnet [1643–1715] when he was Clerk of the Closet. It was left by his son Judge Burnet to his housekeeper who gave it to the Countess of Albemarle's Butler, who gave it to his lady, and her ladyship to Horace Walpole in 1776.'[146] This is a

95

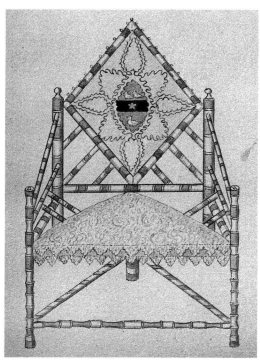

75. Mr Bateman's turned and painted chair by G.D. Harding, 1801

76. A triangular turned chair copied from stained glass by G.D. Harding, 1801

perfect example of Walpole's idea of the pedigree of a work of art. In this case, butlers are as important as bishops and countesses in the chain of pedigree.

Also, as we saw above, the ebony furniture (Plate 72) was believed by Walpole to be Tudor and also to relate to Cardinal Wolsey. There were six ebony chairs and a table in the Holbein Chamber. These pieces did not come from the Conyers sale of 1763. Gray spoke in September 1759 of 'The furnishing of the Holbein Chamber . . . the chairs & dressing table are real carved ebony picked up at auctions'. What these earlier auctions were I have been unable to discover, but Walpole bought eighteen chairs and two tables at the Conyers sale. At the Strawberry Hill sale there were twenty-two chairs and three tables and, as stated in Chapter 2, one ebony chair at least (Plate 36) had escaped well before the sale in 1842.

The bed was divided off from the main part of the room by a pierced screen (Plate 74). The bed was, despite the confined space in which it was housed, of considerable richness. Gray described how Walpole originally attempted to acquire an antique one: 'The bed is to be either from Burleigh (for Ld Exeter is new-furnishing it, & means to sell some of his original household-stuff) of the old tarnish'd embroidery; or if that is not to be had, & it must be new, it is to be a cut velvet with a dark purple pattern on a stone-colour sattin-ground, & deep mix't fringes, & tassels.'[147] Burghley was certainly being refurnished at this date,[148] but in the event Walpole did not buy a bed from the Earl of Exeter. He instead had a new one made by the famous London cabinet-maker William Vile to a design very like that described by Gray: '1760. Oct. 31st. pd Vile's bill for the purple cloth bed . . . 90£.'[149] Walpole described it as 'of purple cloth lined with white sattin, a plume of white and purple feathers on the centre of the tester.'[150] The colour of the hangings very appropriately matched the purple wallpaper. It can be seen in Plate 74, and a watercolour of it also exists showing that Wolsey's hat was hung just beside it.[151]

This purple room must also have been bathed in coloured light from the elaborate stained glass windows. Walpole stated that there were 'In the bow windows some fine painted glass, and the arms of England, and those of George prince of Denmark; the ground is a beautiful mosaic of crimson, blue, and pearls, designed and painted by Price of Hatton-garden.'[152] Gray was impressed by this glass and wrote to Wharton on 28 November 1759: 'the Mosaic at Mr W: it would be no use to you, because it is not merely made of squares put together, but painted in a pattern by Price, & shaded. It is as if little Balustines, or Pomegranate-flowers, were set four together, & formed a lozenge. These are of a golden yellow with a white pearl at the junctions, & the spaces inclosed by them are scarlet, or blew. This repeated makes a Diaper-work, & fills the whole top of the window.'[153]

These windows can just be seen on the right in Plate 74. Though they are fully described,[154] it is not clear whether they are all by Price or whether he mixed ancient glass with his own original productions. Walpole though highly of Price's work: 'William Price, the son now living (He died a bachelor at his house in Great Kirby street hatton-garden, July 16, 1765,) whose colours are fine, whose drawing good, and whose taste in ornaments and mosaic is far superior to any of his predecessors, is equal to the antique, to the good Italian masters, and only surpassed by his own singular modesty.'[155] This glass does not survive at Strawberry Hill.

Walpole was able to use the objects depicted in the glass as sources for his furniture: 'Another chair covered with purple cloth, made from one in a pane of painted glass in the breakfast-room.'[156] The drawing of this chair, which stood in the Holbein Chamber and was covered with purple cloth to match the pervading colour of the room, exists on a sheet with that of another chair, the sheet being labelled by Walpole 'Gothic chairs at Strawberry Hill taken from painted glass there by Mr Bentley.'[157] Watercolours of the two chairs also exist. One was an X-frame chair of a well-known mediaeval type, the best-known example being Queen Mary's Chair at Winchester Cathedral. The triangular turned chair (Plate 76) is again of a late mediaeval type, but the originals never had cane seats; their seats were always solid wood as must have been that depicted in the stained glass. The cane seat must have been a modification by Bentley. If these two chairs still exist one wonders whether they are recognized as interesting mid-eighteenth-century reproductions or are thought to be genuinely mediaeval.

The colour scheme of the room extended to the ancient objects collected to furnish it. Plate 72 shows two blue vases on each side of the fireplace and on the ebony chairs blue cushions. The ebony table served as a dressing table and on it stood 'a bason and ewer of purple and white Seve china.'[158] Also on this table were objects appropriate to a dressing table, namely, 'a tray with four ancient combs; one of ivory is extremely ancient, carved with figures, on one side representing persons bathing and going to bed, on the other, two men and a woman with musical instruments; another comb said to have belonged to the queen of Scots, is of tortoiseshell studded with silver hearts and roses; the two others of tortoiseshell likewise, of which the one with very long teeth belonged to the father of the first lord Edgcumbe, and was used when the large flowing wigs were in fashion.'[159]

Here we see Walpole gathering objects of a range of dates together to make a decorative point. The ivory comb was rare and mediaeval, whereas that made for Lord Edgcumbe was of merely historical interest. None of these combs was the celebrated comb of Queen Bertha (Plate 22) that was in the Small Closet. To anyone spending the night as a guest in the purple gloom of the Holbein Chamber a group of combs would have seemed appropriate furniture for a dressing table.

Walpole's most ancient and important piece of furniture stood in this room (Plate 77): 'A very ancient chair of oak, which came out of Glastonbury-abbey; on it are carved these sentences, *Joannes Arthurus Monacus Glastonie, salvet eum Deus: Da pacem Domine: Sit Laus Deo*, Lord Bathurst had several chairs copied from this'.[160] When Walpole acquired it in 1759, he wrote to Chute on 2 February: 'I am deeper than ever in Gothic antiquities, I have bought a monk of Glastonbury's chair full of scraps of the psalms, and some seals of most reverend illegibility. I pass all my mornings in the thirteenth century, and my evenings with the century that is coming on.'[161]

How Walpole acquired the chair is a mystery, as is its present whereabouts. Walpole took an interest in Glastonbury and indeed owned the standard book on the Abbey.[162] He was certainly the first person to draw attention to this type of chair.[163] Walpole thought the chair, because of its associations, very suitable for ecclesiastical guests. He wrote to Lady Ossory in July 1780: 'I am proprietor of the chair of Joannes Arthurus the monk of Glastonbury, and once made the present Archbishop of Canterbury sit in it at breakfast — but I will reserve it now for a real abbot — It is too much honour for a renegade. If the Pope sends us a genuine Austin, well and good.'[164]

Walpole was in fact remembering events of seven years before. On 7 October 1773 he had written to Lady Ossory: 'Yesterday I dined at George Onslow's with the Archbishop [Frederick Cornwallis, 1713–1783], the Dean of Westminster, a head of a college, two more divines, Lady North, and Madam the Metropolitan. Yesterday they all breakfasted here and Lord North; I enthroned the Primate in the Purple chair from the Holbein room, and it will never be filled with a better prelate.'[165] The Glastonbury Chair also played an amusing part in the Strawberry Hill sale in that George Robins the auctioneer sat in it to conduct the whole sale, and a drawing of him in action survives.[166]

The last object in the room, one that figures prominently in Plate 72, was the carpet, which was quite simply 'A carpet worked by Mrs Catherine Clive, the celebrated comedian'.[167]

The Staircase and Armoury were described by Walpole thus: 'You first enter a small gloomy hall paved with hexagon tyles, and lighted by two narrow windows of painted glass, representing St John and St Francis. This hall is united with the staircase, and both are hung with gothic paper, painted by one Tudor, from the screen of prince Arthur's tomb in the cathedral of Worcester. The ballustrade was

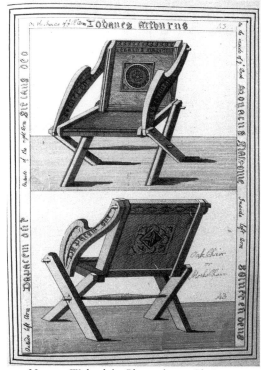

77. Horace Walpole's Glastonbury Chair

78. The Armoury at Strawberry Hill by John Carter, 1788

designed by Mr Bentley; at every corner is an antelope (one of lord Orford's supporters) holding a shield.'[168] The paper appear in the *Accounts*: '1754 . . . pd Bromwich for papering Staircase.'[169] It seems probable that Bromwich supplied all the paper and the papier mâché at Strawberry Hill. He certainly supplied the papier mâché ceiling for the Gallery. Thomas Bromwich traded at the Golden Lyon on Ludgate Hill from at least 1740 until his death in 1787. He had become the Master of the Painters Stainers Company in 1761 and was the most celebrated wallpaper manufacturer of the mid-century.[170]

The paper was put up plain and eventually painted with its Gothic pattern by the appropriately named Mr Tudor, one of Bromwich's employees. Walpole wrote to Bentley on 20 November 1754: 'about the Gothic paper. When you made me fix up mine unpainted, engaging to paint it yourself, and yet could never be persuaded to paint a yard of it, till I was forced to give Bromwich's man God knows what to do it.'[171]

It seems that the whole Walpole circle patronized Bromwich, for Gray wrote to

Wharton on 22 October 1761: 'on rummageing Mr Bromwich's & several other shops I am forced to tell you, that there are absolutely no papers at all, that deserve the name of Gothick'.[172] The decoration of the paper illustrates very well how Walpole and his friends plundered sources by using illustrations rather than by closely examining the actual building or tomb to be copied. Walpole wrote to Bentley in September 1753 after a trip to Worcester: 'The cathedral is pretty ... Prince Arthur's tomb, from whence we took the paper for the hall and staircase, to my great surprise, is on less scale than the paper, and is not brass but stone, and that wretchedly whitewashed.'[173] Walpole and Bentley had in fact taken the design from a plate in F. Sandford's *A Genealogical History of the Kings of England* (1677). Walpole's copy exists with the relevant plate annotated by him and Bentley.[174]

Half-way up the stairs Walpole created his Armoury (Plates 78 through 80). This,

79. The staircase (Walpole, *Description*)

though small in size, was to form an important feature at Strawberry Hill and was an early example in the chronology of Romantic Interiors of the re-creation of a mediaeval-style armoury. In the quotation given earlier, we saw that as early as 1739 the grandeur of the ancient house with its hall hung with armour and weapons was admired by some. But Walpole was one of the first in England to create such an interior in a new Gothic house, there being, of course, surviving examples in ancient houses.

Before the Hall and Armoury were complete Walpole wrote to Mann in 1753: 'my house is so monastic that I have a little hall decked with long saints in lean arched windows and with taper columns, which we call the Paraclete, in memory of Eloisa's cloister ... By next spring I hope to have rusty armour, and arms with quarterings.'[175]

By June 1753 he had acquired some armour for this room, and wrote to Mann: 'a vestibule open with three arches on the landing place, and niches full of trophies of old coats of mail, Indian shields made of rhinoceros's hides, broadswords, quivers, long bows arrows and spears — all supposed to be taken by Terry Robsart in the holy wars'.[176] Sir Terry Robsart was an ancestor of Walpole's who died in 1496, but he does not seem — as Walpole believed — to have taken part in the Crusades.[177]

These pieces of arms and armour were mixed with others of various dates and nationalities: 'Two suits of armour, on one of which is the mark of a bullet; two helmets; a gauntlet; a round leathern quiver; and two pair of stirrups; from Coombe near Kingston in Surry, which seat formerly belonged to the great Richard Neville earl of Warwick ... a beautiful Persian shield, made of rhinoceros's hide ... several other lances, spears, and Indian bows'.[178] But the collection was even more eclectic than the mixture of European and Indian objects would indicate, for it also included American Indian artefacts: 'An American Calumnet; a warriors wreath, and a neck ornament; presents from Governor Pownall'.[179] A 'calumet' is more usually called a 'Pipe of Peace', and Pownall was Governor of Massachusetts from 1755 to 1760.

Several of the most important pieces of armour did not arrive at Strawberry Hill until the early 1770s. They are the shields and the full armour in the niche. The shields were 'Two shields of leather, for tournaments, painted by Polidore; one has the head of Medusa ... They came out of the collection of commendatore Vittoria at Naples, and were sent to Mr W. by Sir W. Hamilton.'[180] They arrived in 1774. Walpole wrote to Hamilton on 19 June 1774: 'they are fine and most charming — nay, almost in too good taste, not to put a Gothic house to shame ... The two that are painted, are in the great style of the best age; and by the Earl of Surry's shield in the Duke of Norfolk's possession which is in the same manner as the form and disposition, though not so bold, I should conclude they are by Polidore, or of that school ... I am going to hang them by the beautiful armour of Francis I.'[181] The Earl of Surrey's shield is indeed very similar to Walpole's two shields, and still exists at Arundel Castle.[182] It was then thought to have been won by the Earl at a tournament in Florence in 1536, and Walpole obviously used this provenance to date his shields. One of the Strawberry Hill shields (Plate 80) is now in the Glasgow Museum and Art Gallery.[183]

The so-called armour of Francis I stood in the niche of the stairs (Plates 78 and 79). 'The armour of Francis Ist. King of France, of steel gilt, and covered with bas-reliefs in a fine taste: his lance is of ebony inlaid with silver; his sword steel; beautifully inlaid with gold, probably the work of Benvenuto Cellini ... purchased from the Crozat collection in 1772.'[184] Walpole wrote to Cole on 23 October 1771: 'I am making a curious purchase at Paris, the complete armour of Francis the First. it is gilt in relief, and is very rich and beautiful it comes from the Crozat collection.'[185] This superb armour was sold in the Strawberry Hill sale to Samuel Pratt, the Victorian armour dealer. It then passed through several collections and is often incorrectly stated to be in the Metropolitan Museum in New York.[186]

Walpole seems to have acquired a number of important objects in Paris, which he

80. The Italian shield from the Armoury (Museum and Art Gallery, Glasgow)

bought at the Crozat sale of 1772, at the Julienne sale of 1767 and at the Caylus sale of 1773.[187] He bought both antique and modern objects. William Cole gives an amusing account of one buying trip which he and Walpole made in November 1765 when they visited two of the best known of the *marchands-merciers* in the rue St Honore:

> We went to the Shop of Madame du Lac, where the Earl of Fife with Mr Sheffield, Son of Sir Charles Sheffield, were making Purchases ... Mr Walpole among other Things, bought 3 most beautiful Vases for a Chimney, of blew Enamel, set in gilt Copper for Mr Chute of the Vine ... From this dangerous Shop we went to another not a whit less so, Mr Poirer's where the China & Toys & fine Cabinets were rather richer & in greater Abundance; being a Magazine of several lower Apartments.[188]

Besides the armour, the Armoury contained several of Walpole's ubiquitous ossuaria (Plate 78) similar to those in the Library (Plate 68). Also, he displayed over the central arch (Plate 78) an oak carving about which he wrote to Henry Lort on 23 December 1780: 'I send you a drawing by Carter, of the head of Henry III, which, I understand from him, Dr Palmer is willing to dispose of for four or five guineas.'[189] Walpole wrote to Cole on 16 June 1781: 'I have placed the oaken head of Henry III over the middle arch of the Armory. Pray tell me what the Church of Barnwell near Oundle, was which his Majesty endowed, and whence his head came.'[190]

The Armoury was small in size and indeed confined to what was little more than a half-landing. Even so it was packed with arms and armour, and, occupying as it did a space on the staircase, it was visible to all who passed up and down the staircase as well as to those in the Entrance Hall. When one accepts that Walpole did not have the space to create a large Gothic ancestral Hall in which to hang these objects, one can acknowledge that he in fact very cleverly created much the same effect in a very small space.

The association of armour with Halls has been mentioned before, but Walpole in actually re-creating the effect in the most public part of his house may well have led others to display armour in this way. In fact, *effect* was exactly what Walpole was striving for. He wished it to appear that Strawberry Hill was a mediaeval house and that the armour hanging on the staircase really was ancestral. As we saw above, he admitted his intentions to his friends when he said that some pieces were 'supposed to be taken by Terry Robsart in the Holy Wars.' There can be no doubt that the visitor viewing the armour in the gloom of the Hall would, unless he were an armour expert, have failed to discern the heterogeneous nature of the collection consisting as it did of American, European and Asian arms and armour. The gloom was achieved during the day by glazing all the windows in stained glass and at night by lighting the staircase by a splendid Gothic lantern designed by Bentley (Plate 81), which was lit by one candle only. The lantern exists in the Lewis collection at Farmington.

The Tribune (Plate 82) and the Gallery (Plate 85) were furnished with much the same mix of objects that I have described for the other interiors, so I shall not describe them at length. The two rooms differ in that the Tribune contained very little furniture, other than several stools and the singular classical cabinet made to house Walpole's miniatures (Plate 58). The room was completed in 1763 and by 1784 was more densely packed with objects than any other interior at Strawberry Hill; seventeen pages of the *Description* are devoted to enumerating them.

Just two of the objects from the Tribune — both now in the Victoria & Albert Museum — will demonstrate the variety and interest of the collection shown there: the celebrated 'point lace' cravat (Plate 83) carved by Grinling Gibbons, the carver whom Walpole admired above all others; and the French Limoges enamel casket of the 1540s (Plate 84), which fitted in well with Walpole's Tudor objects.

By contrast, the Gallery, which was completed in 1763, contained a wide range of

Gothic Lanthorn, designed by Mr Bentley

81. The Lantern of the staircase by G.D. Harding, 1801

82. The Tribune at Strawberry Hill (Walpole, *Description*)

83. A cravat carved in limewood by Grinling Gibbons (Victoria & Albert Museum, London)

furniture, almost all modern, and comparatively few antiquities of the type housed in the Tribune. The Gallery (Plate 85), for instance, housed two japanned commodes and four encoigneurs which were supplied in 1763 by Pierre Langlois, who was then at the height of his powers as a cabinet-maker.[191] One of these Strawberry Hill commodes survives in an American museum.[192]

The most remarkable aspect of the Gallery was perhaps the ceiling. Walpole wrote to George Montagu on 25 March 1763: 'The gallery advances rapidly. The ceiling is Harry VII's chapel in *propia persona*.'[193] This *tour de force* of Tudor Revival vaulting was not, however, carried out in plaster, as might be expected, but in Bromwich's remarkably versatile papier mâché similar to that used in the Holbein Chamber in 1759: '1763 April 2d. pd Bromwich for ye ceiling of the Gallery £115—0—0.'[194]

84. A French Limoges enamel casket, *c.*1540
(Victoria & Albert Museum, London)

Before we move outside, one further interior needs to be briefly noticed. The China Room or China closet opened off the Entrance hall (see Plate 66) and was so packed with ceramics that nine pages of the *Description* are devoted to them, and include the references: 'In the floor some very ancient tyles with arms, from the Cathedral at Gloucester' and 'A tyle from the kitchen of William the Conquerer at caen in Normandy'. On 27 March 1764 Walpole wrote to Charles Churchill: 'the draft of the Conqueror's kitchen, and the tiles you were so good as to send me; and grew horribly afraid lest old Dr Ducarel, who is an ostrich of an antiquary, and can digest superannuated brickbats, should have gobbled them up . . . I weep over the ruined kitchen, but enjoy the tiles. They are exactly like a few which I obtained from the cathedral of Gloucester, when it was new paved; they are inlaid in the floor of my china-room.'[195]

In his two books *A Tour through Normandy* of 1754 and *Anglo-Norman Antiquities* of 1767 Dr Ducarel described what was then thought to be William the Conqueror's Kitchen at Caen, which was paved with fine mediaeval heraldic tiles. These were plundered by several English collectors and brought to England. Three of the Strawberry Hill tiles are shown in Plate 86; the upper two may be from Gloucester and if so were used for the China room floor. The lower one was certainly from Caen, for an identical tile was brought back to England by another collector and shown at a meeting of the Society of Antiquaries of London on 7 February 1788. The collector was John Henniker, F.S.A., M.P., who in his book, which is an incunable of tile literature, illustrates a tile identical to Walpole's: 'These arms belong to the family of Paynel (Plaganelli) who bore on a shield Or, two lions passant gules.'[196] Henniker presented his tiles to the Society of Antiquaries, who still display them in their museum.

Whilst Ducarel was one of the first to draw scholarly attention to the importance of these mediaeval tiles, Walpole was a pioneer in immediately recognizing that they

85. The Gallery at Strawberry Hill by Thomas and Paul Sandby and E. Edwards, 1781 (Victoria & Albert Museum, London)

87. The Cloister at Strawberry Hill by G.D. Harding, 1801

86. Mediaeval tiles by G.D. Harding, 1801

could be used to pave a Gothic Revival interior. The use of mediaeval tiles and of modern re-creations of them was to become universal by the 1840s. Willement was to pioneer the design of Gothic Revival heraldic encaustic tiles in the late 1830s, and Pugin and many other Victorian architects followed his lead.

We now move outside the house. The Great Cloister was joined to the house, but open arches led from it into the garden. It was completed in 1762 (Plate 87), but was not furnished until 1775 when the triangular turned chairs were purchased. Walpole bought these 'ancient Welch chairs' at the sale of Bateman's collection; he had coveted them since the 1760s. On 19 September 1762 he had written to Montagu: 'I did not doubt but you would approved Mr Bateman's since it has changed its religion, I converted it from Chinese to Gothic . . . I envy him his old chairs.'[197] After the Bateman sale he wrote to Lady Ossory on 3 August 1775: 'I have crammed my Cloister with three cartloads of lumbering chairs from Mr Bateman's, and at last am surfeited with the immoveable moveables of our forefathers.'[198]

Walpole also acquired 'two small Welsh armed chairs, painted blue and white, with cushions of point-lace, and on one the arms of Mr Richard Bateman, at whose sale they were purchased;'[199] they were housed in the Star Chamber (Plate 75). It is impossible to say whether these interesting chairs were actually ancient ones rather over-decorated by Bateman with blue 'Barber's Pole' painting, heraldry and lace cushions or were manufactured especially for him. The armorials on the shield certainly look spurious. They were lot 102 on the seventeenth day of the Strawberry Hill sale and were bought by the broker Horatio Rodd. I have been unable to discover their present whereabouts.

These turned chairs, the Glastonbury Chair and the ebony furniture formed a quite distinct group of ancient British furniture and as such represented the most avant-garde aspect of Walpole's collecting activites. I shall be discussing such chairs further in other chapters.

Also attached to the house like the Cloister, but open to the outside through arches, was the Oratory (Plate 88). The 1784 *Description* describes how, 'Entering by the great north gate, the first object that presents itself is a small oratory inclosed

88. The Oratory looking west by John Carter, 1788

89. (right) A French mediaeval bronze angel (Victoria & Albert Museum, London)

with iron rails; in front, an altar, on which stands a saint of bronze; open niches, and stone basons for holy water; designed by John Chute.' The whole arrangement was designed by Chute, but the 'saint' was an extremely rare late mediaeval French bronze angel 34 inches high (Plate 89). Where Walpole acquired this bronze is not known, and he would seem not fully to have appreciated its importance. It had been lost since the Strawberry Hill sale, but fortunately I was able to identify it when it re-emerged in 1977. It was sold at auction[200] and is now in the Victoria & Albert Museum.

I have not dealt with the whole of the interior of Strawberry Hill, but have rather concentrated upon the rooms that best represent different aspects of Walpole's collecting and interior decorating activities. The complexity of these interiors, packed as they were with such a wide range of objects, makes a really thorough study very difficult. Though they contained objects in a wide range of media, certain themes can, however, be discerned. The concentration, for instance, of objects collected especially because they related to Tudor and Elizabethan persons represents one large and coherent group. This would be an even larger group had I also dealt with paintings and engravings. Also, Walpole, like so many of the collectors with whom I shall be dealing, wished each of his objects to be connected with a historical personage and if possible historical event.

But, despite the singular nature of the collections, Strawberry Hill emerges from this study as one of the best-documented eighteenth-century houses in Britain. This is true as far as both manuscript and printed material is concerned, quite apart from the wealth of contemporary illustrations, many of which were commissioned by Walpole himself. How Strawberry Hill related to other houses of its day and how far it was in advance of them is difficult to ascertain, not least because it is so much better documented than most others. The foundations for this study have fortunately been laid recently in an important new book.[201] Very few owners and collectors wrote as much about their activities as Walpole. It is Walpole's writings — perhaps more than his collection itself — that have guaranteed the importance of the house in the eyes of historians.

90. Fonthill in 1813 by Francis Danby

5

FONTHILL ABBEY

I am lost in admiration — and feel that I have seen a place raised
more by majick, or inspiration, than the labours of the human
hand.
                                                    Benjamin West

Few nineteenth-century houses and their collections are as celebrated as
Fonthill Abbey. William Beckford (1760–1844), who created both this remarkable
building and the collection it housed, has been well-served by biographers.[1] They
have, however, concentrated largely upon his singular life; there is no book on
Beckford as a collector.

Fonthill was so vast and the collection so rich that I shall only discuss several of
the best-documented interiors, which fortunately for us contained some of the most
interesting and important objects. Some idea of the scale of the collection is given by
the sale of some of its contents held in 1823, shortly after Beckford had sold the
Abbey.[2] This sale lasted from 9 September until 31 October and included 1,588 lots
of *objets d'art* quite apart from 424 lots of paintings and 20,000 books. The complex
question of the various sales of portions of Beckford's collection has never been
exhaustively investigated, though the major sales have been discussed.[3] As far as we
are concerned here, these several sales are only relevant for the descriptions they give
of the objects that furnished Fonthill.

The building history of the Abbey from the beginning in 1796 until the work
ceased in 1818 with parts still incomplete is complex, but this has fortunately been
lucidly analyzed in print.[4] The first design had a soaring spire (Plate 92). Fortunately
Beckford employed Turner to paint watercolours of the Abbey, and Turner also
sketched it during construction (Plate 93). Beckford and his architect, James Wyatt,
for a decade were constantly making changes to the design, but when the exterior
eventually reached its familiar final form there was no spire (Plate 90 and 94). The
plan (Plate 95) of the finished building — or rather as finished as it ever was — shows
the immense size.

From the available evidence it is impossible to determine the exact measurements
of the structure. Wilton Ely decided that, 'Judging by discrepancies in contemporary
accounts and engravings, the actual height of the tower, like most dimensions of the
Abbey, remains uncertain . . . while Beckford himself claimed that it was 273 feet
high, other opinions range towards 300 feet. The Sublime by definition was
immeasurable.'[5] Some dimensions, however, are known: the door through which
one entered was 30 feet high (Plate 94).

Beckford began to collect actively long before he started the Abbey, for he was
thirty-six years old when the foundation-stone was laid. Even before he had started
to collect on his own account, he possessed the collection he had inherited from his
father: in 1770 Alderman Beckford, the celebrated Lord Mayor of London from
1763 to 1770, died and left him Fonthill Splendens and all its contents. This house,
one of the largest in England, was Palladian in form, being rather reminiscent of
Houghton or Wanstead, but sadly no illustrations of its interiors survive. To judge
from the few descriptions, these were of great splendour and were furnished with
modern objects of the highest quality as well as numerous works of art. For

91. William Beckford aged 21 painted by George
Romney in 1781 (National Trust)

instance, the huge organ from Splendens recently acquired by the Victoria & Albert Museum is in both design and craftmanship of the very highest quality.

Beckford was eventually to demolish Splendens and move some of the contents to the Abbey, selling the rest in three sales in 1801, 1802 and 1807. But before deciding to rebuild, Beckford set about adapting Splendens to his needs, employing both Soane and Wyatt as architects. Again little documentation survives. In 1788 Soane designed the Picture Gallery, the designs for which are in the Soane Museum.[6] A published description of Splendens after Beckford's alterations and before the 1801 sale conveys the splendour of the interiors:

> we enter an anti-room; the chimney-piece, by Bacon, is most delicately sculpted, after a design by Wyatt. This room ... opens into a Library ... In the centre of the Library stands a large Amber-cabinet, which displays every variety of this precious material, from the deepest orange to the palest yellow ... belonged to the Queen of Bohemia, daughter of James the First. Her portrait, and that of her husband, are carved in white amber on one of the drawers ... Adjoining the Library, is ... the Turkish room, as splendid and sumptuous as those magical recesses of enchanted palaces we read of in the Arabian Nights Entertainments. The ground of the vaulted ceiling is entirely gold, upon which the most beautiful arabesques and wreaths of flowers are delineated.[7]

The amber cabinet, as we shall see, later featured prominently at Fonthill Abbey and, being so much of Beckford's taste, was probably collected by him rather than by his father. Similarly, the Turkish room was his own creation, and a design survives by Beckford for a small table in the Turkish style probably for this room. Though this particular apartment seems rather too exotic for rural Wiltshire, it must be remembered that Beckford had published his pioneering arabian novel *Vathek* in 1786.

The extent of Beckford's collection when he moved out of Splendens and into the Abbey is unknown, though there is plenty of evidence of his collecting activities abroad.[8] Following a visit to Geneva in 1777–8, he was frequently on the Continent — in Spain and Portugal in 1787–8 and 1793–5,[9] and, more importantly, in France. He supported the French Revolution, was in Paris in July 1788 and was still there at the fall of the Bastille in July 1789, only leaving for Switzerland in August that year.

He was in Paris again from October 1790 to June 1791, returning in November and staying until May 1793. Then, after a long absence, he returned to Paris from May 1801 until May 1803. At one stage he even considered emigrating to France. In August 1789 he wrote that he was tempted to 'accept the propositions of the National Assembly and fix myself in France.'[10]

Beckford rented for himself the very grandest Parisian *hôtels*, which were, of course, readily available following the Revolution. For his 1789 stay he rented the Hôtel de Clermont at 69 rue de Varenne, which had been elaborately decorated and furnished by the socially ambitious Comte d'Orsay.[11] It was abandoned by the Count at his hasty departure from Paris to exile in Italy. As we shall see, it was from this *hôtel* that Beckford acquired one of his most important pieces of French furniture.

During his 1791–3 stay, he rented a house in the rue de Grenelle in the Fauborg St Germain.[12] He retained this house when he left Paris and stored there his books and works of art, the whole being looked after by his friend the bookseller Chardin, who had also protected Beckford himself when under the threat of arrest that had caused him to flee Paris in 1793.[13] In July 1797 Beckford was able to send his agent Captain Nicholas Williams to Paris to recover these items and purchase still more. Williams returned to England in November.

Beckford returned to the Fauborg St Germain on his next visit to Paris in December 1801. He rented the large and elegant Hôtel Kinsky at 127 rue St Dominique and employed the architect Larsonneur to refurbish the interiors and

92. North-west view of Fonthill Abbey as projected by Charles Wild, c.1799 (Victoria & Albert Museum, London)

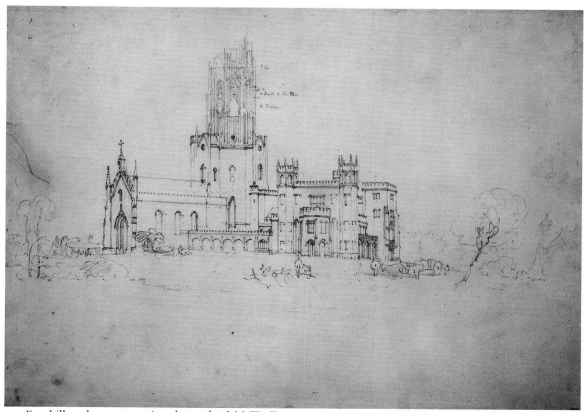

93. Fonthill under construction drawn by J.M.W. Turner, *c*.1803 (Tate Gallery, London)

94. The west and north fronts of Fonthill (J. Rutter, *Delineations of Fonthill* . . . , 1823)

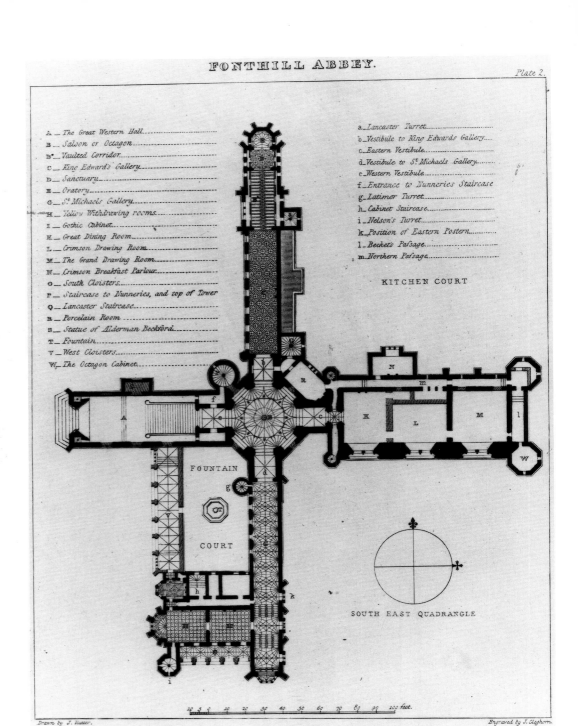

A — The Great Western Hall
B — Saloon or Octagon
B' — Vaulted Corridor
C — King Edward's Gallery
D — Sanctuary
E — Oratory
G — St Michael's Gallery
H — Yellow Withdrawing rooms
I — Gothic Cabinet
K — Great Dining Room
L — Crimson Drawing Room
M — The Grand Drawing Room
N — Crimson Breakfast Parlour
O — South Cloisters
P — Staircase to Nunneries, and top of Tower
Q — Lancaster Staircase
R — Porcelain Room
S — Statue of Alderman Beckford
T — Fountain
V — West Cloisters
W — The Octagon Cabinet

a — Lancaster Turret
b — Vestibule to King Edwards Gallery
c — Eastern Vestibule
d — Vestibule to St Michaels Gallery
e — Western Vestibule
f — Entrance to Nunneries Staircase
g — Latimer Turret
h — Cabinet Staircase
i — Nelson's Turret
k — Position of Eastern Postern
l — Becket's Passage
m — Northern Passage

KITCHEN COURT

FOUNTAIN COURT

SOUTH EAST QUADRANGLE

Drawn by J. Rutter.

Engraved by J. Cleghorn.

PLAN OF THE PRINCIPAL STORY.

The dotted lines represent the Ornamented Ceilings, Groining, &c.

Published June 2nd 1823, by J. Rutter, Shaftsbury.

95. A plan of Fonthill (Rutter, *Delineations*)

reorganize the gardens[14] Beckford lived in the Hôtel Kinsky until 1803, using it as a base for his rapacious collecting activities until his return to England.

Beckford had collected for many years in France. As early as January 1784 when he was only twenty-three he attended the sale of the Duc de la Vallière's celebrated library. Louis-Cesar la Baume le Blanc, Duc de la Vallière, had died in 1780. Beckford wrote: 'I am busied every morn: almost buying books at the Duc de la

Vallière's sale and have the glorious misfortune in general of the Emperor and his Christian Majesty for competitors. Yesterday I bought a rare manuscript in spite of their royal teeth — glittering with gold letters and curious miniatures.'[15]

It must have been a heady experience for the young tyro collector to compete with and best the agents of the Holy Roman Emperor and Louis XVI. The manuscript referred to is now in the Library of Congress. Beckford seems not to have known that an agent of Horace Walpole had also been bidding at the sale for books to furnish the Strawberry Hill Library. Walpole wrote on 3 January 1784 that Mr White, the London bookseller, 'goes to purchase books at the Duc de la Valière's sale. I have given him some commissions at a very high rate.'[16]

The opportunities for collectors during the French Revolution were unique, and when Beckford was unable to visit France himself he employed agents to buy for him. When his agent Williams was in Paris in 1797 Beckford wrote to him on 23 August:

> You are in possession of my Sentiments respecting the Bouillon Collection. No pains should be spared to attempt getting hold of it. I am, in fact, still more anxious about the Japans than the pictures — and surely they might be induced to part with the whole of them in a Lump and for a good price which nobody else *can* or *would* give them — for these small trifling toys cannot be very precious in any eyes except such as are affected by the Japan-mania in a violent incurable degree . . . give Chardin commission to look out for fine Tapestry and look about yourself for some — much will be wanted and I should think might be purchased cheap.[17]

Chardin continued to buy for Beckford after Williams had left Paris. The pictures mentioned were the Bouillon Claudes now in the National Gallery, though it was not Beckford who in the event bought them. Fortunately for Beckford the sale was postponed and did not take place until June 1801, by which time he was again living in Paris. Beckford's 'Japan-mania' was to have a great effect upon the character of his collection[18] and he purchased a number of important pieces at the Bouillon sale. These included the famous Mazarin Chest (Plate 101) and the Van Dieman Box (Plate 102), both now in the Victoria & Albert Museum.[19]

But before leaving Beckford's collecting activities some mention must be made of his close friend and confidant Chevalier Gregorio Franchi (1770–1828), who played a key role in several aspects of Beckford's life.[20] From as early as 1802 Franchi acted as Beckford's agent in the purchase of works of art from both dealers and auctions. Beckford delighted in being encouraged in his excesses by Franchi and wrote to him on 18 September 1813: 'I see from the buying mania which dominates you that we are well on the way to ruin. Oh my God, so many things! I trust to the Saint that they are not junk and unworthy of this sanctuary and refuge of Good Taste.'[21]

Luckily Franchi kept a record of many of the purchases and, when Beckford left Fonthill in 1822 for Bath, made lists of the contents of the cases used to transport the collection. But perhaps most important of all he has recently emerged as the designer of some of the most remarkable metalwork and mounted hardstone objects at Fonthill.[22] In this work Franchi was closely involved with Beckford, who followed the design and manufacture of these pieces with great interest and indeed designed at least one piece himself. Several of these pieces will be discussed later.

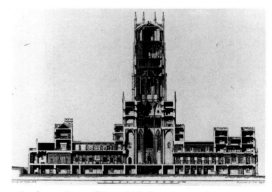

96. A section of Fonthill (Rutter, *Delineations*)

I will not discuss in detail the progress of the protracted building works at Fonthill, but will describe several of the interiors as they were just before Beckford sold the Abbey in 1822. The cost of maintaining the Abbey had been too great for Beckford's dwindling income for several years past. The bulk of this income he derived from his plantations in the West Indies, which were far less profitable than they had been during the the Napoleonic Wars. In fact, the sale of the contents had been planned in 1822,[23] but this was called off when Mr Farquhar purchased both the Abbey and much of its contents. Several books were published at this time to

97. Looking south from King Edward's Gallery across the Octagon and into St Michael's Gallery at Fonthill (Rutter, *Delineations*)

satisfy public curiousity about its interiors, and thousands of people visited the building to view the sales of 1822 and 1823. In 1812 James Storer had published *A Description of Fonthill Abbey*, but almost all of his illustrations were of the exterior. Beckford had, unlike most country house owners, never opened his house to the public; because of his reclusive habits he rarely entertained.

The plan (Plate 95) and the section (Plate 96) show how, starting from the Oratory at the top (north) of the plan, one could progress south through King Edward's Gallery in the direction shown in Plate 97 until one entered the soaring Octagon, which measured 132 feet to the ceiling. From here one looked down the vista of St Michael's Gallery. Plate 107 shows the view from St Michael's Gallery into the Octagon.

From the end of King Edward's Gallery one could see in the distance the oriel window (Plate 108) with the landscape beyond, and Plate 98 shows a view of the Oratory looking north through King Edward's Gallery. Had one stood in the Oratory and looked south towards the oriel at the end of St Michael's Gallery one would have had an uninterrupted vista of 350 feet, the Octagon being in no way visible from a distance.

These Galleries were, like so much of the interior decoration and the furnishings at Fonthill, conceived as an elaborate scheme of heraldic and genealogical decoration. The centrepiece of King Edward's Gallery was a portrait of King Edward III himself (Plates 97 and 98), 'copied by Mathew Wyatt, from one in the vestry of St George's chapel, Windsor'.[24] Edward was chosen in his capacity as the founder of the Order of the Garter. 'The Latimer cross, and the cinque-foil of Hamilton in relievo, in the panels of the ceiling, on the panels of the cabinets, and other furniture. The arms of the soverign founder of the illustrious order of the garter, and seventy-one knights are placed in the frieze of the entablature, from all of whom the present Duchess of Hamilton is lineally descended. They are arranged in the manner of the stall, the earliest dates being placed nearest the central shield.'[25] The Duchess of Hamilton was Susan Euphemia, Beckford's own daughter.

The stalls referred to are those in the Garter Chapel at St George's, Windsor Castle, where, at the same time as working at Fonthill, James Wyatt was carrying out extensive works for George III. He therefore had ready access to copy the heraldry of the Garter stall plates while at Windsor. It is also interesting that Wyatt had been involved in the 1780s with Benjamin West in a scheme at Windsor to house a series of paintings by West of scenes from the life of Edward III. The whole question of this scheme has been recently discussed.[26] Its relevance to Fonthill is obvious. West was, like Wyatt, working simultaneously for both Beckford and the King, and Beckford was not unaware of this.

Beckford's claim to be descended from all the sons of Edward III was quite false, but it provided the *raison d'être* for the decoration of this Gallery. Rutter published Beckford's complete descent in an appendix, stating that, 'Having so frequently had occasion to allude to the splendid genealogical connexions of Mr Beckford, we here subjoin the following Tables.'[27]

The other decorations were equally elaborate. 'In the recesses of the eastern wall are six bookcases, and in the centre a fine alabaster chimney-piece; opposite to, and

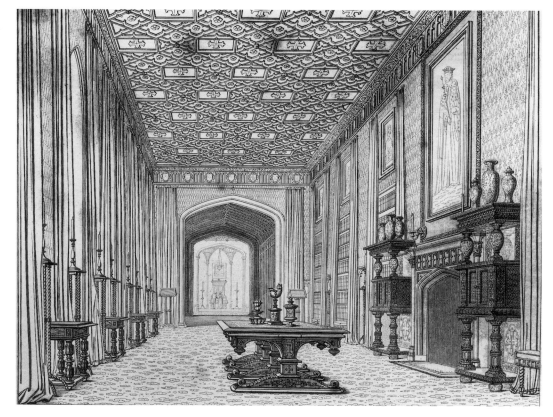

98. Looking north from King Edward's Gallery into the Oratory (J. Britton, *Illustrations ... of Fonthill*, 1823)

corresponding with which are seven pointed windows, with stained glass. A flowered red damask is hung against the walls; purple and scarlet cloth adorn the windows and recesses.'[28] The stained glass was as heraldic as the painted decoration and each of the seven windows contained the arms of the person portrayed in the portrait hung on the opposit wall. With 'the portrait of Edward III . . . on either side are portraits of John of Montford duke of Brittany, the constable Montmorency, Henry VII. Edward IV. and Alphonso king of Naples; and in the top compartments of the windows opposite are brilliantly painted the arms of the personages represented.'[29] Unfortunately this glass does not appear in Plates 97 and 98, the only extant illustrations of King Edward's Gallery.

Stained glass played a very important part in the decoration of Fonthill. It also gave Beckford the opportunity to commission modern artists to carry out work for him. He was not merely a collector of antiquities and ancient paintings, but was throughout his life very active in the support of living painters, sculptors and craftsmen such as goldsmiths and stained glass painters. Beckford commissioned both glass and easel paintings from Benjamin West.

Shortly after the Abbey was started, Beckford contacted the London glass painter James Pearson (c. 1750–1805), who also worked at Strawberry Hill and had worked at Salisbury Cathedral just a few miles from Fonthill.[30]

Farington recounts that on 1 November 1797

> Pearson had said to Wyatt he shd. charge for each figure in painted glass to be copied from Wests Paintings of Saints for the purpose, 100 or 120 or 150gs. Pearson had been mentioned by West to Beckford . . . Beckford calld at Wests to see one of the figures finished; Pearson, accidently on purpose came in — Beckford told Wyatt he soon saw through him . . . Wyatt privately desired His nephew Jeffry Wyatt to write as from himself to Egginton who resides near Birmingham to know his terms for such work. Egginton replied 50 guineas a figure 7 Feet ½ high & 3 feet ½ wide . . . This difference appeared to make Pearsons charge monstrous. Beckford however offers Pearson a figure to execute at 100gs. if He chooses.[31]

Pearson took up Beckford's offer: 'Beckett's Passage — so called from the subject of a lofty painted glass window, in chiaro-oscuro by Pearson, of the celebrated Archbishop, after a design by the late President West.'[32] Beckford also owned the painting by West from which the glass was copied; this is now in the Museum of Art in Toledo, Ohio.[33] The Pearson window was lot 864 in the 1823 sale and survives intact in the Lord Mayor's Chapel in Bristol.[34]

Almost all the other glass in the Abbey was by the Egintons, and Rutter tells us that 'All the stained glass in this Gallery [St Michael's] and the Oak parlour (except the lancet window) were executed by the late Mr Eginton. The lancet window, the windows of the Great Octagon, the Western Hall, King Edward's Gallery and the Oratory, are specimens of the taste and ability of the present Mr William Raphael Eginton, his son.'[35]

Francis Eginton (1737–1805) originally worked with Matthew Boulton at his famous Soho factory in Birmingham, but set up as a glass painter in 1784. He quickly established himself as the pre-eminent glass painter of his day.[36] His son William Raphael was equally celebrated, at first carrying out works in partnership with his father, then later in his own right.[37] Together they painted number of windows at Arundel Castle for the Duke of Norfolk. William's most famous window was his 27-foot-wide copy of Raphael's *School of Athens* painted for the Library at Stourhead; this still survives *in situ*.

Beckford was employing the best and most technically advanced glass painters of his day, who worked from cartoons also commissioned by Beckford, as with the Pearson and West window. Most of this glass was destroyed with the Abbey and it is not known how much Beckford spent upon the glass, but an Eginton account of

99. An engraving of a stained glass window of St Jerome (E. Orme, *An Essay on Transparent Prints* . . ., 1807)

24 April 1799 gives the cost of glass 'Now finished' as £954.[38] The windows at Fonthill were certainly the most extensive stained glass commission ever carried out in a Gothic Revival building up to the 1820s.

Beckford did not confine himself to modern glass, but collected — as Walpole had before him — ancient glass, which he built into windows at the Abbey. In the 1823 sale lots 841–64 were 'Ancient Stained Glass', though as lots 845 and 850 were by Pearson it was obviously not all ancient. Lots 845 and 850 were, however, of great importance, as they each consisted of three large panels of glass from the Château d'Ecouen near Paris. Lot 845 bore 'the cypher and heraldic bearings of Diane de Poitiers, curious and fine from the Château d'Ecouen'. This Renaissance glass was, like so much similar glass, brought on to the market during the French Revolution.

This Ecouen glass may have been acquired by Beckford in 1814, for so avid was he to take advantage of Napoleon's abdication that he sent Franchi to Paris immediately. In reply to a letter of Franchi's, Beckford wrote on 22 July: 'I am a little disappointed with your harvest of lacquer ... and tapestries, arras — all gone to, and the Ecouen glass — thats a mortal blow.'[39] This may of course not be the glass that came to Fonthill but yet more, though after he received this letter Franchi would surely have redoubled his efforts to acquire the glass for his rapacious master.

Some at least of Beckford's Ecouen glass survives in the Lord Mayor's Chapel at Bristol.[40] This Ecouen glass is some of the finest and most important Renaissance glass to survive and both its quality and its historical associations would have appealed to Beckford. A piece of Ecouen glass has recently been acquired by the Victoria & Albert Museum (Plate 100); this came from the collection of Thomas Willement. Willement worked with Eginton at Fonthill, and this piece of glass might well be from the same shipment as that at Fonthill.

100. A panel of Renaissance stained glass from Ecouen (Victoria & Albert Museum, London)

This history of this piece and the similar examples which also bear the arms of Anne de Montmorency, Constable of France (1493–1567), has recently been fully discussed.[41] The relevance of this glass to the interiors at Fonthill is obvious when we remember that in King Edward's Gallery there was both a portrait and a modern heraldic stained glass window devoted to 'Constable Montmorency' in the role of one of Beckford's ancestors.

There was relatively little furniture in King Edward's Gallery; several of the major pieces appear in Plates 97 and 98. The most important was the massive 'TABLE of PIETRE COMMESSE ... about nine feet long, and four feet six inches wide. This grand piece of furniture was formerly in the Borghese palace.'[42] This table still exists at Charlecote Park, having been purchased for that house at the 1823 sale (Plates 185 through 188). This is one of the largest and most important *pietre dure* tables in existence. Although Beckford's provenances for his objects are usually correct, I have never been able to establish the Borghese connection, but no alternative provenance has emerged either.

There is no evidence of when, how or where Beckford acquired it, though Mary Elizabeth Lucy's explanation in her diary does have a ring of truth: she wrote of 'the large Florentine table in the Great Hall, which had originally stood in the Borghese Villa at Rome, from whence it had been taken by the French in the time of Napoleon.'[43] She gives no explanation; perhaps her husband who bought the table directly from Fonthill may have known this provenance as a fact.

Napoleon did indeed remove from Italy to Paris vast quantities of objects and works of art, some of which went back to Italy after the wars, though others were sold in France in 1815 while Beckford was avidly buying. Storer, in his 1812 book, describes many of the major objects at Fonthill, but makes no mention of the table, suggesting that it perhaps did not arrive at Fonthill until after that date.

Had the table had its original massive carved marble base Beckford would certainly have kept it. However, such bases were of far less value than the *pietre dure* top and were frequently left behind when the top was moved any distance. In this case the top itself weighs several tons. The elaborate oak base fits in so well with the iconography of King Edward's Gallery — with Beckford's beloved Latimer cross appearing on the ceiling panels and on the cabinets beside the fireplace as well as on the base itself — that it must have been designed especially for the room. The small oak Gothic tables (Plate 98) that stood on the window piers also bear the Latimer cross. These small tables also went to Charlecote (Plate 186).

Work on the Gallery was well under way by 22 June 1810 when Beckford wrote to Franchi: 'There is a terrible lack of carpets for the Gallery and the ante chamber; but above all there is a lack of silver plaques for the soffit and the large expanse of oak round the portrait of King Edward III.'[44] Both the large and small tables were Tudor in style, and, though there was relatively little modern furniture at Fonthill, most was rather avant-garde in being in the Tudor rather than the Gothic style. The furniture, like the other furnishings, would have been designed in James Wyatt's office until his death in 1813, but there is no evidence that he ever made any designs in the Tudor style. After Wyatt's death Beckford sought architectural help from his relations including Jeffry Wyatt.[45]

Jeffry Wyatt (1766–1840) — later to be called Wyatville — was a well-established architect by the time his uncle James died. There existed a whole tribe of Wyatts who were carpenters, sculptors, painters and architects.[46] In fact a Wyatt painted the portrait of Edward III in the gallery under discussion. From soon after 1800 Jeffry Wyatt had been pioneering the Tudor Revival in, for instance, his restoration and alteration of Longleat from 1801 to 1815 and Wollaton from 1801 to 1823. Any modern visitor to these houses can appreciated how fluent was his handling of Renaissance ornament. Then in 1810 he designed Endsleigh in Devon in the Tudor style and, with the furniture he designed for it, became a pioneer of Tudor Revival furniture.[47] The work at Longleat and Wollaton coincides with the period between James Wyatt's death in 1813 and 1818 when most of the Fonthill works ceased.

Not only is Longleat very close to Fonthill, but Jeffry Wyatt was also working at this time at Hinton House and Marston House in nearby Somerset. He would have had frequent opportunities to visit Fonthill and may well have been involved in the design of the furniture and interiors. If the Borghese Table did arrive in 1815 he could well have designed its base (Plate 188). But it must be remembered that in Franchi — as we have seen — Beckford had an excellent designer always at hand.

The two other major pieces of furniture in King Edward's Gallery were also in the Renaissance rather than the Gothic Revival style. They were two massive cabinets (Plates 97 and 98). 'On each side of the fire-place is a cabinet, carved in imitation of the style of the Elizabethan age, in which singularity if not beauty of design is as conspicuous as extreme labour and excellence of execution.'[48] They were lots 447 and 448 in the 1823 sale: 'A cabinet of carved work, the design in the ancient taste of the reign of Queen Elizabeth with folding doors'. Lot 447 sold for £147 and lot 448 for £157.10.0, both to Pordevan.

I can find no record of a broker called Pordevan, and he might well have been an auctioneer's invention, for the cabinets were actually bought for Beckford himself. They feature in a sale held in Bath as lot 24 in the *Catalogue of Valuable Paintings Magnificent Cabinets & Splendid Furniture from Lansdown Tower . . . by messrs English . . . Milsom Street . . . Jan 4 1841 & Following Day*: A Pair of Cabinets of oak, most elaborately carved in the richest style of Holbein; with folding doors — An upper shelf with most elaborately carved frieze and cornice . . . The formerly adorned *Edward the Third's Gallery* at Fonthill 3 feet wide, 6ft 1 high.'

As the illustration shows, they were used just like their Renaissance prototypes for the display of large pots (see Plates 4 and 5, for instance). Behind their folding doors, however, were stored items from Beckford's vast Library; in 1819 they were described as 'two grand cabinets of oak, richly carved; in these are deposited some of the precious manuscripts belonging to the collection'.[49] The upper part of each had (as can be clearly seen in Plates 97 and 98) mirror glass at the back of the upper section, the bulbous supports only being present at the front. The carved back panels

101. The Mazarin Chest, Japanese lacquer, c.1638 (Victoria & Albert Museum, London)

102. The Van Dieman Box, Japanese lacquer, c.1638 (Victoria & Albert Museum, London)

of the lower part are decorated with large Latimer crosses to accord with the heraldry of the Gallery. Sadly the whereabouts of these pieces is unknown, they were the earliest and most important examples known of fully realized English Renaissance Revival cabinets.

Which cabinet-makers or upholsterers supplied these pieces and indeed the other modern pieces at Fonthill? Two names occur frequently in the Beckford/Franchi letters: they are Edward Foxhall and Robert Hume, father and son. Foxhall was a partner in the firm of Foxhall & Fryer of Old Cavendish Street who had certainly worked at Splendens, for Beckford noted while in Portugal on 6 July 1787: 'I learn from Foxhall that painting and furnishing goes on briskly at Fonthill, that Bacon and Banks are making chimney pieces for me.'[50]

Foxhall may well have been introduced into Splendens by his lifelong friend Soane. Soane designed the facade of Foxhall's shop in Old Cavendish Street and also attended his funeral in 1815. Foxhall certainly executed the elaborate state bed that Soane designed for Splendens, but he also acted for Beckford in the purchase of works of art.[51]

Foxhall, however, frequently exasperated Beckford, who wrote on 30 June 1808: 'To my taste the chairs are unbearable, and I don't see how they can be improved. If we don't hold a general council at Fonthill about furniture we shall never do anything that's worth while. What with Wyatt's apathy and foolish Foxhall's immense incompetance, we shall be throwing away our money in vain.'[52] It is obvious from Beckford's letters that Foxhall got on well with Wyatt, and, despite Beckford's frequent criticisms of him, he played a major part in the furnishing of the Abbey. When Foxhall died in 1815, Beckford wrote: 'I haven't failed to perceive and feel the horror of the loss of Foxhall.'[53]

When Robert Hume the elder died I do not know, but presumably his son worked with him before inheriting the business. The elder Hume had been buying for Beckford since at least 1811, though he may not have been providing furniture at this date,[54] but after the demise of Foxhall he became the main and perhaps the only supplier of furniture to Fonthill. Hume continued to act for Beckford at auctions. on 22 March 1819 Beckford wrote to Franchi: 'I was right in thinking I wouldn't escape a few little purchases ... the divine, gold-mounted little chest painted in the Hindu style (formerly at Gwennap's) ... Hume let me have them for what they cost him.'[55] The broker Gwennap also supplied armour to Abbotsford and Goodrich.

The firm of Hume was listed as carvers and gilders at various addresses from 1807, but from 1831 until 1854, when the firm ceased business, they were at 65 Berners Street. A Robert Hume continued to live at the address until 1870; perhaps this was the younger Hume in retirement. After Beckford moved to Bath in 1822, the firm of Hume continued to work for him and were responsible for furnishing his residences there. The elder Hume was also present at Franchi's tragic death in 1828.[56] The Duke of Hamilton employed Hume to decorate the interiors at Hamilton Palace, and accomplished drawings by him for this work survive.[57] Hume also worked at Charlecote. Others certainly supplied furniture for Fonthill, but Foxhall and Hume played the most important parts.

Only a few other objects are shown in Plates 97 and 98, including several of the 'Suite of 6 gallery stools on ebonized twisted legs stuffed and covered in purple cloth fringed', which sold as lot 451 in the 1823 sale. Also shown are 'ebonized tripods, twisted legs', six of which were lots 477 and 478 at the sale; ensuite was lot 479: 'A large ebonized reading desk, on swivel centre and twisted standards'. The other desk in Plate 98 was lot 480.

As can be discovered from Rutter's two books and the 1823 sale catalogue, several other small pieces of furniture in the Gallery do not appear in the illustrations. There is, of course, a problem about establishing the position of both furniture and objects within the Abbey by using the 1823 catalogue. Though the lots are arranged room by room, this catalogue only records the *status quo* in 1823, a year after Beckford had moved out. He had also taken some objects with him to Bath. Sadly, the 1822 sale catalogue, which records the collection when Beckford was still in residence, was not arranged room by room. Rutter's 1822 *Description* certainly records the disposition of the collection when Beckford was still in residence and, though his *Delineations* was not published until 1823, it was almost certainly finished before Beckford left the Abbey.

John Britton together with his wife stayed at the Abbey with Beckford while he was compiling *Illustrations*, so this too records the situation during Beckford's residence. After Beckford moved out in 1822, it is perfectly possible that Farquhar rearranged some of the smaller objects, but it is unlikely that he moved the larger and more architectural pieces of furniture.

One object of great importance that was listed in Rutter's 1822 book is 'A superb coffer of raised Japan, one of the largest specimens known of this superb quality . . . This unique specimen of Japanese art was formerly the property of Cardinal Mazarin and belonged subsequently to the Duc de Bouillon.' This coffer was still in the Gallery in 1823 when it was lot 576 in the sale and was sold to John Swaby for £131.5.0. Swaby was presumably acting for Beckford, because this coffer turns up again as lot 1165 in the Hamilton Palace sale of 1882, which included many objects inherited from Beckford by his daughter the Duchess of Hamilton.[58] This coffer was 4 feet 6 inches by 2 feet 3 inches and was *en suite* with a somewhat smaller coffer with which it has often been confused.[59] This smaller coffer was lot 147 at Hamilton Palace and is now in the Victoria & Albert Museum (Plate 101).

The present whereabouts of the larger coffer is not known, but, to judge from the one that survives, the two were probably the finest and most important surviving pieces of Japanese lacquer of this later seventeenth-century type. These, along with rest of Beckford's fabulous collection of lacquer, (Plate 102), establish him as the greatest connoisseur and collector of lacquer that this country has produced. Beckford also owned a number of important pieces of French eighteenth-century furniture incorporating Japanese lacquer panels. He also commissioned two remarkable English cabinets incorporating panels from a seventeenth-century Japanese box of the Van Diemen type.[60]

Indeed, as we have seen, lacquer was one of Beckford's earliest enthusiasms. We have already noted his frenzy to buy at the Bouillon sale in 1797 and, while only twenty, he wrote to Lady Hamilton from Paris on 2 April 1781: 'I fear I shall never be half so sapient nor good for anything in this world, but composing airs, building towers, forming gardens, collecting old Japan, and writing a journey to China or the moon.'[61]

While in Paris in 1784 this preoccupation with lacquer grew: 'At the Hotel de la Rochefoucald . . . in the D. de Chabot's snug little apartments which are lined from top to botton with beautiful cabinet pictures, and exhale an odour of old Japan and spiced rose leaves perfectly delectable.'[62] At the 1823 sale King Edward's Gallery contained 28 lots of lacquer quite apart from the Mazarin chests.

But in King Edward's Gallery, as in every room at Fonthill, the startling objects were those standing upon the tables and cabinets. Some of these were small pieces of lacquer, but Beckford's metalwork ranged from Limoges enamels and mediaeval vessels via mannerist and High Renaissance plate to French Baroque and neo-classical plate to the remarkable pieces commissioned by Beckford himself. Many of the latter were partly fabricated from his vast collection of agate, jade, rock crystal and other hard stones.

His ceramics ranged from the earliest and most severe oriental wares to the most elaborate and splendid pieces of eighteenth-century Meissen and Sèvres. His sculp-ture included not only ancient Greek and Roman marbles and bronzes, but also the work of modern sculptors. The pioneering publication on Beckford's historicist plate lists 351 pieces, but the authors consider that yet more remains to be identified.[63] The splendid show these objects must have made amassed upon tables

103. A silver-gilt dish by Samuel Whitford II and William Burwash, 1814–15 (Victoria & Albert Museum, London)

104. An agate cup with silver-gilt mounts, by James Aldridge, 1815–16 (Victoria & Albert Museum, London)

and cabinets is difficult to convey, but Plates 117 and 125 through 127 illustrate a selection.

The agate cup set with rubies and mounted in silver gilt (Plate 104) and the silver-gilt salver (Plate 103), both in the Victoria & Albert Museum, are superb examples of the avant-garde use of arabesque ornament by Beckford and Franchi on the pieces they designed. The agate cup was the first piece of Beckford's historicist plate to be identified and published.[64] It had been bought at the Hamilton Palace sale for the South Kensington Museum by the dealer T.M. Whitehead for the huge sum of £562.4.0 as a sixteenth-century object. When, soon after its purchase, it was discovered to be early nineteenth century it was taken off display, but in 1971 its importance was eventually recognized and it was put on display once again.

The salver is decorated on its whole surface with Beckford's crests repeated over

and over again linked with sixteenth-century-style strapwork. This richly decorative combination of heraldry and Renaissance ornament is unique to these pieces of Beckford plate and appears on a number of pieces.[65] The visual impact of these pieces when combined with ancient pieces of metalwork, hard stone and ceramics on a *pietre dure* table or on the top of an ebony or lacquer cabinet must have been stunning (Plate 125).

The pair of candle sconces under the portrait of Edward (Plates 97 and 98) were part of the Beckford/Franchi plate. The present whereabouts of these sconces is unknown, but an identical pair made for another room at the Abbey survive at Brodick Castle.[66] The candlesticks on the candlestands in the window bays of King Edward's Gallery are from the same group.

Several pieces of ancient metalwork are shown in the published illustrations. The Britton illustration (Plate 98) shows one tall cylindrical vase; Rutter's illustration (Plate 97) shows a pair, but neither book describes these vases as being in the Gallery. Thery were in fact a pair of silver-gilt vases made in 1711 by David Willaume, the Huguenot silversmith, in London. The cylindrical parts are made of carved ivory. The vases are now in the British Museum.[67] Though Rutter shows these vases as in the Gallery, he describes them in the text as in the Grand Drawing Room.[68]

If, however, one consults Rutter's unillustrated 1822 description published the year before in *Delineations*, we find that on the Borghese Table in King Edward's Gallery 'stand two beautiful VASES of CARVED IVORY, with a frieze of infants carved by the celebrated Fiamingo, and superbly mounted with silver gilt. It formerly belonged to the famous Earl of Arundell, and was left by Lady B. Germaine to the late Margravine of Anspach, at whose sale it was purchased.'[69] The Arundel connection was in fact untrue, though the Germaine and Anspach provenance is correct. Hume bought these pieces for Beckford at the auction of the Margravine's collection at Brandenburg on 29 July 1818.[70]

This whole matter illustrates how easily small objects could be moved around at Fonthill. Rutter obviously *saw* the vases on the Borghese Table in 1822, while Beckford still lived at the Abbey, and perhaps had the illustration of the Gallery drawn shortly afterwards. The text of *Delineations* was done later, perhaps in 1823, by which time the vases had migrated to the Grand Drawing Room, and Rutter failed to collate properly the text and illustrations before publication. Britton's illustration shows only one — had one moved by then? — but he does not mention them in his text at all. They are, however, interesting and important pieces of Baroque metalwork.

Also on the Borghese Table in Plate 97 appears a 'magnificent CUP, cover and stem of ivory, sculpted by the celebrated artist Magnus Berg medalist to the Emperor of Germany. The bowl is finely carved with a forest scene. and figures hunting wild animals. On the lid are Diana and her Nymphs asleep amidst animals ... A finely embellished and sculptured figure of hercules forms the stem.'[71] This object sold for £94.10.0 as lot 573 in the 1823 sale; its present whereabouts is unknown. Britton, however, saw at the centre of the table an object which he does not describe, but which Rutter mentions as being in the Gallery in 1823: 'A mounted nautilus upon an ivory plinth carved by Benvenuto Cellini'.[72] This Nautilus, which was set with garnets, vermillions, emeralds, amethysts and a sapphire, was lot 570 in 1823. The ivory base was lot 571. Rutter illustrated the piece along with a selection of the most celebrated objects from the Abbey (Plate 117).

I have described enough examples of the small objects in King Edward's Gallery to give some idea of how it was furnished when Beckford lived in the Abbey. When he moved out in 1822 Beckford left many objects behind so that at the sale in 1823 the Gallery still contained 144 lots excluding books and pictures.

To move north from King Edward's Gallery, as can be seen on the plan (Plate 95), and the view looking north (Plate 97), one passed into the Vaulted Corridor, then the Sanctuary and then into the Oratory. The corridor was conceived as a dramatic contrast to King Edward's Gallery:

We have passed beyond the light, the gold, the marble, and the blazonry: no windows are seen. The crimsoned light which struggles through the richly latticed doors on the sides, and the glimmering of the perspective of the golden arches, are all the apparent illumination. The effect is universal and instantaneous; an involuntary silence falls upon every visitor. The most intense curiosity is only expressed in whisperings no consciousness springs up, that we are approaching a place peculiarly pre-eminent, long before the eye, adapting itself to the gloom, discovers the golden lamp, the fretted ceiling, the candelabra, the statue, and the altar in the distance ... The Sanctuary: we ascend its step, and pause before ... the Oratory ... the walls are covered with damask of the richest dye, where columns, spreading into fans, and shooting their mouldings over the vault, develope a net-work of burnished gold over our heads ... It is a triumph which has never been achieved before in a less area than that of a cathedral.[73]

The elaborate programme of heraldry which started in the Gallery continues in these rooms: 'Vaulted corridor. On the East side is a series of nineteen shields illustrating the descent of Mr Beckford from King Edward I ... on the other side, a similar series, exhibiting his wife Lady Margaret Gordon's descent ... Sanctuary. The Latimer cross woven into the carpet ... Oratory. The Fleur de lis in gold on a purple ground in stained glass.'[74]

In the Vaulted Corridor 'A glimmering light is received through six perforated bronze doors, modeled after those in Henry VII. chapel in Westminster abbey. These doors are hung with crimson curtains, which increase the solemn gloom and effect.'[75] The use of Westminster Abbey as a source continues in St Michael's Gallery where the ceiling is modelled upon that in Henry VII's Chapel. The doors of perforated bronze are still *in situ* at Westminster.

The Oratory was completed by 1812, when it was described and illustrated by Storer (Plate 105): 'From the centre of the ceiling is suspended a golden lamp, elaborately chased. The altar is adorned with a statue of St Anthony, admirably executed in alabaster by Rossi. On each side are lofty stands, upon which are placed

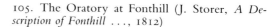

105. The Oratory at Fonthill (J. Storer, *A Description of Fonthill* ..., 1812)

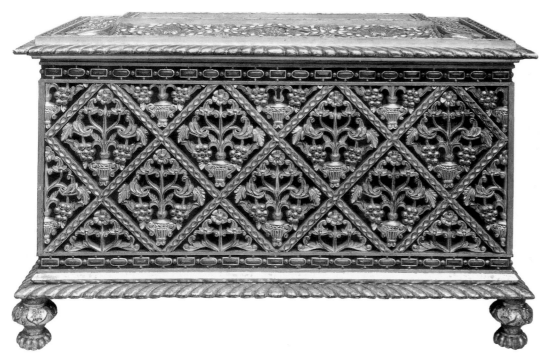

106. A carved, painted and gilded chest (Wallace Collection, London)

candelabra of massive silver richly gilt.'[76] The altar, its candlesticks and the hanging lamp had existed elsewhere in the Abbey before the Oratory was built, for in 1803 Lady Anne Hamilton wrote that an altar 'With the figure of St Anthony upon it holding a child was surrounded by 36 wax lights in gold branches and candlesticks (fm. Auguste at Paris) above glimmers a lamp (fm Green Ludgate Hill) of Beautiful workmanship and Antique form.'[77] The 'golden lamp' was designed by Beckford probably assisted by Franchi. Auguste was Beckford's favourite goldsmith. Although John Charles Felix Rossi (1762–1839) was from 1797 Sculptor to the Prince of Wales and later to George IV and William IV, he was not highly talented.

Beckford often said that St Anthony of Padua was his patron saint and he frequently invoked his help. He had become fond of St Anthony while in Lisbon, where St Anthony is the patron saint. Beckford removed the statue to Bath in either 1822 or 1823, though it may have left the Oratory before eventually leaving the Abbey. Rutter describes how 'The place of the altar, (which was surmounted by an alabaster statue of St Anthony by Rossi) is for the present supplied by a singularly beautiful CABINET of architectural design.'[78]

107. Looking from St Michael's Gallery across the Octagon into King Edward's Gallery at Fonthill (Rutter, *Delineations*)

108. The south end of St Michael's Gallery (Britton, *Illustrations*)

127

Britton in 1823 illustrates the cabinet described by Rutter, yet in his text says that the statue was still in the Oratory. Rutter in *Delineations* also of 1823 does not mention the statue as in the Oratory, but illustrates the splendid altarpiece without the statue. This altarpiece is described as 'of oak, and originally belonged to the Oratory. In the middle compartment stood an alabaster statue . . . The paintings are by Stothard, and their subjects taken from the Book of Tobit . . . The shields are charged with the armorial bearings or Mr Beckford.'[79]

In the Oratory also stood two chests (Plate 106). 'Each side is ornamented by a large and magnificent ROBE CHEST, formed of highly scented wood, externally carved with the rose and thistle, double gilt, and coloured in imitation of gems, with massive wrought handles, hinges, and key, water-gilt, of the times of James I.'[80] These two chests, now in the Wallace Collection, are certainly not of Jacobean date, though Beckford presumably thought they were ancient.

The theatrical religiosity of the Oratory would have been unacceptable in most social circles, except Beckford's, especially as there is no evidence that services were ever held there. It is interesting to recall that the Tribune at Stawberry Hill had a very similar religious ambience, as many of Walpole's visitors noted.

We now retrace our steps down King Edward's Gallery, cross the soaring Octagon and enter St Michael's Gallery (Plates 107 and 108). This part of the Abbey was complete by 23 December 1800 for the grandest and most carefully stage-managed event ever to take place there: the visit of Lord Nelson and Lady Hamilton. Nelson by this date was a national hero following his victory at the battle of the Nile.

Beckford pressed his workmen to complete this part of the Abbey in time for the visit: 'during the dark and inclement season of November and December in that year, it is related that nearly five hundred men were successively employed day and night to expedite the works: and in the darksome and dreary nights of those months, they prosecuted their labours by torch and lamp light.'[81] Enough work was complete by 23 December for the visit to take place and a contemporary description reads like a passage from a Gothic novel by Mrs Radcliffe:

> Slowly wended the train of carriages towards the Abbey as the dusk of evening gathered fast into darkness. It occupied three quarters of an hour by the circuitous route taken . . . the road then lay winding through thick woods of pine and fir illuminated by numberless lamps suspended in the trees, and flambeaux without number carried by the sides of the vehicles . . . The appearance on the arrival of the company at the Abbey, hushed them all into silent admiration . . . the deep shadows falling on the walls, battlements and turrets of the edifice, as they displayed themselves in groups, or, as the light flickering here and there struck the salient parts of the butresses and arches of the great tower until they faded into the gloom above. On the summit, over all, attached to a flag staff fifty feet long waved the broad flag of a vice admiral a compliment to Nelson . . . when dinner was over the company mounted the stairs to some of the apartments above, that had just been completed. The staircase was lighted by certain mysterious looking figures dressed in hooded gowns holding large wax torches . . . a gallery the half of which only was finished and furnished. There too all was in monastic taste, with shrines, reliquaries, and religious sculptures the whole illuminated with wax candles in candlesticks of silver.[82]

The gallery described is St Michael's. The dramatic effect of the lighting and the capacity of the plate glass in the oriel window (Plate 108) to act as a mirror after dark impressed the visitors greatly. 'The long series of lights on either side of the room, resting on stands of ebony, enriched with gold . . . all multiplied and reflected in the great oriel opposite from its spacious squares of plate glass, while the whole reflection narrowed into endless perspective as it receded from the eye, produced a singular and magic effect.'[83] This great event was the only occasion during the

Abbey's existence — except the viewing for the cancelled 1822 sale — when any of those likely to be influenced by the style and form of its architecture and interiors had an opportunity to visit.

Besides Nelson and Sir William and Lady Hamilton, Beckford had invited 'many of the artists, whose works have contributed to the embellishment of the abbey, with Mr Wyatt and the President of the Royal Academy at their head ... with the distinguished musical party beforementioned, and some prominent characters of the literary world, [who] formed together a combination of talents and genius, not often meeting at the same place.'[84]

The P.R.A. was, of course, Benjamin West, who wrote a letter of thanks on 5 January 1801: 'I am lost in admiration — and feel that I have seen a place raised more by majick, or inspiration, than the labours of the human hand ... when the part which remains to be finished, is accomplished, must raise a climax of excellence without an example in the European world — and to give an immortality to the man whose elegant mind has conceived so vast a combination of all that is refined in Painting, Sculpture, and Architecture.'[85] The influence of Fonthill upon the arts and architecture quite apart from the antiquarian interiors of Regency England is too well established to need discussion here, but this one event in 1800 gave it the widest possible publicity in artistic circles.

The Gallery was named 'St Michael's Gallery because the proprietor intended to have its windows painted with the knights of that Order, from whom he traces descent. At the entrance of the Octagon, is a pair of folding doors, of oak, glazed with plate glass ... five pointed arched windows on the west side, three oriels on the east, two of which are over fire-places one of larger dimensions at the south end.'[86] The doors appear in Plate 107. The Gallery was 112 feet long, 13 feet wide and 15 feet high, and the ceiling was fan vaulted, the vaulting pattern derived, like the gates in the Vaulted Corridor, from Henry VII's Chapel at Westminster, the same source Walpole had chosen for the Gallery ceiling at Strawberry Hill (Plate 85).

St Michael's Gallery was decorated in a grander and more elaborately heraldic manner than Walpole ever achieved at Strawberry Hill. 'From the sculptured corbels on each side, clusters of mouldings ... spread over all the ceiling; between them, descend the curtains of scarlet and deep blue, bordered with the regal tressure ... over a crimson carpet, strewed with myriads of white cinque-foils.'[87] The windows, as elsewhere in the Abbey, were of similar elaboration to the rest of the decoration:

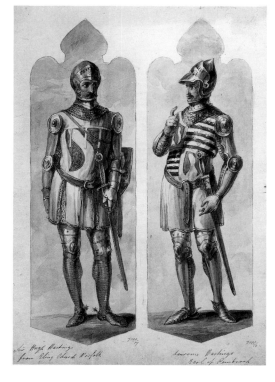

109. A cartoon for stained glass by William Hamilton (Victoria & Albert Museum, London)

> painted glass by Eginton, of arms and historical figures, the latter of which are copied from pictures by Hamilton. The very beautiful window nearest the south end of the gallery is filled with painted glass in five compartments, representing figures of the Venerble bede and Roger Bacon ... A corresponding east window ... in which are figures of St Etheldreda and St Columba ... The south oriel, at the extremity of the gallery ... St Jerome, St Athanasius, St Ambrose and St Augustine. Four other panes enriched with emblazoned shields of four paternal connections of Mr Beckford.[88]

The oriel window figures prominently in Plate 108, and a contemporary engraving of the St Jerome window is shown in Plate 99.

Some idea of the character of the figures in these windows can be gained by examining the coloured cartoons for the similar windows for the Oak Parlour (Plate 109). These are by William Hamilton, R.A. (1751–1801), who was mentioned above as the designer of the St Michael's Gallery glass; all these windows were executed by Eginton. The cartoons, which survive in the Victoria & Albert Museum, depict the first twelve kings following the Norman conquest and twenty knights in armour.

The oriel window very much follows contemporary theories of the picturesque as applied to landscape. Britton described 'the southern oriel window, with its painted glass at top, the large panes of glass below, through which is seen a pleasing prospect

of the distant country.'[89] Lady Anne Hamilton commented upon the prospect in 1803: 'you seem elevated above the world looking over the finest woods, doubly reflected in water.'[90] Thus the neo-mediaeval gloom of the stained glass did not extend to the whole window; when a particularly fine prospect of the surrounding landscape was possible the lower panes were modern plate glass. We will meet again at Charlecote.

As we can see from Plate 107, there was comparatively little furniture in the Gallery itself: 'Eleven ebony tables, with slabs of marble, carrying glazed cabinets of buhl and tortoiseshell, are arranged on each side of the apartment ... A cabinet designed by Holbein.'[91] The tables and cabinets were separate lots in the 1823 sale, and two of the tables and cabinets were purchased at the 1823 sale by George Hammond Lucy for Charlecote, where they survive (Plate 202). These cabinets and their supporting tables were made for Fonthill presumably by Foxhall or Hume.

The tables bear Beckford's Latimer cross in ormolu at the top of Tudor-style twisted ebony legs. The boulle cabinets are in late seventeenth-century French style. They were designed as display cabinets for books and *objets d'art*: 'curiously wrought cabinets, some filled with various rare miniature editions of classical authors, others, with valuable specimens of oriental china.'[92]

The celebrated Holbein Cabinet (Plate 110) was ancient, or at least partly so, and, though it had nothing to do with Holbein, the date and nationality are not wildly at variance with his dates. The cabinet itself is South German and dates from about 1550, the base is later. When and where Beckford acquired it is unknown, but the Holbein provenance might indicate that it was bought in England, especially as it was said to have belonged to Henry VIII. This piece has been in the Victoria & Albert Museum since 1869.[93]

The gueridons in Plate 107 are not mentioned in the several descriptions and were not listed under St Michael's Gallery in the 1823 sale, but from the illustration they seem to be of boulle and probably to be French and date from about 1700. They may, of course, have been reproductions, but Beckford had ample opportunities in France to purchase a long set. At least four others were in the Abbey. There were also in the Gallery several important pieces of lacquer, including 'A box of gold japan, from the Duchess of Portland's collection. Two canteens of japan, from the Duc de Bouillon's collection.'[94]

The character of the furniture in St Michael's Gallery was very mixed. Two stylistic themes have been established: the French boulle style of the gueridons and the display cabinets; and the Tudor style of the ebony tables and the Holbein Cabinet. When however we look at Plate 108 the ebony theme is reinforced here, for even the gueridons instead of being boulle are of ebony. The chairs are 'six curious and interesting ebony chairs, which formerly belonged to the magnificent and haughty Wolsey, and were part of the furniture at Esher Palace'.[95]

The ebony table was 'a table of ebony, with torsel feet, which formerly belonged to Cardinal Wolsey'.[96] Four of these chairs are shown in Plate 108, but there were certainly other similar ebony chairs in the Abbey. The six Wolsey ones were sold in pairs as lots 341, 342 and 343 in the 1823 sale to the ubiquitous Swaby; the ebony gueridons were lot 1230 and the table, lot 1231.

Some of these ebony chairs were certainly retained by Beckford, for at the Hamilton Palace sale lots 169 and 170 were two pairs with the Wolsey provenance. Lot 169 was bought by the South Kensington Museum (Plate 111). Some of the Fonthill chairs had ivory details, as is often the case with such chairs (Plate 255). Some of these chairs were in place by 1800 for Nelson's visit: 'the great saloon which afterwards was called the Cardinal's parlour ... before the arched windows dropped long full curtains of rich purple cloth. Ebony chairs, and tables studded with ivory'.[97]

Beckford and his generation knew the Wolsey connection with these chairs from those that Walpole had owned at Strawberry Hill and which were *in situ* until 1842.

110. The Holbein Cabinet: (cabinet) German, 1550s; (base) English, 1810–15 (Victoria & Albert Museum, London)

111. An Indo-Portuguese ebony chair, mid-seventeenth century (Victoria & Albert Museum, London)

112. An Indo-Portuguese ebony cabinet, mid-seventeenth century (Brodick Castle, National Trust for Scotland)

Indeed as late as 1882, the South Kensington Museum accepted the Wolsey provenance. There were a number of other elaborate ebony Indo-Portuguese pieces of furniture at Fonthill including the Lancaster State Bed now at Charlecote (Plates 207 and 208). There were also a number of ebony cabinets large and small. One which Beckford prized particularly (Plate 112) was at the head of his bed when he died and appears in the painting of his corpse on his deathbed.[98]

Beckford seemed to have a penchant for black furniture. Quite apart from the ebony or the Japanese lacquer, some of his most celebrated pieces of French furniture were largely black. The most dramatic pieces in this group were a pair of boulle armoires (Plate 113), which were the most important pieces of French furniture in his collection. They had been made in the 1660s to the designs of André-Charles Boulle, the celebrated cabinet-maker, very probably for Louis XIV himself.[99]

They were sold by Louis XV in 1751 and were acquired by the famous collector the Duc d'Aumont (1709–1782). They were lot 312 in the sale of his collection and were bought by the Duc de Villequier.[100] How and when Beckford bought them after the Revolution I have not discovered, but he certainly knew that they had belonged to the Duc d'Aumont. They were included in the Fonthill sale, but were bought in for Beckford and went after his death to Hamilton Palace, where they can be seen *in situ* in Plate 129. At the Hamilton Palace sale they were lots 672 and 673 and were sold for the huge sum of £12,000 to the dealer Wertheimer. They then passed once again into a French collection and were presented to the Louvre in 1951, where they are now on display.

These French pieces were not wholly black: the boulle pieces were embellished with brass inlay and elaborate ormolu mounts; the black lacquer panels, with ormolu mounts. When one considers the combination of the rich red textiles, black and gold furniture and huge numbers of gold and silver-gilt objects often enriched with rare gems and hard stones like agate, some idea of the impact that they had on visitors such as West can easily be imagined.

St Michael's Gallery contained a number of pieces of metalwork, mounted hardstone and ceramics, and I will describe a few only. The various accounts of the interiors of the Abbey at night frequently mention the long rows of candlesticks in the galleries. It would seem that Beckford eschewed the use of chandeliers and indeed oil lamps; perhaps he considered candles more theatrical. Oil lamps were thought by Beckford's contemporaries to be perfectly appropriate for Gothic Revival interiors, and the Gothic conservatory at Carlton House, for instance, was lit with Gothic-style oil lamps. Scott was considering gas lighting as appropriate to his Gothic house well before 1820; Beckford continued to use candles.

113. The Duc d'Aumont's armoire probably from the workshop of A.C. Boulle, 1630s

During Nelson's visit, St Michael's Gallery was 'illuminated with wax in candle-sticks of silver upon candelabra, having a most magnificent appearance.' It has recently been perceptively suggested that Beckford was inspired by memories of his visit in 1778 to the Monastery of the Grande Chartreuse,[101] when he was amazed and delighted by 'statues of gold, shrines, and candelabra of the stateliest shape and most delicate execution. Four of the latter, of a gigantic size, were placed upon the steps; which, together with part of the inlaid floor within the choir, were spread with beautiful carpets. The illumination of so many tapers striking on the shrines, censers, and pillars of polished jasper.'[102]

In St Michael's Gallery, not only were there candlesticks on the gueridons, but also on the cabinets (Plate 107): 'Each cabinet supports a pair of silver-gilt candle-sticks, several of them executed by Vuillamy, after designs by Holbein.'[103] These candlesticks were sold in the 1823 sale as lots 922 to 932. There were twenty-four candlesticks in all; their present whereabouts is unknown. Recently a pair to exactly this design, but in ormolu, were auctioned in London (Plate 114).[104] Though there are similarities to Holbein's metalwork, these candlesticks are clearly a product of the Beckford/Franchi design partnership.

There was a wide range of Beckford/Franchi pieces in St Michael's Gallery, both metalwork and mounted hardstones, but there were also several of the most important ancient objects. Two are shown in Plate 108, one on the ebony table and the other on the chimney-piece. The first was the amber cabinet from Splendens: a 'triple Jewel CABINET of amber, in which are seen all the various hues of that precious material; in some parts the palest yellow is suddenly succeeded by the richest orange; in others the tint increases to a garnet red and again declines to a purity almost white . . . made for a Princess of Bavaria in 1665.'[105]

The provenance has changed since being described by Britton when at Splendens; it then described as made for the Queen of Bohemia. Storer in 1812 described it as in the Gallery but, like Britton before him, stated that it had 'Belonged to the Queen of Bohemia daughter of James the First.'[106] Storer describes it as being on the Wolsey table in Plate 108, and some of Storer's phrases such as 'garnet red' and 'purity almost white' are lifted directly by Rutter for his 1822 Description. At all events it sold as lot 1041 in the 1823 sale for the not inconsiderable sum of £115.10.0, and I have been unable to discover its present location.

The other ancient object in Plate 108 stood on the chimney-piece and is shown in Plate 115. It was 'an ancient Reliquary . . . of too much curiosity, antiquity, and rarity to be passed with slight notice only. In Mr Christie's Catalogue it is described as a "Greek shrine of metal, for containing relics, brought by St Louis from

115. A mediaeval Limoges enamel chasse (Metropolitan Museum of Art, New York)

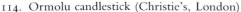

114. Ormolu candlestick (Christie's, London)

Palestine, and had been deposited at St Denys, whence it was taken during the French Revolution" ... Figures representing the Deity, the crucified Saviour, Apostles, with emblems of the Evangelists ... whilst the draperies are enamelled with blue and green colours.'[107]

Britton goes on to mention a very similar chasse that had been published in 1789 by its owner, the antiquary Thomas Astle, in *Vetusta Monumenta*. Interestingly, Astle had purchased this chasse in 1774 at the sale of the collection of Walpole's friend Richard Bateman, but by coincidence he also owned the chasse that had belonged to Stukeley (Plate 9).[108] Walpole also owned a chasse of this type, which is now in the Burrell Collection in Glasgow.

The earliest definite mention of this chasse is in Rutter's *Description* of 1822. It is just possible that this chasse, which has — as is so often the case — rock crystal set into its cresting, is that referred to in a description of Nelson's visit: 'A superb shrine, with a beautiful statue ... with reliquaries studded with brilliants of immense value'.[109] As far as I can discover, Beckford had no other mediaeval reliquary with brilliants. It is likely that the chasse was at Fonthill by 1800 and, though such objects were available in the London trade, the several descriptions of it state that it came from the Abbey of St Denis.

This provenance, like that of so many objects at the Abbey, was given by Beckford to Rutter, Britton and Storer for their published books and to Christie's for the 1822 sale catalogue, which Beckford helped to compile. In many cases, Beckford knew precisely where the objects had come from and in others, by dint of much research, he established a full provenance. He was a formidable linguist and scholar, and in twenty years of checking his provenances I have come to respect his judgement.

The Metropolitan Museum in New York, which now owns this piece, has not yet carried out any extensive research into its provenance, so a few points need to be made which also illuminate both Beckford's collecting methods and the antiquities market of his day. The Treasury at St Denis had, since the Middle Ages, been visited by innumerable tourists. John Evelyn gave an account of his visit of 1643: 'St Denys ... the treasury or Repository to which is esteemed one of the richest in Plate, Jewells, Shrines, Reliques &c in Europe ... The Sacristy, full of large Presses of Plate & Reliques.'[110] There are numerous descriptions of the fabulous riches of the Abbey starting with Abbot Suger's own celebrated account written in the twelfth century.[111] It is, I feel, very likely that Beckford, who spent so much time in Paris, actually visited the treasury before the Revolution.

During the Revolution the Treasury was stripped. 'In the proceedings of the National Convention of France ... November 11 1793. A deputation of citizens inhabiting Franciade, the ci-devant Saint Denis, appeared at the bar, and presented to the Convention the Images of Saints and Kings, which were in their church; the greater part of them were silver, the rest silver gilt.'[112] The whole contents of the treasury accompanied these objects, some were broken up and melted down while others were luckily deemed by the Commission of Monuments to be 'objets de curiosité' and were deposited in the Louvre and the Cabinet de Medailles.

However, to raise money for the government, an auction of treasures from St Denis and the St Chapelle was held: 'The sale took place on the 27th and 28th Messidor an VI (15–16 July 1797) in the Salle d'Anatomie of the Louvre. Though the auction was held, as it was stated by the auctioneer, at a time when transactions of that sort were wholly stagnant, it was a success.'[113]

A rock crystal sold at this auction is now in the British Museum,[114] but, as there is no extant catalogue of the auction, it has not been possible to establish if the chasse was in this sale. The objects retained by the Louvre at the auction, such as the celebrated porphyry and gold eagle that had been presented to St Denis by Suger himself, are still on display in the Gallerie d'Apollon and in the Cabinet de Medailles. Thus, if the chasse did come from St Denis, it was either sold at this sale in 1797 or sold directly by the worthy citizens of Franciade, alias St Denis, in 1793, as some objects certainly were. Although Beckford was in Paris for most of the period 1791–3, he was not there when the 1797 auction took place. Interestingly, his agent Nicholas Williams was in Paris in July 1797 buying for Beckford, and Beckford wrote to him in Paris about the Bouillon Claudes on 11 July.[115]

The archives of the Louvre may one day provide the answer, but as yet there is no evidence other than Beckford's own statement about the provenance of this chasse. The original contents of the Treasury at St Denis have been recently minutely examined in print, but the whereabouts of many objects is unknown.[116] There is a chasse certainly from St Denis in the Louvre which has such similar ornament that it and Beckford's may be said to be *en suite*. The chasse, lot 1263 in the 1823 sale, sold for £27.6.0 to Anne Countess of Newburgh who presented it to the Hon. Robert Curzon of Parham, the armour and manuscript collector (see Plate 48). It later belonged to J. Pierpont Morgan, who gave it to the Metropolitan Museum in 1917.[117]

A chasse and the two other objects singled out as the most important at Fonthill by Britton all appear on the title-page of his book (Plate 116). There is no doubt that Britton had intended to illustrate the Beckford chasse, but in fact he by mistake substituted the celebrated Thomas Astle chasse.[118] All three of these happen to have been in St Michael's Gallery and the chasse and the bottle both also appear amongst the group of the 'Rarest objects of virtu' illustrated by Rutter (Plate 117). The bottle was lot 1293 in 1823: 'of pale sea green oriental china of great antiquity, incrusted with flowers in relief, in compartments with silver gilt spout and handle in the gothic taste. The cover is embellished with paintings in enamel and the arms of Joan of Aragon ... the earliest known specimen introduced from China into Europe.'

As with so many provenances Beckford was correct. The vase dates from *c*.1300 and the mounts from 1381, making it one of the earliest *documented* pieces of Chinese porcelain to reach Europe. I will not deal in detail with or indeed illustrate this object, as it has been fully published elsewhere,[119] and is also known from a

116. The title-page of J. Britton, *Illustrations ... of Fonthill*, 1823

117. A group of objects at Fonthill (Rutter, *Delineations*)

watercolour of 1713 to have been in France at that time. This was painted by the celebrated antiquary Roger de Gaignières.[120] It is presumed that Beckford bought it in Paris after the Revolution. At the 1823 sale it was bought by Hume acting for Beckford for £40.8.6, and it is now in the National Museum of Ireland, but the vital mounts have disappeared.

The other object (Plate 118) illustrated on Britton's title-page (Plate 116) is even more famous and exotic than the porcelain bottle. It was described in the 1822 sale catalogue as lot 46 on the fifth day: 'A vessel of compressed oval shape, formed of a large block of sardonyx hollowed out ... incrusted with vine leaves ... a pair of satyrs heads are sculpted as handles ... executed by a Greek artist in Asia Minor. It is protected at the top by a rim of fine gold.' It was retained by Beckford and finally sold in the Hamilton Palace sale of 1882.

Some time after 1822 Beckford discovered that this vase had once belonged to Rubens and indeed purchased an engraving after a Rubens drawing of the vase.[121] It is now believed that it was made in Asia Minor in about A.D. 400, but where it was housed until Rubens bought it in a street market in St Germain in Paris in 1619 is unknown. In about 1628 Rubens sent the vase to India to be sold, but the ship carrying it was captured by the Dutch and the vase disappeared again until it turned up in Beckford's collection. Where and when Beckford bought it is unknown, but it is now in the Walters Art Gallery in Baltimore, Maryland.

These three spectacular and important objects demonstrate the richness of Beckford's collection and the level of knowledge and energy he expended upon its formation and documentation. He was able to devote his considerable intellect and huge fortune to his collection while most of his contemporaries were active in the political or military life from which his homosexuality excluded him.

St Michael's Gallery and King Edward's Gallery, it must be stressed, were conceived mainly as library rooms despite the fact that they contained many other objects besides books. Beckford's library, though not the largest in his day, was of the highest quality in terms of printed books, bindings and manuscripts. The Fonthill library consisted of about 20,000 volumes, and 'this with the rest of the property was sold in its entirety by the agency of Mr Harry Phillips to the millionaire Mr Farquhar [in 1822] and subsequently under his [Farquhar's] direction by auction, September 1823. Mr Beckford I believe reserved nothing which was there, but at the auction bought some of his favourite books by means of agency.

118. The Rubens Vase (Walters Art Gallery, Baltimore)

His portion of the present library therefore was collected between that period and 1844 the year of his death.'[122] This was written with reference to the Hamilton Palace Library sale[123] by Henry Bohn, who was Beckford's sole bookseller after 1831. The sale in 1882 raised a record sum of £73,000 quite apart from the manuscripts, which were sold privately to the Prussian Government.

As the plan of Fonthill (Plate 95) shows, from the Octagon at Fonthill 'Two very extensive galleries [St Michael's and King Edward's] branching from it, form a part of the principal library; that extending to the south [St Michael's] is one hundred and forty feet long ... Adjoining ... is a very splendid apartment containing, amongst other literary curiosities, a long series of Spanish and Portuguese Chronicles. Two more principal rooms in the second story also have distinct libraries.'[124]

Then conveniently placed at the entrance from the Octagon was the Latimer Tower which by way of a spiral staircase connected these library galleries 'to a suite of apartments over the gallery, and which Mr Beckford occupied as a private sitting-room, library, bed-room, and dressing room.'[125] These apartments can be clearly seen in Plate 96 on the second floor, as can the way in which St Michael's and King Edward's Galleries in effect connect across the Octagon to form an immense and continuous library.

The books themselves, of course, contributed greatly to the richness of the interiors of these galleries by the character and colour of their bindings. As can be seen from Plates 97, 98 and 107, the bookcases took up a considerable proportion of the wall space. These modern bindings carried his heraldic emblems such as the Latimer cross, the cinquefoil and the two crests that are so often engraved on his gold and silver plate.

Beckford often used the following crests: Issuant from a Ducal coronet, Or, an oak tree fructed, proper, the stem penetrated transversely by a frame-saw, also proper, inscribed with the word 'Through' differenced by a shield pendant from a branch of a tree charged with the arms of Latimer, being, Gules, a cross-flory, Or; and, on a wreath of the colours, a Heron's head erased, Or gorged with a collar, flory and counter-flory. Gules; in the beak a fish argent. This latter crest follows the mediaeval heraldic precedent and is in the form of a rebus of the name Beckford, in this case, the heron's beak clutching a fish represents the 'beak fort'.

119. A Beckford armorial binding (Victoria & Albert Museum, London)

Several of these crests appear on Beckford's bookbindings (Plate 119) and, of course, the Latimer cross and the cinquefoil decorate the carpets ceilings, furniture and other parts of the interior decoration in the two galleries in question. It was not unusual for bookbindings to be conceived as part of the scheme of interior decoration. At Audley End in the 1770s, Adam designed a red and gold chequer-board pattern for the spines of the books in the library. I have discussed elsewhere the binding in Plate 119 and its binder.[126] Beckford engaged only the most celebrated binders and in this country employed Christian Kalthoeber, Roger Payne and Charles Lewis, whom Beckford nicknamed 'the Angel'.

Many of the books purchased in France were bound by arrangement with his faithful Parisian bookseller Chardin, who usually employed the celebrated N.D. Derome le jeune. Beckford, a perfectionist in all he did, had very pronounced views concerning bindings: 'This cloth binding is coarse, bungling work, and the lettering on scarlet offensively ugly and glaring *I cannot abide it* ... to be bound in plain, chaste, fragrant russia, as pure and simple as possible, gilt leaves kept large and roughish ... Let it be bound in some little scrap of genuine rough-grained blue morocco, no gold except in lettering.'[127]

That Beckford was concerned not only with the character and quality of the individual bindings, but also with the effect when massed in bookshelves is obvious from a letter to Franchi of 27 August 1817: 'Boletus, with the help of the books recently arrived has done prodigies in St Michael's Gallery. The cabinets contain some six hundred volumes of the greatest beauty, interest and curiosity. A fine spectacle, to make the Dotard tremble if he could see them. The rarest and finest travel books (those of the fifteenth and sixteenth centuries) are now in full view and available: in short, tis a marvel. An intelligent connoisseur could not take a step in this gallery without exclaiming "Indeed, there is nothing like this in the world!"'[128] Boletus was Clarke, Beckford's London bookseller and author of the *Reptorium*, which describes Beckford's library, and the Dotard was Chardin.

Some mention must be made of the use to which the numerous historical, architectural, heraldic and topographical works were put quite apart from the many folios and albums of engraved ornament. Many of these were shelved in the Oak Library. By 1812 there already existed 'an apartment devoted to the use of such artists as are employed in directing the works now carrying on at Fonthill, it contains a collection of the rarest books and prints.'[129] Ten years later Rutter described:

> The Oak Library . . . This room formerly designated 'the board of works,' was devoted to the use of the artists who were employed upon the building designs of Mr Beckford, and his architect, Mr James Wyatt. On the shelves and in the armoires which surround it, the liberality of Mr Beckford had deposited an extensive and costly collection of works in fine arts for their information and study . . . the natural consequence of advantages like these, united with the actual execution of such works as the Abbey, must be, to form artists of more than ordinary ability . . . the present Mr Jeffrey Wyatt was one of the late architect's pupils who enjoyed this rare opportunity . . . A massive library table, covered with purple velvet, two armed chairs, and two candelabra carrying tripod lights, stand in the window recess.[130]

Thus, at the velvet covered library table in the Oak Library Beckford and Franchi with their team of artists and designers pored over both ancient and modern books and prints to ransack the resources of the past for the embellishment of Fonthill — painters like Turner, West, Cattermole, Buckler, Martin, Hamilton and Warwick Smith, architects like the Wyatts, designers like the two Egintons, upholsterers like Hume and Foxhall and antiquaries like Britton. Some came to stay for days at a time. Beckford extended his hospitality to all involved in the creation of the Abbey.

John Britton stayed in 1822 just before the proposed sale:

> Fonthill was placed at the disposal of the amiable and learned Mr Christie, who speedily prepared a Catalogue . . . The auctioneer first made an exhibition of the place in the Summer of 1822 fixing the price of admission at one Guinea for each person. Thousands flocked to see, admire and wonder and Fonthill-fair remained 'the rage' for some months. During this gala I was a resident at the Abbey, with my wife and an artist for nearly a month for the purpose of writing and publishing a volume illustrative and descriptive of the place.[131]

The main users of the Oak Library were in fact Beckford and Franchi who, once Beckford's early travels were over, spent weeks on end together in the Abbey with only the other servants for company.

It was from this Library that Franchi would borrow the books and prints to show to the men who were executing the remarkable objects both he and Beckford were designing. A graphic description of this process survives. W.G. Rogers, the celebrated wood carver, noted: 'Mons Franchi, a man of taste. He would come into the carvers workshop with a volume of Holbein or Aldegraver, select a spoon or handle and have them executed in ivory or ebony as high as he could get talent to bring them, would watch the progress of work day by day, and the question would often be — "if you spent another day on it could you get it finer?"'[132]

Beckford did not mix socially with the 'county' in Wiltshire and almost never had friends to stay at Fonthill. He had for his day, however, an unusually cordial and friendly relationship with the artists, designers and architects whom he employed. Indeed, one very interesting feature of his collecting throughout his long life was his

120. The Grand Drawing Room at Fonthill (Rutter, *Delineations*)

patronage of living and in some cases, as with William Blake and Francis Danby, avant-garde artists and designers.

A room of a very different character, the Grand Drawing Room (Plate 120), was approached from the Octagon through the Great Dining Room and the Crimson Drawing Room (see Plate 95). Besides being the only room other than those discussed so far that was illustrated in contemporary publications, it provides an interesting contrast in that it was furnished with objects which were neither Tudor, Elizabethan nor mediaeval in date or style. The rooms discussed thus far have been profoundly mediaeval or Renaissance in style and contents, but many of the rooms at Fonthill were dominated by Beckford's superb collection of French seventeenth and eighteenth-century furniture and decorative arts.

A few minutes looking through the 1823 sale catalogue demonstrates the extent and quality of this aspect of Beckford's collection. This part of the collection is now scattered throughout the great museums of Europe and America. Curiously, all the illustrations in Rutter, Britton and Storer, save that of the Grand Drawing Room, are not those containing the French objects. Thus this room makes an interesting contrast to St Michael's Gallery and King Edward's Gallery. It is certainly a Romantic Interior in the sense that Beckford applied the same criteria as those used in creating the other rooms, but the ambience of this room would have been felt in Beckford's day to be of a 'Louis Quatorze' character. It was an important room in the context of Fonthill and thus needs to be briefly described.

Rutter describes the Grand Drawing Room thus:

The ceiling beams are carried at their ends by carved and gilt corbels, and the hangings are garter blue silk demask ... the burnished gilt chairs are covered with the same ... A circular table of breche universelle from Malmaison. Four buhl candelabra and candlesticks, with designs from Cellini ... An oriental hookah of carved jade, set with precious stones, formerly belonging to Tippoo Saib.[133]

The table had found its way into the Crimson Drawing Room next door by the time of the 1823 sale. It was lot 1140, 'a circular slab of very rare breech universelle of extraordinary size the diameter being 4ft 8 on a grand and massive standard formed of three bronze dolphins sumptuously gilt . . . This extraordinary slab brought from Egypt by the Emperor Buonaparte and presented to the Empress Josephine and was purchased at the sale of Malmaison in 1816.' It sold for £212 and survives in an English private collection.

Here we see that Beckford's taste in French decorative art was by no means confined to the *ancien régime*, but this table also appealed to his love of exotic minerals. There is no reason to disbelieve the Malmaison provenance, for Beckford had seen Malmaison complete with its collections during his visit to Paris in 1814. He had written to Franchi from Paris on 21 November 1814: 'I like the gallery at Malmaison well enough . . . it is Imperial-like, italianate and comfortable . . . The marble columns at each end of the room give an air of grandeur.'[134]

An examination of the table as it exists today might indicate that the dolphin base is English — though it is impossible to be certain. If this is the case Beckford may only have bought the top at the Malmaison sale. The 1823 catalogue entry could indicate that the slab only came from Malmaison, though the wording is ambiguous. Certainly it would have been the marble that Beckford prized rather than the base.

The Napoleonic theme continued with the large neo-classical carpet which was lot 1546 in the 1823 sale: 'of the celebrated Aubusson Factory, of beautiful and rich antique pattern 25 feet by 24 feet . . . manufacture expressly for the Château de St Cloud in 1814 previous to the abdication of Buonaparte.' It was purchased at the sale by William Bankes for his Dorset house, Kingston Lacy, where it survives in the Saloon.

The seat furniture was also neo-classical and French of the 1780s or 1790s; the sofa is now in the Victoria & Albert Museum. The X-frame stools are also French but probably date from just after 1800. The boulle gueridons are *en suite* with those in St Michael's Gallery and are French of about 1700.

121. Count d'Orsay's desk by J.H. Riesener, *c.*1770 (Wallace Collection, London)

The most important piece of furniture is the roll-top desk (Plates 120 and 121). Curiously Rutter does not describe it, but in the 1823 sale it was lot 1575: 'A matchless and splendid secretaire most elaborately inlaid by Riesner . . . the whole finished and executed with that degree of elaborate care for which this artist is so justly celebrated . . . This princely piece of furniture came from the Garde Meuble at Paris.' It sold for £179, but was bought for Beckford and was sold anonymously by him in 1825 along with the Holbein Cabinet.[135] It is stamped by Riesener and is now in the Wallace Collection.

Beckford, it will be noted, does not say for where or for whom it was made. The theory until 1981 was that it is so similar in quality and splendour to the celebrated 'Bureau du Roi Louis XV' at Versailles that it must have been made for a royal patron. The most likely candidate was Stanislas Lesczynski, King of Poland and father-in-law of Louis XV, and this piece has been frequently published with this attribution.[136]

However, it has recently been established that this remarkable piece was in fact made for the socially ambitious Pierre-Gaspard-Marie Grimond, Comte d'Orsay, who was brash enough to order furniture which vied in grandeur with that at Versailles.[137] Beckford, as we saw above, rented d'Orsay's *hôtel* during his sojourn in Paris in 1789 and may well have fallen for the desk at that time. It is not clear when the furniture was sold from the Hôtel de Clermont, but the Comte died in exile in Italy in 1809 and the story of the dispersal of his collections is predictably complex.[138]

The desk may already have been confiscated and have been in the Garde Meuble by the time of Beckford's return to Paris in 1802. He could have bought it on a subsequent visit. There is no need to dispute his statement that he bought it from the Garde Meuble, which certainly sold confiscated objects. This and the boulle armoires (Plate 113) are the only pieces of Beckford's French furniture I have discussed, but they were the most important pieces in a collection rich in such objects and which was one of the most important such collections ever assembled.

On the table (Plate 120) was lot 1541 in the 1823 sale: 'A matchless specimen of carved jade Stone . . . most superbly mounted in Gold and Silver Gilt as an oriental hookah and set with . . . diamonds, emeralds, opals, avanturine, chrysophas, lapis &c . . . formerly belonged to Tippoo Saib and formed part of the plunder at the taking of Seringapatam'. It sold for £219 and was yet another piece of Beckford's huge collection of mounted hardstones; its present location is unknown.

In the same category was the vase (Plates 117 and 122) which was lot 1567 in 1823: 'A vase . . . the largest known block of Hungarian Topaz . . . mounted with a dragon handle of gold enamelled set with diamonds . . . the undoubted execution of Benvenuto Cellini and intended as a marriage present to Catherine Cornaro whose portrait is in the collection'. This elaborate confection sold for the huge sum of £630 and is now in the Metropolitan Museum in New York. The provenance, the date, the country of origin and the maker of the vase and its mounts are still being debated.[139] The portrait of Catherine Cornaro is now at Apsley House in London.

The Grand Drawing Room contained pictures by West, Rubens, Dou, Berghem and Rembrandt. The Abbey as a whole housed one of the most important collections of paintings ever assembled in this country. These ranged from modern pictures commissioned by Beckford to the whole range of Old Masters. The National Gallery alone has Beckford pictures by Raphael, El Greco, Bellini, Perugino, Velázquez, Wilson, Dou, Orcagna, Cima, Poussin, Lippi and Elsheimer.

Although I have dealt with only a few of the rooms at Fonthill, I have attempted to provide sufficient detail to give a vivid picture of their character. The interiors at Fonthill are grander and more elaborate than any with which I deal in other chapters. In many ways Beckford went his own way and, though the Abbey itself was in the fashionable Gothic Revival style, the character of many of the interiors was quite unlike any others in Britain at this date. The interiors at Strawberry Hill were far

122. The Cellini Cup photographed in 1862 by C. Thurston Thompson

more those of an antiquary of the traditional mid-eighteenth-century type furnished with relics like Wolsey's hat and which Scott would name 'Gabions'; whereas the impact of Beckford's vast collection of mounted rock crystal, jade, enamels, amber, gold and silver must have been more akin to the *Wunderkammers* of Rudolph II's Palace in Prague or the Green Vaults in Dresden.

Snodin and Baker perceptively sum up this aspect of Fonthill: 'Beckford ... intended that his collection should be modelled on the *Wunderkammer* he had seen on the Continent. These qualities were attacked by Hazlitt in his famous criticism of Fonthill; "the specimens exhibited are the best, the most highly finished, the most costly and curious, of that kind of ostentatious magnificence which is calculated to gratify the sense of property in the owner and excite the wondrous curiosity of the stranger". They were precisely those intended by Beckford.'[140]

Beckford was thus not modelling his interiors and the manner in which his collection was displayed on medieval originals, but rather on later sixteenth and seventeenth-century prototypes of the sort discussed in Chapter 1, and, in this, he was ahead of his time. It is unfair perhaps to compare Beckford, the multi-millionaire, with Walpole or Scott, both men of modest wealth. Even though Walpole and Scott owned some *objets d'art* of the same type as Beckford, these they acquired, like most of the other objects in their collections, as relics of historical personages rather than as works of art.

Beckford bought objects — unlike Walpole and Scott he was rarely given them — primarily as works of art or virtuoso craftsmanship in precious and exotic materials. These objects had naturally often been owned by or created for celebrated historical figures, but for Beckford this was an extra bonus and not the main reason for their acquisition. Beckford as a scholar and connoisseur was very interested in establishing the chain of provenance for the objects he collected. Often, as with the Rubens Vase, he purchased an object as a major work of art and only much later established the provenance.

The character of the interiors of the Abbey was, of course, destroyed by the

123. Lansdown Tower with William Beckford's tomb in the foreground

124. The Crimson Drawing Room at Lansdown Tower (Willes Maddox, *Views of Lansdown Tower* ..., 1844)

126. A group of objects at Lansdown Tower (Maddox, *Views*)

125. A group of objects at Lansdown Tower by Willes Maddox, 1844

127. (facing page) A group of objects at Lansdown Tower by Willes Maddox, 1844

dispersal of the collection in 1823. Farquhar lived on there until late December 1825 when 'On Wednesday afternoon about half past three o'clock the Tower, which rose to a height of 270 feet from the centre of the building fell, with a tremendous crash, breaking through a great portion of the roof of the Abbey and instantaneously presenting an immense mass of ruins. Most fortunately no lives were lost.'[141]

That Beckford, the Abbey that he built, and its Romantic Interiors, which he created especially to house a collection built up over forty years of dedicated collecting and research, had considerable influence throughout Europe and America is not in doubt. It is interesting to speculate what the impact would have been if the Abbey had instead been built in the classical rather than the Gothic style. As early as 1804, its style was criticized by Thomas Hope, who at that time was paying court to one of Beckford's daughters. Hope, who had visited Fonthill, wrote: 'I have often regretted that in the new building at Fonthill, where, had the Grecian orders been employed, a mansion might have arisen, unrivalled in the most distant parts of the island, a style had on the contrary been adopted, which subjected every one of its details to disadvantageous comparisons with the cathedral of Salisbury.'[142]

Beckford looked seriously at Hope's publication and justified his choice of style upon the romantic and heraldic grounds which underlie the love of mediaevalism of most of the builders of Gothic Revival houses at this date. These are grounds that Scott or Walpole would have immediately understood. Farington, the painter, noted in his diary: 'West spoke of T Hope's pamphlet . . . He dined at Beckford's last week . . . [Beckford] said Tom Hope was right in his remarks — he said he felt the force of what he observed of the Abbey at Fonthill being a gothic design ill placed within view of Salisbury cathedral, but that he had a particular motive for it. The Gothic windows and compartments afforded him opportunities to blazon and introduce arms of the various great families that did & had existed in Europe from which his daughters are descended or to which they are allied.'[143]

129. An interior of Hamilton Palace in 1882

128. A bloodstone and silver-gilt cup by Paul Storr, 1824 (Barber Institute, Birmingham)

Did Beckford bear the criticism of Gothic in mind when after his move to Bath in 1823 he built his uncompromisingly Grecian Lansdown Tower (Plate 123) to house part of his collection? The splendid interiors of the Tower (Plate 124) certainly provided along with Beckford's house in Lansdown Crescent a splendid setting for that part of his collection removed from Fonthill.[144] The furniture and furnishings of the house and Tower were provided by Hume.

The three pictures (Plates 125 through 127) painted for Beckford in the last year of his life show a number of the most splendid objects that had accompanied him to Bath. The exotic bloodstone bowl mounted in silver gilt by Paul Storr (Plate 128) is just one example. After Beckford's death many of the most important objects were inherited by his daughter the Duchess of Hamilton and were removed to her husband's seat, Hamilton Palace. The boulle armoires can be seen *in situ* at Hamilton Palace in Plate 129.

During most of the nineteenth century when the Gothic Revival was the dominant style, the mediaeval style and character of Fonthill and its singular creator were influential. In 1859 the anonymous reviewer of the first major biography of Beckford demonstrated this influence:

Beckford and Fonthill are names that haunt our memory like the remembrance of an unpleasant dream; for the truths we know of that wayward child of fortune have such an air of unreality about them, that we could wish we did not know them as truths. Beneath these lie surmises, dark and mysterious, which loom like a pall over what remains of the fabric he raised, striking the spectator with awe and sadness ... Thus, after an aimless life passed away, like a comet, William Beckford of Fonthill. Gifted with natural endowments which, by judicious culture, might have exalted him to a high and worthy position among the men of his time, he, gave way to a life of sensuous ease and indulgence ... On the dark side of the character of William Beckford these memoirs shed no light, and none was required.[145]

6

ABBOTSFORD: THE BEGINNING

So it is in the bravura style of building or if you will what a
romance is in poetry or a melo-drama in modern theatricals . . .
                                        Walter Scott

Abbotsford was created by Sir Walter Scott between 1812 and his death
in 1832. In its day it was far better known than Strawberry Hill had been during
Horace Walpole's lifetime. Scott, while engaged in the works at Abbotsford,
certainly admired Walpole's creation of Strawberry Hill. In his introduction to the
1821 edition of Walpole's Gothic novel *The Castle of Otranto*, Scott wrote of
Walpole:

> his studies, bore evidence of a taste for English antiquities, which was then
> uncommon. He loved, as a satirist has expressed it, 'to gaze on Gothic toys
> through Gothic glass,' and the villa at Strawberry-Hill, which he chose for his
> abode, gradually swelled into a feudal castle, by the addition of turrets, towers,
> galleries and corridors, whose fretted roofs, carved panels, and iluminated
> windows, were garnished with the appropriate furniture of scutcheons, armorial
> bearings, shields, tilting lances, and all the panoply of chivalry . . . when Mr
> Walpole began to exhibit speciments of the Gothic style, and to show how
> patterns, collected from cathedrals and monuments, might be applied to
> chimney-pieces, ceilings, windows, and balustrades, he did not comply with the
> dictates of a prevailing fashion, but pleased his own taste, and realized his own
> visions.[1]

Scott was, however, fully aware that what had been avant-garde in Walpole's day
was almost too fashionable in his: 'The Gothic order of architecture is now so
generally, and, indeed, so indiscriminately used, that we are rather surprised if the
country-house of a tradesman retired from business does not exhibit lanceolated
windows, divided by stone shafts, and garnished by painted glass, a cupboard in the
form of a cathedral-stall, and a pig-house with a front borrowed from the facade of
an ancient chapel.'[2] Scott, as we shall see, did not think of Abbotsford as being in the
Gothic Revival style as defined here.

There are a number of similarities between Strawberry Hill and Abbotsford.
Scott, like Walpole, could hardly have imagined the criticism that was to be levelled
at every aspect of their houses by the archaeological mediaevalists of the Victorian
period. Walpole used papier mâché for his fan vaults and painted them to look like
stone and plaster, whilst Scott created Gothic ceilings in plaster and grained them to
look like oak. They both took mediaeval motifs and used them in a literal way
without adapting them to their new purpose, and, as we saw above, Scott even
praised Walpole for plundering the resources of cathedrals in this way. Both with
great enthusiasm incorporated ancient carvings of wood and stone which might well
deceive the visitor. They each took modest existing houses and extended them,
cramming them with an eclectic assemblage of armour, furniture, stained glass and
other objects transforming their rooms into densely packed Romantic Interiors.

The earliest and most reasoned attack on Abbotsford came from John Ruskin, who was deeply distressed by his first visit to Abbotsford in 1838. Ruskin was a lifelong and ardent admirer of Scott and his works. The index to the Library Edition of his works contains hundreds of references to Scott, but here we find the nineteen-year-old Ruskin exhibiting that hatred of sham and the un-archaeological approach to the Middle Ages, which Georgian Gothicism represented, which was to emerge so strongly in such works as *The Seven Lamps of Architecture* of 1849.

In 1838, only six years after Scott's death, Ruskin was contributing a series of articles to J.C. Loudon's *Architectural Magazine* under the pseudonym Kata Phusin. He wrote to Loudon in September that year concerning his contribution to the January 1839 number:

> I took my notebook with me to the place, intending Abbotsford to be the subject of No. 1 of a series . . . to be called the Homes of the Mighty . . . The house itself commences with a horrible-looking dungeon keep, which rises full four feet above the level of the roof . . . Next comes a large flat side of wall, into the middle of which, twenty feet from the ground, is built the actual wooden door of the old Tolbooth of Edinburgh, with lock, bars, and all, classically decorated with an architrave, etc. The spectator, after sundry speculations upon the mode of access to this celestial door, and much conjecture as to the mode in which very little boys get at the knocker, goes round to the grand front, which is a splendid combination of the English baronial, the old Elizabethan, and the Melrose Gothic — a jumble of jagged and flanky towers, ending in chimneys, and full of black slits with plaster mouldings, copied from Melrose, stuck all over it — the whole being tied together with tremendous stone cables, gracefully coiled and knotted, and terminating with an edifying combination of nautical and botanical accuracy in thistle tops. When we enter-through a painted glass door into a hall about the size of a merchantman's cabin, fitted up as if it were as large as the Louvre, or Ch. Ch. hall Oxford — the first thing with which we are struck is a copy of a splendid arch in the cloisters of melrose. This arch exquisitely designed for raising the mind to the highest degree of religious emotion, charged with the loveliest carving you can imagine, and in its natural position combining most exquisitely with the heavenward proportions of surrounding curves, has been copied by Scott in plaster and made a *fireplace* . . . This was, to me, the finishing touch, for it proved to me at once what without such proof not all the world could have convinced me of, that Scott, notwithstanding all his nonsense about moonlight at Melrose, had *not* the slightest feeling of the real beauty and application of Gothic architecture.[3]

See Plates 133 and 134 for the elevation referred to by Ruskin.

In the event Ruskin under his pseudonym published a long essay on the proposed Scott memorial for Edinburgh,[4] although the letter quoted was not published until after Ruskin's death. He was wrong in one particular: the fireplace in the hall is stone not plaster, but much else in the house was sham in Ruskin's terms. It is also certainly the case that, even during the first phase of the Abbotsford works twenty years before Ruskin was writing, advanced architects had abandoned what Professor J.M. Crook has christened the 'motif mongering' approach of Walpole's generation which allowed forms like the Melrose arch to be utilized for fireplaces.

Scott himself was personally responsible for choosing most of the features criticized by Ruskin, including the acquisition and siting of the Tolbooth door. It must be said in Scott's defence that his pioneering efforts to create a specifically Scottish version of the Gothic Revival meant little to Ruskin, whose knowledge in 1838 of Scottish mediaeval architecture was rudimentary to say the least.

Whilst I shall deal with the whole question of the creation of Abbotsford from an architectural and decorative art point of view, to the Victorians the fame of Scott, the literary genius, outweighted the criticisms of mediaeval theorists such as Ruskin.[5] Indeed Abbotsford, more than all the other houses I shall deal with, transcends all considerations of architectural quality — though it has a great deal — and, to use Ruskin's term, it is certainly one of 'the homes of the mighty'. It is one with Shakespeare's birthplace or Robert Burns's cottage where admirers come to muse in an attempt to understand their hero better. Indeed it was Shakespeare who put Charlecote on the tourist map, not the Lucy family. The very special status of Abbotsford late in Scott's life was described in 1829:

> Abbotsford, Roxburghshire; the seat of Sir Walter Scott, Bart. The accompanying View possesses more than an ordinary share of interest, owing to the literary fame of the ingenious owner of the Mansion. In all ages the favoured spot of seclusion, selected by men of transcendant genius in any department of the Fine Arts or Belles Lettres, has been an object of particular curiosity: and a view of Pope's Villa, at Twickenham, or Thomson's House at Kew Green, will ever continue to inspire the most pleasurable emotions and to interest the feelings of the enlightened part of the community. Abbotsford, the residence of the most amusing and prolific writer of the present day, has likewise particular claim to notice in point of architecture.[6]

Well over a million copies of his books had sold world-wide by Scott's death. Today we tend to remember the novels only, but well before the first, *Waverley*, came out in 1814 his poetry had established him as a major figure in the European Romantic movement. A reviewer of Marmion noted as early as 1808 that Scott's 'genius, seconded by the omnipotence of fashion has brought chivalry again into temporary favour; but he ought to know that this is a taste to evidently unnatural to be long prevalent in the modern world. Fine ladies and gentlemen now talk, indeed, of donjons, keeps, tabards, scutcheons, tressures, caps of maintenance, portcullisses, wimples, and we know not what besides.'[7]

In the event chivalry stayed in fashion and Scott's influence upon painters such as Delacroix and Bonington was considerable;[8] luckily his influence upon French painters has been dealt with.[9] Thackeray, after a visit to the Paris Salon of 1840, wrote amusingly of Scott's impact:

> Nevertheless Jacques Louis David is dead. He died about a year after his bodily demise in 1825. Romanticism killed him. Walter Scott, from his castle of Abbotsford sent out a troop of gallant young Scotch adventurers, merry outlaws, valiant knights, and savage highlanders, who, with trunk hosen and buff jerkins, fierce, two handed swords and harness on the back did challenge, combat and overcome the heroes and demigods of Greece and Rome ... down goes Ajax under the mace of Dunois; and yonder are Leonidas and Romulus begging their lives of Rob Roy Macgregor. Classicism is dead.[10]

Thus many visitors came to Abbotsford to see Scott, his house and collections and it was his poems that brought them, the Waverley novels being by 'The Great Unknown' until 1826, though well before that date Scott's authorship was an open secret. These visitors took away with them memories of Abbotsford and it was in this way rather than through published illustrations that its fame and influence spread. Many of the visitors were famous in their own right — like Wordsworth, Turner, Wilkie, Maria Edgeworth and Sir Humphrey Davy.

As early as 1818 the tourists were becoming a problem. Lockhart describes how, 'On returning to Abbotsford, we found Mrs Scott and her daughters doing penance under the merciless curiosity of a couple of tourists ... They were rich specimens — tall, lanky young men, both of them rigged out in new jackets and trowsers of the Macgregor tartain; the one, as they had revealed, being a lawyer, the other a Unitarian preacher, from New England ... Scott signifying that his hour for dinner approached ... he bowed the overwhelmed originals to his door.'[11] Scott's natural hospitality almost overcame him and later that evening he said to his wife, 'Hang the Yahoos, Charlotte — but we should have bid them stay dinner.'[12]

By 1825 Scott was forced to take up a less hospitable stance, as Captain Basil Hall, the explorer who was spending Christmas at Abbotsford that year, wrote:

> Some conversation arose about stranger tourists, and I learned that Sir Walter had at length been very reluctantly obliged to put a stop to the inundation of these people, by sending an intimation to the inns at Melrose and Selkirk to stop them, by a message saying it was not convenient to receive company at Abbotsford, unless their visit had been previously announced and accepted. Before this the house used to be literally stormed: no less than *sixteen* parties all uninvited, came in one day ... The tourists roved about the house, touched and displaced the armour, and I daresay (though this was not admitted) many and many a set carried off some trophy with them.[13]

Scott continued to welcome generously those who came with letters of recommendation. As late as August 1830 when he was in failing health he was visited by the young Robert Gilmor from Baltimore, Maryland. Gilmor recorded in his diary: 'and finally into his little sanctum sanctorum ... advancing to a corner he [Scott] took up a cane and presenting it to me said "If you wish to take away with you something as a memento of Abbotsford and myself here is a cane I have used for many, many years" I was truly enchanted with this testimonial of his esteem.'[14]

It is also remarkable that, even though he limited the casual visitors, he was able to entertain so many celebrated contemporaries and still find time to write such a prodigious amount.

It would seem that the young Scott showed precocious interest in the past and its artefacts, for in 1777, aged seven, 'When taken to bed last night, he told his aunt he liked that lady. "What lady?" says she. "Why, Mrs Cockburn; for I think she is a virtuoso like myself". "Dear Walter", says Aunt Jenny, "What is a virtuoso?" "Don't ye know? Why, its one who wishes and will know everything".'[15]

In terms of the rediscovery of Scottish culture and antiquities Scott was born at an opportune moment. The mania for the culture of ancient Greece and Rome was abating to some extent by the time Scott was in his teens. Certainly the Scottish enthusiasm for classical literature and architecture was still — and would remain for another thirty years — strong, but a new and genuine interest for things Scottish was emerging. The Society of Antiquaries of Scotland was founded in 1780 and volume one of its publications *Archaeologia Scotica* appeared in 1792. This whole world of Scottish antiquities of the late eighteenth century is fascinating and very relevant to Scott's intellectual development.[16]

Edinburgh late in the eighteenth century was a centre of intellectual excellence of European significance; some of its inhabitants like the philosopher David Hume had no deep interest in the Scottish past. Others like Lord Monboddo, while publishing works of international importance such as his *Ancient metaphysics* (1779–99) and *Of the Origin and Progress of Language* (1773–92), took a close and increasing interest in the Scottish past and antiquities. Monboddo met and corresponded with the young Icelandic scholar Grim Thorkelin about Northern antiquities; Thorkelin was many years later to be the first editor of that great Northern epic *Beowulf*.[17]

Scott was to realize the importance of the connection between Norse and Scottish literature and was in 1814 to publish his account of the Eyrbiggia Saga. Scott was also deeply influenced by Bishop Percy's 1770 translation of Paul Henri Mallet's book *Northern Antiquities*. From his early teens Scott had taken a deep interest in ancient legends and ballads, which led to an interest in the surviving artefacts of which he soon began to form a collection. But Scott was also a pioneer folklorist and in 1784 at the age of thirteen he 'first became acquainted with Bishop Percy's Reliques of Ancient Poetry ... I remember well the spot where I read these volumes for the first time. It was beneath a huge platanus tree ... in the garden.'[18] Scott was soon to conceive the idea that there must be ballads to be collected in Scotland.

In 1792 Scott was called to the Bar and in that year at a County Court dinner at

Jedburgh he met Robert Shortreed, the Sheriff Substitute of Roxburghshire, who remained a close friend until his death in 1829. Shortreed related that he and Scott 'made Seven raids a' thegither, and our first expedition was in the Autumn of 1792 ... Dr Elliot of Cleugh-head had a great turn for that kind o' lore himsel, and when Sir Walter cam in quest o' that kind o' thing he got all that the Doctor then had collected.'[19]

These 'raids' were into Liddesdale, the valley of the river Lyd in the southern corner of Roxburghshire, a wild and underdeveloped area at this date with no roads. It was here that Scott collected many unrecorded ballads, coming into contact with many survivors of the 1745 Jacobite rebellion, and from them and many other singular country characters he gleaned material for his poems and novels.

Scott also seized the opportunity to collect antiquities for his growing collection. Shortreed told how 'In one of our expeditions we spent a haill day at Hermitage Castle ... we had wi' pickaxes and shovels to see gin we could licht on the Cowt o' Keeldar's grave ... Sir Walter was very anxious to find Cowts remains, for he was a gigantick size, and he thocht there wad may be some auld-warld weapons buried along wi' him.'[20] The castle ruins belonged to the Duke of Buccleuch to whom Scott was related. Cowt of Keeldar was a local mediaeval hero who had been killed near Hermitage Castle; they did not find the grave, though Scott at this time acquired one of his most prized relics. Shortreed related: 'It was that season that Sir Walter got the large old Border Warhorn from Dr Elliot [the ballad enthusiast] and which you may have seen hangin' in the Armoury at Abbotsford. He was very *great* I remember when he was master o' *that* relic. I believe it was found in Hermitage Castle. The Doctor got it out o' the clutches o' one o' his farm servants who had used it mony a lang day as a creesh [grease] horn for his scythe! It had been found in great preservation, wi' its original chain hoop and mouthpiece, all of iron.'[21] This horn is still at Abbotsford (Plate 175).

The objects acquired during these raids were a bonus, but the real purpose was to collect ballads. These Scott published in 1802–3 as *Minstrelsy of the Scottish Border, consisting of Historical and Romantic Ballads, collected in the Southern counties of Scotland*, which has been reprinted a number of times since and is an important milestone in the history of British folklore.[22]

There are several indications that Scott's interests as a collector were, during the 1790s, moving away from the usual pattern of his day towards Scottish antiquities. The Abbotsford collection is particularly strong in Scottish objects. Until the mid-1790s Scott collected mainly Greek and Roman coins, but on 9 May 1795 he wrote to his fellow coin collector Charles Kerr, the Laird of Abbotrule, that he had met 'a Dr Jamieson from Forfar, a man of Letters an author and a poet ... and a remarkably fortunate collector of coins of which he has a scarce and valuable selection ... He has been of late obliged to part with several of his coins in order to purchase Books ... They are a few Scotch and some of the most beautiful and scarce Roman and Grecian Denarrii ... Now as I have compleatly given up the Roman line ... the Scottish coins which are all that I care for.'[23]

Even before he had a house of his own Scott had created a small Romantic Interior to house his collection. Lord Jeffrey (1773–1850), the future Lord Advocate of Scotland, editor of the *Edinburgh Review*, became a close friend of Scott's after they met at a meeting of the Edinburgh Speculative Society in 1791. Jeffrey late in 1791 called upon Scott

and found him 'in a small den, on the sunk floor of his fathers house in George's Square, surrounded with dingy books', [a footnote adds] ... I may add here the description of that early *den*, with which I am favoured by a lady of Scott's family: — "Walter had soon begun to collect out-of-the-way things of all sorts. He had more books than shelves; a small painted cabinet, with Scotch and Roman coins in it, and so forth. A claymore and Lochaber axe, given him by old Invernahyle, mounted guard on a little print of Prince Charlie; and Broughton's Saucer was hooked up against the wall below it.'[24]

Here we have a mention of both Scottish and Roman coins and of two veritable Jacobite relics. The saucer had been saved by Scott when his father had purposely broken its cup after Mr Murray of Broughton, the Pretender's secretary during the '45 had drunk from it.[25] Alexander Stewart of Invernahyle (1707–1795) was like Broughton a client of Scott's lawyer father and an old Jacobite who — or so he told Scott — was out in both the '15 and the '45. Whether he had been out in the '15 at the age of eight is open to debate, but he had certainly taken an active part in the '45 of which he gave Scott graphic accounts.[26]

Invernahyle's stories were later to form the basis for parts of *Waverley* and *Rob Roy*, and an axe with this provenance was no mean acquisition for the young Scott. It is not definitely identifiable at Abbotsford, where there are certainly Jedburgh or Jeddart axes, and I would suggest that Scott's female relation had confused a Jedburgh axe with a Lochaber one, this being very easy to do.[27] It is unlikely that Scott would have disposed of such an important relic. Here at this early stage in Scott's collecting career we see, as at Strawberry Hill, the importance of personal gifts as a source of supply at least as important as purchases.

In 1798 Scott moved into his own house; in 1801 he moved to another house in the same street, 39 Castle Street (Plate 130), where he was to live until 1826. Here he spent the Legal Terms, which bound him to Edinburgh for large parts of the year, and it was here that his collection grew until he could house it properly at Abbotsford.

From 1804 until he purchased Abbotsford in 1811 he also kept some of his collection at Ashiestiel, a house he rented in Selkirkshire. Scott wrote to George Ellis on 1 August 1804: 'I had this farm-house to furnish from sales, from brokers' shops, and from all manner of hospitals for incurable furniture.'[28] Eventually the collection Scott housed there was moved to Abbotsford. On 30 June 1814 he wrote to M.W. Hartstonge from Edinburgh: 'I am packing up all my Museum to send it to Abbotsford and am writing in the midst of boxes filled with broadswords, targets, pistols, lances, & daggers.'[29]

Some objects probably stayed at Castle Street or perhaps new acquisitions sometimes stayed there rather than going to Abbotsford, for in 1818 after the Armoury at Abbotsford was completed, Lockhart described the Edinburgh house;

> at this time occupied as his *den* a square small room behind the dining parlour in Castle Street ... The walls were entirely clothed with books; most of them folios and quartos, and all in that complete state of repair which at a glance reveals a tinge of bibliomania ... all stamped with his *device* of the portcullis, and its motto, *causus tutus ero* — being an anagram of his name in Latin ... The only table was a massive piece of furniture which he had had constructed on the model of one at Rokeby ... The room had no space for pictures except one, an original portrait of Claverhouse which hung over the chimneypiece, with a Highland target on either side, and broadswords and dirks (each having its own story) disposed star-fashion round them ... I have mentioned all the furniture of the room except a sort of ladder ... by which he helped himself to books from his higher shelves. On the top step ... a venerable tom-cat ... usually lay.[30]

There is not, as far as I can discover, any contemporary illustration of this room, though many of Scott's friends must have known it.

The table mentioned was in fact the knee-hole desk now in Scott's Study at Abbotsford (Plates 162 and 163). It could have been moved to Abbotsford in 1824 when the Study there was completed, but it probably was moved when Scott sold Castle Street in 1826. The story of the desk is an interesting one: Scott wrote on 23 May 1810 to his friend J.B.S. Morritt of Rokeby in Yorkshire with whom he had

130. Scott's house at 39 Castle Street, Edinburgh (J.G. Lockhart, *Memoirs ...*, 1839)

just been staying: 'You know I fell in love with your Library table and now that The Lady has put crowns into my purse I would willingly treat myself unto the like ... Now were I to send to your Upholsterer (not to mention I have forgot his local habitation and his name) ... the terms to be ready money on the things arriving here.'[31]

The 'Lady' was Scott's poem *The Lady of the Lake* which had been published in May, the very month of the above letter. The poem sold very well: 20,000 copies went in the first few months.[32] Morritt's cabinet-maker turned out to be none other than the well-known Mr Gillow of Lancaster. Scott wrote to Morritt on 9 August 1810: 'I must not omit to tell you that gillows table has arrived and gives great satisfaction. Every one that sees it likes it so much that I dare say I shall have some commissions to send him. His Bill did not much exceed yours being about £30 ready money.'[33]

The full details are given in the surviving accounts: 'July 7th 1810. Pack for W. Scott Esq., Castle Street, Edinburgh case containing mahogany beauroe writing table Double Elevating tops cupboard in center compleat writing drawers ... 2 yards green Baize to preserve top.'[34] It is interesting to note that Gillow had made the piece with commendable speed: even if Morritt had ordered it as soon as he received Scott's letter of 23 May, the piece was completed and ready for packing in little over a month. Perhaps the author of *The Lady* was a valued new customer? It is curious, then, that Scott never ordered any more furniture from Gillow.

This desk was not specially designed for Scott. Gillows had been making desks of this type since at least the 1780s, for they often occur in their records. One appears in 1810[35] and could be that supplied to Scott; it is illustrated, but no customer's name appears. These desks are ingenious and useful objects, which is presumably what appealed to Scott. The dummy upper drawer front drops down and becomes a writing surface[36] and the top becomes a double sloping writing surface.

Having dealt with the housing of Scott's collection prior to Abbotsford and with the acquisition of some of the objects, let us turn to the creation of Abbotsford. Scott wrote to Morritt on 1 July 1811: 'We stay at Ashiestiel this season, but migrate the next to our new settlements. I have only fixed upon two points respecting my intended cottage one is that it shall stand in my garden ... the other that the little drawing room shall open into a little conservatory in which ... shall be a fountain.'[37]

So even before he had actually moved, Scott was starting to plan alterations to the small farmhouse that was to become Abbotsford. The idea of attaching a conservatory to the house was a rather advanced one for this date. Scott was well aware of the modern theories of picturesque garden planning, knowing for instance the works of Uvedale Price, and was himself to write an essay, 'On Landscape Gardening'.[38]

He was excited at becoming a landowner; he wrote to Lady Abercorn on 5 July 1811: 'I have bought a small farm about £150 a year prettily situated upon the banks of the Tweed so now I am a *Laird* at your Ladyships service and I want your advice about planting and building a cottage.'[39]

One friend, however, sounded a note of caution, which, as we saw above, was to prove all too well founded. Joanna Baillie wrote on 9 July 1811: 'So you have become the Laird of Abbotsford ... But don't let all the idle Travellers, who come to visit the country and the ruins which you have made famous, make an Inn of your house for their own convenience and that they may boast in their stupid Tours afterwards of the great attentions they received from their friend Mr Scott.'[40]

In May 1812 the family and their collection decamped from Ashiestiel to Abbotsford and, in a letter to Lady Alvanley, Scott gave an amusing account of the scene:

The neighbours have been much delighted with the procession of my furniture, in which old swords, bows, targets, and lances, made a very conspicuous show. A family of turkeys was accommodated within the helmet of some *preux* chevalier of ancient Border fame; and the very cows, for aught I know, were bearing banners and muskets. I assure your ladyship that this caravan, attended by a dozen of ragged rosy peasant children carrying fishing-rods and spears, and leading poneys, greyhounds, and spaniels, would, as it crossed the Tweed, have furnished no bad subject for the pencil, and really reminded me of one of the gypsey groups of Callot upon their march.[41]

Some idea of the size of the collection and household furnishings that Scott had crammed into his small rented house is given in a letter to Daniel Terry dated 9 June 1812: 'we had twenty four cart-loads of the veriest trash in nature.'[42] Though at Abbotsford there was very little more room than at Ashiestiel, he wrote to John Murray on 25 July 1812 that he was packing 'a few other books for my hermitage at Abbotsford where my present parlour is only twelve foot square & my book press in liliputian proportion.'[43]

Scott wrote in similar vein to Lady Abercorn on 2 September 1812: 'We are all screwed into the former farmhouse — our single sitting room is twelve feet square and the room above subdivided for cribs to the children — an old coal-hole makes our cellar, a garret above a little kitchen with a sort of light closet make bedroom and dressing-room decorated — lumbered, my wife says — with all my guns, pistols, targets, broadswords, bugle-horns and old armour.'[44]

Abbotsford was a small and unprepossessing house when Scott bought it (Plate 131); it was even smaller than Strawberry Hill had been when Walpole purchased it. Scott, in obliterating totally the original house, was to act exactly as Walpole had done. It is not my purpose here to deal in detail with the new house with which Scott gradually replaced the old in terms of its exterior, nor to deal with the Scottish houses that relate stylistically to it. Abbotsford has recently been admirably placed in its architectural context by James Macaulay.[45] But it is necessary to say a little about how its style evolved and who were those responsible for it, especially as these same individuals were closely involved with the interiors.

This group of Scott and friends Macaulay likens to Walpole's 'Committee of Taste' at Strawberry Hill: 'Among this latter day Committee of Taste, ideas for the advancement of Scott's house were bandied around. Every detail was discussed either at meetings or, more usually, in letters so that while much factual information and insight can be gained into the making of Abbotsford, it is, at times, very difficult to discover the source of the motivation behind the many changes.'[46]

This group consisted of James Skene of Rubislaw (1775–1864), lawyer, laird and amateur artist;[47] Daniel Terry (1780?–1829), actor, manager and probably failed architect; Edward Blore (1787–1879), artist, architect and antiquary;[48] William Atkinson (1773–1839), architect; William Stark (1770–1813), architect; and George Bullock (1782/3–1818), sculptor, entrepreneur and cabinet-maker.

Blore and Atkinson, as nationally known architects, need no introduction;[49] Stark died young and had little impact at Abbotsford. Bullock's work was confined to the interiors and furniture, so more of him later. Skene was the closest friend of Scott's in the whole group and he spent a great deal of time in Edinburgh living in a series of houses near Scott's house. They saw each other frequently.

Terry became a friend of Scott's and was to act as his *defacto* agent who searched London for antiquities and furnishings besides chasing Atkinson, Blore and Bullock when needed. He was to adapt and act in a number of stage versions of Scott's novels. Scott was to help him with these adaptations and called them 'Terryfications'. Scott had seen him act in his friend Joanna Baillie's play *The Family Legend* in Edinburgh in 1810. Scott wrote to Joanna Baillie on 30 January 1810 of 'A Mr Terry who promises to be a fine performer.'[50]

Scott soon met Terry and 'Scott's intimacy with that gentleman began to make very rapid progress from the date of his first purchase of Abbotsford. He spent

131. Abbotsford in 1812 (Lockhart, *Memoirs*)

several weeks of that autumn [1811] at Ashiestiel, riding over daily to the new farm, and assisting his friend with advice, which his acquirements as an architect and draughtsman rendered exceedingly valuable, as to the future arrangements about both house and grounds.'[51]

The clue to the nature of Terry's architectural experience emerges in a letter Scott wrote to Richard Heber on 11 June 1812: 'Mr Terry of the Haymarket [Theatre] lately of the Edinr theatre a man of uncommon powers . . . He is a great student of the old dramatists and has helped me to pass many a pleasant sunday evening . . . He was bred under Wyat & is a beautiful draughtsman. If you give him a breakfast in your *reduit* at Westminster you will be pleased with him.'[52]

The Wyatt one would presume would have been James Wyatt, but in fact 'During five years he [Terry] was a pupil of Samuel Wyatt the architect; . . . Terry left him to join in 1803 or 5 the company at Sheffield under the management of the Elder Macready.'[53] Samuel was the elder brother of James Wyatt, and five years in his busy office would have given Terry a very good grounding in architecture. An intriguing possibility emerges: as we shall see, Terry was on intimate terms with Atkinson who had trained in James Wyatt's office in the late 1790s; could they have known each other since that time?

In 1815 Terry married for the second time; his wife was Elizabeth Nasmyth, the daughter of the well-known Scottish artist Alexander Nasmyth. Elizabeth had great talent as a designer and artist and was to design some of the stained glass windows for Abbotsford. Terry certainly retained a close interest in architecture and became friendly with his father-in-law, who besides being an artist was involved in landscape gardening. Terry wrote to Scott on 16 September 1818: 'Mr Nasmyth has frequently dwelt upon the possibility of gradually opening up the way for myself as an architect & spoke of uniting his landscaping with mine in such an undertaking.'[54]

A specifically Scottish style of architecture was not at first considered for Abbotsford; Scott, on buying the house, 'immediately, I believe by Terry's council, requested Mr Stark of Edinburgh, an architect of whose talents he always spoke warmly, to give him a design for an ornamental cottage in the style of the old English vicarage-house. But before this could be done, Mr Stark died.'[55] Stark did in fact produce some plans before his death in 1813, for Scott wrote to Terry in September 1812: 'I have lacked your assistance, my dear sir, for twenty whimsicalities this autumn. Abbotsford, as you will readily conceive, has considerably changed its face . . . We have got up a good garden wall, complete stables in the haugh, according to Stark's plan, and the old farm-yard being enclosed with a wall, with some little picturesque additions in front.'[56] Shortly after this he started to incorporate ancient fragments into the house and its grounds.

Scott wrote to Hartstonge on 29 October 1812: 'I have just finished a well constructed out of a few of the broken stones taken up in clearing the rubbish from Melrose Abbey . . . It makes a tolerable deception and looks at least 300 years old. In honor of an old Melrose saint I have put an inscription in a Gothic Latin verse.'[57] Scott had a lifelong connection with Melrose Abbey, which is only a mile or two from Abbotsford.

Scott wrote to Terry on 10 November 1814 to report progress: 'I wish you saw Abbotsford, which begins this season to look the whimsical, gay, odd cabin, that we had chalked out. I have been obliged to relinquish Stark's plan, which was greatly too expensive. So I have made the old farm-house my *corps de logis*, with some outlying places for kitchen, laundry, and two spare bedrooms, which run along the east wall of the farm-court, not without some picturesque effect. A perforated cross, the spoils of the old kirk of Galashiels, decorates an advanced door, and looks very well.'[58]

Scott was himself learning the principles of the Gothic Revival in architecture and decoration; he wrote to Morritt on 13 July 1813: 'My present intention is to be at Drumlanrig about the 25th where I shall see what the Duke of Buccleugh is making of his new domain and lend him some of my Gothic knowledge if he will accept it to put his castle into repair.'[59] By the time the major scheme of alteration was started at Abbotsford Scott was knowledgeable enough to contribute in a very positive way.

His friend Skene gave him help at the outset; the following account, though dated by the editor July 1818, describes the events of 1816: 'at this time Sir Walter was still living in the old farmhouse, which was very small indeed consisting only of two small public rooms . . . he had built a kitchen and small bedroom and dressing room in a detached building . . . One morning Skene proposed to him to connect this building . . . to the house by building a small addition to the drawing room. Sir Walter was delighted with the idea, and set to work immediately to measure the ground and make plans which were afterwards much enlarged, but the ground plan was as concocted at first.'[60]

Scott wrote to Terry on 12 November 1816:

I was made very happy to receive him [Bullock] at Abbotsford, though only for a start; and no less so to see Mr Blore, from whom I received your last letter . . . I have had the assistance of both these gentlemen in arranging an addition to the cottage at Abbotsford, intended to connect the present farm house with the line of low buildings to the right of it. Mr Bullock will show you the plan . . . Mr Blore has drawn me a very handsome elevation, both to the road and to the river . . . This addition will give me a handsome boudoir . . . a handsome dining parlour . . . a study for myself, which we design to fit up with ornaments from Melrose Abbey. Bullock made several casts with his own hands — masks, and so forth, delightful for cornices, &c.[61]

At this point George Bullock must be mentioned, for, as we see from the above quote, he is making plaster casts and was to supply furniture, joinery, ancient armour and to advise on several other aspects of the new interiors. He started life as a sculptor while also dabbling in antique dealing and then dealt in marble and set up a cabinet-making firm first in Liverpool and then in London. Recent research has established him as one of the most important Regency cabinet-makers.[62] He was quite widely employed in Scotland and collaborated with Atkinson at Bowhill.[63] Bullock's brother William, the naturalist and proprietor of the Egyptian Hall, Piccadilly, helped George in many ways and was to help Scott obtain armour for Abbotsford after George's death.[64]

When Scott wrote to Joanna Baillie on 26 November 1816 he was still unsure quite which style his house should be: 'The front I intend shall have some resemblance to one of the old fashioned English halls which your gentlemen of £500 a year lived comfortably in in former days.'[65] On 28 December he wrote to Terry of:

the trouble the Abbots den is like to cost you all. Mr Atkinsons plans are very ingenious indeed & would promise in many respects better interior accommodation than those which with Blores assistance I have hammered out of Mr Skenes original idea. The exterior of Mr Blores plan I prefer as being less Gothic & more in the old fashioned Scotch stile which delighted in notch'd Gable ends & all manner of bartizans . . . I am satisfied the interior may be greatly improved & at any rate should be anxious to have the views of you three ingenious gentlemen concerning the mode of fitting up . . . You will easily conceive the extreme importance which I consider as attached to Mr Atkinsons advice. I never in my life saw any thing so well arranged as the offices at Bowhill.[66]

Scott had the Duke of Buccleuch to thank not only for the introduction to Atkinson, but also for the fact that it was the Duke who had brought Blore to Scotland. Terry wrote to Scott on 15 July 1816 to introduce 'Mr Blore a gentleman now employing his pencil upon Melrose Abbey for the Duke of Buccleugh.'[67] Indeed Atkinson and Bullock seem to have found Scott a more interesting client than the Duke. Scott wrote to Terry on 24 October 1817: 'The Duke says my building engrosses, as a common centre, the thoughts of Mr Atkinson and Mr Bullock and wishes he could make them equally anxious in his own behalf.'[68]

Scott wrote to his steward William Laidlaw in December 1816: 'I have got a very good plan from Atkinson for my addition but I do not like the outside, which is modern Gothic, a style I hold to be equally false and foolish. Blore and I have been at work to *Scottify* it, by turning battlements into Bartizans and so on. I think we have struck out a picturesque, appropriate and entirely new line of architecture.'[69] On 28 February 1818 Scott wrote to Lady Compton: 'So it is in the bravura style of building or if you will what a romance is in poetry or a melo-drama in modern theatricals ... It is in short a sort of pic-nic dwelling for its ornaments have been pillaged from all sort of buildings — I shall only mention Galashiels old kirk and the tolbooth of Edinburgh the cross of one and the gateway of the other being transported to the banks of the tweed.'[70]

The conclusions to be drawn from all this debate about Scottifying the house are very interesting. Scott at first wanted a house in the English vicarage style, which would have looked like any one of dozens of such houses that appear in the English architectural pattern-books of the period, and indeed large numbers were actually built. This is presumably what Atkinson's design mentioned above resembled, for he had himself published a number of such designs in his book *Views of Picturesque Cottages* of 1805.

132. The entrance front of Abbotsford before the farmhouse was demolished (National Library of Scotland, Edinburgh)

Scott had by this time identified the real differences between late mediaeval Scottish and English buildings and with Blore's help adapted Atkinson's elevations to fit in with these principles. Scott perceptively defined these essential principles in a letter to Terry of 28 December 1816 when he talked of 'old fashioned Scotch style which delighted in notch'd gable ends and all manner of bartizans.' These two motifs were by the mid-nineteenth century to become the two most common clichés of the Scottish 'Baronial' style, — indeed the example of Abbotsford was crucial in the creation of this style. However, the use of these motifs at Abbotsford (Plates 133, 134 and 135) set it apart from most of its contemporaries, which are in distinctly English Gothic Revival or Tudor style.

Scott had discerned these Scottish characteristics by 1814 when he published *Waverley*. Here the picturesque and ancient seat of the Baron of Bradwardine, the castle of Tully-Veolan, is described thus: 'half hidden by the trees of the avenue, the

133. The entrance front of Abbotsford drawn by J.M.W. Turner in 1831 (Tate Gallery, London)

134. The entrance front of Abbotsford (W.H. Fox Talbot, *Sun Pictures in Scotland*, 1845)

135. Abbotsford from across the Tweed in 1878 by John Valentine

high steep roofs and narrow gables of the mansion, with ascending lines leading into steps ... It had been built at a period when castles were no longer necessary, and when the Scottish architects had not yet acquired the art of designing a domestic residence. The windows were numberless, but very small; the roof had some non-descript kind of projections called bartizans, and displayed at each frequent angle a small watch tower, rather resembling a pepper box than a Gothic watch-tower.'[71]

So here we have both 'bartizans' and 'notched gable ends' three years before the additions to Abbotsford were started. Scott's use of the word 'bartizan' has led to misconceptions. Claire Lamont in her excellent new edition of *Waverley* tells us that Scott is said to have introduced the form into English.[72] This she takes from the *Oxford English Dictionary*: 'apparently first used by Sir Walter Scott and due to a misconception of a seventeenth century illiterate (Scottish) spelling of Bertisene for Bertising.'

However, 'There is no reason for fathering this particular form upon Scott, or describing as "illiterate" a spelling which Scott could find in quite ordinary literary sources'.[73] The *Scots Magazine* explains the matter fully and describes a bartizan as a 'small open turret corbelled out over the angle of a building with battlements.'[74] Also quoted is a Scott letter of 1818 which contained a drawing by Scott of a bartizan[75] — sadly the drawing is not illustrated and the letter is not extant. Two bartizans can be clearly seen above the front door of Abbotsford (Plate 134) these are on the 1822–5 addition.

By 22 September 1818 the first phase of the work was almost complete. John Murray the publisher wrote that Scott 'has nearly completed the centre and one wing of a castle on the banks of the Tweed where he is the happiness as well as pride of the whole neighbourhood.'[76] The house at this date must have looked very peculiar with the new additions built but dwarfing the original cottage. The singular drawing (Plate 132) shows the house at this stage, though the tower is shown higher than it actually is. This drawing must date from between 1818 and 1822 when the next phase started. Lockhart describes the house in October 1818: 'It had a fantastic appearance — but being a fragment of the existing edifice — and not at all harmonizing in its outline with "Mother Retford's" original tenement.'[77]

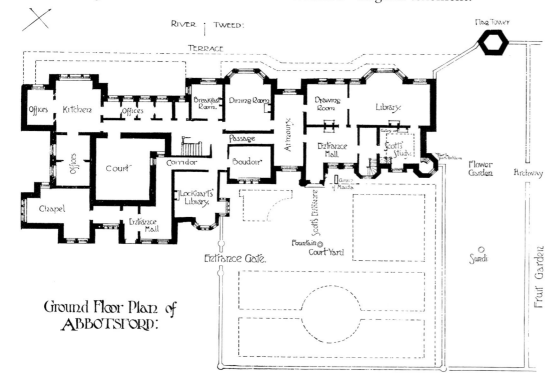

136. The plan of Abbotsford today

137. *The Invasion of the Sanctum* by W. Fettes Douglas, 1874 (Museum and Art Gallery, Dundee)

138. *The Antiquary and Lovel entering the Sanctum* by Robert Herdman, 1867

The plan today (Plate 136) shows the relationship one to the other of the rooms I shall describe. The new additions gave Scott a proper Armoury (Plate 148) and Study (Plate 151), a large Dining Room (Plate 144) and the Conservatory he had planned as long ago as 1811. All these rooms except the Study retained their function when the next phase of the building was completed in 1825. The Study moved to the new Study (Plates 162 and 163), which interestingly was in floor area almost the same size as the old. However, the books Scott had kept in his old Study could now expand into the purpose-built Library. The old Study became the Breakfast Parlour. How the two downstairs rooms in the old farmhouse were used between 1819 and 1822 is unclear, though one at least presumably acted as a drawing room — a new one not being provided until the next phase of the building.

One interesting feature of the planning is that no particularly grand staircase was added in the 1817–19 wing, and in the next phase the main staircase' provided was a relatively small one crammed into a tower (see Plate 136). This might be another deliberately Scottish feature; it is unthinkable that an English house of the date and relative grandeur of Abbotsford would not have had a suitably grand staircase. But if one looks at the late mediaeval Scottish houses that Scott sought to emulate, such as nearby Traquair, they usually have only small tower staircases. Did Scott perhaps consider the English formula 'Modern Gothic'?

I shall deal with the ground floor rooms at Abbotsford only, those upstairs being furnished mainly with family furniture. Lockhart tells us that 'The same feeling was apparent in all the arrangement of his private apartment. Pictures of his father and mother were the only ones in his dressing-room. The clumsy antique cabinets that stood there, things of a very different class from the beautiful and costly productions in the public rooms below, had all belonged to the furniture of George's Square. Even his father's rickety washing-stand, with all its cramped appurtenances, though exceedingly unlike what a man of his scrupulous habits would have selected in these days, kept its ground.'[78]

The Study was the most personal of Scott's rooms in the first phase of the additions, and it was in this room that he wrote when at Abbotsford. Though he continued to write in Edinburgh, too, it was in this room between 1819 and 1825, when he moved to the new Study, that he wrote large sections of *Ivanhoe, The Monastery, The Abbot, Kenilworth, The Pirate, The Fortunes of Nigel, Peveril of the Peak, Quentin Durward, St Ronan's Well* and *Redgauntlet* as well as numerous other works. The Allan painting of 1831 from which the engraving (Plate 151) was taken purports to show this Study.[79] The architectural detail is largely fanciful, though actual objects, like the Byron Urn (Plate 140), the Shakespeare bust (Plate 143) and weapons now in the Armoury, had actually been in the Study.

When the building work was in progress he wrote to Terry on 29 October 1817: 'I have changed my mind as to having doors on the book-presses, which is, after all, a great bore. No person will be admitted into my sanctum, and I can have the door locked during my absence.'[80] The term 'sanctum' had already been used by Scott in that novel which is central to the understanding of Abbotsford and Scott's collecting activities, *The Antiquary*.

The central character of the novel, the Antiquary of the title, is Jonathan Oldbuck of Monkbarns, a character based partly upon Scott himself, but mainly on several of Scott's friends, the most important of whom was George Constable (1719–1803).[81] The novel was published in 1816, having been written just when the interiors at Abbotsford were being planned. In it Scott described Oldbuck's

sanctum sanctorum, my cell I may call it . . . Mr Oldbuck had, by this time, attained the top of the winding stair which led to his own apartment, and opening a door, and pushing aside a piece of tapestry with which it was covered, his first exclamation was, 'What are you about here, you sluts?' A dirty bare footed chambermaid threw down her duster, detected in the heinous act of arranging the *sanctum sanctorum*, and fled . . . 'You'll be poisoned here with the volumes of dust they have raised' . . . 'but I assure you the dust was very ancient, peaceful, quiet dust, about an hour ago, and would have remained so for a hundred years' . . . It was a lofty room of middling size, obscurely lighted by high narrow latticed windows. One end was entirely occupied by bookshelves, greatly too limited in space for the number of volumes, placed upon them . . . while numberless others littered the floor and the tables, amid a chaos of maps, engravings scraps of parchment, bundles of papers, pieces of old armour, swords, dirks, helmets, and highland targets. Behind Mr Oldbuck's seat, (which was an ancient leather-covered easy-chair, worn smooth by constant use) was a huge oaken cabinet . . . The top of this cabinet was covered with busts . . . The walls of the apartment were partly clothed with grim old tapestry . . . The rest of the room was panelled, or wainscotted, with black oak . . . A large old-fashioned oaken table was covered with a profusion of papers, parchments, books, and nondescript trinkets and gegaws, which seemed to have little to recommend them, besides rust and the antiquity which it indicates. In the midst of this wreck of ancient books and utensils, with a gravity equal to Marius among the ruins of Carthage sat a large black cat . . . The floor, as well as the table and chairs, was overflowed by the same *mare magnum* of miscellaneous trumpery.[82]

139. *Jonathan Oldbuck, l'Antiquaire* by Godefroy Durand (Walter Scott, *Illustre l'Antiquaire* . . ., 1882)

As has been noticed recently,[83] Scott in this description of Oldbuck's *sanctum* reworks a description he had written in 1815 for his novel *Guy Mannering*, but had removed before publication. It describes the study of Jon Clerk of Eldin (1728–1812), the artist, engraver and author of *An Essay on Naval Tactics* (1782), who was another of the prototypes for Oldbuck. This description survives in a manuscript in the Pierpont Morgan Library:

The table at which he sate was coverd with a miscellaneous collection of all sorts — pencils paints and crayons (he draws most beautifully) clay models half finished or half broken, books letters instruments specimens of mineralogy of all sorts, vials with chemical liquors for experiments, plans of battles ancient and modern, models of new mechanical engines maps and calculations of levels sheets of music printed and written in short an emblematical chaos of literature and science. Over all this miscellany two or three kittens . . . gambold.[84]

Cats seem an essential part of Scott's conception of a *sanctum*, especially when we remember the presence of Scott's own cat in the description of his study at Castle Street. There are many illustrations of Oldbuck in his *sanctum* in illustrated editions of *The Antiquary*. An 1882 French edition[85] portrays him with his cat (Plate 139). A number of paintings and engravings also illustrate the moment when Oldbuck and his guest Lovel enter the *sanctum* (Plates 137 and 138). The painting executed in 1836 not long after Scott's death and entitled *The Antiquary's Cell* (Plate 31) is directly inspired by the description of Oldbuck's *sanctum*.

While on the subject of Oldbuck's collection, I must deal with Scott's projected catalogue of his own collection. The scheme only emerged late in Scott's life, for as late as 1828 he was worried at the idea of such catalogues. Though he admired what Walpole had accomplished at Strawberry Hill, when a Mr Stewart came to visit him to collect material for an entry on Abbotsford for Neale's *Seats* — quoted above — Scott wrote in his Journal on 4 January 1828: 'I must take care he does not in civility over-puff my little assemblage of curiosities. Scarce any thing can be meaner than the vanity which details the contents of china closets — basins, ewers and Chamber-pots. Horace Walpole with all his talents makes a silly figure when he gives an upholsterer's catalogue of his goods and chattles at Strawberry Hill.'[86]

As early as 1812 his friends had begun to compare his collection to Walpole's. Joanna Baillie wrote to Scott on 4 March 1812: 'We shall see there [at Abbotsford] some years hence a collection like that at Strawberry Hill — the collection of a poetical, sentimental antiquarian . . . with contributions from your numerous admirers rather than purchases from curiosity brokers.'[87] It is also interesting that she makes the point that so many objects were gifts rather than purchases.

But in the summer of 1831 when Scott's health was deteriorating and his mental capacity to write another novel in doubt, Cadell, his publisher, 'suggested very kindly, and ingeniously too, by way of *mezzo-termine*, that before entering upon any new novel, he should draw up a sort of *catalogue raisonnee* of the most curious articles in his library and museum. Sir Walter grasped at this, and began next morning . . . under the title of "Reliquae Trottcosienses, or the Gabions of Jonathan Oldbuck".'[88]

This title would seem to be a variation of that originally proposed, for Cadell had written to Scott on 6 September 1830: 'I hereby place at your command by these presents, the sum of seven hundred and fifty pounds, for the right to print five thousand copies of a little work entitled Reliquiae Trotcosienses. Being the Sweepings of the Study of the late Jonathan Oldbuck of Monkbarns. Edited by Duncan Oldbuck Mac Intyre nephew and Heir of the esteemed person. To be printed in a neat size and to sell for fifteen shillings in boards and in 2 volumes.'[89] The work went quickly at first, for Scott wrote to Cadell on 22 September: 'I should like to know how Reliquae Trottcosienses stands. About 200 pages are written.'[90]

No illustrations are mentioned and certainly nothing elaborate by way of illustrations could be expected in a fifteen shilling book. There is evidence, however, that they might have been intended, for, though Lockhart stated that the idea for the book had been Cadell's, Scott had written months before, in February 1830, to the artist Abraham Cooper: 'I have a plan to assist the widow of an old Friend Dan Terry [who had died in 1829] of the Adelphi theatre with some drawings from the interior of Abbotsford & an account of the few curiosities it contains.'[91] Even before Terry died Scott had written to Lockhart on 3 April 1829: 'As to poor Terry I see nothing to pray for but a speedy release . . . I thought something might be made descriptive of the trumpery here with vignettes &c which might be got up for Mrs Terry's advantage with your assistance. I could finish the thing in a week.'[92]

It would seem, therefore, that the idea for 'Reliquae' was originally Scott's and was later taken up by Cadell. Lockhart is often in error on such details, but in this case there was little excuse, for the above letter was actually addressed to him. As late as 26 January 1832 Scott could write: 'Let me see what I have on the stocks . . . *Trotcosiana Reliquia* — [£] 2,500.'[93] This was written in Naples shortly before Scott returned mortally ill to die at Abbotsford on 21 September. It is sad that the work was never finished; to judge from the fragment published later, it would have been fascinating to all Scott enthusiasts.[94] The illustrations would have been particularly interesting and would have spread the influence of Abbotsford even more widely.

To unravel the rest of this complex story, in *The Antiquary*, Oldbuck's sister is married to a Captain M'Intyre. Thus the son mentioned in the novel is none other than Duncan Oldbuck MacIntyre, the imaginary editor mentioned above. The work was to be called 'Reliquiae Trotconsiensis'. Oldbuck, in his lengthy disquisition upon the history of his house, Monkbarns, discusses its original builder: 'he was a mitred abbot . . . you'll see the name of the Abbot of Trotcosey, *Abbas Trottocosiensis*, at the head of the rolls of parliament in the fourteenth and fifteenth centuries.'[95]

The word 'gabion', which was added to the title of the work after its original conception, normally has the meaning of a basket used in fortification.[96] Scott, however — on what evidence he does not say — defines it as 'curiosities of small intrinsic value, whether rare books, antiquities, or small articles of the fine and useful arts.'[97]

But to return to Scott's own *sanctum*, all the evidence points towards a neatness and order in the arrangement of the books and collection, with little dust, ancient or otherwise, to be seen and no piles of objects on the floor — in fact the exact antithesis of Oldbuck or Clerk of Eldin's *sanctums*. Though the character and habits of Oldbuck have often been taken as a guide to Scott's own, care must be taken in jumping to such conclusions. Lockhart in his description of the study at Castle Street

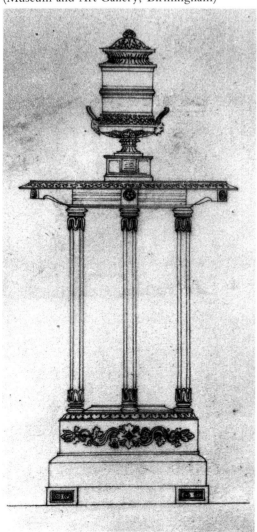

140. The design for the Byron Urn and stand (Museum and Art Gallery, Birmingham)

says that, far from Scott scattering his books on the floor, they were 'all in that complete state of repair which at a glance reveals a tinge of bibliomania. A dozen volumes or so, needful for immediate purposes of reference, were placed close by him on a small movable frame — something like a dumb-waiter. All the rest were in their proper niches.'[98]

The order that Scott imposed upon his collections at Castle Street also prevailed at Abbotsford. Until the large Library was completed in 1825 many of Scott's books were housed in his Study. There is to my knowledge no good description of the contents of the Study at this time. One can see from the plan (Plate 136) or indeed from the room, which exists unchanged in shape today, that when one counts out the space taken up by the door, two windows and the fireplace in a room 15 feet 6 inches by 12 feet there is relatively little space left for armour, books, furniture and pictures. The bookcases seem to have been quite large, for Scott wrote to his builders on 30 January 1818: 'I have the pleasure to send you the full drawings of my book-room. The front of the standards & the sides [of the bookcases] where exposed to view as also the ornament along the top to be of oak — the rest of fir which we will after wards paint to oak colour.'[99] It is even possible that the books overflowed into the Dining Room until the Library was finished in 1825. Scott wrote to Terry in March 1817: 'I incline to have book presses in the dining room as well as the study: my books are growing too many for me here.'[100] There is no indication that these were ever built.

One object that seems likely to have stood in the Study between 1819 and 1825 was the splendid and important neo-classical silver urn presented to Scott by Byron. Scott in 1815 was the most famous British poet and had only in the previous year published *Waverley*, his first novel, anonymously. Byron was only later to overshadow Scott as a poet. Scott wished to meet Byron, but felt that they might not get on together. In the spring of 1815, John Murray, who published both Scott and Byron, brought them together while Scott was in London. They met in Murray's famous drawing room in Albemarle Street and became friends. Scott wrote:

141. Bullock's stand for the Byron Urn

> I saw Byron for the last time in 1815 . . . He dined, or lunched with me at Longs, in Bond Street. I never saw him so full of gaiety and good-humour, to which the presence of Mr Mathews, the comedian, added not a little. Poor Terry was also present . . . I never saw Lord Byron again. Several letters passed between us — one perhaps every half-year. Like the old heroes in Homer, we exchanged gifts. I gave Byron a beautiful dagger mounted with gold, which had been the property of the redoubted Elfi Bey . . . Byron sent me, some time after, a large sepulchral vase of silver. It was full of dead men's bones, and had inscriptions on two sides of the base. One ran thus: — 'The bones contained in this urn were found in certain ancient sepulchres within the long walls of Athens, in the month of February 1811'. The other face bears the lines of Juvenal — 'Expende — quot libras in duce summo invenies? — mors sola fatetur quantula sint hominum corpuscula.'[101]

Murray had suggested to Byron that he should have an inscription to Scott engraved upon the vase, but Byron wrote to Murray on 9 April 1815: 'I have a great objection to your proposition about inscribing the vase — which is, that it would appear *ostentatious* on my part.'[102] Scott quickly had it engraved 'The gift of Lord Byron to Walter Scott.'[103]

Scott at some time before 1818 ordered from George Bullock a stand for the vase. Scott wrote to Terry of 'the very handsome stand for Lord Byron's vase, with which our friend George Bullock has equipped me.'[104] This stand was made in Bullock's workshop (Plate 141) and a version of it with the urn standing upon it is shown in Plate 140; this tracing of a lost drawing is in an album of such tracings from Bullock's workshop which survives in the Birmingham Museum and Art Gallery.

The stand as executed differs slightly from the design; when I published the design in 1977 I stated that 'This stand . . . is clearly seen in late nineteenth-century photographs of the library, but it is not now in the house.'[105] In 1981 the stand or an identical one was discovered in an antique shop.[106] The designer of the stand is not documented, but it was probably Bullock himself. The urn has always remained at Abbotsford and it still contains in a black velvet bag the 'Attic bones': it and its stand are now back in the Library where they were placed in 1825.

Another object that was very probably in the Study is mentioned by Scott in a letter to Terry: "This addition will give me: — first a handsome boudoir in which I intend to place Mr Bullock's Shakespeare, with his superb cabinet, which serves as a pedestal.'[107] Scott refers elsewhere to the Study as a 'Boudoir'.[108] A tracing (Plate 142) of the pedestal from the Bullock tracing-book survives as does the pedestal and bust (Plate 143). In the centre of the drawer immediately below the bust is an oval ebony plaque with the initials *WS* in brass. It was a curious coincidence and one which appealed to Scott that he shared Shakespeare's initials. The pedestal was with Scott by 22 November 1816 when he wrote to Morritt:

> One of our first occupations was to unpack Shakespeare and his superb pedestal, which is positively the most elegant and appropriate piece of furniture which I ever saw. It has been the admiration of all who have seen . . . its arrival has made a great sensation. There is really great taste in the form and colouring of the cabinet and it would do Bullock immortal honour were it not to be suspected that it was executed under the direction of a certain classical traveller. The value which [I] set upon it as *your* gift . . . now I have only to arrange a proper shrine for the Bard of Avon since you have fitted him with an altar worthy of himself . . . The figure came safe, and the more I look at it the more I feel that it must have resembled the Bard much more than any of the ordinary prints.[109]

The pedestal was in fact made from wood grown on Morritt's own estate. Scott in his own description speaks of 'a handsome cabinet also wrought out of Rokeby yew, and serving to contain an exact cast of the poet Shakespeare taken by Mr Bullock from his monument'.[110] The 'classical traveller' is Morritt himself, who was constantly travelling in Greece. He was a member of the Society of Dilettanti and a founder member of the Travellers Club. In 1800 he published *Additional Remarks on the Topography of Troy*.

The cast of Shakespeare's monument at Stratford was made by Bullock at the instigation of the antiquary and publisher John Britton:

> In the year 1814 I incited Mr George Bullock to make a cast of the *Monumental Bust* of the Poet . . . and had an equally faithful copy in mezzotint engraved . . . Intimate with Walter Scott, Benjamin West P.R.A., and Dr Spurzheim, Mr Bullock invited these gentlemen and myself to breakfast in Tenterden Street, shortly after his return from Stratford; on which occasion the host took a cast from the head of Scott . . . [Scott was asked to] give his opinion of the bust [of Shakespeare] . . . he remarked, the unnatural space between the nose and the upper lip. This all agreed manifested some error in the sculptor, until Bullock, looking at Mr Scott said his features had the same peculiarity . . . and when a pair of compasses was employed to settle the question, and the modern bard lost his wager by a quarter inch.[111]

Dr Spurzheim was a German phrenologist who would, in keeping with contemporary phrenological theory, have looked for physical similarities shared by the two great British bards. Phrenology was making a great impact upon sculptors at this date and, as a trained sculptor, Bullock probably knew Spurzheim.[112]

If R.B. Wheler of Stratford is to be believed, Scott's Shakespeare may have been Bullock's original cast: 'Mr George Bullock . . . visited Stratford in December last, with such sentiments as animate the connoisseur, and made the first complete cast of the whole bust . . . To multiply the casts from Mr Bullock's first, and consequently valuable mould, will now be impossible; for after that which he has in London, and one which I possess (the latter only half way down the body of the bust) were made, the original mould was broken up and thrown into the Avon.'[113]

One must presume if this is true that Bullock gave his original cast to Scott; other casts must have been taken later, because numbers of full-size casts exist, as we shall see elsewhere. A copy of the engraving Britton speaks of, signed in ink by Britton himself, hangs at Abbotsford next to the bust. Britton presumably sent Scott an impression. Scott was a great admirer of Shakespeare: the references to him in Scott's letters quite apart from those in his published works run into hundreds. It is thus entirely in character that Scott should have been so delighted with the bust and its elegant pedestal. In 1825 these were to find a place in the new Library in a specially created niche.

The Dining room (Plate 144) Scott himself described as

a quiet apartment not very large, yet ample enough for all the common wants of a private family, and capable of accommodating a larger company of guests than the proprietor would wish to see together. The dimensions of the room are 30 feet in length and seventeen in breadth The ceiling is not above twelve feet in height, and is apparently supported by ribs of carved oak, which nevertheless are only stucco but so ingeniously moulded and panelled and tied with ornaments and escutcheons at the places where they cross each other that they can hardly be distinguished from more permanent material ... the dining room contains a beautiful dining table ... there are however certain peculiar gabions, and that name may be conferred upon such paintings as hang upon the walls. The proprietor has no judgement at all to enable him to prize them as works of art and merely treasures them for some hobby horsical point and for accommodation.[114]

142. The design for the pedestal for the bust of Shakespeare (Museum and Art Gallery, Birmingham)

143. The Shakespeare bust and pedestal

CABINET FOR WALTER SCOTT ESQ

165

Scott's remarks about his attitude to pictures apply throughout Abbotsford. Scott owned some pictures of artistic consequence, like his Turners, but his pictures are mainly of historical and antiquarian interest. Even those of artistic merit he collected for these reasons, any artistic merit being a bonus.

The Dining Room is shown in Plate 144; this photograph was taken in 1971 since which date the Mona marble chimney-piece has been stripped of its paint. The ceiling ribs are now painted white rather than grained as originally; thus they do not give the impression of an oak ceiling. Early in the planning of the new works the size of the Dining Room was decided upon. Scott wrote to Terry of 'a handsome dining-parlour of 27 feet by 18, with three windows to the north, and one to the south — the last to be Gothic, and filled with stained glass.'[115] In the Dining Room as built there is no window to the south (see plan, Plate 136), the wall with the sideboard alcove is in fact the south wall. The Dining Room does not have stained glass in any of its windows.

In the spring of 1818 final plans were being made. Atkinson wrote to Scott on 7

144. The Dining Room at Abbotsford in 1976

March: 'The working drawings for the dining room ceiling ... will be sent in the course of the week ... you mention that you can get casts of corbels for niches at Melrose [Abbey] that will do for the dining room ... I wish you would send me a rough drawing of the corbels with dimensions without which I cannot possible design the niches to suit.'[116] As we saw above, as early as 1816 Bullock, while visiting Abbotsford, had taken plaster casts of the sculpture at Melrose.

The niches (Plate 144) mentioned were intended for oil lamps. These lamps do not survive, but they were probably similar to the Gothic lamps in Gothic niches which Bullock and his associates designed for several other Gothic houses. Scott wrote to Terry on 30 April 1818: 'Mr Atkinson has kept tryst charmingly, and the ceiling of the dining-room will be superb. I have got I know not how many casts, from Melrose and other places, of pure Gothic antiquity.'[117]

As we have seen, the plaster ceiling was grained to look as though it was carved from solid oak. This graining was carried out — as was all the other painted work — by the Scottish decorator David Ramsay Hay of Edinburgh. Hay was a very interesting character who started his career as an apprentice house painter with the celebrated Scottish painter David Roberts and was later to form an important collection of Roberts' work.

By 1820 Hay had his own firm, which he made the most famous in Edinburgh. He also published a series of books on colour and colour theory including *The Principles of Beauty in Colouring Systematized* (1845) and *Original Geometrical Diaper Designs* (1844). It is typical of Scott, who was most generous with his help for friends, that he should help promote Hay's career and artistic education on the strength of his work at Abbotsford. Hay wrote to Scott in April 1823: 'do me the honour of accepting the old cabinet which accompanies this as a trifling mark of the gratitude which I feel, for the kindness and liberality with which you encouraged my early efforts in painting and especially for the trouble you had the goodness to take in getting me admitted to the Drawing Academy and by your valuable advice directing my future pursuits to that line of business in which by the aid of your support and recommendation I have been so successful.'[118]

Hay, many years after Scott's death, wrote a fascinating account of the work he had done at Abbotsford:

[Scott]abominated the common-place daubing of walls, panels, doors, and win-dow-boards, with coats of white, blue, or grey ... He desired to have about him, wherever he could manage it, rich, though not gaudy hangings, or substantial old-fashioned wainscot work, with no ornament but that of carving, and where the wood was to be painted at all, it was done in strict imitation of oak or cedar ... He ordered me to paint the dining-room ceiling, cornice, niches, &c. in imitation of oak to match the doors, window-shutters, and wainscoting which were made of that wood; to emblazon some small shields in the bosses of the ceiling, with their heraldic metals and colours, and to fix four pictures on certain parts of the wall ... These, after being fixed to the wall by a narrow moulding of oak, were to be surrounded with an imitation of a carved frame of the same material, painted in light and shade upon the flat plaster. To cover the remainder of the wall he gave me an Indian paper of a crimson colour, with a small gilded pattern upon it. This paper he said he did not altogether approve of for a dining-room, but as he had got it in a present ... I observed to Sir Walter, that there would be scarcely enough to cover the remainder of the wall ... he replied, that in that case I might paint the recess for the sideboard in imitation of oak ... These orders I received early in March 1820 and with eight assistants commenced their execution on the 20th.[119]

Hay goes on to tell how in the event the recess was papered, but Scott returned from England, 'having seen in some ancient houses in England these recesses fitted up in real oak, [and] he was convinced it was the proper style.'[120] So the recess finally ended up grained as oak. So effective was Hay's graining that Scott's friend Mrs Hughes reported that the ceilings were 'all incrusted with roses, leaves, fruit, groupes of figures, imitated in plaister, and painted like oak with such exactness that it is impossible to detect it without scraping it; an operation in which Sir Walter found a sceptical Swiss Baron engaged one morning, when he came down earlier than his guest expected.'[121]

In August 1817 Scott was concerned about the design of new chairs probably for the Dining Room. He wrote to Atkinson on the 17th: 'Mr Blore was with me for a day and he was to see you in ten days or so. I think you and he will hold a committee of chairs'.[122] By October he was concerned about storage space in the Dining Room: 'I expect Mr Bullock here every day, and should be glad to have the drawings for the dining-room wainscot, as he could explain them to the artists who are to work them . . . I should like if the pannelling of the wainscot could admit of a press on each side of the sideboard. I don't mean a formal press with a high door, but some crypt, or, to speak vulgarly, *cupboard*, to put away bottles of wine, &c. You know I am my own butler.'[123]

Work on both the Dining Room and the others in the wing and their furnishings proceeded steadily throughout the winter of 1817 and the spring of the next year. Then suddenly on May 1818 Bullock died. Scott was very distressed by this event, and he wrote to Terry on 4 May:

> I received with the greatest surprise, and the most sincere distress, the news of poor George Bullock's death. In the full career of honourable . . . taste and talent, — esteemed by all who transacted business with him, — and loved by those who had the pleasure of his more intimate acquaintance . . . It comes as a particular shock to me, because I had, particularly of late, so much associated his idea with the improvements here, in which his kind and enthusiastic temper led him to take such interest; and in looking at every unfinished or projected circumstance, I feel an impression of melancholy which will for some time take away the pleasure I have found in them . . . It must have been a dreadful surprise to Mr Atkinson and you who lived with him so much.[124]

Terry and Atkinson after some delay arranged for Scott's outstanding orders to be completed. Terry wrote to Scott on 16 September 1818: 'I was with Atkinson a few mornings ago arranging & providing for your [illegible] as best we can for poor Bullock's concern is entirely to cease & in another week or two is to be sold up. Mr Bridgens is gone to Italy and all the rest gone to the Devil I believe — The Thing is no more — but we will take care of you.'[125] Work, it would appear, went slowly, but by 12 April 1819 'your chairs sideboard, glazing etc, etc, are all in progress.'[126] Bullock's business was finally sold in May 1819[127] and Terry wrote to Scott on 18 June: 'The concern is entirely sold off and the accounts closing — your other articles are making under Mr Atkinsons direction by the workmen formerly employed at Bullock's.'[128]

A list of all the furniture Scott had ordered for Abbotsford is given in a letter to Terry of 17 June 1818: 'the following articles will I think include all the furniture which we shall want immediately from Hanover Square. Two sets of Marbles parlour & Armoury. Sideboard & Dining tables. Chairs for eating room (To Mr Atkinsons taste & yours). One four post bed, one couch bed. The drawings were returned to Mr Buggin's [Bridgens] & marked by me. Three grates dining room Armoury & study with fire irons corresponding. Chairs or stools for Armoury. I suppose two chairs & two stools would do: they should be in character.'[129]

Terry wrote to Scott on 16 September 1818: 'I mentioned that the colours of marbles we thought for the dining room . . . the red mona.'[130] Bullock had been the lessee of a marble quarry on Mona, the Isle of Anglesea in Wales, and from this quarry Bullock's Mona Marble Works in London had supplied the public with two types of marble: a red Mona, which resembled porphyry and was used in the Dining

Room fireplace at Abbotsford, and a green Mona, which resembled Verde Antique and was used for the top of the Byron stand (Plate 141). A number of pieces of Bullock's furniture have Mona marble tops; a dwarf cabinet in the Victoria & Albert Museum has a green Mona top.

Considerable debate over the Dining Room furniture took place, for Scott wrote to Terry in July 1818: 'I do not much like the chairs & sideboard of which I received the draught from London: they are very expensive two guineas & a half, a common chair without any simplicity or propriety merely a series of unnecessary knobs & carved work: this is between ourselves. I trust Blore will hit upon something more simple for the Gothic style, plain & handsome. I think I could do it myself if I could draw.'[131]

Terry wrote on 16 September 1818: 'The chair designed by our friend Blore would be about three times the expense of the other that is about 10–11 guineas & is not very practicable into the bargain the conception of a heavy-sitting nether end would be likely to destroy its fabrication completely — Blore does not seem to be aware of the difference between *turning* and *carving* . . . do you wish any alteration to your sideboard.'[132]

Scott replied: 'I renounce Blores chair but would like a plainer pattern than the others; they are I think *knobbish* & out of character. Something less affected would please me better & the same applies to the side board. I do greatly affect the plain & massive & would prefer the side board made of very handsome wood with plain massive legs in the stile of the sketch of Robert Bruces table which I sent up last year: the knobs look very fritterish.'[133] Then on 20 October Blore wrote to Scott: 'I presume that Mr Terry will by this time have laid before you the various designs which have been made for the chairs & sideboard.'[134]

By 3 June 1819 the chairs had still not been made and Scott asked his friend Adam Fergusson to seek out Terry in London and 'ask him what is doing about my dining room chairs . . . for I shall not without them have the use of what Slender calls "mine own great parlour" this season'.[135] Terry wrote to Scott — perhaps prompted by Fergusson — on 7 June 1819: 'The pattern chair is made but I do not altogether like the effect in execution, it must have a few alterations the sideboard and wine sarcophagus will be handsome.'[136]

In September the sideboard finally arrived at Abbotsford and Scott wrote to Bullock & Co. on the 19th: 'The sideboard came safe and is extremely beautiful.'[137] He had to wait a little longer for the other furnishings of the Dining Room. Terry wrote to Scott on 5 November 1819:

I was yesterday at Mr Atkinson's & have to inform you that the conclusion of all your Abbotsford chattels is well nigh ready to dispatch a dozen chairs are finished all but the stuffing your carpet is made and I hope that you will like it much it will finish off the dining room with appropriate beauty. The stand also for the leaves of the dining table is done all but polishing and these with the fire irons & lamps for the niches and sideboard I believe contain all that is in expectation.[138]

The dining table Scott described as

of Scottish oak with room for thirty people and clouded in the most beautiful style. On this last subject and apropros of the set of dining tables these are more valuable for more reasons than one. They were made of particular parts of the growth of certain very old oaks which had grown for ages . . . in the old and noble park at Drumlanrig Castle, these trees were sold . . . Bullock who happened to be in attendance at Drumlanrig . . . the set of tables designed for Abbotsford was accordingly taken in hand . . . a case made also by Bullock out of the roots of elm and yew trees which had grown in the woods of Rokeby completed the set.[139]

As can be seen from the complex correspondence quoted here, it is impossible at

145. Design for the dining chairs (Victoria & Albert Museum, London)

146. Richard Bridgens's scheme for arranging the armour at Abbotsford, 1817

the moment to establish an individual designer for the Dining Room furniture. Blore, Atkinson, Terry, Scott, Bullock and Bridgens were all involved: perhaps to accept joint authorship is the best solution. Richard Hicks Bridgens (1785–1840), also involved in the Armoury, was a designer and architect who worked for Bullock. They were both, for instance, involved in furnishing Aston Hall near Birmingham,[140] a job Bridgens continued after Bullock's death. In 1825 and 1838 two editions of a book entitled *Furniture with Candelabra and interior decoration, applicable to the embellishment of modern and Old English Mansions* were published; it consists of designs by Bridgens. Numbers of these designs by Bridgens also occur in the Bullock workshop tracing-book in Birmingham.[141]

Also in the Print Room of the Victoria & Albert Museum are six chair designs inscribed 'W. Scott Esq.', one of which (Plate 145) is for the Abbotsford Dining Room chairs as executed; the others are probably alternative designs. These water-colour designs are all by the same hand, and tracings of several occur in the tracing-book and in *Furniture with Candelabra*. It may be that they are all by the hand of Bridgens, but this does not necessarily mean that they are his own designs. One, indeed, is probably by Blore. Bridgens, like any other artist designer employed in a workshop such as Bullock's, would have been called upon to produce finished watercolours for clients to see from rough designs by other architects and designers associated with the firm. That Bridgens was himself an interesting furniture designer is evident from his work at Aston Hall, but I feel that on the present evidence he did not play a major role in the design of the Abbotsford furniture.

Before we leave the Dining Room there is the question of the carpets and curtains. Scott at first thought of obtaining the curtains in Edinburgh. He wrote to Terrry on 18 April 1819: 'hangings, curtains, &c I believe we shall get as well in Edinburgh as in London; it is in your joiner and cabinet work that your infinite superiority lies'.[142] But they seem to have come from London, for Terry wrote to Scott in July 1819: 'the carpets are in hand & the curtains for the dining room and armoury nearly done'.[143] Terry wrote about the carpet on 7 June 1819:

enclosed is a plan of the dining room with the carpet marked upon it with Mr Atkinson's note which accompanied it I decidedly agree with him in condemning the common Brussels tho it sounds so much cheaper as I know by such experience that there is little wear in it & that the moment it begins to wear it looks very shabby. The real brussels wears well to the end & will certainly outlast 4 of the common, to line the sides & windows with oak coloured drugget & the passing across the sideboard with oak colour oil cloth, will be much better as well as handsome for the carpet as it is so much more easily removed for the purpose of cleaning.[144]

Work on the Armoury went on in tandem with the Dining Room and the Study, similar personalities being involved in the design work. Scott's armour collection in 1825 was to be spread throughout the Entrance Hall and the Armoury. Hay decorated the Armoury in March and April 1820 at the same time as the other rooms. he wrote of 'The small armoury adjoining [the Dining Room]. He directed to be painted altogether in imitation of oak.'[145] Scott wrote to Terry on 23 January 1818:

I am quite feverish about the armoury. I have two, pretty complete suits of armour-one Indian one and a cuirassiers, with boots, casque, &c. many helmets, corslets, and steel caps, swords and poinards without end, and about a dozen of guns, ancient and modern. I have besides two or three battle-axes and maces, pikes and targets, a Highlander's accoutrement complete . . . horns, pikes, bows and arrows, and the clubs and creases of Indian tribes. Mr Bullock promised to give some hint about the fashion of disposing all these matters; and now our spring is approaching, and I want but my plans to get on.[146]

DESIGN FOR THE ARRANGEMENT OF AN ARMOURY NOW ERECTING AT ABBOTSFORD
THE SEAT OF
WALTER SCOTT ESQ.R

George Bullock was by 1818 well versed in the whole business of arranging and displaying armour to the best mediaeval effect (see Plate 49).[147] Terry wrote to Scott on 24 April 1818:

> I have been to see the Laird of the Red Barn and the King of the Marble Island since I communicated to them your last dispatches you no doubt have received proofs of their attention by the arrival of everything necessary to keep the tide of work in full flood at Abbotsford ... Bullock's design for the arrangement of the armour I think beautiful. There is an excellent drawing of it gone to Somerset House exhibition so London people will have some notion of the romantic charms of your Scottish retirement. It will be an unrivalled little retreat for convenience and delightful elegance.[148]

Bullock with his Mona marble connections was often called by Scott 'The King of the Marble Island'; 'The Laird of the Red Barn' may be James Skene of Rubislaw, Scott quickly replied on 30 April 'My Dear Terry, — Your packet arrived this morning. I was much disappointed not to find the Prince of the Black Islands' plan in it, nor have I heard a word from him.'[149] Bullock was dead by the time Terry received this letter.

The drawing referred to is the watercolour that was shown at the Royal Academy exhibition at Somerset House. The catalogue lists 'An Armoury at Abbotsford the Seat of Walter Scott'. This watercolour survives at Abbotsford (Plate 146) and is signed 'R. Bridgens 1818'. The suit of Indian armour which Scott referred to above is clearly seen on the left of the watercolour.

Scott had described the armour to Terry on 28 December 1816:

> the armour of the celebrated Jalabad Sing Son of Nadir Shah which is most beautiful & compleat with head piece & hood of mail, shirt of Do., noble arm pieces & gauntlets, plate armour for back breast & sides, sword battle axe & target. I think it worth while to have a masque painted exactly like a common masquerade vizor with an Indian copperer's visnomy such as we see in Malcolms

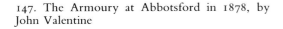

147. The Armoury at Abbotsford in 1878, by John Valentine

148. Sir Walter Scott in his Armoury by Henry Stisted, 1826

history of Persia or Elphinstones account . . . I believe it will be rather a pleasure than a trouble to you to get me such a masque.[150]

Nadir Shah of Persia, 'The Conquerer' (1688–1747), had conquered Afghanistan.[151] The armour as displayed had the mask which presumably Terry had obtained for Scott; it is no longer on display at Abbotsford. In this letter we see Scott's wide historical knowledge and that use of standard reference books which he was to deploy with such effect in carrying out the research for his novels. He is not here dealing with his familiar Scottish past, but with the history of Persia.

As with the furnishing of the Dining Room, Scott's friends rallied round following Bullock's death. Scott wrote to Terry on 25 July 1818: 'I expect Blore every day here . . . the antique corbeils on the ceiling [of the Armoury] . . . you never saw such delightful grinners. I have transferr'd almost all the masques from Melrose to my roofs & they look delightful. Mr Atkinson has given me hope that Mr Buggins [Bridgens] may himself be in Scotland to supply poor Bullock's place. If not I shall have Allan's assistance in grouping the armour.'[152] Several of the 'grinners' in the Armoury can be seen in Plate 147. William Allan, the artist of Plate 151, is the Allan referred to. Scott wrote to Atkinson on 17 August 1818 — Bridgens not having appeared — 'The plaisterers are busy with the armoury & I hope to get the armour pretty well arranged even if I should not have the advantage of Mr Bridgens important assistance.'[153]

Scott wrote to Terry about a month later:

The armoury is boarded: but what is to be done next? If any particular kind of paper is to be put over it you had better bring or send it down. If we had that & the marbles & windows the arms could be hung up while you are here. Pray look what sort of hooks &c ought to be used for disposing these trophies. In Scotland we are not clever at devices of that sort . . . In particular I am puzzled how to hang a full suit of armours against a wall. I am impatient to see the stained glass. I hope it will be pack'd & sent off as soon as possible.[154]

Boarding the walls allowed hooks for the armour to be driven in easily at the appropriate points, this being impossible with a conventional lath and plaster wall. The walls were then grained to resemble oak by Hay and his painters. This same technique of hanging armour was to be used later in the Entrance Hall.

One important feature of the Armoury was the stained glass. Initially Scott certainly thought in terms of purchasing ancient glass, as Walpole had done at Strawberry Hill. Indeed the fashion for incorporating ancient glass into houses old and new was widespread by this date. In the end all the Abbotsford glass was especially designed. It was largely heraldic (Plates 148 and 149), though a number of figurative roundels and small human figures were included. There were no full-length figures of the type which Beckford was commissioning at just this time for Fonthill Abbey, though Beckford also used throughout Fonthill immense quantities of heraldic glass very similar to that at Abbotsford. The Abbotsford glass may have been designed by Terry's wife, who, as I have mentioned, was a talented artist, a talent inherited or encouraged by her artist father.

The Terrys married in June 1815 and on 15 July Terry wrote to Scott:

Mrs Terry is at length returned to her easel our visitors are departed & quite singular labour is again embarked upon we have upon the frames three transparencies the designs of two are already outlined & are armour clad men in appropriate landscapes for the third we are yet undetermined & should like to know if there be *particular armorial bearings* trophies or any thing pertaining to any familiar subject, which would please you to ornament your cottage museum with, it there be pray describe or sketch it in any rough way and the best shall be done with it.[155]

These transparencies could refer to cartoons for stained glass, but they more probably refer to transparent painted roller blinds of the type popular at this time. Thomas Sheraton in one of his books illustrated a splendid painted blind in the form of a Gothic lancet window filled with stained glass. Also Edward Orme's *An Essay on Transparent Prints* of 1807 fully describes such blinds. Terry had written to Scott on 11 May 1816: 'I will now take my leave neither your sketches of the scenery of Guy Mannering nor the window blinds for Abbotsford are forgotten with the restored health of the artist [Mrs Terry] they will be proceeded with.'[156]

But by November 1816 stained glass was certainly being designed, for Scott wrote to Terry: 'About my armorial bearings: I will send you a correct drawing of them as soon as I can get hold of Blore; namely — of the scutcheons of my grandsires on each side, and my own. I could detail them in the jargon of heraldry, but it is better to speak to your eyes by translating them into coloured drawings, as the sublime science of armory has fallen into some neglect of late years, with all its mascles, buckles, crescents, and boars.'[157]

By 26 September Scott could write to Terry: 'you may be sure I shall be most anxious to hear that "my fathers arms Old Harden's Crest" have escaped from the furnace as Shadrach, Meshach & Abednego of yore; the windows in which they are to be inserted will I presume fall to be placed in the armoury'.[158] The Armoury windows were not finished until almost a year later (Plate 149). Terry wrote to Scott on 16 September 1818: 'I think you will like your windows with your arms, old abbots, knights and the Stirling heads with their coloured borders and ornaments I assure you they cut a very lightsome and gay figure & will throw a beautiful light upon the room. I shall bring down with me instructions from the fountainhead — Bridgens drawing of the Armoury [Plate 146] comes with the windows & when we are together I trust we may be able to do something towards the actual arrangement of your collection.'[159]

The reference to 'Stirling heads' relates to the book *Lacunar Strevelinse: A Collection of Heads, etched and engraved after the carved work which formerly decorated the roof of the King's Room in Stirling Castle* published in 1817. Several of the roundels including Margaret Tudor and King James V were copied in the stained glass at Abbotsford and several survive. Shortly after this, Mrs Terry and her father came to inspect progress. Scott wrote to Lady Compton on 23 October 1818: 'Naesmythe and his daughter Mrs Terry have arrived here unexpectedly.'[160]

Finally in September 1819 the Armoury was finished and the armour arranged, for Scott wrote to Terry on the 28th: 'Prince Leopold honoured us with a visit a few days since, and was much pleased with Abbotsford, and especially with the Armoury, which by dint of the new acquisitions now makes a very handsome appearance. We use it much as a sitting-room, being now compleated and in order.'[161]

The only other part of the ground floor of this phase of the building works which I have not mentioned is the Conservatory. Scott had planned a conservatory ever since he first purchased Abbotsford. It can be seen as built in Plates 133 and 134, on the immediate left of the front porch. It was abolished in the 1853–7 alterations, as can be seen in Plate 136. It was never a success from a horticultural point of view even though it faced south. During its planning Scott was worried that it would be too dark for the plants.

Scott wrote to Terry in March 1817: 'Before leaving the green house I pray leave to state my doubt whether, considering the eminence in front which intercepts so much of the morning sun the three windows in front will be sufficient to keep the plants in a healthy state.'[162] As we saw in Scott's letter to Morritt of 1811, he originally intended that the Conservatory should open off a drawing room, but of course no new drawing room was added to the house at this stage. Other problems arose if the Conservatory opened directly into a room: 'We must attend that the greenhouse should have its entry distinct from the house, otherwise the *taxing man* will charge it as windows. This may be done by having a sashed door in the centre.'[163]

149. Heraldic stained glass in the Armoury at Abbotsford

As I have said, Scott was aware of the modern theories of gardening, but just at this time in 1818 J.B. Papworth was discussing the whole matter in print:

A Gothic Conservatory Designed to be connected with a Mansion ... The conservatory is distinguished from the green-house by the circumstance of its affording protection only to the plants; whereas the latter is used for rearing them ... it should combine with the breakfast or morning sitting-room, to which it is properly applicable ... It is attached occasionally, but improperly, to the dining and drawing rooms; because, as is well known, plants absorb in the evening a large proportion of that quality of vital air that is essential to human existence.[164]

Though Papworth talks of a 'Gothic' conservatory, whether having the Conservatory at Abbotsford opening off that profoundly Gothic room, the Armoury, was an architectural or horticultural solecism can only be guessed at. Perhaps Scott, but certainly trained architects like Atkinson and Blore, would by 1818 have known that Scott's earlier idea of having the Conservatory open off a drawing room was unacceptable. On Papworth's definition, it is even doubtful that it was a Conservatory rather than a green house; Scott certainly used the word 'Conservatory' in 1811.

Scott, however, wrote to Terry on 28 December 1816: 'The Green-closet, for it cannot be term'd either a Green-house or a Green-Room, has not indeed room enough to swing a cat in but I am no botanist or florist & if it holds a few bow pots for Mrs Scott through the season it will serve well enough.'[165] Whatever one calls it, to have such an addition to one's house was in 1818 very fashionable — as Scott well knew — and not incompatible with the 'Old Scotch Style' of the house.

176

Another of Scott's proposals was at this time even more advanced than the Conservatory, to light Abbotsford with gas. This was almost unheard of in a country house in 1817 when Scott put the idea forward. He wrote to Terry on 29 March: 'I have some thoughts of adopting the Gas lights should I find on an accurate enquiry that they emit no smell. In other respects the saving & beauty is immense. Now suppose I do adopt this mode of lighting I intend to have the principal rails of my balustrade cast hollow & to finish at top with a fleur de lys or thistle with burners . . . lighting the burners at the top of the rails you have an extempore illumination at pleasure.'[166] It was not in fact installed at this stage. One would like to know where he saw it demonstrated. Perhaps he found it too smelly? It was not until 1823 that Scott installed gas at Abbotsford, still a very early use for a country house.

Though most of the new rooms were habitable by 1819 there must have been considerable disruption when Hay's men did their painting in the spring of 1820, but from that date Scott and his family were able to occupy and enjoy the enlarged house.

150. The Armoury in 1989 (Country Life)

7

ABBOTSFORD: THE COMPLETION

*What a romance of a house I am making which is neither to be
castle or abbey (God forbid) but an old Scottish manor-house.*
                                                    Walter Scott

In 1822 work started on the final phase in the enlargement of
Abbotsford. If one compares Plate 132, of the house with the old cottage still
standing, with Plates 133 and 134, the expansion of the house to almost twice its size
in 1822 is apparent. The Fox Talbot photograph is particularly interesting in that it is
an accurate record of the house as finally completed by Scott, and when compared to
the plan (Plate 136) shows the extent of the Hope/Scott additions of 1853–7. The
photograph is also fascinating in that it and his others taken at the same time seem to
be the first photographs of a country house ever taken in Scotland. Fox Talbot had
earlier taken photographs of his own house, Lacock Abbey in Wiltshire, but in 1845
he published his second book of photographs, *Sun Pictures in Scotland*, which include
the Abbotsford views. *Sun Pictures* has no text, but the rare published prospectus
states that 'Most of the views represent scenes connected in some way with the life
and writings of Sir Walter Scott'.

In March 1820, while Hay was working on the decoration of the newly completed first phase, Scott was already planning the next. He wrote to his wife: 'I have
got a delightful plan for the addition at Abb. which I think will make it quite
complete and furnish me with a handsome library and you with a drawing room and
better bedroom with a good bedroom for company &c. It will cost me a little hard
work to meet the expence but I have been a good while idle.[1]

Scott was in London in July 1821 for the coronation of George IV and when he
returned to Abbotsford 'he brought with him the detailed plans of Mr Atkinson for
the completion of his house . . . throughout there were numberless consultations
with Mr Blore, Mr Terry, and Mr Skene, as well as with Mr Atkinson and the actual
builders [Smiths of Darnick] placed considerable inventive talents . . . at the service
of their friendly employer.'[2]

Blore, with whom Scott was in close contact at this time because of Blore's
drawings for Scott's part-work *Provincial Antiquities*, wrote to Scott on 12
November 1821 offering his help: 'I am extremely glad to learn that you have made
satisfactory contracts for your building I hope I need not add that it will at all times
afford me sincere pleasure to aid your wishes in the progress of the work provided
you should feel disposed to avail yourself of my services.[3]

Late in 1821 work had progressed sufficiently to render the demolition of the old
farmhouse necessary, as Scott wrote to W.S. Rose on 18 December: 'I am going to
Abbotsford on Saturday to sign the downfall of the old cottage and its verdant
porch, which I shall not do without a sigh. I would write an elegy, but it is out of
fashion.[4] On 7 February 1822 he wrote to Lord Montagu: 'The poor old cottage is
now [demolished] which I do not think of with entire stoicism.'[5] He wrote again to
Lord Montagu on 27 March: 'It is worth while to come were it but to see what a
romance of a house I am making which is neither to be castle or abbey (God forbid)
but an old Scottish manor-house. I believe Atkinson is in despair with my whims.'[6]

151. Sir Walter Scott, Bart., in his Study by
William Allan, 1835

179

Scott also 'had collected from all quarters whatever sculptured stones or inscriptions from old Scottish buildings could be procured to insert in the walls, and as most of these are in some respect historical, he took great delight in narrating the events and history of the persons to which they referred'.[7] He did not, however, stop at Scottish inscriptions, for he also incorporated Romano-British inscriptions into the structure.[8]

By August 1823 the work was still not complete externally, for J.L. Adolphus noted on a visit that Abbotsford

> had not yet had time to take any tint from the weather, and its whole complication of towers, turrets, galleries, cornices, and quaintly ornamented mouldings, looked fresh from the chisel, except where the walls were enriched with some really ancient carving or inscription. As I approached the house, there was a busy sound of mason's tools: the shrubbery before the windows was strewed with the works of the carpenter and stone-cutter, and with grotesque antiquities, for which a place was yet to be found ... The drawing-room and library (unfurnished at the time ...).[9]

But by 18 February 1824 Scott could write to Terry: 'About July, Abbotsford will, I think be finished, when I shall, like the old Duke of Queensbury who built Drumlanrig, fold up the accounts in a sealed parcel, with a label bidding 'the deil pike out the een of any of my successors that shall open it?'[10] Hay reports that 'The building was sufficiently advanced by the beginning of 1824 to admit of the painting being commenced. I therefore with ten assistants repaired to Abbotsford on the 21st February for that purpose ... Sir Walter was often at Abbotsford during the progress of the work.[11] Late in 1824 the building work was, except for a few minor details, complete.

Two major changes in approach characterize the new and final building stage. First, though in the earlier phase of the building ancient carvings were incorporated into the structure, no ancient fragments were incorporated into the interior. This was to change in the second phase in which considerable quantities of ancient woodwork were used inside the house. Second, all the furniture provided by Terry, Atkinson, Bullock and Blore for the first phase was newly made, though neo-classical in form in some rooms and Gothic in others: the Shakespeare pedestal and the Byron stand were classical and the Dining Room furniture, Gothic. These London advisors neither provided nor encouraged Scott to look for ancient pieces of furniture. He did in fact acquire in Scotland one or two pieces of ancient furniture before 1819 and he was of course acquiring large quantities of ancient arms, armour and antiquities throughout his whole life. But the emphasis was to change after Bullock's death, and in the rooms of the second phase most of the furniture was to be ancient.

Also by 1822 the antique trade had, as discussed in Chapter 2, developed considerably from its state in 1815, and ancient furniture was far more easily available than when the earlier rooms were being furnished. Outside London shops hardly existed in 1822. Hay describes how 'there were no shops in Edinburgh, such as those where old carvings can now [1847] be so easily obtained — for I believe Sir Walter Scott's adoption of these articles as a decoration, gave the first impulse to that rage for them which has since existed, and which is now so well responded to by all who deal in other antiquities.'[12]

Scott, when he initially embarked upon his new rooms, thought in terms of having furniture especially made, but for some reason looked not to Atkinson, Blore or even Terry who were all helping with other furnishings, but wished to find a furniture pattern book to which he could turn for ideas. He wrote to Terry on 5 October 1822: 'Pray is there not a tolerable book on upholstery — I mean plans for tables, chairs, commodes and such like. If so I would be much obliged to you to get me a copy.'[13] Terry replied:

I have hunted London for a book on furniture & have ascertained that there is none of any character. Hope's is merely his own house — which is entirely grecian & there is a french one of Bonaparte's Palaces but not one of a style pertaining with your castle . . . I have been hunting thro' a variety of old brokers shops I have seen numbers of articles of exquisite beauty & character for your purposes & from the prices asked should indeed recommend the principle portion of your furniture (I mean the tasteful) to be so obtained . . . I have been making these voyages of discovery thro' brokers . . . you might have some occasion to come to London that I might pilot you thro' them to make choice of such goods as were necessary after your own Fancy. But should you not Mr Atkinson & I will do the best for you, not to spend but — save all the money we can — in furnishing conundrum Castle . . . any article of furniture which these extraordinary reportoires of ancient matters cannot supply, as there is no book to aprise us will be best invented by a committee of your own ingenious friends therein skillful, after your own wishes.[14]

Terry was indeed right about pattern books: the two to which he refers were Thomas Hope's *Household Furniture* of 1807 and C. Percier and P. Fontaine's *Recueil de décoration intérieures* of 1812, which were rather out of date by 1822 and both completely neo-classical in character. By the end of 1825 the first part of Bridgens' *Furniture with Candelabra* was in print and contained a number of suitable designs. But it was not until A.W.N. and A.C. Pugin's *Gothic Furniture* appeared in 1827 that a pattern book was completely devoted to Gothic Revival furniture suitable for houses such as Abbotsford.

Though Scott was purchasing only in England at this time, his taste for ancient objects was well known to all his friends. Morritt wrote from Florence in November 1823: 'How I wish you would come here, for I have been rummaging old stores such as you delight in and turned out such morsels of tilting armour, old cabinets, carved work by Benvenuto Cellini and gimcracks of various sorts as we have been meat and drink to you for at least a twelve month.'[15]

This advice concerning the compelling reasons why ancient furniture was the best buy for Abbotsford convinced Scott, and this aesthetic was applied to the new rooms. However, a few pieces of modern furniture such as fire-screens were provided, and an 1878 photograph of the Drawing Room (Plate 152) shows a small round table made by Bullock, which must by then have strayed in from elsewhere. The two chairs are early Victorian, and the curious sofa is either altered from a 1760s example or a neo-Georgian one of the 1870s. If the former, it may have been bought by Scott as old, but I can find no record of it in the letters. It would have been usual for a drawing room in Scott's day to have had at least one sofa, but more probably two.

Earlier reservations about the installation of gas having been overcome, Scott must by now have had access to a local Scottish expert in gas technology. At this date few such existed anywhere. Indeed Edinburgh was probably in advance of London in this new technology. One possibility is the man responsible for the advanced hot air heating system installed at Abbotsford at the same time as the gas. Scott wrote to Terry on 14 February 1823: 'I have got a capital stove (proved and exercised by Mr Robison, who is such a mechanical genius as his father, the celebrated professor).'[16] This was Sir John Robison (1778–1843), son of Professor John Robison (1739–1805), secretary of the Royal Society of Edinburgh from 1828 to 1840. He 'specialized in the application of hot air to warming houses, and of gas to the purposes of illumination'[17]

Scott certainly knew Robison, for so interested did Scott become in the potential of the new gas technology that in 1823 he became the chairman of the newly formed Edinburgh Oil Gas Company; Robison became the deputy chairman. Scott was interested in the possibilities of investment which gas offered and wrote late in 1823:

'I am concerned in an Oil Gas Compy. to no great extent however but one must find something better than land to invest money in at present.'[18]

By the autumn of 1823 the gas plant was installed and in operation; the work being carried out by James Milne of Edinburgh.[19] Scott wrote to Maria Edgeworth on 22 September following her recent visit to Abbotsford: 'We are all here much as you left us, only in possession of our drawing-room and glorious with our gas-lights . . . it is soon like to put wax and mutton-suet entirely out of fashion.'[20] He wrote to his son Walter on 22 October:

> Our Gas establishment is now perfect and in full brilliancy I never saw a house so completely and beautifully lighted both in sitting rooms passages and bedrooms. I do not think on the whole it will prove oeconomical because the machinery for making the gas costs a great deal in the first instance and then though the gas is itself easily manufactured and very clean yet this cheapness is an encouragement for great liberality not to say extravagance in the use of it. But then your house is twenty times lighter for the same expence so that one gains a great deal in comfort and brilliancy and the servants are clear of all this endless trouble of cleaning argand burners.[21]

Scott extolled the virtues of the new system: 'a gallon of the basest train-oil, which is used for preference makes a hundred feet of gas . . . in our new mansion we should have been ruined with spermaceti oil and wax-candles, yet had one-tenth part of the light . . . I never saw an invention more completely satisfactory in the results.'[22]

Lockhart described the effect of the new lighting system:

> The effect the new apparatus in the dining-room at Abbotsford was at first superb. In sitting down to table, in Autumn, no one observed that in each of three chandeliers (one of them of very great dimensions) there lurked a little tiny bead of red light. Dinner passed off, and the sun went down, and suddenly, at the turning of a screw, the room was filled with a gush of splendour worthy of the palace of Aladdin; but, as in the case of Aladdin, the old lamp would have been better in the upshot. Jewelry sparkled, but cheeks and lips looked cold and wan in this fierce illumination; and the eye was wearied, and the brow ached, if the sitting was at all protracted. I confess, however, that my chief enmity to the whole affair arises from my conviction that Sir Walter's own health was damaged, in his latter years, in consequence of his habitually working at night under the intense and burning glare of a broad star of gas, which hung, as it were, in the air, immediately over his writing-table.[23]

The gas fitting in Scott's Study to which Lockhart refers still exists (Plate 163).

It seemed curious to Virginia Woolf that Scott the antiquary and historical novelist who lived in a Gothic or 'Old Scotch' house should so easily accept or indeed pioneer the use of so modern an amenity. She discusses this in her essay written in 1940, and entitled 'Sir Walter Scott: Gas at Abbotsford'.[24] But, as Walpole was at pains to explain, Strawberry Hill though mediaeval in style was very modern and convenient as a dwelling. We shall see that Charlecote Park despite its Elizabethan character had hot air central heating installed at much the same time as Abbotsford. Also the two examples of country houses mentioned by Mark Girouard as having early gas lighting systems were both in the Gothic style: Tortworth by S.S. Teulon and Abney partly by Pugin.[25]

Indeed Pugin, the leading protagonist of the application of mediaeval 'True Principles', shared with Butterfield, Street and G.G. Scott an enthusiasm for the use of gas light in all Gothic Revival buildings including churches. Certainly Scott and most of the creators of the Romantic Interiors with whom I deal had no desire to live in a mediaeval or even old-fashioned way in their houses any more than their contemporaries who lives in neo-classical houses wished to emulate the domestic arrangements of the ancient Greeks or Romans.

152. The Drawing Room at Abbotsford in 1878

Scott wrote in January 1828 of Abbotsford: 'It is a kind of Conundrum Castle to be sure and I have great pleasure in it, for while it pleases a fantastic person in the stile and manner of its architecture and decoration it has all the comforts of a commodious habitation.'[26] The descriptions by visitors often stress the comfort of Abbotsford and, with respect to gas, these constitute some of the earliest descriptions of its effect upon domestic life. The artist William Bewick wrote of a visit: 'The brilliant gaslight, the elegance and taste displayed throughout the beautiful apartment [Drawing Room] the beautiful costume of the ladies, with the sparkle and glitter of the tea-table . . . a sense of luxury of a home and fireside . . . Then attending me to my room, and turning up the gaslight, he [Scott] said "You see, here is the gas lighted ready for you; you can keep it burning all night by turning it down thus to the size of a pin's head; and if you wish for a light during the night turn it up again".'[27]

Meanwhile work on the Drawing Room (Plate 152) was under way and Scott wrote to Terry on 10 November 1822:

Hawl the second is twenty-four pieces of the most splendid Chinese paper, twelve feet high by four feet wide, a present from my cousin Hugh Scott [who worked for the East India Company], enough to finish the drawing room and two bed-rooms . . . The mirror should, I presume, be placed over the drawing-room chimney-piece; and opposite to it I mean to put an antique table of mosaic marbles, to support Chantrey's bust. A good sofa would be desirable, and so would a tapestry-screen, if really fresh and beautiful; but as much of our furniture will be a little antiquated, one would not run too much into that taste in so small an apartment.[28]

Terry replied on 8 March 1823: 'I think you still may have the drawing room to inhabit by the Summer, if you wish it and will still keep my eye watch for a reliable and striking mirror. Your chimney pieces for this and the library are in hand with the grates and all appurtances . . . In the drawing room some fancy must be indulged and the taste of lady Scott consulted.'[29] This is one of the few examples of any reference to Lady Scott's wishes.

183

153. An Indo-Portuguese ebony chair, c.1800

A year later Scott was still without his mirror. He wrote to Terry in a slightly exasperated way on 13 March 1824: 'We are now arrived here, and in great bustle with painters, which obliges me to press you about the mirrors. If we cannot have them soon, there is now an excellent assortment at Trotters ... I will hardly again endure to have the house turned upside down by upholsterers and wish the whole business ended, and the house rid of that sort of cattle once for all.'[30] Trotters were the best-known Edinburgh firm of upholsterers, where it may even have been Lady Scott who saw the mirrors, the Drawing Room being the only room in which she had a say over the furnishings.

The amount of time Scott spent in the consideration of each and every detail was immense. On 18 February 1824 he wrote to Terry concerning several aspects of the Drawing Room:

> On the side of the window I intend to have exactly beneath the glass a plain white side-table of the purest marble, on which to place Chantrey's bust ... these memoranda will enable Baldock to say at what price those points can be handsomely accomplished ... I am much obliged to Mr Baldock for his confidence about the screen ... The stuff for the windows in the drawing-room is of the crimson damask silk we bought last year. I enclose a scrap of it that the fringe may be made to match ... I refer to Mr Atkinson about the fringe, but I think a little mixture of gold would look handsome with the crimson.[31]

Edward Holmes Baldock of Rathbone Place, London, has been dealt with fully elsewhere.[32] The mention of Sir Francis Chantrey relates to the famous bust of Scott which he sculpted and which now stands at the end of the Library. Scott presumably knew that Chantrey intended to give him a duplicate of the bust and had decided to place it in the Drawing Room. The offer was finalized in 1825, for Scott wrote on 16 May 1825: 'Chantrey the great Sculptor was with me a day before I left Abbotsford ... He has made Lady Scott a present of the fine bust he cut of my poor noddle three years ago ... It is reckond (the subject out of the question) a fine piece of Sculpture in point of execution.'[33]

The bust took over three years to arrive, Scott wrote to Allan Cunningham, his friend and a pupil of Chantrey, on 28 June 1828: 'I must not fail to acknowledge the safe arrival of the valued treasure you so kindly forwarded ... There is a great dispute about the place to be selected however we have chosen a good one pro tempore ... There is only one capital place in the House & that is at the further end of the library. But it is already occupied by a cast of Shakespeare's tomb and bust from Stratford upon Avon and I cannot think of dispossessing them for a successor so unworthy.'[34] After Scott's death his son replaced the Shakespeare bust with the Chantrey bust; the Shakespeare bust and its Bullock pedestal were moved to the Drawing Room.

Despite Scott's protestations about not having the furniture in this room 'too antiquated', he managed to fit in several ancient pieces. He wrote of this room:

> The apartments of this house designed for the reception of friends are, like the fortunes of the possessor, formed upon a limited scale ... when this apartment is inadequate to the accommodation of our fair friends, especially if dancing or a musical party be in contemplation, we have only to open the door between the drawing room and the library in order to obtain all the space necessary for the purpose, at least in a poor man's house. The furniture of the drawing room consists of curious antique ebony chairs, an antique cabinet said to have been part of the furniture which found its way out of the Palace of Falkirk, and verifying by its appearance its alleged antiquity.[35]

The cabinet was still in the room in 1878 (Plate 152). It has always been said to have belonged to the Marquis of Montrose and to have been left behind by him after his defeat at the battle of Philiphaugh. It is in fact a Flemish cabinet of the late seventeenth century with an early nineteenth-century base and is now in the Armoury.

The ebony chairs (Plate 153) are still in the Drawing Room, but do not appear in Plate 152. The cabinet may be that which Scott described to Terry on 21 February 1817: 'I have in my offer and think I shall buy it: an ebony cabinet six feet wide.'[36] The chairs are probably those referred to by Terry in his letter to Scott dated 3 February 1823:

> I have in my eye 12 light and beautiful chairs with two armchairs to match fit for any drawing room in the kingdom made of *solid* ebony richly polished and fitted up with new cushions of crimson damask china silk of your own pattern light and elegant in appearance as you will see by the sketch I enclose but weighty strong and servicable as if of iron the price in Mr Atkinson's opinion nothing for such articles is certainly higher than you would pay for common cane chairs and commonplace mahogany furniture but then Ah me! Sir! would you? could you be content with such inferior sitting accommodation in such a room in such a castle — they are £7.00.0 each the armchairs the *same* and will last as long as the castle walls themselves.[37]

The armchairs are unusual, probably dating from about 1800 and of Dutch or Portuguese East Indian manufacture. These chairs and the ebony cabinet represent part of the furniture mentioned above as being ancient or at least second-hand rather than especially designed for the second phase of Abbotsford.

154. The Library at Abbotsford in 1831 by William Allan (National Galleries of Scotland, Edinburgh)

155. The Roslin Drop

The work on the Library (Plate 154) was also in progress, and Scott described the room as

> a sizable chamber, which more frequently than I could wish is given up to the purposes of ordinary society. But a house such as I was able to build in respect of extent had not space enough to afford a drawing room exclusively for social functions. The library is therefore rather more than 40 feet long by 18 feet broad. It is in appearance a well-proportioned room, but unless varied by some angles it would want relief, or, in the phrase of womankind, would be inexcusibly devoid of a flirting corner. To remedy this defect an octagon is thrown out upon the northern side of the room which corresponding to the uses of the whole apartment, contains two book presses . . . its roof, on a level with that of the hall is sixteen feet high, and the presses rise to a height of 11 feet, having a space of 5 feet accordingly between the top of the shelves and the ceiling. This was a subject of great anxiety to me. A difference of 6 feet in height all round a room 40 feet long would have added greatly to my accomodations. But on the other hand a bulky and somewhat ancient person climbing up a height to pull a book down from a shelf 13 feet high is somewhat too much in the position of a sea boy in the dizzy shroud.[38]

Scott had planned a new Library from as early as 1818 and had obviously discussed the matter with Atkinson, for the latter wrote to Scott on 7 March 1818: 'there is a great objection to placing the door from the armoury opposite the Dining Room Door, as it would be in the new library when built'.[39] During the planning stage of the new Library Blore wrote a singular letter to Scott on 10 August 1821: 'I have paid a visit to Lord Guilford's library with which I am much pleased. As soon as Terry and I can spend an hour or two together we shall employ it in preparing something of the kind gothicized for your consideration.'[40] The appearance of Lord Guilford's library and what it was that recommended it as a model for that at Abbotsford is a puzzle.

Frederick North, 5th Earl of Guilford (1766–1827), was a friend of Scott's, for Scott wrote on 20 July 1824 to his own son, who was visiting Kent: 'If Lord

Guilford had been at home and had known you were in the neighbourhood he would have been civil to you for I know him very well but he is seldom resident in the country.'[41] Any library built for Guilford would almost certainly have been uncompromisingly neo-classical, for he is described thus by J.M. Crook: 'Lord Guilford, a vintage eccentric who dressed Greek and prayed Orthodox and is still remembered in Corfu as the founder of the Ionian Academy and first President of the Philomuse Society'.[42]

He was also a friend of that arch-classicist C.R. Cockerell, but I can find no record of Cockerell or any other architect building a library for him either at his country seat in Kent, Waldershare Park, or at his London house. Blore, however, certainly felt that a gothicized version of some such library would be suitable for Abbotsford. Without knowledge of the original, it is, of course, impossible to say if any of its characteristics were reproduced at Abbotsford.

Scott was also exploring other possibilities for decorating the proposed Library, for he wrote to Archibald Constable on 20 September 1821: 'You have such a genius for finding out all that your friends want that perhaps you may light on some old oak panelling in the course of your researches. I should like much to make a purchase of that kind for fitting up my future library.'[43] This panelling was not forthcoming; the Library was built of new materials without the inclusion of ancient carving.

A year later the Library was under way and Terry in October 1822 wrote to Scott: 'I dined on Sunday with Mr Atkinson and we settled the designs of the ceilings the drawings of which you will have in a few days after which the bookcases may be proceeded with as quickly as possible.'[44] Terry wrote to Scott again on 18 November: 'You will by now have received a large volume of drawings for the library and think that you will now approve of its appearance t'will be a noble room indeed the ceiling I think very handsome and the bookcases are made as spacious now as possible what with the oratory — the bow windows — & with a large table or two which may be made with great elegance & utility to hold books round their sides. I believe you will find more space than you at present require.'[45]

The oratory referred to was to be in the Study (Plates 162 and 163). Scott had received the drawings and wrote to Terry on 10 November 1822:

I got all the plans safe, and they are delightful. The library ceiling will be superb, and we have plenty of ornaments for it, without repeating one of those in the eating-room. The plan of shelves is also excellent, and will, I think for a long time, suffice my collection ... Hawl third is a quantity of what is called Jamaica cedar-wood, enough for fitting up both the drawing-room and the library, including the presses, shelves, &c: the wood is finely pencilled and most beautiful, something like the colour of gingerbread; it costs very little more than oak, works much easier, and is never touched by vermin.[46]

As the work progressed Scott in consultation with his friends constantly modified the details of the room, writing to Terry on 9 January 1823: 'I give up the Roslin drop in the oratory — indeed I have long seen it would not do. I think the termination of it may be employed as the central part of Mr Atkinson's beautiful plan for a recess in the library, by the by, the whole of that ceiling, with the heads we have got, will be the prettiest thing ever seen in these parts.'[47]

The 'Roslin Drop' (Plate 155) is taken directly from Roslin Chapel, which along with Melrose Abbey provided most of the interior details at Abbotsford. Blore had drawn the interior of Roslin and his drawing was engraved on 1 August 1821 and published in Scott's *Provincial Antiquities* as plate 206. This shows the 'drop' *in situ*. Scott was a lifelong admirer of the singular and exotic interior of Roslin and in his epic poem *The Lay of the Last Minstrel* of 1805 he devoted nine stanzas to the chapel.[48] In his notes to the poem written in 1831 he spoke of 'the chapel, which is in the most rich and florid style of Gothic architecture. Among the profuse carving on the pillars and buttresses, the rose is frequently introduced, in allusion to the name.'[49]

Later in January 1823 when Scott was concerning himself with the Libary curtains, he wrote to Terry on the 9th: 'in the library we shall have a superfine crimson cloth from Galashiels, made out of mine own wool . . . I wish these curtains to be made up on a simple useful pattern, without that paltry trash of drapery, &c &c. I would take the armoury curtains for my pattern, and set my own tailor, Robin Goodfellow, to make them up.'[50] The curtains did not progress quickly, for a year later Scott wrote to Terry, on 18 February 1824: 'I think the curtains for the library, considering the purpose of the room, require no fringe at all . . . As for the library, a yellow fringe, if any.'[51] The curtains were not made by Goodfellow, who died in sad circumstances in 1824;[52] they were in fact made by Messrs Potts and Collinson of London.[53]

The exact form of the curtains cannot now be established, as they no longer exist, though Plate 154 shows them reasonably clearly. The ever resourceful and inventive Atkinson was able to help with the curtain trimmings, as Terry wrote to Scott on 3 February 1823: 'I have begged Mr Atkinson to send you a specimen of some of his invention made of *packthread* gilt in oil gold which washes with soap and water & a brush when grown dull to its first brightness and comes *very* reasonable & looks remarkably bold and handsome.'[54]

Once the curtains had been dealt with the question of an appropriate carpet was considered, Terry wrote to Scott on 8 March 1823: 'I should think for the library a large and first rate Turkey carpet would be far the most preferable it would cost if properly set about very little more than our own first rate carpets and will wear for five and twenty years and still be excellent in texture if this can speak for appearance.'[55] The carpet in the Library had gone by 1878, as a photograph taken in that year shows.

The chimney-pieces in the first phase of the house differ from those in the second, the former being made from Mona marble provided by Bullock; the latter, from conventional Italian marble. Terry wrote to Scott on the subject of marble in March 1823:

> Your chimney pieces for this [Drawing Room] and the library are in hand with the grates . . . and rare specimen of Italian breschia marble of singular warm and harmonious brown red and at a price of common marble, it had been in the proprietors marble yard a long time and got there through some accidental purchase beneath its value of which the buyer and the seller were equally ignorant. Mr Atkinson thinks highly of it we must not indeed expect to find marble marked so cheap as our poor friend Bullock's who sold his marble at no profit to you but Mr Atkinson is most cautious to plan & estimate to the most economical scale & to select the most reasonable artificer.[56]

The library chimney-piece as executed could well be made from the Breschia marble mentioned here; it is still *in situ*. The work progressed slowly but surely throughout 1823 and Scott could report to Terry on 5 February 1824: 'our Christmas gambols came off gaily, and how they danced in the new library till moonlight and starlight and gaslight went out'[57] On the 21 February Hay and his men started to decorate the Library:

> The whole of this ceiling, with its pendants, was painted in imitation of the cedar — of which the fittings were made, but the wall between the top of the book-cases and ceiling gave Sir Walter a great deal of concern. This formed a narrow stripe all round the apartment, and it could not be done in any of the usual modes of wall decoration, as the book-cases were actually part of the fittings of the room, and had not the slightest appearance of being placed against the wall like pieces of furniture. At last the idea of a piece of painted imitation drapery

hanging from the cornice was suggested to him, and he at once adopted it. It was painted of a sombre hue of green, in order to relieve the red hue of the cedar, which it effectually did; and that it might also partake of the richness of the backs of the books with which the cases underneath it were filled, it was embellished with devices in gold colour. Sir Walter often said that this was the only part of the decorative painting that he could not come to a decison upon in his own mind, but when he saw it finished he expressed himself highly gratified.[58]

The painted lambrequins to which Hay refers survive intact and can be seen clearly in Plate 156. Such *trompe-l'oeil* painted decoration would have deeply offended Ruskin and Pugin with its intent to deceive. Interestingly, though, there are many mediaeval precedents for painted representations of fabrics draped and hung on walls; however, to what extent Hay and Scott knew these is uncertain.

The carpenters must still have had work to do after Hay's painters had finished, for Scott wrote to Cadell on 16 April 1824: 'I wanted him to come and help me to

189

arrange my books but I cannot get the carpenters out of the Library.'[59] The work must have been completed shortly after this, for Scott wrote to Miss Clephane on 12 May 'I had the horrible labour of arranging all my books in a new bookroom yet it was still a kind of labour of love.'[60]

Now we turn to the furnishings of the room. Here even more than with the Drawing Room Scott acquired ancient pieces of furniture especially for the room. The most prominent position was occupied by the Shakespeare bust and its splendid pedestal (Plate 143) in the niche especially designed for it (Plate 154).

A considerable number of contemporary descriptions of Abbotsford exist, and though most include very similar descriptions of the major antiquities and interiors, close collation of one with the other often yields information unique to one account. Most accounts include a description of the Shakespeare bust, but only one describes how 'After dinner Sir W took us into a splendid library, well filled and handsomely furnished. At the top of the room in a niche was a cast from the celebrated bust with lines on his tombstone beneath "Stranger, respect these stones, and curst be he that meddles with my bones" which sir W repeated with that peculiar beauty and pathos which made his recitation of poetry one of the most thrilling things of the kind I ever listened to'.[61] These lines do actually occur on Shakespeare's tomb, but, as Plate 143 shows, they do not appear on the pedestal itself. Was there a plaque or label attached to the pedestal? It so it does not survive.

As previously mentioned, Scott's son replaced the bust and pedestal with the Chantrey bust of Scott after Scott's death. Did his son also make a more subtle allusion to his father's death? It has not been noticed before that the crossed thyrsii, which on the design (Plate 142) point upwards as one would expect, now (Plate 143) point downwards. Is this merely a mistake made when at some time they were taken off for cleaning or were they reversed in the way that classical torches are often reversed to denote death?

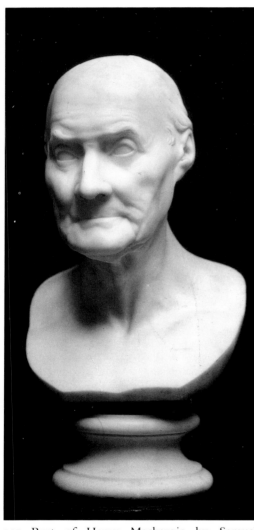

157. Bust of Henry Mackenzie by Samuel Joseph, 1822 (National Galleries of Scotland, Edinburgh)

A close reading of the contemporary accounts also yields details of another interesting piece of sculpture that was in the Library at one stage. In October 1825 'At the other end [from the Shakespeare bust] of the library was a bust of Henry Mackenzie, the author of "The Man of Feeling" one of the chief writers in the Lounger and Mirror. The bust looked a strong likeness of an intellectual looking *very* old who was then alive and who Sir W said was the living link between the literature of the last and present generation.'[62]

This is the only reference to the presence of the bust in the Library; at a later date it was in the Breakfast Parlour, previously the Study: 'the breakfast parlour, in which by the way stood the bust of Mackenzie'.[63] This latter location is confirmed by a description of 1829: 'breakfast room ... there is a bust of Henry Mackenzie, by Joseph of Edinburgh ... the library ... the only bust is that of Shakespeare'.[64]

Several points emerge: Henry Mackenzie (1745–1831), the author of the novel *The Man of Feeling*, was a friend of Scott's; Scott wrote an essay about him in 1822.[65] The bust is not now at Abbotsford and curiously there is no mention of it in Lockhart or in Scott's letters, so when he acquired it and when it left Abbotsford are unknown. Samuel Joseph (1791–1850) was a celebrated sculptor who in 1826 helped to found the Royal Scottish Academy and who in 1825 sculpted what in many people's opinion is the best bust of Scott.

Only one bust of Mackenzie by Joseph is known (Plate 157) and is dated 1822. It was given to the Scottish National Portrait Gallery on its foundation in 1882, but the earlier history of the bust is unknown. I would suggest that it is likely to be the Abbotsford bust; Joseph rarely carved duplicates.

Scott purchased for the Library in 1823 one of his most spectacular pieces of furniture (Plate 158). Terry wrote to him in early January that he had found 'One of the most solid and superb ebony escritoires I ever saw or think ever was in London it is entirely plain I mean from gilded ornaments Sir but exquisitely carved in panels & mouldings extensive roomy in ever possible division ... I think from my re-

158. The ebony roll-top desk

memberence far exceeding yours at Castle Street in extent and convenience & would certainly complement most nobly your new Library the price is a 100 guineas.'[66] Scott wrote immediately to Terry:

> I am completely Lady Wishfort as to the escritoire. In fact, my determination would very much depend on the possibility of showing it to advantage; for if it be such as it set up against a wall, like what is called, *par excellence*, a writing-desk, you know we have no space in the library that is not occupied by book-presses — If, on the contrary, it stands quite free — why, I do not know — I must e'en leave it to you to decide between taste and prudence ... Perhaps the slightest sketch of the escritoire might enable me to decide. If I could swop my own, which cost me £30, it might diminish my prudential scruples.[67]

Scott is here referring to his Gillow desk, which was not worth secondhand anything like the £30 he paid for it, and though Terry was to offer to dispose of it Scott in fact kept it and it is now at Abbotsford. Terry wrote to Scott in February 1823:

> I have decided to receive the escritoire it is so splendid & complete a specimen of ebony furniture that altogether it is a somewhat of a highish price I should have always regretted its loss & if you had seen it I am sure so would you ... The back of it however did not satisfy me as equal to the rest & as it is to stand in centre of the room I have searched about among the hidden stores of such curious art and selected with great good luck some more rich and corresp specimens of ebony carving of form and designs so exactly corresponding to the rest that they will look as if restored to their original place this will add a little to the cost & take

191

about a fortnight or three weeks to complete ... As to your old one [desk] in Castle Street, if you wish me to get rid of it and will let it be packed and sent to me.[68]

The alterations were completed quickly, for Terry wrote on 8 March: 'your escritoire and seven ebony chairs to match sailed on Thursday ... in unpacking the escritoire first unscrew the board TOP & then the sides & wheel it out into the room at once as it stands when the circular part of the escritoire is thrown up the writing board covered with leather draws out ... the linen cover will keep it nicely whenever you leave Abbotsford.[69]

The desk was not an ancient one. It could just possibly date from the late eighteenth century, but it is more likely to have been constructed from old pieces of carved ebony shortly before Scott purchased it. It was certainly altered for Scott, as we saw above.

The probable source of the piece was Baldock's shop in Rathbone Place, as Terry's letter of 3 February ended: 'I shall send Baldock's receipt properly stamped.'[70] Baldock was supplying objects for the Drawing Room and, as we saw in Chapter 5, Baldock supplied ebony objects to Fonthill Abbey. He was noted for the ebony furniture he sold, and much of this was constructed or altered in his workshop. This also emerges from his activities in connection with the Royal Collection.[71]

It would seem that the desk did not immediately go into the Library. The celebrated comedian C.J. Mathews (1803–1878) went to stay at Abbotsford with his father the actor and friend of Scott, Byron and Terry. Mathews was at this time

159. The consulting desk

training to be an architect under A.C. Pugin and wrote on 20 January 1826 that Scott took him from the Library into the Study next door: 'He took me into it being an architect, to show me his comforts, and there I saw a mysterious sable ebony bureau! doubtless containing the steam-engine, loom, water wheels, or whatever machinery it may be with which he manufactures the patent novels.'[72] It seems likely that, until Scott moved out of Castle Street on 15 March 1826[73] and moved the Gillow desk to Abbotsford for use in the Study, the ebony desk saw service in the Study. It was certainly in the Library at the time of his death, not free-standing but against the bookcases (Plate 154); it is now in the Drawing Room.

There were two other desks in the Library. One was what Scott referred to as his 'consulting desk' (Plate 159). He wrote to Archibald Constable on 15 May 1823: 'I wanted too something of a consulting desk. But none of these things are in any hurry and will serve to amuse you in your walks.'[74] He also wrote to Terry on 18 June 1823 'Has an old-fashioned consulting desk ever met your eye in your rambles? I mean one of those which have four faces, each forming an inclined plane, like a writing desk, and made to turn round as well as to rise, and be depressed by a strong iron screw in the centre ... choicely convenient, as you can keep three or four books, folios if you like open for reference. If you have not seen one, I can get one made to a model in the Advocates' Library.'[75]

Terry wrote back: 'I poke about as constantly as I may for materials for a discerningly handsome & antique consulting desk and have been consulting with Mr Bridgens.'[76] There seem to be no more references to this desk, but the four monopodia and the carved boss out of which the desk was eventually constructed very probably came from London, though whether via Terry or Constable and whether Bridgens provided a design are unknown. The whole was, however, constructed and the new top made: 'Joseph Shillinglaw, a joiner at Darnick was a clever carver in wood ... it was he who made Sir Walter's revolving desk.'[77] Shillinglaw also made the large Gothic library desk (Plate 154), though the designer is unknown. Lockhart wrote: 'The great table in the library, for example (a most complex and beautiful one) was done entirely in the room where it now stands, by Joseph Shillinglaw.'[78]

160. The Venetian carved armchair

The other important pieces of furniture in the Library are the two elaborately carved chairs (Plates 154 and 160), discovered by Archibald Constable. Constable wrote to Scott on 31 May 1822: 'I went yesterday to the shop of a curious person — Mr Swaby of Wardour Street — to look at an old portrait ... I found at the same place two large elbow-chairs, elaborately carved, in boxwood — with figures, foliage etc, perfectly entire. Mr Swaby, from whom I bought them, assures me they came from Rome. There were originally ten of them. He had just sold six to the Duke of Rutland for Belvoir Castle, where they will be appropriate furniture. The two which I have purchased would I think, not be less so in the Library at Abbotsford.'[79]

Constable gave the chairs, the portrait — which was of James IV of Scotland — and a mosaic slab all purchased from Swaby to Scott as a present. Constable, who was at this time Scott's publisher, had reported earlier in the above letter that 7,000 copies of *The Fortunes of Nigel* had been sold by 10.30 a.m. on the first day of publication, so he could afford to be generous!

The mosaic slab I will deal with later. Constable wrote on 11 July 1822: 'the chairs from the Borghese Palace ... There were ten chairs in all brought to England by the Abbé Alotti, as Mr Swaby informs me. He sold six of them to the Duke of Rutland for Belvoir Castle. Two of them went to Newstead, and the others are here accounted for.'[80] Swaby's letter to Constable and the shipper's receipt survive. Swaby wrote on 6 July 1822: 'Sir I have this morning sent off the chairs mosaic slab & portrait to Sir W Scott.'[81] The shipper's receipt shows that, like most Scott's antiquities and furniture purchased in London, these objects went by sea: 'Leith & Berwick Wharf, opposite Burr Street, Lower, East Smithfield ... Received to be shipped on board the Old Shipping Company's Smack Queen Charlotte, Geo Crabb master for Leith'.

The chairs are still at Belvoir, but the pair that Byron bought for Newstead are no longer there. The details Swaby gave to Constable are fascinating — the Abbé Alotti was in fact the Abbé Celotti who was involved with Baldock in the importation of the Borghese Table for Fonthill Abbey. On the flyleaf of a copy of the Fonthill sale catalogue in the library at Charlecote is a note by Celotti which relates to the table, but which also states that he had told Baldock he had also imported 'Brustalon chairs'. It seems likely, therefore, that the Swaby chairs were those imported by Celotti along with the table. The Abbotsford chairs are of very high quality and manifestly in the style of Brustalon. They are fine enough to have come from his workshop, though without documentation one can go no further.[82]

This completes the description of the Library furniture and furnishings, but mention must be made of the important collection of books which the room was created to house. It is also convenient to deal here with the books to be found in the Study and elsewhere. Scott's books are still on the Library shelves at Abbotsford and are of crucial importance for the study of any and every aspect of his life and work. These books were collected in the main not as rarities — though some were indeed rare — but to form a working scholarly library. It is difficult for scholars today to understand the problems of their early nineteenth-century predecessors working away from London, Oxford or Cambridge. Edinburgh was indeed better served by libraries than many English cities. But generally speaking Scott like other scholars had to collect the books himself; thus all his interests, preoccupations and sources are demonstrated by the books on the shelves in his Library.

Scott, as his own footnotes amply demonstrate, needed sources for many of the descriptions and historical facts in his novels, but for his non-fiction works like the nine volume *Life of Napoleon* published in 1827 reference books were even more crucial. He made great use of periodicals and ephemeral pamphlets as well as books. In his Study in 1826 'on the table and about the floor lay several volumes of the *Moniteur* and other French *Journeaux* and pamphlets with which he is assisting himself in his 'Life of Bonaparte'.[83] Scott spoke of 'the working room and study in

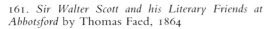

161. *Sir Walter Scott and his Literary Friends at Abbotsford* by Thomas Faed, 1864

162. The Study in 1832 by William Allan
(National Galleries of Scotland, Edinburgh)

addition to my library where I keep around me the dictionaries and books of reference which my immediate needs may require me to consult'.[84]

Scott was justifiably proud of the comprehensive nature of his collection of books: 'In branches of information I would only say that my collection of historical works relating to England and Scotland in particular, is extensive and valuable, as indeed the reprints of the London booksellers.'[85] Fortunately soon after his death a complete catalogue of the library was published, the compiler stating: 'The collection not being formed upon a general plan, embracing all departments of human knowledge, but mainly confined to the two great heads of History and Belles-Lettres'.[86] This catalogue, as well as listing the 20,000 or so books in great detail, also gives the location of the book presses throughout the house. We learn, for instance, that the Breakfast Parlour contained appropriately the 'Novels and Light Literature'. There is not space here to discuss the books in the collection that relate to Scott's collection of antiquities and from which he gleaned the knowledge about these objects. These books appear in the catalogue along with the *belles-lettres*.

The Library was to be the setting for the painting by Faed of *Sir Walter Scott and*

his Literary Friends at Abbotsford (Plate 161). Sadly this imagined galaxy of literary talent, which included Crabbe, Hogg and Wordsworth, had never attended Abbotsford all at the same time. The engraving of the picture was published in both London and New York, and in America it inspired the painting *Washington Irving and his Friends at Sunnyside* by Christian Schussele.[87] Sunnyside was Irving's house in Tarrytown near New York City. Both Fennimore Cooper and Irving, who knew Scott, are depicted in the painting along with others including Poe, Longfellow and Hawthorne.

Scott described the Study (Plates 162 and 163) as

a private apartment 16 feet high, like the others, 20 feet long by about 14 broad ... a small gallery filled up with oaken shelves running round three sides of the study and resting upon small projecting beams of oak. The gallery and its contents are accessible by a small stair about three feet in breadth which gains room to ascend in the southward angle of the chamber, and runs in front of the books, leaving such a narrow passage as is sometimes found in front of balustrades in old convents ... a small door encloses a staircase which leads about seven paces higher and by another private entrance reaches the bedroom story of the house, and lands in the proprietors dressing room. The inhabitant of the Study, therefore if unwilling to be surprised by visitors, may make his retreat unobserved by means of this gallery to the private staircase.[88]

All the visitors' accounts stress the utilitarian character of this room: 'I was in the *Sanctum Sanctorum* of the all creating author of *Waverley*. The room was plainly furnished, with a table and a couple of chairs, and bookshelves all round, full of books *in use*, not in ornamental bindings like those in the large library.'[89] Scott was proud of his secret staircase; he 'had in his mind a favourite cabinet of Napoleon's at the *Elysee Bourbon* where there are a gallery and concealed staircase'[90] The idea as originally suggested by Scott was that 'This staircase might be made to hang on the door and pull out when it is opened, which is the way abroad with an *escalier derobé*'.[91] The Napoleonic staircase was apparently of this latter type.

As can be seen from the plan (Plate 136), an oratory was proposed, but the octagonal space was not eventually fitted out in the quasi-religious way Scott suggested. He had written to Terry on 10 November 1822: 'Mr Atkinson has missed a little my idea of the oratory, fitting it up entirely as a bookcase, whereas I should like to have had recesses for curiosities, — for the Bruce's skull — for a crucifix, &c, &c; in short a little cabinet instead of a book-closet.'[92] The skull was housed instead in the Hall. The whole gallery idea seems to have been Scott's own, conceived partly to house his growing book collection. He wrote to Terry on 9 January 1823: 'I have at present some doubt namely, the capacity of my library to accommodate my books. Should it appear limited (I mean making allowances for future additions) I can perhaps, by Mr Atkinson's assistance, fit up this private room with a gallery.'[93] On 18 June he again wrote to Terry: 'I enclose you a plan of my own for a gallery round my own room, which is to combine that advantage with a private staircase.'[94]

There were several pieces of furniture in the room. The Gillow desk, dealt with above, was from 1826, and the desk chair (Plates 162 and 163) could date stylistically from any time after 1816 or 1817. The chair is a comfortable utilitarian object of no particular aesthetic interest and, though similar chairs were made by Bullock, Trotters of Edinburgh made them also. The large court cupboard (seen against the lower back wall in Plate 162) probably dates from the 1660s. It now has four bays, the two right-hand ones with solid doors being ancient; the other half with its latticed doors was made to match at some point between its acquisition in 1823 and Scott's death.

Scott acquired the ancient part late in May or in June 1823 from his friend Thomas Shortreed of Jedburgh. Scott wrote to Shortreed: 'Dear Tom, I send the cart as agreed, for the buckshead and the wardrobe [cupboard] ... I send my carpenter for

163. The Study at Abbotsford in 1989 (Country Life)

164. The Armada Chair by Edward Blore (British Library)

165. The Robroyston Chair

fear either of these valued and curious articles shall receive injury.'[95] A note in the margin of the letter states: 'The wardrobe is the old oak one which stood behind Sir Walter's chair in his study.'[96] It would seem likely that the cupboard was extended in width soon after it was purchased.

The other cabinet in Plate 162 does not appear to be mentioned in the letters, but would seem to date from the mid-eighteenth century and is of no great interest. This may have been a piece of family furniture. The bust which stands upon it is not the Chantrey of Scott or the Joseph of Mackenzie temporarily misplaced from its usual position, both these being mounted on a socle. The bust here quite clearly has cut off sides, it was probably the plaster cast of Chantrey's bust of Wordsworth which, though in the Hall in the 1870s (Plate 168), was not there in the 1830s (Plate 167).

The last items of furniture that were in the Study in Scott's day are two chairs. One was drawn by Blore, who inscribed his drawing 'Chair at Sir W. Scott's — Chair at Abbotsford supposed to have been saved from the wreck of the Armada' (Plate 164). This is probably the chair Scott referred to while on his voyage to the Shetland Islands, for he wrote from Fair Isle on 10 August 1814: 'In this place, and perhaps in the very cottage now inhabited by Mr Strong, the Duke of Medina Sidonia, Commander-in-Chief of the Invincible Armada, wintered, after loosing his vessel ... Mr Strong gave me a curious old chair belonging to Quendale, a former proprietor of the Fair Isle, and which a more zealous antiquary would have dubbed "the Duke's chair" I will have it refitted for Abbotsford however.'[97] The chair is a perfectly standard English or Scottish chair of the 1660s and cannot possibly date from the 1580s. Scott himself was sceptical of the legend. There is a very similar chair in the Victoria & Albert Museum which came from Holyrood Palace, so Scott's chair is more likely to be Scottish.

The other chair in the Study (Plate 165) is of great interest. Lockhart records the following legend on the brass plate on the back of the chair: 'This chair made of the only remaining wood of the House of Robroyston in which the matchless Sir William Wallace "was done to death by felon hand for guarding well his father's land", Is most respectfully presented to Sir Walter Scott as a small token of gratitude by his devoted servant Joseph Train.'[98] Train (1779–1852) was an exciseman and a poet who frequently provided Scott with tales and legends for use in his novels and also provided important antiquities for Abbotsford. Sir William Wallace the Scottish patriot had been executed by the English in 1305. Train wrote of the chair:

As the ruin [at Robroyston] was about being taken down to make way for the ploughshare, I easily succeeded in purchasing these old stumps [the ends of rafters] from the farmer ... these pieces of wood were seemingly so much decayed as to be fit only for fuel; but after planing off an inch from the surface, I found that the remainder as hard as a bone, and susceptible of a fine polish ... It was modelled from an old chair in the Palace of Hamilton, and is nearly covered with carved work, representing rocks, heather, and thistles, emblematic of Scotland, and indented with brass, representing the *Harp of the North*, surrounded with laurels, and supported by targets, claymores, Lochaber axes, war horns, etc.[99]

It is a tribute to Scott's popularity that there were scenes of great rejoicing during the transport of this remarkable relic. Train wrote: 'many persons in Kirkintilloch yet remember how triumphantly the symbolic chair was borne from my lodgings to the bank of the Great Canal, to be there shipped for Abbotsford, in the midst the town-band playing "Scots wha hae wi' Wallace bled", and surrounded by thousands'.[100] Scott was predictably delighted and wrote to Train on 26 May 1822: 'I found the curious chair which your kindness destined for me safe here on my return from Abbotsford. It is *quite* invaluable to me who am filling up an addition to my house in the country with things of that antique nature.'[101]

In 'Gabions' Scott devotes three pages to a description of the Hall and the 1888 catalogue devotes fourteen of its forty-five pages to enumerating 108 of the choicest pieces of armour and arms there displayed.[102] The densely packed walls of the Hall are clearly shown in Plates 166 through 168 and 171. One important drawing, which brilliantly captures the character of the Hall (Plate 166), was that made by Turner when he came to stay with Scott at Abbotsford in 1831.[103] He filled his 'Abbotsford Sketchbook' with views of Abbotsford (Plate 133) and the surrounding countryside. After Scott's death he came back to Scotland and did drawings for Lockhart's *Memoirs* (Plate 130).

Scott's own description of the Hall must be quoted, for, although the descriptions of visitors almost all describe the Hall, Scott's is obviously of prime importance and was also written late in his life when the Hall was complete.

166. The Entrance Hall at Abbotsford, drawn by J.M.W. Turner in 1831 (Tate Gallery, London)

The walls from the floor to the height of eight feet are panelled with black oak which was once the panelling of the pews belonging to the church of Dunfermline . . . In this panelling are inserted many pieces of carved oak of the same work. The west side of the hall is furnished with long windows, which are filled with

167. The Entrance Hall *c*.1830

THE ENTRANCE HALL, ABBOTSFORD. 1544. IV.

168. The Entrance Hall at Abbotsford in 1878 by J. Valentine

painted glass representing the arms of different families of the name Scott . . . The ceiling of the hall is about 16 feet high, is vaulted and ribbed, and decorated with a line of escutcheons going round both sides of the hall, with the following inscription in black letter 'These be the Coat Armouries of ye Clannis and men of name keepit the Scottish marches in ye days of auld. They were worthie in their tyme, and in their defens, God thaim defended'. The name of each one is above the proper escutcheon . . . a large range of schields running east and west along the top of this hall, understood to be the various escutcheons belonging to the proprietor . . . on the right side of the hall . . . two species of presses or cupboards . . . are of the pulpit and precentors desk of Mr Ebenezer Erskine . . . the purpose of keeping a few bottles of wine cool in hot weather, when we sometimes for the sake of taking our family meal *al fresco*, make use of the hall instead of our dining room . . . the carved panelling is terminated by a sort of festoon extends a space of about four feet high, not panelled with Dunfermline wood, but with strong fir painted the colour of oak. This is easily penetrated with nails or hooks of iron, and the space is reserved for the occupation of such gabions as their size and character recommend to this situation. They are generally arms both Gothic and modern, offensive and defensive, together with the spoils of wild animals [Plate 169], mineralogical specimens and other articles . . . The massive chimney piece of this hall with the works of the chisel does great honor to the execution of the artist from Darnick who modelled them in freestone from what is called the Abbots seat in the cloister of Melrose.[104]

Hay carried out all the painted decoration, both here and in the Armoury. 'Before hanging up the armour, or placing the full suits of mail in the niches, Sir Walter was most anxious to have all the steel and iron secured from rusting . . . This I accomplished by having all the coats of mail and warlike instruments cleaned with rotten-stone and water, and, when perfectly dry, placing them before a good fire, and giving them a thin coat of the clearest copal varnish. I saw them fifteen years thereafter without the slightest mark of rust upon them and I believe they remain so till this day [1847].'[105]

It is impossible to deal here with the whole collection displayed in the Hall, and I will thus be selective while giving a picture of the character of the Hall, the most complex and exciting room at Abbotsford. There are only two large pieces of furniture in the Hall, a table and a chest (Plates 168 and 170). The table was constructed from the mosaic slab which, as mentioned earlier, had been purchased from Swaby by Constable at the same time as the 'Brustalon' chairs. The plain oak Gothic base was possibly designed by Atkinson.

The chest (Plate 170) is an Italian late sixteenth-century cypress wood chest on early nineteenth-century feet. I have been unable to discover when Scott purchased it, but it is reputedly the chest in which Ginevra was entombed, as related in the story of 'The Mistletoe Bough'. The story is retold in the poem 'Ginevra' by Scott's friend Samuel Rogers, which appeared in the collection of poems entitled *Italy* published in 1830.

The collection of arms and armour is of great interest and importance in its own right, and, though one excellent and scholarly article has been written about it,[106] it has never been fully studied. The collection falls into two groups: those pieces relating to Scottish historical figures and those pieces with international appeal, whether European or oriental (Plates 172 through 174). The former group, not surprisingly, had pride of place, and several of the historical figures who had once owned them appear in Scott's poems or novels.

Scott, as we have already seen, had begun to acquire weapons as early as 1791 when he displayed his Lochaber axes, etc., in his den in his father's house. As time went on, weapons came from more exotic sources; his friend the poet, polymath, orientalist and autodidact John Leyden (1775–1811)[107] wrote to him from Poolo Penang on 24 November 1805: 'Besides I must tell you of the collection of Indian arms and armour that I have made to illustrate the cottage [Scott's rented cottage]

169. The overdoor at the west end of the Entrance Hall

170. The Ginevra Chest, Italian, *c.*1600

171. The Entrance Hall at Abbotsford in 1989
(Country Life)

with, and which I am greatly distressed how to have sent . . . a polygar spear 18 feet long and a Nair bow eight feet long which might have served Robin Hood himself . . . there are creeses, waved and plain and poisoned, and polygar daggers.'[108]

Leyden's untimely death in 1811 meant that many of these pieces never found their way to Abbotsford, but some did. Scott wrote to the poet Southey on 10 April 1811: 'Poor Jack of Leyden sent me some months ago a precious gage d'amitie in the shape of a poisoned creeze the hilt as brilliant as that of Excabbar.'[109] Scott had several Malayan krises; that with a wavy blade in Plate 148 *may* be that from Leyden. The two weapons 'A Polygar's knife' and 'A Persian Dagger' on the left in Plate 172 could also have come from Leyden.

But such pieces were also easily available on the English market by the mid-eighteenth century. Many were brought back to this country by employees of the

East India Company as souvenirs. Horace Walpole had acquired Indian weapons for Strawberry Hill, and I have already described how Scott purchased a suit of Persian armour on the open market.

One of the interesting features of Scott's collecting is the way in which he realized that history was not just a matter of past events. Most collectors only wish to acquire objects relating to persons or events of the relatively distant past, such objects having become by common consent rare and important. Scott by contrast was aware that important historical events were happening all the time and he wished to illustrate and commemorate these in his collection. He owned objects relating to Scottish battles of the earlier eighteenth century, but in his own time it was the campaigns of Napoleon — of whom Scott was to write a biography — that dominated world history.

Scott in 1813 attempted to acquire a relic of one of the heroic participants in the Napoleonic struggle. Matvei Ivanovich Platov (1757–1818), was hetman of the Don Cossacks who had played such an important part in Napoleon's defeat in Russia.[110] Scott wrote to Miss Clephane on 12 May 1813: 'Platow at the request of a friend is sending me a Cossack pike weilded by one of his prime warriors — So much for gem crackery.'[111] Unfortunately the object was destroyed in another battle before it could reach Scott. He wrote to Lady Abercorn on 6 November: 'An English officer who was known to this renowned partisan begged one of his lances to add to my collection of arms but I believe it was lost when the French re-entered Hamburgh.'[112]

To Scott's delight, though he never acquired the lance, he actually met Platov and Czar Alexander at dinner while in Paris in 1815. He wrote to his wife: 'Old Platoff was presented to me and we said a world of pretty things to each other by signs. Apparently he took me into great friendship for meeting him the other day on horseback he dismounted gave his horse to one of his Cossacks embraced me with great affection.'[113]

Scott's presence in Paris stemmed directly from his fascination with contemporary historical events, for as soon as he heard the news of the victory at Waterloo, with his typical mixture of imagination and journalistic acumen, he persuaded his publisher to fund a visit to the Continent to describe the battlefield. His account was published anonymously in 1816 as *Paul's Letters to his Kinfolk*, but previously he had published in October 1815 his poem *The Field of Waterloo*, the profits of the first edition going to a fund for the widows and orphans of the soldiers killed in the battle.[114] Scott's descriptions of the battlefield and of Paris occupied by allied troops make interesting reading. Not only did Scott meet Platov, but also the Duke of Wellington, who became a firm friend. Scott took the unique opportunity to acquire various relics of the battle, which are still displayed at Abbotsford (Plate 173).

He arrived at Waterloo just too late to pick up relics free from the battlefield and had instead to buy them.

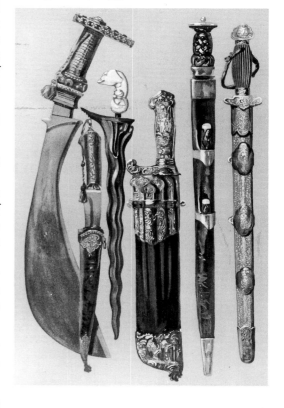

172. Various weapons (M.M. Maxwell Scott, *Abbotsford . . .*, 1893)

> All ghastly remains of the carnage had been either burnt or buried and the reliques of the fray which yet remained were not in themselves of a very imposing kind. Bones of horses, quantities of old hats . . . But the great object of ambition was to possess the armour of a cuirassier . . . The victors had indeed carried off some of these cuirasses to serve as culinary utensils, I myself have seen the Highlanders frying their rations of beef or mutton upon the breast-plates . . . But enough remained to make the fortunes of the people of St John, Waterloo, Planche-noit, &c. When I was at La Belle Alliance I bought the cuirass of a common soldier for about six francs; but a very handsome inlaid one, once the property of a French officer of distinction which was for sale in Brussels, cost me four times the sum.[115]

The weapons from Waterloo from a collector's point of view had a perfectly unassailable provenance, but only collectors such as Scott with the imagination to see the historical implications of these modern objects could benefit.

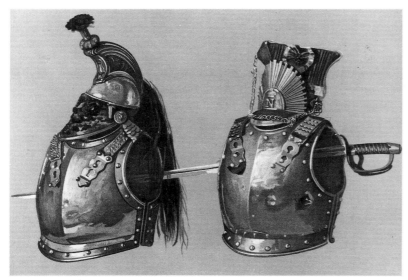
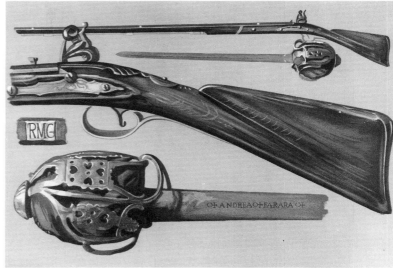

173. Relics from Waterloo (Scott, *Abbotsford*)

174. Rob Roy's gun and sword (Scott, *Abbotsford*)

Scott was later to acquire a more macabre reminder of the battle: on the mantelpiece in the Hall in Scott's day were 'Two models of the skull of Shaw, the famous Lifeguardsman who killed six men at Waterloo'.[116] The importance that Scott and his contemporaries accorded to phrenology has been discussed above, and this explains the presence of the models of Shaw's skull, though how Scott acquired them is a mystery. Scott knew of Shaw, for in 1815 he spoke of 'Shaw, a Corporal in the Life Guards, well known as a pugilistic champion and equally formidable as a swordsman. He is supposed to have slain or disabled ten Frenchmen with his own hand, before he was killed.'[117]

The interest in both phrenology and relics combined in the acquisition of the other plaster cast of a skull that appears with those of Shaw in Plate 168; those of Shaw are readily recognizable in that they lack their jaw bones. This other cast, which today is on the left of the mantelpiece, is of the skull of the celebrated Scottish hero Robert the Bruce (1274–1329). Bruce's tomb in Dunfermline Abbey had been discovered by chance in 1818 during building operations. The tomb was opened on 5 November 1819 and the skull removed for the inevitable phrenological examination before being reinterred. A cast was taken at this time by W. Scoular, a pupil of Chantrey's, and it is from this that Scott obtained a cast.[118] Appropriately, the panelling used in the Hall (Plate 171) also came from Dunfermline.

The most evocative of Scott's Scottish relics were probably Rob Roy's gun, sword and dirk; the gun and the sword appear in Plate 174. The only other Scottish weapon Scott prized as highly was the Marquess of Montrose's sword. He acquired the gun as early as 1811, for he wrote to Hartstonge on 22 December of 'the purchase of a small lot of ancient armour and other curiosities (Rob Roy's gun among other things) the stock in trade of a Virtuoso who is leaving off collecting'[119]

Shortly after, through the good office of his publisher John Ballantyne, he acquired the Montrose sword: 'the present proprietor was selling his library or great part of it and John Ballantyne the purchaser wishing to oblige me would not conclude a bargain which the gentleman's necessity made him anxious about till he flung the sword into the scale'.[120]

Both Rob Roy's sword and dirk are inscribed 'Andrea Farara' (Plate 174), a puzzling, but charismatic figure in the history of Scottish swords. He is mentioned in Scott's novels. When Jonathan Oldbuck and his sister prepare to defend Monkbarns against a supposed French invasion, weapons from Oldbuck's collection are the only ones to hand: '"Whilk o' them, Monkbarns?" cried his sister, offering a Roman faulchion of brass with the one hand, with the other an Andrea Ferrara without a handle. "The langest, the langest," cried Jenny Ritherout, dragging in a two-handed sword of the twelfth century.'[121]

In *Waverley* we learn that the hero's '" father and uncle are both imprisoned by the government on my account". "We'll put in bail, my boy; old Andrew Ferrara shall lodge his security; and I should like to see him put to justify it in Westminster-hall".'[122] Scott in a footnote in a later edition tells us that 'The name of Andrea de Ferrara is inscribed on all the Scottish broadswords which are accounted of peculiar excellence. Who this artist was, what were his fortunes, and when he flourished, have hitherto defied the research of antiquaries.'[123]

Scott's interest in these swords led to further acquisitions. He was given by Joseph Train in 1824 'an Andrea Ferrara found of the field of battle near Falkirk'.[124] In June 1830, in the company of friends, Scott went to the battlefield of 'Preston pans . . . We saw two broad swords found on the field of battle, one a highlander's, an Andr[e]w Ferrara.'[125] These swords were presented to Scott by the local laird, who owned them.

Scott was greatly helped in the early 1820s in his acquisition of arms and armour by Sir Samuel Rush Meyrick. An important unpublished series of letters from Meyrick to Scott survive. Those from Scott sadly do not. The identity of Ferrara is widely discussed in these letters. Meyrick wrote to Scott on 10 March 1821: 'I am induced to ask you for information relative to Andrea Ferrara and the basket hilted swords of the highlanders.'[126] On 20 March he again wrote to Scott: I have gleaned the following oral information respecting Andria Farara, but which I should like to see warranted by any documentary evidence.'[127]

On 5 October, after a visit to Scotland, Meyrick again wrote to Scott 'to return my sincere thanks to you and your family for the kind civilities shewn to me while in Edinburgh . . . The Andrea Ferrara which you were so kind as to add to my sons collection of armour was viewed in the highlands with the utmost delight and performed the office of an introduction.'[128] Such was still the fame of the name Ferrara in the Highlands in the 1820s! Homage to Scott's gift to Meyrick and his son was paid in Skelton's two elegant folios devoted to the Meyrick collection: 'A Scotch basket hilted sword, the blade stamped with the name of Andria Ferara; . . . This specimen was added to the collection by Sir Walter Scott Bart.'[130]

Scott and Meyrick did not come any closer to solving the puzzle of Andrea Ferrara and his influence in Scotland than did later scholars.[129] Fortunately the mystery has very recently been cleared up by new research in Italy which has uncovered a contract dated 1578 for a swordmaker called Zanandrea of Ferrara to supply swords to a London swordmaker.[131]

Scott was all the while learning from Meyrick and seeking his help in purchasing objects. He was constantly encouraging Meyrick to publish his scholarly discoveries relative to Meyrick's own collection and to the subject in general. Meyrick wrote to Scott on 21 August 1821: 'Your hint relative to the catalogue raisonnee shall not be thrown out in vain, but I must render the chronological arrangement a little more perfect by a few more purchases ere I think of preparing any thing of the kind for the press.'[132]

Meyrick did venture into print in 1823, for Scott wrote to Terry on 29 October: 'Have you seen Dr. Meyrick's account of the Ancient Armour? — it is a book beautifully got up, and of much antiquarian information.'[133] The title-page of this, the principal vade-mecum of armour scholars for the next hundred years, carries the date 1824,[134] but it was available for Meyrick to present to his friends late in 1823. Scott received his copy late in October, at which time Meyrick also presented a copy to the Society of Antiquaries of London.

In the preface Meyrick singles out for especial thanks two of his friends: 'the useful hints of his much esteemed friend, that most able and critical antiquary, Francis Douce Esq., and the valuable communications on all that related to Scotch armour from one no less to be admired for his private virtues than his boundless

175. The Hermitage Castle Horn (Scott, *Abbotsford*)

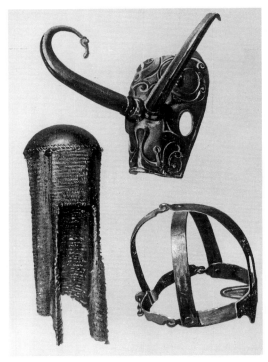

176. Bronze mask, the branks and a steel skull cap (Scott, *Abbotsford*)

177. A case of curiosities in the Library at Abbotsford

talents, his good friend Sir Walter Scott, Bart.'[135] One intriguing fact about the book is that the title-page and a number of plates were designed by none other than Richard Bridgens. Either Scott or Blore — the architect of Goodrich — could have introduced him to Meyrick. Through the good offices of friends like Terry and Meyrick, Scott was steadily buying armour right through both the building phases at Abbotsford. The pieces thus acquired are usually documented in the letters and described in the 1888 catalogue, most are still *in situ* in the Hall and Armoury.

But to turn to other objects in the Hall, on the mantelpiece by 1878 (Plate 168) was a boulle clock of the 1740s that does not relate in style to any other object in the Hall — it is still there today. Robert Cadell, Scott's publisher, gave the clock to Scott, who wrote to Cadell on 4 October 1828: 'We were equally gratified and surprised by the arrival of the superb time-piece ... There are grand discussions where it is to be put, and we are only agreed upon one point, that it is one of the handsomest things of the kind we ever saw.'[136] It was originally placed in the Drawing Room,[137] where it would have accorded better with the decoration than it does in the Hall.

In front of the fireplace stands an ancient bronze pot (Plates 167 and 168), the story of whose acquisition Scott so amusingly tells in 'Gabions'.[138] Another ancient Scottish relic that hung prominently in the Hall was the 'war horn' (Plate 175) acquired in one of Scott's 'raids' into Liddesdale while compiling *Minstrelsy*. The most important object in archaeological terms that Scott ever acquired was the curious bronze mask (Plate 176) given to him by Joseph Train. 'He [Train] at that time [1829] sent a visor of brass, founded in a morass at Torrs, in the parish of Kelton in the stewartry of Kircudbright.'[139] There has been discussion since Scott acquired this singular object about its date and whether the horns were an integral part or were added later. The mask now at Abbotsford is a copy; the original is now in the Royal Museum of Scotland in Edinburgh.

Not all the objects hung in the Hall were pieces of arms and armour, for several sets of horns played an important part. The largest pair hung over the west door (Plate 169) and were given to Scott in 1823 by Thomas Shortreed. Andrew Shortreed related that 'the bucks head considered the finest in Scotland ... was found in Doorpool Moss in Jed Forest one of the Abbotrule farms — It used to hang in our Dining Room at Jedburgh. It was greatly prized by us all but Sir Walter's repeated eulogies & wistful glances at length prevailed.'[140]

Some of the horns, though less dramatic, were more exotic. To Scott's surprise a cargo of horns arrived from South Africa. He wrote to Terry on 18 June 1823: 'The quantity of horns I have for the hall would furnish the whole world of cuckoldom; arrived this instant a new cargo of them, Lord knows whence.'[141] He eventually discovered that they had come from South Africa and had been sent by Thomas Pringle, the Scottish poet, to whom Scott wrote on 24 October 1826: 'The curiosities you had the kindness to send me from the Cape reach'd me in perfect safety and form a most important and valued part of the decorations of an old (new) Gothick entrance hall hung with armour antlers &c &c.'[142] Several of these horns can be seen in Plate 168.

Other curiosities as well as horns arrived from exotic sources, of which Constable wrote on 7 September 1824: 'A friend in London was so good as to give me for your museum some relics recently brought from Peru, found in the tomb of one of the Incas.'[143]

I have not the space to deal with the many small objects in Scott's collection; these did, however, form a very important aspect of the whole scheme of interior decoration at Abbotsford. Many of the accounts mention these smaller objects and some are listed in the 1888 catalogue. Those shown in Plate 177 were by this date in a special octagonal showcase in the bow window of the Library and are all listed in the catalogue. In the centre of the case was 'Napoleon First's Blotting-Book'. This and the case are still in the Library.

I have dealt with the interiors at Abbotsford at more length than those of the houses considered in other chapters for several reasons: they are far better documented; they survive virtually intact and can thus be carefully studied; and they are also more densely packed with objects than even the rooms at Strawberry Hill. Furthermore, Scott, by virtue of his international reputation as a poet, novelist, historian, as the chronicler of the whole antiquarian movement in the *Antiquary* and as the creator of Abbotsford, occupies a crucial and central position in the whole world of Romantic Interiors. Abbotsford, I would suggest, is the most influential and highly developed of the suites of Romantic Interiors that I shall discuss.

As we have seen elsewhere, the more intellectually vigorous and strong in personality was the owner, patron and collector of the building in question, the more complex, exciting and highly wrought are the interiors. Though Scott had the unlimited help of Blore, Atkinson, Skene, Terry, Bullock and several other friends, there is no doubt that he was the guiding genius and the impresario who actually created Abbotsford. It is due to Scott that the style is 'Old Scotch' rather than that of another Regency Tudor or Gothic villa of the well-known English variety.

It was Scott's personality and fame that brought him so many of the objects, whether by gift or purchase, and also directed much of the collecting towards 'gabions' relating to Scottish history. Nowhere can his range of interests be so immediately perceived than in the contents of his Library shelves; we have here not an artistic and literary squire like George Hammond Lucy of Charlecote, but a figure of international standing who created a house that reflected his own view of the past. Scott started out as an obscure Scottish advocate and rose to international fame, moving by stages through rented cottages to end his life in suitably baronial style at Abbotsford.

As his fame as a literary figure grew, the influence of all he did grew with it, including the fame of his embellishments at Abbotsford. Scott was constantly amazed at his own fame and wrote in his journal on 15 February 1827: 'I have a letter from Baron von Goethe . . . But Goethe is different and a wonderful fellow, the Ariosto at once, and almost the Voltaire of Germany. Who could have told me 30 years ago I should correspond and on something like an equal footing with the Author of the *Robbers*.'[144]

He wrote back to Goethe on 9 July 1827: 'I have a stately antique chateau to which any friend of Baron von Goethe will be at all times most welcome with an entrance hall filled with armour which might have become Jaxthansen itself and a gigantic bloodhound to guard the entrance.'[145] Scott had in 1799 translated and published Goethe's *Goetz von Berlichingen*, and Jaxthansen is a town mentioned in Goetz. Sadly, Goethe was by this time too old to travel to Scotland, and he died in 1832 while Scott — shortly before his own untimely death — was on his way to visit him.

Huge numbers of tourists have visited Abbotsford since Scott's death and they are to this day welcomed to the house by his descendants. The house is a remarkable monument to both Scott himself and the Romantic Movement to which he belonged. Some, though, have always been saddened by such historic shrines. Nathaniel Hawthorne described the house at length after visiting it in 1857 but felt that

> I do abhor this mode of making pilgrimage to the shrines of departed great men; there is certainly something wrong in it, for it seldom or never produces (in me, at least,) the right feeling. It is a queer truth, too, that a house is forever after spoiled and ruined, as a house, by having been the abode of a great man. His spirit haunts it, as it were, with a malevolent effect, and takes the hearth and hall away from the nominal possessors, giving all the world (because he had such intimate relations with all) the right to enter there.[146]

8

CHARLECOTE PARK

As I contemplated the venerable old mansion, I called to mind
Falstaff's encomium on Justice Shallow's abode.

Washington Irving

Charlecote Park is one of a large group of late mediaeval, Tudor and
Elizabethan houses which have until recently been accepted as surviving relatively
intact from the original period of their construction and furnishing. But upon closer
examination such houses frequently turn out to have been 'modernized' in the later
seventeenth or eighteenth century, this work having been lost without trace when
they were redecorated and refurnished during the early nineteenth in the style in
which they were originally built.

In many cases the essential documentation has not survived in the family archives,
and only a structural survey or contemporary accounts by visitors give some clue to
the alterations. Fortunately the changes which took place at Charlecote Park in the
eighteenth and nineteenth centuries are well-documented by surviving bills,
inventories, letters and published material.[1] Most of the furniture and furnishings
collected in the nineteenth century survive along with some of those from the earlier
periods.[2]

Charlecote has been the seat of the Lucy family since the twelfth century and the
property of the National Trust since 1946. The present house, built some little
distance from the previous house, was begun in 1551 and completed in 1558. It was
built for Sir Thomas Lucy (d.1600), who was knighted in the Great Hall in 1565 by
Robert Dudley, Earl of Leicester.[3]

In August 1572 Queen Elizabeth spent two nights in the house. The Royal
accounts state: 'and also for making ready Sir Thomas Lucy's house by the space of
two days, *mensis Augusti anno xiiij Regine predicta* as appeareth by the bill, signed the
L. Chamberlain & x. xvs. viid'.[4] The Queen came to Charlecote from nearby
Kenilworth Castle where she was staying with her close friend Robert Dudley. This
royal visit alone would have provided quite sufficient historical evidence to prompt
the nineteenth-century alterations at Charlecote, but even the Queen's visit takes
second place to the international fame of Charlecote because of its connection with
William Shakespeare (Plate 178)

One of the earliest accounts was published in the introduction to Rowe's famous
1709 edition of Shakespeare's works:

[Shakespeare] had, by a misfortune common enough to young fellows fallen into
ill company; and amongst them, some that made a frequent practice of Deer-
Stealing engag'd him with them more than once in robbing a Park that belong'd
to *Sir Thomas Lucy of Cherlcot*, near *Stratford*. For this he was prosecuted by that
Gentleman, as he thought somewhat severely; and in order to revenge that ill
usage, he made a Ballad upon him. And this, probably the first Essay of his
poetry be lost yet it is said to have been very bitter, that it redoubled the
prosecution against him to that degree, that he was obliged to leave his business
and family in *Warwickshire*, for some time and shelter himself in London.[5]

178. Shakespeare and Sir Thomas Lucy (J. Nash,
The Mansions . . ., 1839–42)

Elsewhere Rowe informs us: 'In the *Merry Wives of Windsor* he [Shakespeare] had made him [Prince Hal] a Deer Stealer that he might at the same time remember his *Warwickshire* Prosecutor, under the name of Justice *Shallow*; he has given him the very near coat of Arms which *Dugdale* in his Antiquities of that County describes for a family there.'[6] The 1823 edition of Rowe includes a so-called Shakespeare ballad, the first verse of which runs

> A parliamente member, a justice of peace.
> At home a poor Scare-Crowe, at London an asse,
> If Lowsie is Lucy, as some volke miscalle it
> The Lucy is Lowsie whatever befall it.[7]

This poem seems to have been published as early as 1778: 'first published by Steevens in 1778 from manuscript collections for a life of Shakespear made by Oldys'.[8] The relevant section of *The Merry Wives of Windsor* reads thus:

SHALLOW Ay, cousin Slender, and *Cust-alorum*.

SLENDER Ay, and ratolorum too; and a gentleman born, master parson; who writes himself *armigero*; in any bill, warrant, quittance, or obligation, *armigero*.

SHALLOW Ay, that we do; and have done any time these three hundred years.

SLENDER All his successors, gone before him have done't; and all his ancestors, that come after him may; they may give the dozen white luces in their coat.

SHALLOW It is an old coat.

EVANS The dozen white louses do become an old coat well; it agrees well, passant; it is a familiar beast to man, and signifies — love.[9]

These laboured puns concerning luces and louses and coats of arms, which become flea-ridden garments, link the ballad quoted above and the passage from the play. The allusions to armigerous families and to a *custos rotulorum* seem to make their meaning even more obscure. All becomes clear, however, when we consider that Sir Thomas Lucy was certainly a *custos rotulorum* and that his coat of arms as displayed in the heraldic stained glass windows made for the hall at Charlecote included 'Gules three lucies haurient Argent, two and one'.[10]

The arms (Plate 181) include three young pike rising for air, 'haurient' in fact. The country name for a pike is Luce and thus the arms include — as is so often the case with mediaeval heraldry — a rebus in that the Lucy family is represented by a Luce. Fish were frequently used in late mediaeval and Tudor heraldry, and Plate 181 is taken from Thomas Moule's book *The Heraldry of Fish* of 1842, which deals with the whole subject including the Lucy arms. The Lucy crests and arms were to play an important part in the decoration of the interiors of nineteenth-century Charlecote (Plate 180).

As we have seen, stories concerning Charlecote and Shakespeare were extant by the early eighteenth century, but the one great event that brought droves of both tourists and fashionable Londoners to Warwickshire was the Shakespeare Jubilee. This was organized by David Garrick at Stratford-on-Avon in 1769, and George Lucy of Charlecote (1714–1788), in his capacity of Lord High Sheriff of Warwickshire, played a prominent part in the festivities. Gainsborough even painted a portrait of Garrick embracing a bust of the immortal bard, a copy of which still hangs in the Library at Charlecote. Many of the visitors to Stratford travelled the four miles to Charlecote to examine the site of Shakespeare's deer-stealing escapade. George Lucy used this event as an excuse to entertain both his London and his

179. A bird's-eye view of Charlecote in 1690 by Jan Stevens (National Trust)

local friends at Charlecote, all of whom henceforth associated Charlecote with Shakespeare.[11]

George Lucy did not, however, at this time change his attitude to his house in the light of its strong links with important events in the distant past. He felt no compulsion to preserve the interiors as they were, in piety either to Shakespeare or to his own ancestors. He was not so driven by the prevailing fashion for modernization that he wished for a totally new house and he said as much in a letter of 14 April 1765: 'But what have I to do (who am happy to have a good old house) but make it decent and to content myself with that.'[12] In fact making 'decent' required considerable changes, which had largely taken place by the time of the Jubilee. It is not clear to what extent that Elizabethan interiors still survived in the 1750s, but what did survive was — except for the Great Hall — replaced by provincial Georgian work.

Many of the bills for the work survive, including the 'Estimate by William Hiorn for work to be done for George Lucy Esq., in fitting up the dining and drawing room at Charlecote £186.12s.4d 10 March 1762'.[13] The alterations were extensive. 'Between 1763 and 1769 all the old wainscoting was taken out of the principal rooms. [George Lucy] decided on a chaste white marble chimney-piece from Messrs. Gilliam Taylor of Piccadilly and Hyde Park Corner for the drawing room . . . new doors with moulded architraves, for an "enrich'd cornice", for Norway oak sashes and frames . . . the finishing colour dead white . . . In the dining-room at the foot of the great staircase the ceiling was raised and a carved stucco cornice run round it. It was lined with shallow fielded panels to match those on the stairs, painted white.'[14]

Though it would seem that the Great Hall was left relatively untouched, the other

Lord · Lucy   Thomas Lord Lucy   Antony Lord Lucy   Sir William Janne Dawa bter to Antony Lord Lucy   Welton Webid

ANNO DNI
·1558·

180. The original stained glass in the Hall at Charlecote (Country Life)

rooms in the house must have had the appearance of smart new Georgian interiors. The visitors to the house during the Jubilee would have been unable to gain — should they have wished to do so — any clear impression of the character of the interiors in Shakespeare's day.

Even the seventeenth-century gardens, so clearly shown in a painting of *c.*1690 (Plate 179), had by 1769 been destroyed by 'Capability' Brown. Brown's work had been carried out in the early 1760s, though at that date he had so much work on hand that he was a difficult man to hurry. In April 1761 George Lucy, who was in Bath having his portrait painted by Gainsborough, wrote: '12 April . . . Mr Brown was here on Sunday last and staid until Tuesday, when he called upon me, not upon business as he said, but to enquire after my health and told me he should not be at Charlecote till May, which I suppose will be June at soonest. I did not know how to construe his visit, I told him the time was elapsed for a second payment which he said was no matter as he did not want money, but upon my offering a £100 note he pulled out his pocket book and carried it off with him.'[15] The original of the agreement between George Lucy and Brown does not survive, but details of its contents do.[16]

It would seem, therefore, that both Charlecote and George Lucy could bask in the reflected glory of Shakespeare's involvement in the history of the house and its family even though most of the interiors and the gardens had been recently modernized. It appears that the visitor in 1769 in search of glimpses of Elizabethan England was comparatively undemanding when it came to tangible relics of the English past.

It may well have been that part of the explanation lies in the fact that the lack of general awareness of the actual history of ancient English architecture and interior decoration made people unsure what they were actually looking for. There were no books to inform the amateur concerning the finer points of Elizabethan architecture and interior decoration, but the mere fact that Shakespeare was *known* to have been involved with Charlecote made the house a shrine even in its modernized form.

Following the Jubilee, the fame of the house in no way diminished, though the visitors slowly became aware that alterations had taken place. For instance, in 1795 Samuel Ireland, in a book packed with Shakespearean lore, described the house and family thus: 'This house was built by Sir Thomas Lucy, Knight, in the first year of Queen Elizabeth's reign. It is of brick, with stone coins, and still makes a venerable appearance, although it has, in many parts, particularly in the forms of the windows, been modernized. The grand front at the entrance is nearly in its original state; and the great outer-gate, the inner part of which is seen in the annexed view, is a handsome specimen of the Gothic style used at the period of its erection.'[17]

The best description of the interior at Charlecote prior to the alterations of the 1820s was that published by the American Washington Irving in 1820. Irving came to Stratford as tourist and described his visits to all the places associated with Shakespeare:

181. The Lucy arms in 1558 from the stained glass at Charlecote (Thomas Moule, *The Heraldry of Fish*, 1842)

> The front of the house is completely in the old style; with stone shafted casements, a great bow-window of heavy stonework, and a portal with armorial bearings over it, carved in stone. At each corner of the building is an octagon tower surmounted by a gilt ball and weathercock ... As I contemplated the venerable old mansion, I called to mind Falstaff's encomium on Justice Shallow's abode ... I was courteously received by a worthy old housekeeper who, with the civility and communicativeness of her order, showed me the civility and communicativeness of her order, showed me the interior of the house. The greater part has undergone alterations, and been adapted to modern tastes and modes of living: there is a fine oaken staircase; and the great hall, that noble feature in an ancient manor-house, still retains much of the appearance it must have had in the days of Shakespeare. The ceiling is arched and lofty; and at one end is a gallery, in which stands an organ. The weapons and trophies of the chace, which formerly adorned the hall of a country gentleman, have made way for family portraits. There is a wide hospitable fireplace, calculated for an ample old-fashioned wood fire, formerly the rallying place of winter festivity. On the opposite side of the hall is the huge gothic bow-window with stone shafts, which looks out upon the court yard. Here are emblazoned in stained glass the armorial bearings of the Lucy family for many generations, some being dated 1558. I was delighted to observe the quarterings the three *white luces* by which the character of Sir Thomas Lucy was first identified with that of Justice shallow ... I regretted to find that the ancient furniture of the hall had disappeared; for I had hoped to find the stately elbow chair of carved oak, in which the country squire of former days was wont to sway the sceptre of empire over his rural domains, and in which it might be presumed the redoubted Sir Thomas sat enthroned in awful state when the recreant Shakespeare was brought before him ... I was gratified by the civil entreaties of the housekeeper and butler, that I would take some refreshment: an instance of good old hospitality, which I grieve to say we castle-hunters seldom meet with in modern days. I make no doubt it is a virtue which the present representative of the Lucys inherits from his ancestors.[18]

Irving's description sums up what attracted so many visitors to Charlecote. There was a particular combination of historical and literary associations which, though they had taken place in the distant past, had imbued the house with that special though indefinable atmosphere that pervades so many ancient buildings. The interiors seen by Irving had survived untouched since George Lucy's alterations of the 1760s. The Lucy line died out at his death in 1786, and the house and estate were inherited by the Reverend John Hammond, a cousin of George Lucy, who had been his secretary and companion for some years prior to his death.

John Hammond was fifty-three years old when he inherited; he married in 1788 and in 1789 changed his name by King's sign manual to Lucy.[19] The first of two sons, George, was born in 1789. John Hammond Lucy lived the life of a quiet country gentleman and was content to dwell in the house he inherited; he made no changes. He died aged ninety on 12 January 1823. The house by this date was in a neglected state. The 1760s decoration and furnishings had become very worn and threadbare; even when new they had not been of the highest quality. The Great Hall and any of the other ancient interiors that still existed were, along with the exterior

182. The entrance front at Charlecote (William Rider, *Views in Stratford-on-Avon and its vicinity illustrative of the biography of Shakespeare . . .*, 1828)

183. The entrance front in 1985

fabric of the house, in a very decayed state. This was the house inherited in 1823 by the thirty-four year old George Hammond Lucy (Plate 184). The entrance front at this date is shown in Plate 182 (and see Plate 183).

George Hammond Lucy — I shall drop the Hammond in future — was educated at Harrow and Christ Church, Oxford, and became a Member of Parliament in 1820 when his father purchased for him one of the seats for the 'rotten borough' of Fowey in Cornwall, which he retained until 1830. As soon as he inherited Charlecote he began to seek a wife and on 2 December 1823 he married Mary Elizabeth Williams (Plate 184).

Mary Elizabeth had been brought up in an ancient house in Flintshire called Bodelwyddan, which had been classicized by her father Sir John Williams soon after 1800. It fell to her brother John to gothicize it, thus transforming it into Bodelwyddan Castle, which in 1988 was so splendidly refurbished as a branch of the National Portrait Gallery.[20] Mary Elizabeth left a splendid description of the feudal welcome accorded to her and her husband when they arrived at Charlecote on 16 December:

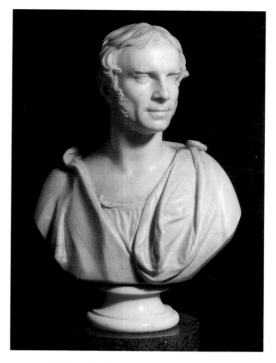

> It was dusk when we drove through the park gate, and there was a torchlight procession of the tenantry drawn up by the gateway to welcome us, and some were on the flat leaden roof of the building, with flambeaux in their hands, to cheer and hurrah as we passed underneath. The church bells were still ringing forth their merry peals, and the house itself blazed with lights from every window. The domestics all marshalled in line in the great hall to receive and have a look at their young mistress . . . It was very different then to what it is now, and the old hall did indeed look as Washington Irving said, 'as it might have done in Shakespeare's time', with its old worn stone floor, its small panes of glass, and old window-frames creaking and rattling with every gust of wind; and so cold! oh, so cold! — no hot air then![21]

But before we consider the alterations hinted at in the above description, George Lucy's extensive purchases from the Fonthill Abbey sale must be considered. Between his accession to the estate and house at Charlecote and his marriage, Lucy made some of the most important purchases of his life. The presence at Charlecote of the largest group of Fonthill Abbey objects still associated with a country house greatly enhances the importance of the collection today.

George Lucy's activities as a large-scale buyer at the sale in 1823 immediately established him in the eyes of his contemporaries, both collectors and dealers, as a bona fide collector. Whether George Lucy went to the viewing of the proposed Fonthill sale of 1822 is unrecorded; it was perhaps lucky for him that this sale was called off, for before the 1823 sale took place he had inherited Charlecote and the considerable fortune that went with it.

184. George and Mary Elizabeth Lucy by William Behnes, 1830 (National Trust)

He certainly seems to have been fascinated by William Beckford's sublime Abbey; he subscribed to Rutter's book on the Abbey.[22] Also, like the thousands of other visitors to the Abbey to view the sale, George Lucy was amazed by the scale and splendour of the building and its furnishings. The collection was quite simply the most important and extensive one ever to have been sold in England to that date. The elaborate series of heraldic stained glass windows which Beckford had commissioned to illustrate his descent from King Edward III and the complex heraldic carpets and ceilings (Plates 97, 98 and 108) certainly appealed to George Lucy and no doubt encouraged his growing passion for heraldic decoration.

The sale of furniture and *objets d'art* started on 23 September, the eleventh day of the sale, but it was not until lot 333 on the thirteenth day that George Lucy started to bid; his last bid was lot 1524 on the thirty-second day. He recorded only the lots on which he bid *successfully*; he may well have missed others, the prices being generally very high. He bought 64 lots in all out of a total of 1,566 lots of furniture and *objets d'art* for a total of £3,431.10.6. Though this figure represents something over 12 per

185. The Great Hall at Charlecote (S.C. Hall, *The Baronial Halls and Picturesque Edifices of England*, 1848)

186. The Great Hall in 1985

cent of the £43,869.14.0 raised from the whole sale, when one subtracts from the sale total the £13,249.15.0 realized for the 424 pictures, George Lucy emerges as one of the major buyers of *objets d'art* at the sale. It was the case, however, that one piece of furniture cost more than half of his outlay, whereas all the other objects except two cost him less than £100 each

The expensive object was lot 446 on the fourteenth day: 'A MAGNIFICENT TABLE OF PIETRE COMMESSE, the center being an oval specimen of mammillated oriental onyx, surrounded by parterres of rare and beautiful *jaspers* and *breccia*, with broad border of bold arabesque, of various costly and uncommon marbles, belted with variegated marble. It is mounted on a superbly carved frame of oak, about 9 feet long and four feet wide . . . This superb piece of furniture was formerly in the Borghese Palace.'[23] It had stood in King Edward's Gallery at Fonthill (Plates 97 and 98).

Its dramatic purchase was described by Mary Elizabeth; 'but first "the table", for which there were many bidders; but the most formidable were the King, George the Fourth, and the Marquis of Westminster. It was "going, going", many times, but when the sum mounted up to one thousand eight hundred guineas there was dead silence; and George Lucy being the last to call out so high a figure, the table was his.'[24] The table has stood since 1823 in the centre of the Great Hall (Plates 185 through 187).

The 64 lots that George Lucy purchased consisted of 31 of oriental ceramics, 2

European ceramics, 14 oriental lacquer, 4 metalwork and 13 furniture. I have been unable to discover how he acquired his taste for oriental ceramics and lacquer. It might be that as oriental objects played such an important part in the scheme of interior decoration of Beckford's Gothic Abbey, George Lucy decided that they would be equally appropriate for Charlecote.

In the choice of the 13 pieces of furniture a pattern can be discerned. The great table had an oak base in the Tudor style (Plate 188), and the *pietre dure* top was of sixteenth-century date (Plate 187), the whole piece thus being appropriate for a sixteenth-century house. The carved oak Gothic Revival tables were also stylistically appropriate for the house (Plate 186). They had stood with the *pietre dure* table in King Edward's Gallery at Fonthill (Plate 98). The rest of the furniture was either ebony or ebonized; such furniture was considered at this time to be Tudor.

It is also interesting that several of the Beckford pieces including the Borghese Table and the oak tables bore the Latimer cross, one of Beckford's crests (Plate 188), which to the unheraldic eye was very similar to the cross crosslets of the Lucy family (Plate 192) and was shortly to be widely used in the interior decoration of Charlecote. How and where these Fonthill pieces were displayed at Charlecote when they arrived in 1823 I have been unable to discover, but, as we shall see later, they were shortly to play an important part in the interiors created in the 1830s.

The Fonthill purchases were the only ones George Lucy was to make without close consultations with his wife. But together they seem to have bought little except paintings, or to have very much altered Charlecote in the first years of their marriage. Mary Elizabeth had her first three children at this time, a son in 1824 and daughters in 1826 and 1828. The last description of Charlecote before it was altered dates from this period. Appropriately, it was written by Walter Scott, who came with his daughter on 8 April 1828:

188. The base of the Borghese Table

> Learning from Washington Irving's description of Stratford that the hall of Sir Thomas Lucy, the Justice who renderd Warwickshire too hot for Shakespeare and drove him to London was still extant, We went in quest of it. Charlecote is in high preservation and inhabited by Mr Lucy, descendant of the worshipful Sir Thomas ... While we were surveying the antlered old hall with its painted glass and family pictures, Mr Lucy came to wellcome us in person, and to show the house, with the collection of paintings, which seems valuable and to which he had made many valuable additions ... This visit gave me great pleasure; it really brought Justice Shallow freshly before my eyes — the luces in his arms which do become an old coat well were not more lively plainly portrayed in his own armorials in the hall window than was his person in my mind's eye.[25]

It is interesting that though Scott came because of the Shakespeare connection, Irving's book put the idea into his head. There is one intriguing difference between Scott's and Irving's descriptions of the Hall. Irving remarked that 'The weapons and trophies of the chace which formerly adorned the hall of a country gentleman, have made way for family portraits'. Scott described 'the antlered old hall'. This may indicate that the re-creation of the interior character of the Hall had begun by 1828, prompted perhaps by Irving's comment that antlers would once have adorned the Hall. Scott does not mention the presence of weapons, but the Hall was shortly to have both weapons and antlers (Plate 186).

In 1829 work began on what Mary Elizabeth called the 're-edifying' of Charlecote: 'A.D. 1829. In the spring we were obliged to turn out of Charlecote for a time, as we were pulling down the old offices and building the present kitchen, servants' hall, &c., and adding on the western front the dinner-room and the library. On the 16th of May we started for a two months' tour on the Continent.'[26]

The frequent use at this period of the word 're-edify' is important in that it does not, nor was it intended by those who used it, mean restoration in the modern sense. It meant rather the transformation of an ancient and decayed structure into a sound and modern one which was at one and the same time decorated and furnished in an appropriately ancient style, but capable of functioning as a comfortable family house.

In most cases neither the owner nor his architect attempted or indeed wished to restore the house and its contents and interiors accurately to the state in which the original builder had left it. The term 're-edify' in fact had a Shakespearean source very appropriate for Charlecote. In act 3, scene 1, of *Richard III* Richard himself says of the Tower of London that Julius Caesar 'did my Lord, begin that place; whch since, succeeding ages have re-edified.'

At Charlecote both the owner and his architects had a very clear idea of their concept of the past and its artefacts, but they also knew to what extent they were willing to adapt the modern life style to the occupation of an ancient building. The Lucys felt the need for a new kitchen, servants' hall, dining room and library and therefore added them to the old house and, like Walpole and Scott before them, wished to live in an ancient yet comfortable house.

The architect chosen to work on the house was Benjamin Dean Wyatt, the architect of Stafford House, London (1822–7), and Apsley House, London (1828–9). Wyatt's splendid elevations still exist at Charlecote, but were never executed. Instead George Lucy employed Charles S. Smith, a pupil of Sir Jeffry Wyatville. Smith seems to have worked almost exclusively in Warwickshire.[27] But, as has been observed, George Lucy 'paid Charles Smith £300 for his plan and proceeded to be his own architect'.[28] Smith was in fact involved in some way with the work through the 1830s; a letter from him to George Lucy dated 27 May 1835 relates to payment for the plaster ceilings of the Library and Dining Room. It is unclear whether the designed or had the ceilings made; it is even possible that he acted as a contractor.[29]

The Library and Dining Room wing was added to the back of the house (Plate 193) and was built of dark blue brick with stone dressings, no attempt being made to match the red brick of the original house. The alterations carried out to the entrance front in the 1850s were, however, executed in red brick. The work on the exterior of the new rooms was not completed until late in 1835. The family moved back into the house on 2 October 1830,[30] though they were to co-exist in the house with the builders until at least 1837.

There is ample documentation for the decorating and furnishing of the two new rooms, which survive intact to this day (Plates 195 and 199). A careful examination of this material throws a great deal of light upon the way in which such schemes were realized in the 1830s. A number of different individuals were involved including designers, craftsmen, cabinet-makers and antique and picture dealers. It may be that George and Mary Elizabeth organized the whole project using all these individuals as sub-contractors. The documentary evidence points to the controlling genius being Thomas Willement, working closely with the Lucys and Charles Smith.

Willement at this date was at the height of his powers as a heraldic artist, interior decorator, antiquary, decorative painter, stained glass restorer and designer.[31] How George Lucy met him is unknown, but his passion for heraldry may have brought them together. George Lucy's interest in the history of his family was to find full expression in the interior decoration of his house. This interest was described by Mary Elizabeth: 'He was fond of the study of heraldry, and took great pains in tracing the pedigree of his ancestors. I have known him travel miles after a marriage certificate or register of a birth. He had the fine emblazoned Lucy pedigree book compiled at the Heralds' College, and would not allow a thing to be inserted without being authenticated.'[32]

The title-page of the pedigree book is elaborately illuminated on vellum (Plate 189); the whole book is similarly decorated. In his heraldic researches George Lucy would certainly have come across Willement's book *Regal Heraldry: The Armorial Insignia of the Kings and Queens of England from Coeval Authorities* (1821). George Lucy

189. George Lucy's genealogical album

might also have met Willement through the two commissions he had carried out in Warwickshire before he worked at Charlecote; these both date from 1825 and were a window in the church at Leamington Priors and a window in Grendon Hall,[33] the former about six miles and the latter about twenty-five miles from Charlecote.

A number of letters from Willement to George Lucy survive; they cover the period 1830–9 and document much of the work that he designed and carried out. While the work was under way on the new wing, changes were taking place in the Great Hall. These seem to have been under Willement's control. It also seems to have been the case that while the work at Charlecote was in progress, Charles Smith and Willement — far from being rivals — were probably co-operating elsewhere.

Smith was working at Stoneleigh Abbey, Warwickshire: 'Alterations for 1st Lord Leigh, including Gothic Entrance Hall etc 1837–39.[34] In 1837 on the page that faces the description of Willement's work in the Library and Dining Room at Charlecote, it states that Willement provided for Stoneleigh Abbey 'ELEVEN Windows in the corridor, containing the various alliances of the family.'[35] These windows sound very similar in character to those at Charlecote.

The work in the Great Hall started with the bay window (Plate 185). The stained glass (Plate 180) which had been so admired by Irving and Scott, but criticized by Mary Elizabeth because it fitted so badly in its frames that it let in the cold, was in a parlous state: 'The whole of the ancient stained glass in thew windows of the great hall repaired and re-leaded, eight additional panels executed to complete the series of descendants ... very considerable painted decorations through the whole mansion.'[36]

There is no evidence concerning the disposition of the glass in the bay window before 1830. Willement's bill of 1830–1 describes '28 large compartments of ancient glass taken to pieces, the arms, ornaments etc repaired with new pieces new leaded with ground glass and cemented'.[37] The glass was arranged at the top of the bay window so that the major part of the window could be filled with plate glass to bring more light into the Hall and allow a view of the gardens from indoors as had been the case at both Strawberry Hill and Fonthill.

Willement described his plan in a letter to George Lucy: 'December 7 1830 ... the arrangement I have followed is to place all the coats of arms connected with the *Lords* Lucy in the first window. Those of Lucy of Charlecote in the *center* of the bay with their wives in the *two sides* of it. The new ones will then fill the 3rd window.'[38] Willement described the new arrangement of the twenty-eight old panels and the eight new ones. The new panels culminated with the following arms 'Gules semee of crosslets, three lucies haurient Argent, impaling, Argent, two boxes counter salient in saltire Gules, a mullet for difference "George Lucy Esquier Wedyd Mary Elizabeth daughter of Sir John Williams Knt".'[39]

As was so often the case during the nineteenth century, a title appropriate for the ancient family was also felt desirable. Willement was consulted and wrote to George Lucy: 'July 11 1831 ... If you are seriously disposed to investigate the Lucy Barony I would advise you to consult with Mr N.H. Nicolas ... who is exceedingly conversant with such matters and is engaged in nearly all similar claims before the House of Lords. The late recovery of the Devon Earldom was entirely by him ... I should consider his opinion quite final.'[40]

So crucial to an understanding of George Lucy's attitude and that of many of his contemporaries to their mediaeval ancestors is the question of reviving titles that we must examine the scheme to claim the Lucy barony. The barony was created in 1320 in Northumberland, but went into abeyance when the third baron died in 1369 without a male heir. The connection between the Lucys of Charlecote and the Northumbrian family is obscure. 'Sir William Dugdale surmises that SIR WILLIAM LUCY, the 1st ancestor of the LUCYS, of CHARLECOTE, Co. Warwick, who bore the surname of Lucy, did so because his mother might have been the heir of some branch of this baronial family of Lucy.'[41]

Willement's heraldic work had brought him into close contact with Nicolas on a number of occasions. Sir Nicholas Harris Nicolas, G.C.M.G., F.S.A. (1799–1849), of the Inner Temple 'devoted himself almost entirely to antiquarian literature, particularly in the departments of history, genealogy, and heraldry, and the works which he produced in quick succession bore witness at once to his critical acumen and his almost unparalleled industry . . . As a barrister, the business of Sir Harris Nicolas was confined to claims of peerage before the House of Lords . . . His favourite branch of study was that which connected itself with the history and antiquities of the country, with the genealogy and descent of our ancient families.'[42] He wrote thirty-seven books, contributed to books by others, and wrote many periodical articles. Among his books were *Report of the Proceedings on the Claim of the Earldom of Devon in the House of Lords* (1832), *Notitia Historica* (1824) and, his first, *Catalogue of the Herald's Visitations . . . in the British Museum* (1823).

The establishment of the claim to the earldom of Devon astonished the legal world. Nicolas's skill becomes clear when the tenuousness of the claim is considered: 'William Courtenay Viscount Courtenay of Powderham . . . on the 14th May 1831 he was declared Earl of Devon by the House of Lords under the rem. in the creation of that Earldom 3 Sep 1553 . . . he being *collaterally* h. male to the grantee inasmuch as his grandfather's grandfather's grandfather's grandfather (all of them unconscious of their right to such dignity) Sir William Courtenay (who d. 1555) was a very distant cousin and h. male of the grantee 1553, whose ancestor in the *seventh* degree was this Sir William's grandfather's grandfather's grandfather's grandfather.'[43]

The best description of Nicolas's activities and character is to be found in Disraeli's novel *Sybil* of 1845. The character of Baptist Hatton, Esq., Inner Temple, is, I would suggest, closely based upon Nicolas, though whether his rooms in the Temple resembled the appropriately Romantic Interiors described here I have been unable to discover:

> He is an heraldic antiquary; a discoverer, inventor, framer, arranger of pedigrees; profound in the mysteries of genealogies; an authority, I believe, unrivalled in everything that concerns the constitution and elements of the House of Lords . . . at present all the business of the country connected with descents flows into his chambers. Not a pedigree in dispute not a peerage in abeyance, which is not submitted to his consideration . . . Sir Vavasour Firebrace is seated in a spacious library that looks upon the Thames and the gardens of the Temple. Though piles of parchments and papers cover the tables, and in many parts intrude upon the Turkey carpet, an air of comfort and taste pervades the chamber. The hangings of crimson damask silk blend with the antique furniture of oak; the upper panes of the windows are tinted by the brilliant pencil of feudal Germany while the choice volumes that line the shelves are clothed in bindings which become their rare contents . . . 'I can make a peer,' said Mr Hatton leaning back in his chair and playing with his seals . . . 'which will give you precedency over every peer on the roll, except three (and I made those), and it will not cost you a paltry twenty or thirty thousand pounds.'[44]

The matter of precedence was considered to be of great importance at this date with respect to the Devon title. 'AN OLD SUBSCRIBER' wrote to the *Gentleman's Magazine*: 'Lord Courtenay having established his right to the Earldom of Devon under the grant to Edward Courtenay 28 Sept. 1553, it seems to remain a question whether the present Earl is entitled to the precedence of 1553 only, or to the original precedence of 1335 (which would constitute him premier Earl), their being a clause in the patent of 1553 granting to Edward Courtenay the same precedence any of his ancestors being Earls of Devon had heretofore enjoyed.'[45] The precedence referred to was the order in which the peerage follow the monarch in the coronation procession.

Either the potential cost or the fact that George Lucy's claim to the Lucy barony was even weaker than that of the Courtenays to the earldom of Devon presumably deterred him in the end from any such attempt. It must have been the Courtenays' success that initially prompted George Lucy; the timing points to this. Willement's letter quoted above is dated 11 July 1831. The Devon claim was established on 14 May. It is not clear whether George Lucy actually consulted Nicolas or made up his own mind against proceeding. The very fact that George Lucy even contemplated spending such a large sum of money in this way while already involved in expensive works at Charlecote demonstrates the importance he and his contemporaries accorded to titles that linked their families to their remote mediaeval ancestors.

Work on the Hall windows at Charlecote did not proceed quickly. In a letter of 21 September 1836 Willement demonstrated his subtle and sensitive attitude to his work on the old glass: 'The coat of Valence is variously *drawn* . . . the lead across the manche [of Hastings] was placed there to strengthen the piece which was broken in the last time of burning but which turned out so fine in colour that I was loth to give it up, and as the work generally is to imitate the old designs I imagined that a repairing lead here and there would not be a serious detriment to the glass.'[46]

This letter certainly refers to the old glass in the Hall bay window; the heraldic references given above prove this. The great care which Willement and George Lucy lavished upon the restoration of the glass is evident here in their desire to match the new parts to the old. While rearrangement and restoration of the old glass was being carried out, newly designed coats of arms were being translated into glass to bring the Lucy pedigree up to date (Plate 190).

George Lucy wrote: 'Copy of letter addressed to Mr Willement December 9 1836 — on receipt altered *Label* under coat of *Valence* & some alterations in the last three stained glass windows in Great Hall . . . I wish I could entirely approve the Hall window but its not equal to expectation. The first shield Arnold & Lucy is not only fine in the ruby that predominates it wants however something occasionally introduced about the centre window, the date 1605 in this glass is right but in the next shield Lucy & Kingsmill you have not rectified the date.'[47] The Valence shield was old glass, the two other references were to new glass.[48]

While this work on the glass continued, the Hall itself was being extensively altered: a new fireplace was constructed (Plates 185 and 186) and the windows in the western wall on each side of the fireplace were replaced by doors leading to the new Dining Room and Library. The open-timber roof was replaced by a new and richly grained and stencilled ceiling, and the organ, its gallery and the old wainscot admired by Irving and Scott were all swept away. This work was completed in 1837. Willement's bill gives the details: 'Painting & Gilding at Charlecote . . . £504 14s 4d'.[49] Except for the marble floor laid in the mid-1840s, the room has survived unchanged until today (Plate 186). By 1837 the walls were hung with the portraits Irving had admired supplemented with the weapons and the trophies of the chase, whose absence he had noted.

The Borghese Table along with those it had stood with at Fonthill were given pride of place in the Hall. The only other furniture was a set of six chairs and another table (Plate 191) which like the Borghese Table was a splendid *pietre dure* top for which a modern carved oak base was made (Plate 192). This table, which is fortunately well documented, was purchased in 1824 from Thomas Emmerson, the well-known picture dealer, of 20 Stratford Place (north of Oxford Street).

The Lucys had been buying from him since at least 1823. 'The two beautiful pictures by P. Wouvermans and Teniers' own "Wedding Fete", hanging in the drawing room . . . were purchased for £3,000 by George Lucy, in 1823, from Thomas Emmerson.'[50] He continued to sell pictures to George Lucy right up to his death in 1845; in 1844 he wrote concerning a Van Dyck, a Giorgione and a Canaletto.[51]

Emmerson wrote concerning the table on 13 January 1824:

chance has thrown in my way a remarkable fine Florentine slab, which I have secured — it had just been cleared from the Customs House by a merchant in the City and I had intelligence of it from my broker before it has been seen by any person, the size is 5 feet 8 inches long by nearly 4 feet wide and with the exception of yours the [Borghese Table] which I consider unique and remarkable, it is the finest I know — the design and colour are beautiful and the materials most precious — the centre oval piece is of fine mamiliated Jasper ... in short it is worthy to be in the same mansion with 'The Table' it was met with by accident in Germany where it had been many years in the family of an Italian Banker, by the gentleman of whom I got it who was travelling on business there — the price is Five Hundred Guineas which I consider very cheap ... I think a stand might be made for it in the country from your own, which would serve as a model ... T. Emmerson.[52]

A base was certainly made which closely followed Emmerson's suggestion: this can be seen by comparing it (Plate 192) with the end of the Borghese Table (Plate 188). The only significant difference between the two is that the Beckford Latimer cross on the Borghese Table becomes the Lucy cross crosslets on the base for the Lucy table. There is no documentation concerning the making of the base.

The top is certainly one of the most interesting and important in England and, though much smaller than the Borghese Table, is of a more interesting design. Willement considered this *pietre dure* top important enough to record in a water-colour in 1831, which has listed upon it the various marbles of which it is made.[53]

The only other furniture in the Hall, a set of six chairs (Plates 185 and 186), was not purchased until long after the Fonthill pieces and the Emmerson table. These

were purchased from the broker Samuel Isaacs: '27 Feb 1837 ... the same person has 6 fine carved hall chairs of the period of Louis XIV — for which he asks 80G — but will take £70. They are very finely cut and are of old dark wood, I should think pear tree.'[54] They were in fact probably Dutch and were in the style associated with Daniel Marot and date from c.1710. The Louis XIV dating was thus very accurate, in that Louis died in 1715.

Isaacs, who traded from 131 Regent Street on the left-hand corner of its junction with Leicester Street, described himself variously as 'Importer of paintings china and curiosities' and 'Dealer in jewelery and bronzes'.[55] He, like Emmerson, stayed in contact with the family and as late as August 1871 he wrote to Mary Elizabeth: 'Dear Madame, when last I had the pleasure of seeing you I said I had some small specimens of china which I forgot to bring with me & of which I begged your acceptance.'[56] The chairs seen in Plate 185 are the original ones, but those seen in the Hall today (Plate 186) are reproductions made in the 1920s when the originals were sold to an American museum.

The finishing touches were not given to the Hall until just before George Lucy's death and were the result of George and Mary Elizabeth's trip to the Continent in 1841–3. 'It was at Florence we bought the large vase and doves in alabaster by Pisani, the design taken from the celebrated, vase found by Cardinal Furetti in Adrian's Villa.'[57] The source of this design is actually a mosaic of doves drinking.

The vase can be seen in Plate 186 along with the pedestal. 'George Lucy purchased at Rome the fine Cipplino pedestal, on which the alabaster vase with the doves stands in the oriel window in the great hall, and for which, with the beautiful red porphyry one, on which my bust now stands, he only gave 275 piastres; also the pedestal of Egyptian porphyry, on which his own bust is placed.'[58] These two busts (Plate 184) were sculpted in 1830 by William Behnes; they were dispatched to Charlecote on 6 October 1830.[59]

Finally, the 'old worn stone floor', which Mary Elizabeth had complained of in 1823, was replaced by the present marble floor: 'thence to Venice. It was there that George Lucy purchased the red and white marble which now paves the great hall.'[60] Holme & Co. wrote to George Lucy: 'Venice 5th April 1843. Sir, By the schooner "Kate" about to sail from Venice to London we have shipped the marble pavement you ordered when in Venice.'[61]

While all this work was proceeding in the Hall, the Library and Dining Room were being built, decorated and furnished (Plate 193). The two rooms interconnect, the Library being entered by a door on the right of the Great Hall chimney-piece and the Dining Room by one on the left. The chronology of the construction of these two rooms can be established from the letters and bills. George Lucy noted 'materials that have been purchased for the two new rooms with the workmanship and the building ... began April 1833'.[62] He also gives a list of firms which tie in with bills and letters from those firms; for instance, Browne & Co. of the Scagliola Works, University Street, London, supplied the fireplaces for the two rooms in July 1835, and William Summers, stove manufacturer, of 105 New Bond Street, supplied the two grates in November 1837 'to drawings' probably by Willement.[63]

Willement supplied the glass, but was delayed by Charles Smith who, as the following letter shows, was still involved in the works. Willement wrote to George Lucy: 'Oct 23 1835 ... when I saw Mr Smith at Hampton [Lucy] he desired that I should not proceed with the Glass for the new rooms until I heard from him what the exact size should be, will you be so good as to hasten his finding the dimensions as it would be most convenient to me to put them in hand directly.'[64] Some of the glass at least was at Charlecote by October 1836: 'Oct 5 1836 all the glass was in place in both rooms: '1837 ... Nine very large armorial compartments in the library nine others in the dining room shewing the descent of Sir John Lucy Knight who built Charlecote House in the reign of Queen Elizabeth'.[66]

The finely carved Elizabethan-style bookcases in the Library (Plates 194 through

192. The base of the Lucy Table

191. .(facing page) The top of the Lucy *pietre dure* table (Country Life)

193. The exterior of the Library and Dining Room at Charlecote

225

196) were carved by J.M. Willcox, the celebrated Warwick carver.[67] His bill survives and shows how long the work took: 'Apr 27 [1835] To carving mouldg small leaf to go round windows and doors of Library ... 1837 Feby 2. To carving Fatia board for bookcase and chimney piece complete except the arms ... July 28 [1837]. To carving 3 coats of arms with shield & fixing for chimney piece in Library ... July 15 1839 to making two bookshelves for library complete.'[68]

One of the most splendid features of these two rooms is the wallpaper (Plate 201) designed and supplied by Willement. That for the Library was supplied in 1837: '15 pieces of brown flock Elizab[ethan] paper on embossed metal ground';[69] it survives *in situ*. This paper, like most of the Willement papers in the house, has a gold leaf ground. Willement wrote on 17 February 1832 concerning similar papers to be hung in the bedrooms: 'I suppose your Paper Hanger is accustomed to the hanging of flock and metal papers, which requires very great care, and they should have very smooth & stout lining papers under them and the joints well rubbed down before the printed paper is applied. I trust that if well hung the effect of all three patterns will be very handsome and very well suited to the style of your house.'[70] It may well be that the local paper-hanger was unable to cope, for Willement's bill of July 1832 includes the item: 'Expenses of two paper hangers to and from Charlecote £6.18'.[71]

The responsibility for the design of the splendid armorial carpet with semée of luces, cross crosslets and an elaborate border 'Ducal coronets Gules with boar's heads argent between two wings sable' is almost certainly Willement's, though no documentation concerning its design and manufacture has come to light. This carpet can be clearly seen in Plates 195 and 196. Willlement may well also have designed the bookcases in the Library; he certainly designed the armorials on the chimney-piece, these were carved by Willcox: 'July 28 1837 carving 3 coats of arms with shields & fixing for chimney piece in Library'.[72] The Library ceiling was — like that in the Dining Room — probably chosen rather than designed, for it is likely to be a reproduction of an actual Elizabethan ceiling. Willement, with his considerable knowledge of sixteenth-century interiors, may well have made the choice.

The purchase of the major pieces of Library furniture took place in 1837. I have already quoted from a letter of 1837 relating to the purchase of the Hall chairs;[73] this letter was written to George Lucy by William Buchanan, the famous dealer in paintings. He was still active in 1846 when he wrote after George Lucy's death to Henry Spencer Lucy. Buchanan had supplied a number of George Lucy's most important paintings and said in this letter, 'I have seen my friend Mr Holford this morning who informs me he *has heard* it is your intention to dispose of a portion of your collection of pictures.[74] George Lucy certainly chose a talented dealer, who by the time of his involvement at Charlecote had written a major book on picture dealing,[75] and it was said of him 'that by that year [1896] ... upward of a third of the pictures in the National Gallery had passed through Buchanan's hands'.[76]

Buchanan did not, however, deal in furniture, as his letter to George Lucy explains: '24 Feb 1837 ... I have just seen a very magnificent wardrobe of inlaid woods ... which has been offered to me for a very trifling sum in my opinion considering its condition and elegance. It is in the hands of a Jew ... I am no purchaser of such articles, but your fine old home at Charlecote immediately occurred to me and I think it may be worth your notice if you are still looking after objects of this kind.'[77]

The Jew was the same Samuel Isaacs of Regent Street from whom George Lucy bought the Hall chairs, and he immediately bought the cabinet: 'Isaacs marquetrie wardrobe £50.00'.[78] George Lucy reacted in this case with the speed any passionate collector will understand; Buchanan replied to a letter from him: 'London 27 February 1837 ... I have the pleasure of receiving yours of Saturday this morning with the enclosure of a cheque for £50 with which I immediately went to the possessor of the fine piece of marquetrie which I was afraid might have escaped me and instantly secured it.'[79]

194. The Library at Charlecote in about 1870

195. (below) The Library in 1985 (Country Life)

198. (facing page) The ebony and ivory furniture in the Library (Country Life)

196. The Library at Charlecote in 1985

197. The Dutch marquetry cabinet

This very fine cabinet is still at Charlecote (Plate 197) and can be firmly attributed to the celebrated Amsterdam cabinet-maker Jan Van Mekeren (1658–1733). Interestingly, George Lucy was in good company in considering such a cabinet suitable for his ancient house, for at much the same time very similar cabinets were being purchased for Burghley, Belton and Kingston Lacy.[80] Where it was placed when it arrived at Charlecote is unrecorded; by 1891 it stood at the foot of the main staircase and may well have stood there from 1837.

Buchanan, after dealing with the wardrobe, continued:

But now for a chance! which has never occured to you in all probability before and never may occur again. Having paid the Jew his money I was led into a room where he showed me what I must fairly confess to you surprized me, not only from the beauty and elegance of the objects themselves, but from my belief that the history given on them is true . . . He has lately purchased from an old mansion in Norfolk, the name of which he will not give — and the proprietors name he is pledged to secrecy never to give. The set of 8 chairs *armchair couch* and pair of cabinets which were made a present of by Queen Elizabeth to the Earl of Leicester, and were formerly at Kenilworth . . . They are massive solid ebony *richly inlaid* with the tooth of sea horse . . . price demanded for the whole set 800 £ but he told me he would taken 500 gs . . . They are indeed *magnifique*. They cost Queen Elizabeth as history goes 2,000 pieces of gold.[81]

The suite was quickly purchased for less than even the 500 guineas demanded — 'Isaacs Black Library chairs sofa & Cabinet 488.5.6.'[82] — and placed in the Library (Plates 196 and 198). These pieces had a very special appeal for the Lucy family, Queen Elizabeth having come to Charlecote on her famous visit when she was staying at Kenilworth with the Earl of Leicester. Willement designed special needlework upholstery for the chairs and sofa;[83] these were worked by Mary Elizabeth, and the cover on the sofa has the initials *ER* worked on it (Plate 198). Alas, the suite does not date from the sixteenth century and is not even English. It

was made in Batavia or Goa in the later seventeenth century and relates to the turned ebony chairs discussed elsewhere.

Two other major pieces of furniture, both tables, were purchased for the Library at this time. One was an elaborate marquetry writing desk (Plate 195) made up from two late seventeenth-century tables combined with new elements to make a complete piece of furniture. It seems likely, however, that George Lucy bought the desk as a genuinely old piece. Underneath is a label which reads 'Robinson Decorator and Furnisher a l'Antique. Importer of and Dealer in Ancient Furniture, Pictures, Bronzes, Sculpture, Armour, Carvings, Books, Curiosities &c. 27 Oxford Street and 56 Rathbone Place'. The bill exists and shows that the desk cost £47.5.0, and George Lucy noted elsewhere 'June 30 1837 Robinson . . . Library Tab . . .'[84]

The other table bought at this time was a marquetry octagon table decorated with crossed *L*'s (Plates 195 and 196) after the manner of French royal furniture. George Lucy intended the *L*'s to symbolize Lucy, but whether he thought that this was an antique French royal table is unclear. The bill reads: 'E.H. Baldock Chinaman by appointment to his Majesty Hanway Street Oxford Street 1837 . . . June 17 — a very beautiful inlaid octagon Table with Drawer and place for ink 52.10.0.'[85]

Baldock, the well-known dealer we have met before, and whose shop was about 100 yards from Robinson's Rathbone Street premises, had supplied china and plate to Charlecote since at least 1826. He had also supplied objects to William Beckford for Fonthill Abbey and to Sir Walter Scott for Abbotsford.[86] Several other tables of this type are known: one was sold by Baldock to the Duke of Buccleuch in 1840[87] and another is in the Victoria & Albert Museum. They would all seem to date from the period 1825–40 and were probably made by or at least for Baldock.

The remainder of the Library furniture included comfortable modern armchairs covered with loose covers printed with an Elizabethan-style strapwork pattern of the same character as the Library wallpaper and, like the wallpaper, designed by Willement (Plate 194). The spectacular Gothic Revival argand oil lamps that stood upon the ebony cabinets (Plate 194) were supplied to the house sometime after 1833 by Hancock & Rixon.[88]

These were probably identical to ones they had already supplied: '8 Dec 1824 . . . Hancock Shepherd and Rixon No. 1 Cockspur Street, Charing Cross . . . 1 Pair of Bronze Gothic richly wrought Lamps on Handsome Pedestals £23.2s.'[89] This firm was well known for its lamps, having already supplied lamps to the Duke of Wellington's houses, Apsley House and Stratfield Saye in the 1820s.

The most important picture in terms of furnishing the Library was of Queen Elizabeth (Plate 194). A splendid oak frame was made by the cabinet-maker Hume — whom we met at Fonthill — probably to Willement's design, though the bill does not mention this: 'May 1836 To making and Richly Carving in best wainscot a suitable Frame to the Portrait of Queen Elizabeth 43.10.0 . . . Robert Hume'.[90]

Close to the portraits on top of the bookcases stood a series of Greek vases. These seem an odd choice for a house like Charlecote. George Lucy felt, however, that they would enhance his collection, and they are in fact of considerable quality and importance and were carefully chosen, presumably to stand in the Library in their present positions. They were not all purchased, as might seem likely, on one of the Lucy trips to Italy. Some were bought there in 1842, but a number were bought from Browne of London in September 1838.[91]

The collection of books in the house when George Lucy inherited was of considerable interest, many of them having been purchased in the sixteenth or seventeenth century,[92] but the large new Library greatly exceeded the old in size, and new books were therefore needed to fill Willcox's splendid shelves. George Lucy went to William Pickering, the great bookseller, bibliographer and publisher,[93] to find suitable books, for he certainly shared the belief that

An antiquary without books is like a steamer without paddles — no progress, no work — lost and floundering in sand and mud . . . we would therefore recom-

199. The Dining Room at Charlecote in 1985 (Country Life)

mend our readers, who may wish to furnish themselves with antiquarian books to do as we do, and to resort to the old-bookshops of London ... Mr Pickering, 177 Piccadilly — a sort of Golconda to him who looks for diamonds of antiquity. You may spend two or three hundred pounds there in a morning and come home with a cart load of folios, quartos, and miniature duodecimos.[94]

In November and December 1838 George Lucy spent £331.8.6 with Pickering. His purchases included 'Shakespeare's Merry Wives ... Walton's Angler ... Common Prayer Baskerville ... Puffendorff Historia ... Brittons works ... Walpoles Anecdotes of Painting ... Guillims Heraldry'.[95] By the late 1830s Pickering was going to stay at Charlecote and wrote:

London Oct 1839. Sir, I should be wanting in my duty were I not to thank you & Mrs Lucy for your kind attentions when at Charlecot I shall not very soon forget what I saw there, although from description I expected much still with truth I can say that it exceeded my expectations, your restorations are all in keeping combining utility with elegance & durability, & it does not appear to me likely

200. The Dining Room at Charlecote in 1985

that you will ever have to undo or do again any part that you have restored. When you have finished I think it will bear comparison with any seat of its style in the Kingdom . . . As to your library I can readily understand that you will by degrees furnish it with books . . . the substantial restorations must of course occupy your time as well as lighten your purse and be first considered . . . I am always delighted with the Tudor period — the Literature — the portraiture — the architectural carving & painting on glass & furniture are to my taste, more truly English than at any other period.[96]

It may well have been Willement who introduced Pickering and George Lucy, for Willement had known Pickering since at least 1828 when he created a window at 'Chancery Lane London at the Residence of William Pickering Esq. Nine compartments containing, within ornamental frames, the arms of Chaucer, Gower, Shakespeare, Spencer, Sidney, Bacon Newton and Milton'.

The work on the Dining Room was progressing at much the same speed as that on the Library. Willement supplied in 1837 an even richer wallpaper than that in the Library: '23 pieces of rich paper various coloured flocks on embossed metal ground at 5/yard and hanging do all close £71.17.6'.[97] This elaborate paper can be seen in Plates 199 through 201. Willement designed a much more elaborate carpet than that for the Library, closely following the design and colours of the wallpaper.

The richly moulded plaster ceiling is very closely based upon that in the King James Drawing Room at Hatfield House. A published illustration had been available since the appearance in 1834 of Henry Shaw's book on Elizabethan architecture.[98] Willement was a close friend of Shaw's and in fact several of the plates in this book were drawn by Willement. But to complete the Charlecote connection, it was published by none other than William Pickering himself. The Dining Room ceiling might therefore either be a direct copy of that at Hatfield or be taken from Shaw's illustration.

The most important piece of furniture in the dining room of a great mediaeval or Elizabethan house was considered by Willement and his fellow antiquaries and scholars to have been the great 'buffet'. Therefore George Lucy attempted to

201. The Dining Room Wallpaper (Country Life)

discover a piece of the correct type and found in the hands of Edward Baldock — the supplier of the octagonal Library table — what purported to be an ancient piece. This was a sideboard with splendidly carved oak panels. The panels were indeed ancient, but the object itself could not have been made before the 1820s when sideboards of this form were first designed to supersede the side table and its attendant pedestals. Baldock's bill reads '1837 . . . June 17 . . . a fine large carved oak sideboard £45, adding brackets to Do and altering date £2.10.0'.[99]

Baldock presumably sold this as a genuinely ancient object and then for an extra charge obligingly altered the carved date on the back — from what, is unknown — to 1558, the date when the building of Charlecote was completed. This sideboard moved to the Hall, where it stands today (Plate 186), in 1858 when Willcox's famous Charlecote Buffet (Plate 199 and 200) was purchased for the Dining Room. The smaller *pietre dure* table discussed above was thus displaced from the Hall by the Baldock sideboard and was moved to the Library, where it still stands today.

A large set of dining chairs in the style of the 1660s, though considered at this date Tudor, was ordered for the Dining Room. They were probably designed by Willement and were supplied by Thomas Bott of 28 Margaret Street, Cavendish Square: 'Dec 8. [1837] To 22 Antique oak chairs for Dining room the back & front legs and stretchers turned & twisted, carved pateras highly polished the seats and backs stuffed in the best manner and covered with super fine scarlet Utrecht velvet ... two very handsome large Elbow chairs ... to correspond with other chairs ... £158.13.6'.[100] The term 'Antique' must mean the style rather than that they were actually considered old; the velvet seats are still intact and in good condition.

The two marble-topped tables on either side of the chimney-piece were the most innovatory pieces of furniture designed for the house. Their massive slab ends pierced with patterns derived from strapwork designs of the sixteenth century (Plate 199) relate to several coeval tables from Aston Hall where Richard Bridgens was the designer.[101] The Aston Hall example was published in Bridgens' book *Furniture with Candelabra* of 1825.

Willement certainly drew some of the illustrations in this book and almost certainly designed the Charlecote tables, but his link with Bridgens is obscure. Tables of this type were certainly considered in the 1830s to be appropriate for Elizabethan-style rooms and were designed for a number of houses in which Salvin and/or Willement were involved. More work needs to be done on these interesting objects and the respective roles of Willement, Salvin and Bridgens.

I have dealt at length with the decoration and furnishing of the Hall, Library and Dining Room because these were the rooms upon which so much care and attention were lavished by George and Mary Elizabeth. There were other rooms on the ground floor, but it seems that family life revolved around these three main rooms. I have not mentioned a Drawing Room, for, as so often seems to be the case in the 1830s and 1840s, the Library preformed the dual role of Library and Drawing Room. It is particularly relevant that when Samuel Carter Hall visited the house in July 1845 he remarked, 'The new apartments consist of a dining-room and drawing room serving also as a library'.[102]

Even after Mary Elizabeth had refurbished the eighteenth-century Drawing Room in the 1850s (Plate 202), it was separated from the Hall by the Billiard Room. The late Sir Brian Fairfax Lucy, who died in 1974 aged seventy-five, told me that he remembered clearly that this later Drawing Room was used mainly by guests who could descend into it down a staircase which led directly to it from the bedroom floor above. He also remembered that most of the social activities of the family in his youth including the taking of tea were still carried on in the Library rather than the Drawing Room.

The evidence for the disposition of the furniture and other objects in the rooms has been detailed above. When the National Trust took over the house in the 1940s the furniture and other contents were rearranged in what was then considered an appropriate way. The show rooms were subsequently rearranged in the manner shown in Plates 186, 195, 196, 199, 200, 202 and 207 by John Hardy and me in 1973. There seems to be no surviving inventory of the contents of each room at George Lucy's death, but extensive use was made during the reordering of 1973 of the very full inventory taken in 1891 just after Mary Elizabeth's death.[103]

It is important to summarize here the evidence relating to their contents before 1850. The appearance of the Hall was recorded in 1845 (Plate 185): the Beckford *pietre dure* table stood in the middle and the smaller *pietre dure* table at the end. As we saw above, this smaller table was displaced in 1858 by the Baldock sideboard, itself displaced from the Dining Room by the Willcox buffet. The Library was photographed in about 1870 (Plate 194).

In some records as in the Bott bill for chairs, the Dining Room is specifically mentioned. We then have George Lucy's own list: 'Fixtures and Furniture for the New Dining Room and Library ... Bott dinner room chairs ... Isaacs Black Library chairs & sofa & cabinets ... Baldock Library Table, dining R sideboard ... Isaacs Marquetrie wardrobe ...'[104] The wardrobe is a puzzle. There was no wall space in the Library; it could have stood in the Dining Room, but, as we saw above, it seems to have been in the staircase hall for a very long while. Mary Elizabeth's

202. The Drawing Room at Charlecote in 1985
(Country Life)

book of 1862[105] gives details of the placing of some objects, and these are almost all
still in the same place in the 1891 inventory. On the evidence it would seem
reasonable to assume that very little change took place in the Library, Hall and
Dining Room between the date of their furnishing and the 1891 inventory.

Where the bulk of the Fonthill objects were displayed before Mary Elizabeth's
refurnishing of the Drawing Room in the 1850s cannot yet be established. Many of
them were certainly displayed in the Drawing Room when her book was written in
1862 and were once again placed in these positions in 1973 (Plate 202). The three
cabinets at the end of the room (Plate 205), that on the right and the *pietre dure* casket
on the table (Plate 203) are all from Fonthill. In the Drawing Room there are also a
number of pieces of oriental ceramics with eighteenth-century French ormolu
mounts (Plates 204 and 206).

On the floor above, in the Ebony Bedroom stood another Fonthill object (this
was not bought from the 1823 sale). It appears in the catalogue but went to join the
rest of Beckford's collection in Bath. It was sold by Beckford through English, the
Bath auctioneers and cabinet-makers, to George Lucy. English's bill of June 1837
states: 'To the Lancaster State Bedstead and hangings formerly at Fonthill — also

235

203. A *pietre dure* casket from Fonthill, Italian, *c.*1750 (Country Life)
204. A Chinese bowl, *c.*1740, with French ormolu mounts, from Fonthill (Country Life)

205. A *pietre dure* cabinet from Fonthill, Italian, *c.* 1640 (Country Life)

207. The furniture from the Ebony Bedroom, now in the Billiard Room at Charlecote

a paliasse — 2 mattresses — feather bed bolster & two pillows & silk Quilt [£]136.10.0.'[106]

It would seem that George Lucy was in contact with English about other objects, for English had written to George Lucy on 10 July 1832: 'I was at Erlstoke Friday last, the effects are worth seeing some pictures fine and genuine . . . it was thronged to suffocation not less than 1,600 persons admitted on that day.'[107] The Watson Taylor sale at Erlestoke included a number of objects Watson Taylor had bought at the Fonthill sale, which presumably explains George Lucy's interest, though he seems not to have bought anything at the sale. The Ebony Bedroom has been put to other use and the Billiard Room is now furnished with its contents (Plate 207). The Lancaster State Bed itself (Plate 208) is made of ebony and was created for the Lancaster bedroom at Fonthill. It was constructed from a seventeenth-century Indo-Portuguese bed, or even a pair of sofas like that at Cothele (Plate 18), with ebony posts added for Beckford.

208. The headboard from the Lancaster State Bed

I have said little concerning George and Mary Elizabeth's two continental tours, which were from May to July 1829 and October 1841 to May 1843. Mary Elizabeth published an account of this second tour.[108] The objects they purchased were usually small, but they enliven the rooms at Charlecote even so. On the 1829 tour, for instance, 'We crossed the Simplon, and arrived at Milan on the 9th of June. It was *there* we got, for *one* English sovereign, in an old broker's shop, the beautiful pair of candelabras which now stand in the drawing room; and for the cleaning and gilding of which my dear husband afterwards paid to Hume, Berners Street, London, one *hundred* sovereigns.'[109]

These are the tall candlestands (Plate 202) on which now stand 'the pair of exquisite candelabras, with figures holding four lights, standing on a base of white marble', which were bought in Paris in 1843,[110] where they also bought 'The three rare and beautiful vases in Manganesi Rose de Russie . . . which now stand on the chimneypiece in the library'[111] (Plate 194).

In Naples in 1842 they bought 'The six lapis lazuli candlesticks now in the library. They were very old and dirty, and the shopkeeper with a most grave face, assured [George Lucy] they had been taken out of Pompeii.'[112] Two of these can be seen on

206. (facing page) A Chinese vase, and a Japanese bottle, c.1740, both with French ormolu mounts, from Fonthill (Country Life)

the mantelpiece in Plates 194 and 195, as can a purchase made in Rome in 1842, 'The casket panelled with fine ancient Florentine pietra dura he [George Lucy] got for 224 piastres; it now stands on the centre table in the library.'[113] These two continental tours encompass neatly George and Mary Elizabeth's large-scale collecting activities, coming as they do, one before they began the transformation of Charlecote and the other when the building and furnishing were finished.

The range of furniture and other objects collected for Charlecote was confined in terms of country and date in the following way: the majority of objects range in date from 1550–1720 and are mainly Italian, Dutch, oriental and English. The ebony pieces were, as I have said, deemed to be English by George Lucy and his contemporaries. It would seem that a conscious effort was made by George and Mary Elizabeth to acquire objects suitable for an Elizabethan house. There were none of the mediaeval objects such as enamels, ivories and furniture of the type collected for other houses during the 1820s and 1830s.

Many of the owners of Elizabethan houses filled them with both mediaeval and Elizabethan objects mixed together, but this was not the case at Charlecote. The only piece of 'old oak' carved furniture was the Dining Room sideboard, whereas many other houses were packed with such pieces. George Lucy did not incorporate ancient pieces of panelling and carving or stained glass in the interiors he was creating, neither were they hung with ancient tapestries. He used instead new Elizabethan-style wallpapers, carpets and stained glass in the new rooms; he did not even attempt to spread out the ancient stained glass from the Great Hall to the new rooms. Charlecote is thus a very good example of an ancient house very largely furnished with antique objects especially collected for it, but where the modern furnishings and interior decoration cannot easily be mistaken for old work.

George and Mary Elizabeth paid close attention to the progress of the work of re-edification, which in fact lasted for half of their married life. It will be seen from the material quoted that George Lucy very carefully selected from the objects offered to him by dealers and he seemed to have struck up friendships with a number of them. He also chose the best craftsmen and designers, Willcox and Willement both standing at the head of their profession.

Shakespeare was responsible for the fame of Charlecote, and justice was certainly done to his memory by George and Mary Elizabeth. But the Shakespeare legend certainly brought informed visitors and scholars such as Irving and Scott to the house, and their interest and comments gave great encouragement to George and Mary Elizabeth to re-edify the house in the most sensitive, creative way. The appearance of instant antiquity achieved by such a successful re-edification certainly convinced another tourist, Nathaniel Hawthorne:

> All about the house, and the park, however, there is a perfection of comfort and domestic taste, and an amplitude of convenience, which must have taken ages, and the thoughts of successive generations, intent upon adding all possible household charm to the house which they loved, to produce. It is only so that real homes can be produced; one man's life is not enough for it.[114]

9

GOODRICH COURT

In Abbotsford is united the castle and the monstery, with
something of the fanciful, fairy spirit of Border legends. At
Goodrich Court we dream of Froissart and his chronicles of
arms and chivalry.   Thomas Roscoe

Sir Samuel Rush Meyrick (1783–1848) (Plate 209) has already made his
appearance as the friend of Sir Walter Scott who gave most help in building up the
collection of arms and armour at Abbotsford. The extent of this help is apparent
from the surviving letters written by Meyrick to Scott. Though Meyrick was born
in London, he always claimed that he was descended from the family of Meyrick of
Bodorgan on the Isle of Anglesea. Thus he could claim such celebrated ancestors as
Dr Rowland Meyrick, Bishop of Bangor (1505–1566), and his son Sir Gelly
(1556–1601), who was executed for his close association with Robert Earl of Essex.[1]
Meyrick identified strongly with Wales, devoting both his first book, *The History
and Antiquities of the County of Cardigan*, of 1810 and his last, *Heraldic Visitations of
Wales*, of 1846 to aspects of the Principality.

He was nevertheless brought up in London and went to Queen's College,
Oxford. After his marriage in 1803 he was disinherited by his father, whose
considerable wealth devolved upon Sir Samuel's son Llewelyn. But the premature
death of Llewelyn in 1837 meant that Sir Samuel eventually inherited his father's
fortune, by way of his son. Luckily Llewelyn had shared his father's passion for
armour and provided the money to create the celebrated collection I shall describe.

To earn a living Meyrick had become a barrister in the Ecclesiastical and
Admiralty Courts. He was elected a fellow of the Society of Antiquaries of London
in 1810 and over the next thirty years or so published numerous articles in the
Archaeologia, several of which describe objects in his and his son's collection. In
1817, of instance, he published an illustration of an ancient crozier head he had
recently purchased in France and which he had exhibited at a ballot at the
Antiquaries Rooms in Somerset House on 29 January 1816. This crozier is now in
the British Museum.[2]

The collection grew apace and was at first housed at 3 Sloane Terrace, Chelsea,
but then at 20 Upper Cadogan Place where he 'gradually accumulated a very large
collection of armour which not only filled the garrets, the staircase, and the back
drawing-room, but even encroached upon the bedrooms'[3] — a situation that would
have been familiar to Oldbuck himself! By the mid-1820s the Meyrick collection of
armour and antiquities was known throughout Europe, attracting many visitors to
Cadogan Place.

Two of the most interesting were the artists Eugène Delacroix and Richard
Bonington who came on 8 July 1825. Plate 210 shows a drawing which Delacroix
made of several of Meyrick's most important pieces of armour. At least two other
Delacroix drawings of Meyrick armour survive, one in the Louvre and one at
Breman.[4] The Breman drawing is dated 9 July, which might indicate a second visit,
though it could have been drawn the next day from memory. A watercolour by
Bonington of the suit of armour shown in Delacroix's Louvre drawing is in the

209. Sir Samuel Rush Meyrick in 1834 by Henry
Brockedon (National Portrait Gallery, London)

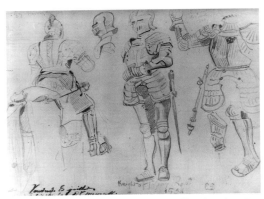

210. Armour from Meyrick's collection in 1825 by Delacroix (Wallace Collection, London)

British Museum.[5] This latter suit is the celebrated Buckhurst Armour (Plate 238) now in the Wallace Collection.[6]

Delacroix wrote to Théophile Thoré on 30 November 1861 that he and Bonington 'met again in England in 1825, and we worked together making studies at Dr Meyrick's: this was a famous English antiquarian who had the finest collection of armour there has ever been.'[7] Both Delacroix and Bonington were to depict armour from Meyrick's collection in their historical painting.[8] Interestingly, both artists also depicted Meyrick pieces in paintings of scenes from Scott's novel *Quentin Durward*.[9]

Even before the creation of Goodrich we see this celebrated collection making a direct contribution to the improved accuracy with which armour was represented in the works of two major artists. Meyrick himself was well aware of the direct influence his collection could have on the Romantic artists who were painting mediaeval subjects. Indeed collections of classical antiquities had been used in this way since the Renaissance. Less than a year after the visit of Bonington and Delacroix, Meyrick wrote in connection with the publication of the first part of a book devoted to the Meyrick collection:

> To Artists, it appears to me, the work will be invaluable; for there now exists a feeling for correctness of costume and accessories, both here and on the Continent . . . that cannot be retrograde. The taste with the publick is in its commencement, but it is daily gaining ground, and when once they have become confident judges in these matters, they will no longer tolerate anachronisms. Foreigners and natives are continually drawing from my sons collection; and at least six pictures, painted by as many of the English who stand at the head of their profession, will grace the walls of the ensuing exhibition at Somerset-house. These paintings have been ordered by the first among our nobility who patronize the arts, and all the authors of them declare that they never could have satisfactorily performed their engagements without access to this collection.[10]

The book in question was eventually published in two splendid folio volumes in 1830, but was previously issued in parts first announced in January 1826.[11] The first part, entitled *Engraved Illustrations of the Antient Arms and Armour, from the Collection of Llewelyn Meyrick LLB, FSA, After the Drawings and with the Descriptions of Dr Meyrick, By Joseph Skelton FSA*, was reviewed in April 1826.[12] The reviewer stated that it was a work 'which, when completed, cannot fail, from the high character that Collection has obtained, to be generally acceptable, and more particularly useful to the Antiquary, Historian, and Artist'.[13] When part XIII was reviewed in October 1828 the title included the words 'from the collection at Goodrich Court.'[14]

Meyrick had already made his name as an arms and armour scholar with the publication in 1823 of his three volume work *A Critical Inquiry into Antient Armour, as it existed in Europe but Particularly in England*. Sir Walter Scott thought highly of this book. On publication it immediately established itself as a standard work, and it has remained so until today. Claude Blair, Britain's most celebrated armour scholar, has written that Meyrick's *Inquiry*, 'for the first time, provided a chronological survey of the development of European armour based on a study of early documents and illustrations and, to a more limited extent of actual specimens of armour . . . it is no exaggeration to say that all subsequent works on the subject stem ultimately from it.'[15]

After the publication of this book not only artists, writers and historians, but also stage designers turned to Meyrick for advice. J.R. Planche, the herald and dramatist, was in 1823 asked by the actor–manager Charles Kemble to 'make the necessary researches, design the dresses, and superintend the production of "King John" . . . Fortunately I obtained, through a mutual friend, an introduction to Doctor afterwards Sir Samuel Meyrick, who had just published his elaborate and valuable work . . . He entered most warmly and kindly into my views, pointed out to me the best authorities, and gave me an introduction to Mr Francis Douce.'[16]

This production at Covent was — due to its historical accurary — a great success. 'Receipts of from 400L. to 600L. nightly soon reimbursed the management for the expense of the production, and a complete reformation of dramatic costume became from that moment inevitable upon the English stage.'[17] Here we clearly see how interdependent in the 1820s were this small circle of British antiquaries. Planche tells us that 'In 1834, my "History of British Costume" — the result of ten years' of diligent devotion to its study of every leisure hour ... was published ... That I am indebted for all this to the counsels and encouragement of Mr Douce and Sir Samuel Rush Meyrick I shall never cease gratefully to proclaim.'[18] Planche's work joined Meyrick's *Inquiry* as a crucial source for writers and painters.

Meyrick was thus a natural choice to reorganize the Horse Armoury at the Tower of London. He had criticized the arrangement of the armour in the Tower in his *Inquiry* in 1823 and was eventually called upon to remedy these defects. The Line of Kings in the Horse Armoury had been a famous features of the Tower since the late seventeenth century, being mentioned by a German visitor in 1694.[19] In 1706–7 another German visitor described the 'Place where the Kings of England are in full Proportion on Horseback, with the proper armour they use in Battle.'[20] By 1750 the line consisted of sixteen equestrian figures of kings from William the Conqueror to George I.

Meyrick was annoyed not to have been consulted over the design of the newly erected buildings for the Horse Armouries and wrote:

> Nor have I had any thing to do with the new building for the Horse armoury, erected without any knowledge of how effect is produced, with the exception of substituting some of Mr Willement's painted glass for the childish and tasteless *ornaments* of two out of four circular windows. You may remember that the row of kings, as it was called bid defiance to truth. One of my objects was, therefore, to restore the suits of armour to their real dates. Having ousted William the Conqueror, Richard I, Edw III, John of Gaunt, and Henry V ... As a tribute most justly due to the Master General of the Ordnance under whose auspices the improvement, as I trust I may call it has been effected, I have taken care the exhibition should commence and terminate with the spoils of Waterloo.[21]

The Master General was, of course, the Duke of Wellington. Meyrick's friend Sir Walter Scott had arranged his spoils of Waterloo along with his ancient armour at Abbotsford before the Tower was reorganized, and Meyrick himself was later to do the same at Goodrich.

The mention of Willement is interesting. It may well be that Meyrick made his acquaintance over the work at the Tower, and Willement was to work for Meyrick at Goodrich. Willement recorded that in 1826 he supplied to 'The Tower of London. In the horse-armoury, two armorial windows erected by order of the Hon. the Board of Ordnance, immediately after the chronological arrangement of the armour had been completed by Sir Samuel Rush Meyrick.'[22] Meyrick wrote in 1827 to the Secretary of the Board of Ordnance that 'If the armour at the Tower be not the most splendid in Europe it is now the only collection that is truly and historically arranged.'[23]

Shortly after he had completed his work at the Tower, Meyrick was called to Windsor Castle and on 30 April 1828 it was announced that 'the armour at Windsor, previous to its new arrangement in the King and Queen's guard chambers, is to undergo a revision his majesty was pleased to command Dr Meyrick's attendance on this day for the purpose of inspecting it ... and after honouring him with a long private audience, directed him to undertake its superintendance.'[24]

The armour collection at Windsor was an important one which included many pieces with unusually secure provenances, and Meyrick's undertaking provided him the opportunity to examine them closely. In 1832 King William IV knighted Meyrick 'in consequence of the services rendered by him in the very able and masterly arrangement effected under his superintendance of the armoury in the Tower of London and that at Windsor Castle. He [Meyrick] was dubbed a knight bachelor on the 22d Feb.'[25]

By 1832 Meyrick's standing as Europe's leading arms and armour scholar rested not only upon his pioneering publications, but also upon his practical experience of rearranging two of the important European collections of armour. His influence is apparent upon the assembling and the display not only of the armour collections of his contemporaries in this country, but also of those collections made during the rest of the century. He counted as friends most of the celebrated antiquaries of the day, men such a Willement, Blore, Scott, Douce, Phillips, Shaw and Planche. He also knew his fellow lawyer Sir Nicholas Harris Nicolas and provided notes for his book *The Siege of Carlaverock* published in 1829.

In his *Inquiry* Meyrick, after discussing the armour in the Royal Collection and the Tower, gives an interesting list of private collections of armour, but notes that 'there are few in England ... Llewelyn Meyrick Esq, has a large and probably the most instructive collection in Western Europe.'[26] The collections he singled out were Belvoir Castle, Chatsworth, Warwick Castle, Eaton Hall, Castle Howard, Wardour Castle, Cothele, Penshurst, Battle Abbey, Costessey, Middle Hill, Abbotsford and Brancepeth Castle. Middle Hill was the Worcestershire home of Sir Thomas Phillips.

Meyrick was in the early 1820s helping Scott to collect armour for Abbotsford though in fact Scott also presented an ancient sword to Meyrick. Meyrick wrote to Scott in April 1821: 'My dear Sir Walter, I am sorry to say that I did not succeed in getting anything for you at the sale. Every lot you marked went for twice the money ... I have sent you the form and measurement of my sons lance so that by removing the head of the pike which you purchased your carpenter will be enabled to make an exact resemblance.'[27]

Meyrick wrote again on 5 July: 'I hope you received the memoir I sent by the hands of Mr Allan who expressed himself highly pleased with my son's armoury.'[28] The Allan referred to was William Allan, the artist who was to depict the interiors of Abbotsford (Plates 151 and 154). So here we find an artist using the Meyrick collection as an historical source several years before the visit of Delacroix and Bonington.

But, as far as Goodrich is concerned, the most important letter was written by Meyrick to Scott on 5 October 1822 following a trip Meyrick had made to Scotland:

> my sincere thanks to you and your family for the kind civilities to me while in Edinburgh ... Notwithstanding what you say in that beautiful work on Scottish Scenery and Castles, all the numbers of which I possess respecting rendering an old ruin habitable, I am now fully in pursuit of that object, hoping to attain it within a years time. But I assure you you need not dread demolition for unless I would make it fit to live in without the slightest alteration, even cutting an additional window, I would forbear and build my residence within view. If therefore I succeed in making such a purchase it will be with perfectly antiquarian motives. My son and myself are most highly delighted with your country and nothing but its great distance from the Southern capital makes me prefer the principality for our Summer residence.[29]

The book Meyrick referred to was Scott's *Provincial Antiquities and Picturesque Scenery of Scotland* in which a number of celebrated castles are illustrated. The remark about purchasing a property within a year of 1822 and a Welsh one at that is interesting. Did he have the ruined castle at Goodrich in mind so early? It would indeed seem that Meyrick had negotiated to purchase Goodrich for some years and that this started in 1822, as his letter to Scott indicates. Confirmation comes in a letter Meyrick wrote to Douce on 12 April 1823: 'I returned this morning having travelled all night from Herefordshire. We have found the very thing to suit us, so

211. Goodrich Court in 1845 (C. Nash, *The Goodrich Court Guide*, 1845)

212. The north elevation in 1828 by Edward Blore (RIBA Drawings Collection, London)

213. The Courtyard in 1828 by Edward Blore (RIBA Drawings Collection, London)

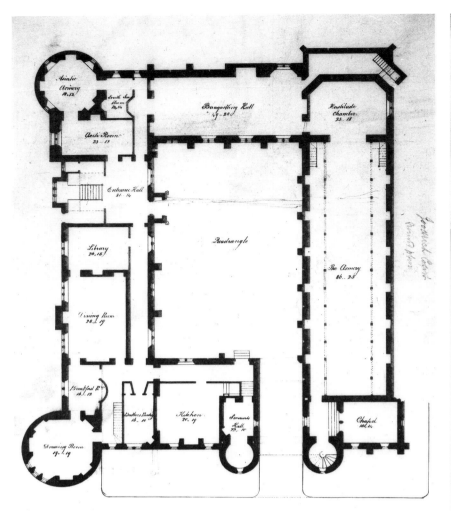

214. Plan of Goodrich in 1828 by Edward Blore
(RIBA Drawings Collection, London)

215. The entrance to Goodrich in the 1940s

exactly that it seems made on purpose. This is Goodrich Castle ... I have set an attorney to work ... Should you be able without inconvenience to put your hand on that volume of Grose which contains Goodrich I shall be very much obliged by the loan of it for this evening.'[30] It is amusing to see Meyrick the scholar consulting the works of an antiquary of the previous generation; the book in question was Grose's *Antiquities*, which contains two illustrations of Goodrich.[31]

The protracted negotiations to purchase eventually broke down, and Meyrick started to build Goodrich Court nearby. His obituary states: 'About the year 1827 Dr Meyrick having vainly endeavoured to purchase the ruins of Goodrich castle on the banks of the Wye, (the owners of which, some single ladies, were advised to ask a very exhorbitant price for ruined walls, on a barren rock, almost the only product of which consisted in the gratuities of tourists to the tenant, who acted as their *cicerone*) was induced to buy the opposite hill, and to erect thereon a new mansion, which he styled Goodrich Court.'[32] It would have been very interesting if Meyrick had actually restored an ancient castle in the manner he described to Scott, for his letters betrays a far greater sensitivity to ancient buildings than was usual in the 1820s. It is also interesting that Meyrick eventually, as he described to Scott, did actually build a new house overlooking a ruined castle.

Meyrick wrote to Douce on 28 March 1828: 'after next spring my armour will be in Herefordshire I have bought the land adjoining the castle at Goodrich on the Wye and not choosing to wait longer for the ladies decision am about to build instantly a dwelling in the style of Edward 2nd under the superintendence of the first gothic architect of the age my friend Edward Blore ... I will show you the plans etc of what will be termed "Goodrich court".[33]

Goodrich was started in 1828. 'From the Hereford Gazette we learn that Dr Meyrick and his son have determined that their own collection shall form an object on the tour of the Wye, and that the first stone of *Goodrich Court*, destined to contain, it was laid by the latter on St George's day.'[34] Further details are given in the guidebook (Plate 211) written by Charles Nash:

> The following is a copy of the inscription on the plate deposited under the foundation-stone: 'Goodrich Court, erected under the superintendence of Edward Blore, Esq., F.S.A., Architect, by Samuel Rush Meyrick, L.L.D., F.S.A. The first stone laid by Llewelyn Meyrick, Esq., L.L.D. and F.S.A., his only son, in the presence of Francis Martin, Esq., F.S.A. Windsor Herald, this 23d of April, 1828 the anniversary of St George'. Three years afterwards on the same day of the month of April, 1831, the last stone was fixed in the southern bartizan and the external work finished.[35]

Nash's title-page informs us that he was Secretary of the Hereford Mechanic's Institution and he advertises in the book as 'Stationer, Bookseller, Bookbinder, Engraver and Music Seller, 18 Westgate Street, Gloucester.'

The story of the construction of Goodrich has recently been very clearly told,[36] and there are several other contemporary sources besides Nash.[37] Though the exterior was indeed completed in 1831, a commendably short time for a building of this scale. The interiors were complete well before Meyrick wrote to Douce on 21 October 1833: 'It is a great nuisance that Blore did not make the roof of the armoury water-tight before he gave it up to me. The rain comes in, in every part and I am forced to prevent the armour being completely spoilt to move it into the banquetting hall.'[38]

Blore's north-eastern elevation is shown in Plate 212, the Courtyard in Plate 213 and the ground floor plan in Plate 214. The distant view was described in 1828: 'a building of stone of the very best masonry, and of the architecture of Edward II ... It crowns a commanding eminence, flanked by a hanging wood, the skirt of which is washed by a bold sweep of the celebrated river Wye. Of a character suited to the romantic scenery in which it is placed, it is highly creditable to the taste and talents of that skilful architect, whom we have often had occasion to notice, Edward Blore.'[39]

Thomas Roscoe perceptively linked Goodrich with Abbotsford and, of course, Blore was also involved at Abbotsford: 'Goodrich Court. I may well apply to this mansion the term used regarding Abbotsford; this is, indeed, "a romance in stone and lime". But the characters of the romances are different. In Abbotsford is united the castle and the monastery, with something of the fanciful, fairy spirit of Border legends. At Goodrich Court we dream of Froissart and his chronicles of arms and chivalry.'[40]

The house was from the first open to interested visitors, for as we saw both Meyrick and his son intended that it should be part of the 'Wye Tour'. Roscoe described how 'the visitor arrives at the principal gateway, which is approached over a drawbridge, (not intended to be raised) and is furnished with a portcullis and flanked by two round towers [Plate 215]. The surrounding battlements, turrets, loopholes, and machicolations look bristlingly on the defensive.'[41]

'Having rung the bell of the grand entrance door, their summons is answered by one or other of the domestics (male and female) whose vocation it is to conduct the strangers through the rooms and explain the more important curiosities as they pass along. You are requested to insert the name and residence of one of the company, with the number of your friends, in a book in the first room.'[42]

The first room seen by visitors was the Entrance Hall (Plate 216), which measured 21 by 13 feet by 12 feet high. 'The authority for the flattened roof is a chapel on the

216. The Entrance Hall (J. Skelton, *Engraved Illustrations of Antient Arms and Armour ...*, 1830)

247

south side of Rochester Cathedral of the time of Edward II, of which period is the whole style of architecture throughout the building: the fire-place an adaptation of a monument at Winchelsea and the chairs of the state one of Edward I.'[43] This quotation and several that follow are, with a number of the illustrations, taken from Skelton and Meyrick's famous book on the collection as displayed at Goodrich.

Though the printed book was published in two volumes in 1830, it was first issued in parts. Parts I to IV were reviewed in January 1827.[44] In October 1828 part XIII was reviewed[45] and this part included the illustrations of the Entrance Hall (Plate 216) and the Hastilude Chamber (Plate 221). If one compares these dates with the date of the laying of the foundation-stone in April 1828 and the completion date of 1831 it is obvious that the several rooms (Plates 216, 220, 221 and 222) were illustrated by Skelton before they actually existed. This remarkable fact is confirmed by Planche, who stated that the Skelton plates were

> from drawings made to scale by himself [Meyrick] . . . and engraved long before the completion of the building and yet when it was completed, and the entire magnificent collection of armour had been brought down from Cadogan Place, London and arranged in the rooms that had been specially constructed for its reception, every article, to a single dagger or gauntlet occupied the exact positon in which it appeared in the engravings, just as though the drawing had been carefully made after they had been placed there instead of some years previous to the erection of the walls they hung upon.[46]

Planche may be exaggerating when he says some years, for, as we saw, the house was under construction when the engravings were published. The drawings, however, may well have been in existence for some time.

But to return to the Entrance Hall: 'This room is lighted by a window containing various armorial bearings of the Meyrick family and the inner [Hall] by an oriel on the first landing place of the staircase, in the glass of which is the whole length portrait of Meuric ab Llewelyn, Esquire of the body to Henry VII'.[47] These windows were, like a number of others at Goodrich, designed by Willement[48] who also supplied some of the elaborate wallpapers in the house. That on the staircase (Plate 217) besides the armoured figure depicts the Meyrick arms and in the quarries is the Ragged staff Fired, which was one of Meyrick's badges and which also occurs on the Breda ceiling (Plate 223). Sadly none of Willement's glass for Goodrich survives, but several of the designs are in the British Museum.

Meyrick, after describing the hunting implements seen over the arch in Plate 216, stated:

> The trophy over the right-hand door, leading to the banquetting hall is composed of Scotch weapons . . . Between the chairs is a two handed sword of state, with halberds on each side, and in the passage . . . beyond the fire-place, a nich containing spoils from Waterloo . . . The authority for placing cross-bows and other weapons in the entrance hall of a mansion, is found in the inventory . . . of Sir John Fastolffe in the time of Henry VI, and there are many reasons to conclude that the practise was of far more antient date.[49]

The Scottish weapons probably owe their presence to Meyrick's friendship with Scott and, as I have described, Scott at Abbotsford arranged in his Hall a number of weapons from Waterloo. As we shall see elsewhere at Goodrich, Meyrick displayed modern weapons associated with important historical events, for he like Scott believed that history was still in the making.

The whole question of the display of arms and armour in interiors is a complex one; indeed arms and armour were a vital ingredient in the furnishing of Romantic Interiors. At Goodrich arms and armour were not merely part of a more general collection of antiquities, but the whole building was created around them. Meyrick's point about placing weapons in an entrance hall is an important one. He believed

217. Willement's stained glass window depicting Meuric ab Llewelyn (Royal Commission on the Historical Monuments of England)

that until the seventeenth century 'Weapons for the chace and for armed peasantry hung up in readiness in the halls of our old mansions, but were never so placed for the mere purpose of ornament'.[50]

Meyrick again refers to the Fastolffe inventory of 1459, which had been published in 1827 and relates to the objects at Caister Castle, the family seat. Meyrick had, along with his friend Douce, helped with the editing of this fascinating manuscript. 'At the castellated abode of so distinguished a commander, the catalogue of armour may be expected to be copious ... The great hall was furnished with eleven cross-bows, a boar-spear, and a target.'[51]

Thus, though Meyrick knew that in a mediaeval castle of the stylistic date of Goodrich, armour would not have been arranged as he arranged it, he made a conscious choice to act counter to the historical precedents which he had published. His aims were at least as didactic as they were antiquarian or aesthetic. When, long after his death, from 1868 to 1871 the collection was displayed at the South Kensington Museum, Planche wrote of 'the collection of European arms and armour, which for historical interest, and (what is of even more importance to the institution to which it is at present confided) for *educational purposes*, I believe to be unrivalled in England or on the continent. The grand object of its founder was INSTRUCTION and his old friend and grateful pupil rejoices in the fortunate occurrence which has enabled him to assist in its further development.'[52] Meyrick had written:

A due knowledge of armour is absolutely necessary to all who undertake the task of topographers, in order to correctly describe a monumental effigy, a painting on glass or an antient seal; from thence it is that the true date, if wanting can be ascertained. It is equally instructive, from the same cause, to the antiquary and is in a great degree serviceable to the historian. The utility of a collection formed on the principle of that at Goodrich will be evident, when it is considered that there is no surer criterion of date than costume, and recollected that down to the time of Charles II our ancestors represented every subject they had to produce in the fashion of their own time.[53]

The Line of Kings at the Tower had, as we have seen, been arranged in a didactic way since the seventeenth century. But Meyrick's own research took him back to the sixteenth century, and he concluded that 'It was Emperor Charles V who, with all the ideas of parade that had distinguished Maximilian, first collected armour for the purpose of show, and this he placed in the Castle of Ambras in the Tyrol; Ferdinand his brother and successor, added to its extent. Previously the arsenals contained weapons and munitions of war for actual service and the suits kept in closets thence termed *armoires*.'[54] The Ambras collection is still one of the most celebrated assemblages of arms and armour and antiquities in Europe and as such had wide influence on Meyrick and his generation of collectors.

As Meyrick knew, it had been collected by several of the Hapsburg dynasty, namely, Maximilian I (1459–1519) and his grandsons Charles V (1500–1558) and Ferdinand I (1503–1564). It was, however, Archduke Ferdinand II (1529–1595) who as State Prince of the Tyrol from 1563 until his death arranged the Ambras collection in a new and revolutionary way.[55]

While Ferdinand was Governor of Bohemia from 1547 to 1563, He began collecting on a large scale in Bohemia, his special interest being armour. On the one hand coats of mail represented for him the historical personality of their one-time owners, and on the other, he valued them as pieces which reminded him of the events at which they had been worn. They constituted an imaginary collection of heroes, which he later called his 'honourable company'. While he was in the Tirol the Archduke was gradually able to arrange his collections ... in Ambras Castle near Innsbruck in an orderly exhibition ... In the *Kunstkammer* a series of ancient objects was included which had belonged to his great forbears.[56]

Luckily an inventory of the Ambras collection was taken a year after Ferdinand's death, but Meyrick could not have seen this, as it was not published until the later nineteenth century. Neither could he have seen the collection *in situ* at Ambras, for, by the time he and Llewelyn visited Vienna in 1823, he was to record that 'The suits from the Chateau of Ambras have been removed to the Palace of the Little Belvidere ... so far as finding the figures wielding the sword and poising the lance, all the weapons are in a separate compartment: while with the exception of eight on horseback the suits are placed on two shelves one above the other in places like pigeon-holes.'[57]

But Meyrick had noted in 1824:

Of the Ambras collection a folio volume of description, with plates was published in 1601, entitled Armamentarium Heroicum Ambrasianum, by James Schenck, and a copy having been lent to me by my worthy friend Mr Douce ... From the costume of the figures we learn that they could not have been set up above forty years before the date of this work; the shoes, particularly, where armour is wanting, being all of the middle of our Elizabeth's reign. The number of statues, independent of two or three Asiatics not in armour is 108 and they are thus named and armed.[58]

Meyrick goes on to list all the figures, giving the actual date of the armour in which they were clad. In dating the shoes to about 1560 Meyrick demonstrated his considerable knowledge of armour and costume, for, as we saw, Ferdinand started to set up the figures when he became Prince of the Tyrol in 1563. It was the first Latin edition of *Armamentarium* that Douce had lent to Meyrick.[59] At some stage after 1824 Meyrick acquired a copy of the German edition of 1603, for this appears in the sale catalogue of his library.[60]

218. The exterior of Schloss Ambras (J. Schrenken, *Ambrasische Helden Rustkammer ...*, 1735)

219. The Armoury at Ambras (Schrenken *Ambrasische*)

There was an interesting later edition,[61] which depicts Ambras itself framed by weapons from the collection (Plate 218). There is also a portrait of Archduke Ferdinand, the background of which shows the gallery containing armed figures (Plate 219). But also listed in the sale of Meyrick's library is a copy of a work of 1760 by John Keysler which describes the Ambras collection when it was still *in situ* in the castle.[62]

For instance, at Ambras 'coats of armour and the weapons made use of by several famous princes and noblemen ... to every armour they have annexed the image, name and titles of the great personage who wore it'.[63] Keysler went on to describe the eighteen closets of curiosities and antiquities at Ambras. The actual form of the displays of armour at Ambras has recently been carefully examined,[64] as has the character of the collections of curiosities and antiquities.[65] But from the evidence I have given here the influence of the form of display of the armour at Ambras in the furnishing of Goodrich is obvious and indeed is confirmed by Meyrick's own publications.

To return to Goodrich, despite the mediaeval character of the Entrance Hall, there was one classical antiquity: 'The lamp which lights this stair case is of Greek art and made for the Romans, as it was dug out of the ruins of Herculaneum ... The female masks and horses' heads, with which it is adorned are in the very best style, as well as the Janus-head, which forms the lid.'[66] This lamp forms the frontispiece to volume II of Skelton.

Turning left from the Hall the visitor entered the Asiatic Ante Room, which opened into the Asiatic Armoury (Plate 220). 'One of the principal subjects here [in the Armoury] is the Luti Pindarrie on his Arabian steed ... The apellation of Luti is derived from the circumstance of his letting himself out "to hire," receiving pay from such power as engages him.'[67] 'The horse was carved, and the whole arranged from a drawing by captain Grindley, whose taste and knowledge have been proved by his interesting publications.'[68] Captain Grindley was in fact R.M. Grindlay, who wrote on India.[69]

The history of the armour described is fortunately recounted in a letter written by Meyrick to the painter William Etty who seems — like several artists I have mentioned — to have collected armour in a modest way. Meyrick wrote on 19 February 1838:

> I return you many thanks for the promise of being the first to have the offer of your long bellied suit of armour in case you should feel inclined to part with it. I think you likewise purchased your trowsers of mail with circular kneecaps at Gwennaps ... if you have a mind in the warm weather to take a trip hither ... bring a young lady with you you can make studies from a chronological series of armour and chronological series of finished apartments that might become useful to you hereafter ... I suppose you aware that the mounted Pindarrie was bought for me at Gwennap's sale.[70]

Gwennap was a well-known London armour dealer. The Meyrick collection was being utilized once again by an artist to whom the chronological arrangement was important. Etty seems not to have had a large collection of armour, for his studio sale after his death included only two complete suits of armour as lots 878 and 978 as well as several lots of weapons.[71] The advice that Meyrick gave Etty on how to clean and preserve his armour would strike terror into the heart of modern armour conservators:

> The varnish should be copal and whenever you find it setting too yellow for the lights you want a little spirits of turpentine will take it all of and you can put some on afresh. This is the way I preserve the armour here ... The Indian way of cleaning mail is to put it in a sack with bran and slaked lime and then shake it about; the antient European one to put it into a barrel placed on a frame horizontally like a barrel churn with sand and lime and by turning it round thus procure the brightness. Oil is very well in the first instance toward getting off the rust, but sandpaper must be afterwards used or emery.[72]

Copal varnish was frequently used to preserve armour, and Hay used this method at Abbotsford.

Meyrick was interested in modern weapons with an interesting history, so in the Ante Room was 'an interesting modern Affghan sword taken from the person of Prince Hyder Khan, Governor of Ghunznee, son of Dost Mohammed Khan, when he was made prisoner on the 23rd July 1839'.[73] The engagement referred to was the capture of the city of Ghunznee in eastern Persia by British troops commanded by Sir John Keane during the Afghan War of 1838–42.

While Goodrich was being built, the reorganization of the armouries at the Tower of London continued and by late 1829 'The last stronghold of humbug the Spanish Armoury has yielded to the strong and repeated remonstrances of Dr. Meyrick, and the spoils of the Armada have vanished ... the whole will be called the "Asiatic Armoury".[74] It is thus difficult to establish to which armoury the name 'Asiatic' was first applied, but the term was certainly Meyrick's.

The Asiatic Armoury at Goodrich was 18 feet 6 inches square. 'Over the fire-place, inlaid in an Asiatic ornament, is one of the glazed tiles which occupied a place in the walls of the Alhambra Palace, in Spain.'[75] All the decoration in this exotic room was Islamic in character. 'The ceiling which has gilt stars on a blue ground, the cornice and the papering of the room are from antient Persian Illumination.'[76] Meyrick was a pioneer in the use of Islamic ornament in this way, well before Owen Jones and his generation began to advocate its use. Meyrick in his own description of Plate 220 states that 'Looking through the arch of the anti-room a soldier in mail armour of Delhi is seen kneeling in an attitude of homage to an Indian Rajah, who is seated cross-legged on his couch with one hand resting on a mace, and wearing the coat of plate'.

The visitor then entered the South Sea Room, 'which is filled with the rude

220. The Asiatic Armoury at Goodrich (Skelton, *Engraved Illustrations*)

weapons, feathered cloaks, etc., of the islanders of the Pacific Ocean. Among these is a war cloak made from the plumage of the Tropic bird, brought from the Sandwich Isles by Captain Cooke . . . and a cap with the representation of the whale fishery upon it, from Nootka Sound, engraved in the plates to his third voyage, and formerly in the Leverian museum.'[77] The celebrated Leverian Museum was described in print in 1790 and several caps identical to Meyrick's were described in detail.[78] The collection was sold in 1806, and one of the caps was then easily identifiable.[79]

Two of these caps probably found their way into William Bullock's collection, from the sale of which Sir Walter Scott purchased objects for Abbotsford. Meyrick bought armour from this sale and the two caps, which are listed as lots 7 and 9.[80] One cap of this type survives in Liverpool Museum. It is illustrated and the whole matter of Bullock's Museum and the Captain Cook objects has been fascinatingly discussed in print recently.[81] The ethnographical curiosities collected by Cook on his voyages are today of immense historical significance and the inclusion of such objects in Meyrick's collection is another illustration of its wide-ranging nature.

Meyrick attempted to order the ethnographical items in the same scholarly and precise way as the European ones. He stated that 'It has been almost equally difficult to particularize the first locality of the weapons from the Pacific ocean, owing to the same careless application of the term *South-sea* but all that reference to books, catalogues and engravings could produce has been made available to give authenticity to the statement of particular islands or coasts as the places from whence the articles have been brought.'[82] Did Meyrick know that Nootka or King George's Sound was on the coast of North America rather than in the midst of the Pacific ocean?

After the South Sea Room the visitor entered the Banquetting Hall, which was 49 feet by 20 feet:

> over the entrance door is the Minstrels Gallery. At the upper end, upon an elevated floor, instead of a high table, stands a billiard table . . . The chimney piece is well carved in Painswick stone, with the equestrian figure and armorial bearings of Aylmer de Valence. On a lecterne, or reading desk, is placed a fine copy of the *Nuremburg Chronicle*, 1493, in its original binding . . . In the oriel, in painted glass, are representations of William and Aylmer de Valence, successively owners of Goodrich Castle in the reigns of Henry III. and Edward I.[83]

The glass was supplied by Willement in January 1844: 'Two effigies of the Valences in armour with their coats and shields bearing arms resting on painted bases all in stained glass . . . 22.10.0.'[84] Willement had also provided some years previously in 1828 'Various armorial circular compartments for the windows of the banquetting hall'.[85]

The inclusion of a billiard table might seem a modern touch, but there are certainly seventeenth-century precedents for billiard tables in the halls and other public rooms of grand houses. Ham House and Knole are two well-documented examples, with the billiard table itself even surviving at the latter. In the 1840s Pugin was also to include a billiard table in his scheme for the Cromwell Hall at Chirk Castle (Plate 256), not many miles from Goodrich.

The nature of most of the other furnishings of the Banquetting Hall is unrecorded and, unusually for Goodrich, there was no armour on display. However, 'In niches are casts from the effigies of Edward II. and his mother on their monuments, and instead of half pannelling, dwarf bookcases, contain an extensive collection of useful, rare, and valuable volumes. Folding-doors on the right of the billiard table lead to the HASTILUDE CHAMBER.'[86]

The name of the Hastilude Chamber (Plate 221) is derived from 'hasta', a spear, and 'ludus', to play. Though this sounds like late-Georgian antiquarianism, the term 'hastilude' means literally spear play. This appeared in print as another name for a

221. The Hastilude Chamber at Goodrich (Skelton, *Engraved Illustrations*)

tournament as early as 1586 according to the *Oxford English Dictionary*. This room was 25 feet long, 17 feet 6 inches wide and 18 feet high and was

fitted up to represent a jousting match. Two combattants are engaged within the lists, while five others are waiting for their turns. On the steps, before the royal box, at the back of which is tapestry . . . of Henry VI, are two heralds: one holds a sword as a reward for a successful comer; the other a helmet, the guerdon for a tenant who awaits the effect of his challenge. On the left of the whole is the tree usually set up for holding the emblazoned shields of the combattants.[87]

After this room was furnished as engraved in 1830, further figures were added, those of 'guards in the costume of Henry VIII, charged with the badge of the ragged staff fired, [These costumes] were the dresses of the javelin-men who formed the escort of Sir Samuel Rush Meyrick, when High Sheriff of the county of Hereford, in the year 1834'.[88] These costumes relate to one of Meyrick's revivals of what he considered the feudal grandeur appropriate to his standing as High Sheriff: 'In 1834 he served the office of High Sheriff of Herefordshire, and made his year conspicuous by a revival of the ancient display of the javelin-men, duly harnessed, and other pageantry.'[89] Here is yet another example of Meyrick incorporating the material evidence of a recent historical event — indeed one which he created himself — into his display at Goodrich.

Next on the line of route was the Grand Armoury (Plate 222), which was 86 feet 6 inches by 25 feet,

222. The Grand Armoury (Skelton, *Engraved Illustrations*)

with its oaken roof . . . the antient British arms and the unbroken series of guns from the first invention to the fire-lock are absolutely unique, while the Greek and Roman armour cannot fail to be highly interesting. Above these glass-cases are the emblazoned banners of Edward II. . . . which have been selected from these knights holding lands in the county of Hereford . . . The oaken columns which support the gallery, are surrounded by weapons of all other known kinds, and between them, and also in the niches, are placed ten suits on horseback, and several on foot, from the time of Edward III. to that of James II., being the most comprehensive and instructive collection of the kind . . . king Charles Ist in an original buff jacket and gorget, with his armour on the floor of a tent, and his crown and helmet on the table attended by his standard bearer . . . The face and hand of king Charles which rests on a rapier, were painted by H.P. Briggs, Esqr., R.A.[90]

Not every visitor to Goodrich, however, was happy with the naturalistic arrangement of the arms and armour. Thomas Roscoe commented:

I think this is a splendid collection seriously injured by the puerile style of its arrangement: such as the introduction of dilapidated doll faces into the visors . . . To me, the sight of a vacant suit of armour is a strange and solemn thing . . . Another circumstance very annoying amid one's enjoyment in this palace of antiquity, is the severe reflection on the ignorant and mischievious propensities of my countrymen *and* women, conveyed in the numberless tickets and placards scattered through all the public rooms, reiterating the request, '*Don't touch any thing*'. It is pinned to banners, wafered to walls, stitched on hero's garments.[91]

By contrast Louisa Twamley visiting in 1838 wrote: 'though the intrusion of such things as wooden figures, and rather hetrogeous drapery, destroys the thoughtful and even solemn character which such assembled records of by-gone times and men cannot but create, it admirably serves to show how they appeared'.[92]

Though one perhaps deplores the intrusion of didactic material into the displays to satisfy a curious public, anyone with any experience of presenting to visitors a complex historic building and collection will appreciate Meyrick's dilemma. Du Sommerard used lay figures at the Cluny at much the same time as Meyrick (Plate

223. The Breda ceiling in the Library at Goodrich (Royal Commission on the Historical Monuments of England)

8). Indeed debate about displaying armour, and indeed costume, empty or on a lay figure, is still a live issue in museums today.

In the Grand Armoury we again see Meyrick's concern with recent historical events: on display were 'many of the insurrectionary weapons wrested from the rioters at the (so called) Chartists' *emeute* at Newport, during the night of Sunday Nov. 4, 1839 . . . presented by the authorities of that port to this collection'.[93]

The Chapel next to the Armoury was the last of the rooms shown to the public. The plan (Plate 214) shows that the ground floor also included a Library, Dining Room, Breakfast Room and Drawing Room, but sadly no illustrations of these interiors in Meyrick's day exist. All of these rooms were, however, crowded with objects from Meyrick's collection. Built into the Library was the largest ancient object at Goodrich (Plate 223): 'The oak ceiling . . . The foliage of the design and the frieze round the room, is supposed to be the premier specimen of the kind in this country. It was removed here from the Breda government-house in Holland, and was by Italians executed expressly for the Spaniards in the time of Henry VIII.'[94]

The Library also housed part of Meyrick's extensive collection of books and manuscripts.[95]

The Dining Room was hung with paintings and 'papered with crimson-coloured flock, the pattern trellice work and fleurs de lis'.[96] This elaborate paper was probably designed and supplied by Willement, who was designing equally elaborate papers for Charlecote Park in the 1830s (Plate 201). On 7 May 1842 he supplied to Goodrich '35 pieces of paper hanging Fleur de lis yellow and black on deep satin (Printed from own blocks by H&A) 21.0.0.'[97] It was usual for the person who commissioned a special block-printed wallpaper to retain the block himself to protect the privacy of the design. The block would then be lent to whichever firm was chosen to print or reprint the paper.

The Dining Room was packed with ancient objects, but the sideboard and chairs were made especially — presumably to Blore's designs. 'The sideboard of the time of Edward II is copied from one in Harewood Castle; it is sculptured oak, ornamented with the emblazoned armorial bearings of William de Valence, owner of Goodrich Castle in Edward I's reign ... The chairs are of oak, corresponding with the style of the architecture.'[98]

224. Mediaeval Limoges enamel candlestick (Rijksmuseum, Amsterdam)

The Breakfast Room was:

> furnished in the gorgeous style of queen Anne's time. The plaster-work of the ceiling is rich in pattern and highly ornamented with gilding, two paintings, by H.P. Briggs, R.A., in imitation of ... Verrio, representing Venus and Neptune ... The pannels on the walls, enclosed within gilt frames, are of green and brown silk, on which are bouquets of flowers in tambour work. The window curtains and hangings ... All these, as well as the gilt pier-table, the stand of that in the centre of the room, supporting choice curiosities of the period, the looking glasses, Seve and Dresden porcelain, the splendid clock, &c., being originals of the time of queen Anne.[99]

The decoration and furnishing of this room were truly revolutionary for its date; it is certainly the earliest example of the Queen Anne Revival that I have encountered. The so-called Queen Anne Revival is normally associated with the 1870s and 1880s, but here is an example created well before the accession of Queen Victoria. It is the intensely archaeological character of the room that is so interesting, especially the imitations of Verrio.

Henry Peyronet Briggs (1791–1844) actually stayed at Goodrich, for Planche wrote that 'With Peyronet Briggs, who in 1835 ceased to paint history and took up portraiture, I passed much happy time at Goodrich Court, the seat of our mutual friend Sir Samuel Meyrick sketching together on the banks of the Wye in the morning and in the evening making studies from suites of armour, or mediaeval carvings in wood and ivory in the Doucean collection.'[100] A portrait of Meyrick by Briggs had been shown at the Royal Academy in 1829 and hung in the Banquetting Hall at Goodrich, but I have been unable to discover where it is now. He also painted one of Planche which was shown in the Academy in 1835 and is now at the Garrick Club. Briggs was a painter celebrated in his day for both history painting and portraiture.[101]

The Drawing Room, as can be seen from the plan (Plate 214), was in the tower at the opposite end of the entrance front to the tower that housed the Asiatic Armoury. In complete stylistic contrast, it was mediaeval in decoration and contents. 'This room contains a number of curious missals. A pair of spiked copper enamelled candlesticks 700 years old, inkstands &c. ... The fireplace is taken from that beautiful specimen of the end of Edward II's reign, in Prior Crawden's house at Ely.'[102] These candlesticks were not part of the Douce collection, but were bought by Meyrick himself. They still survive in the Rijksmuseum in Amsterdam (Plate 224) and have recently been published as being not mediaeval, but rather an 'Interpretation neo-mediaeval de l'Oeuvre de Limoges'.[103]

Their history is interesting. Meyrick exhibited them at the Society of Antiquaries of London on 20 May 1830, dating them to the twelfth century and saying that they 'were purchased at Aix-la-Chapelle, at the house of a travelling dealer, so it was impossible to ascertain their original locality'.[104] It is likely that Meyrick purchased them while in Aix in July 1823. They were also illustrated in colour by Shaw as Plate L. They eventually passed with so many objects from Goodrich into the Spitzer collection in Paris. At the auction of that collection in 1893 the South Kensington Museum had commissioned a French dealer to bid for the candlesticks, but he was outbid by a continental collector who bought them for £32.

It is highly unlikely that anyone on the Continent was faking such sophisticated examples of Limoges enamel in the 1820s in the vicinity of Aix-la-Chappelle, especially when genuine pieces were so cheap, and they are actually likely to be mediaeval, as Meyrick thought. Whatever their date, they must have looked splendid in the elaborately decorated context of the Drawing Room.

> The room is octagonal, six of the sides being composed of niches. In one of these is a large mirror, another is occupied by a piano-forte, the case of which is from an elegant design by Mr Blore, and on the walls of the remainder are the following paintings, after the manner of that period by Mr John Coke Smith, a rising young artist of great talents. The legend of St George and the Dragon; the romance of Sir Tristrem; the tale of the Comtesse de Vergi; and the tale of the Tournament of the White Garment; the second and third being from ivory carvings formerly in the possession of Francis Douce, esq., the eminent antiquary, and now, by his munificence, belonging to Sir Samuel.[105]

The idea of painting in imitation of mediaeval wall paintings — though to become commonplace in the 1850s — was unusual in a Gothic Revival building in the 1830s. Meyrick set about choosing the iconography and finding suitable prototypes in his characteristically direct yet scholarly fashion. He consulted Douce, the leading scholar and collector of mediaeval manuscripts. Meyrick wrote to Douce on 8 March 1830: 'I once mentioned to you my intention of painting in two of the recesses of the drawing-room in Goodrich Court subjects from the old romances. I will therefore trouble you to tell me what might have been the most favourite subjects in the reign of Edwd 2nd — and next whether you have any of that period — I should prefer such as have knights and ladies.'[106]

It emerges from the letters that Meyrick called upon Douce, who showed him both suitable manuscripts and ivories. Meyrick wrote to Douce on 19 March: 'as my servant is going into your neighbourhood I . . . have directed him to call for the Fabliaux you are so kind as to lend me . . . You have delighted me exceedingly with the pretty romance and its illustrative sculpture in ivory . . . I shall be very impatient on Thursday next to resume acquaintance with its companion Tristam de Lyoness.'[107]

John Coke Smith seems not to have made his mark as an artist. He may be J.C. Smith, the miniaturist who was painting in the late 1830s; did he perhaps die young? The use of Sir Tristram as a subject was to be taken up later by the Pre-Raphaelites and Burne-Jones in their paintings and Morris and Tennyson in their poems. It is impossible to establish how influential Meyrick's mediaevalizing wall paintings were, but as the house was open to the public and they were described in print they were certainly well known.

It would also be interesting to know what Blore's piano looked like: was it Gothic or Tudor in style? There is to my knowledge no extant piano of the 1830s in either of these styles with which to compare it. A.C. Pugin had, however, published a design for a Gothic grand piano as early as 1827 in his book *Gothic Furniture*, though there is no evidence that this was ever executed.

The other piece of Gothic furniture mentioned as in the Drawing Room was 'The oak table in the centre . . . from the only remaining specimen of the kind, which is

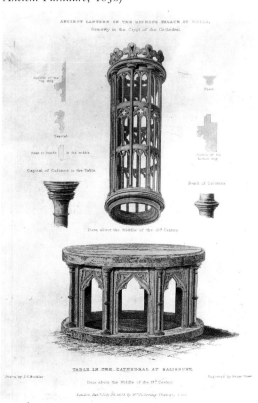

225. The Salisbury Table (H. Shaw, *Specimens of Ancient Furniture*, 1836)

preserved in the Chapter-house at Salisbury'.[108] The Salisbury Table is shown in Plate 225, and it appeared as Plate XLVI in Shaw's *Specimens*. The original table still exists at Salisbury, though its actual date is in dispute.

Shaw's *Specimens* has been mentioned elsewhere and I have discussed it in print,[109] but it is especially relevant here for two reasons: first, that the title-page states 'With descriptions by Sir Samuel Rush Meyrick' (the scholarly twenty-six page introduction is in fact by him); second, that eight of the seventy-four plates portray objects at Goodrich. For example plate LV illustrates several pieces on one plate: 'Furniture of a Fireplace, time of Elizabeth, Do time of Charles 1st ... The highest subject in the plate represents the furniture of the fire-place in Sir Gethley's [Gelly's] chamber' (Plate 233).

Shaw's book was first issued in monthly parts from 1832 to 1835 and published as a book in 1836, and its impact over the next decade upon both the Romantic Interior and the antique trade was enormous. The prospectus circulated prior to the publication of the first part issue stated:

Although the names of most articles of furniture used in the middle ages occur in various antiquarian publications, no attempt has hitherto been made to produce a series of graphic representations of them ... The Antiquary who desires a perfect idea of any article of furniture mentioned in Froissart, Chaucer, or Shakespeare, the architect who wishes for standard authorities for the restoration or imitation of ancient buildings; the painter ... the histrionic manager ... will it is hoped patronize and support a publication of which the object is the gratification of their respective wants and tastes.

Meyrick wrote in his introduction: 'The fact is, that modern furniture is too poor ... for however beautiful the elegant simplicity of Grecian forms, these are not of themselves sufficient to produce that effect that should be given to the interior of an English residence.'[110] Meyrick was speaking with the experience of creating Goodrich fresh in his memory, and in fact when he wrote, though the building was complete, the furnishing of the interiors was not. Meyrick favoured not only ancient furniture, but also ancient fireplace furniture (Plate 233) and candlesticks (Plates 224 and 226).

He was fascinated by both the history and the function of the furnishings he had collected. Plate 226 shows a 'Candlestick of brass gilt of the close of the 12th century, probably the earliest known specimen with a nozzle'.[111] These ancient utilitarian furnishings also encompassed a Renaissance inkstand (Plate 229) and a singular salt-cellar (Plate 227). Even the clocks were suitably splendid and ancient, that in Plate 228 was German late sixteenth century.

This completes the description of the ground floor, but a little needs to be said concerning the first floor. From the Gallery of the Grand Armoury one entered the Doucean Museum:

Francis Douce, Esq., by his will dated 22nd of August 1830 made this bequest: — 'I give to Dr Meyrick all my carvings in ivory or other materials, together with my miscellaneous curiosities ... in the fullest confidence that he will think it worth while to devote some small apartment in his noble mansion at Goodrich Court' — ... Sir Samuel has caused three chambers to be appropriated to the reception of these ... altar-pieces, croziers, miniatures, scriptural paintings, seals, caskets in wood and ivory, and metals, tapestries, drawings, engravings, engraved tablets, religious boxes, boxes for domestic uses, diptychs, paxes, and infinite miscellanies.[112]

Meyrick had been a close friend of Douce's and had frequently invited him to stay at Goodrich. He wrote to Douce on 12 August 1831: 'a bed awaits you at Goodrich Court although we are not as forward as I could wish ... Planche is coming down so you need not want a companion.'[113] Eventually Douce went to stay at Goodrich,

226. A mediaeval candlestick (C.J. Richardson, *Studies from Old English mansions* ..., 1848)

227. A salt cellar (Shaw, *Specimens*)

228. (following page) A German sixteenth-century table clock, painted by C.J. Richardson in the early 1840s (Victoria & Albert Museum, London)

The clock of the time of Elizabeth at Goodrich Court
Herefordshire.

8304
13

258

Inkstand of Limoge enamel mounted
in Ormolu of the time of Hen: 8th
at Goodrich Court

830H
23.

Développemens des Ornemens, Figures et Inscriptions placés sur la Crosse de Ragenfroi;
Elu Evêque de Chartres, vers l'an 941.

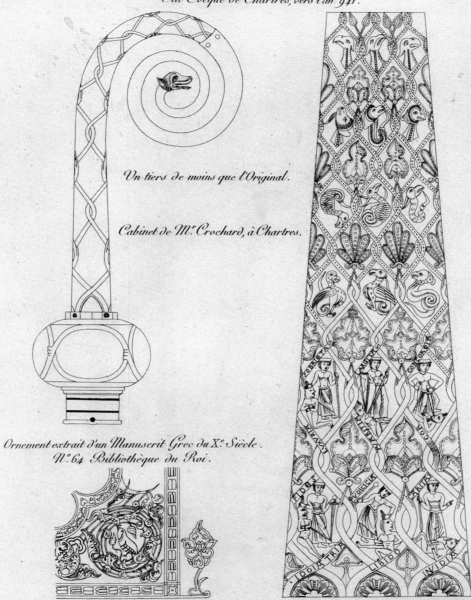

Un tiers de moins que l'Original.

Cabinet de Mr. Crochard, à Chartres.

Ornement extrait d'un Manuscrit Grec du Xe. Siècle.
No. 64 Bibliothèque du Roi.

Willemin direxit.

Amédée Peré del. et sculpt.

✠ FRATER WILLELMVS ME FECIT

for Meyrick wrote to him on 2 September 1831: 'I am quite delighted that you have fixed a time that I may expect you which I shall most anxiously do on the 10th.'[114]

Douce was obviously sufficiently impressed with the house to leave Meyrick much of his collection. 'His very curious Museum illustrative of the arts and manners of the middle ages he bequeathed to Dr Meyrick, to whose beautiful mansion of Goodrich Court he had paid a visit not long before.'[115] The Douce collection was a rich and important one. Together the two collections made the furnishing of the interiors far richer at Goodrich than Meyrick had originally intended or indeed could ever have afforded from his own resources. Sadly there are no illustrations of the Doucean collection *in situ* at Goodrich. Some objects were displayed in the rooms created for them, others were mixed with the furnishings of the living rooms.

Fortunately Meyrick published a description of the collection after its arrival in 1834 following Douce's death.[116] The combined collections may well have been at that time the most important collection of mediaeval and Renaissance objects in Britain. The collection deserves further study, and I will illustrate several objects to give some idea of its richness.

The watercolour painted by C.J. Richardson in the early-1840s (Plate 229) depicts one of the many important Douce enamels: 'An hexagonal inkstand of Limoges enamel on copper, mounted with ormolu. The subjects taken from the story of Hercules are well drawn and in brilliant colours . . . The height of the inkstand is 3½ inches, and its date about Edward the Sixth.'[117] Where this object is now I have been unable to discover.

The twelfth-century enamelled crozier (Plate 230) had also belonged to Douce: 'The head and ferrule of an ancient crozier . . . formerly in the possession of M. Crochard at Chartres. The head is engraved in Willemen's work who has assigned it with no better evidence than the assertion of its French possessor, to Ragenfroi Bishop of Chartres in 941. The costume proves it to be a century and a half later.'[118]

229. (previous page) A French Limoges enamel inkstand of the sixteenth century, painted by C.J. Richardson in the early 1840s (Victoria & Albert Museum, London)

230. (facing page) A French mediaeval crozier (N.X. Willemin, *Monumens Français* . . ., 1839)

231. The Douce casket (Wallace Collection, London)

261

232. A mirror at Goodrich (Shaw, *Specimens*)

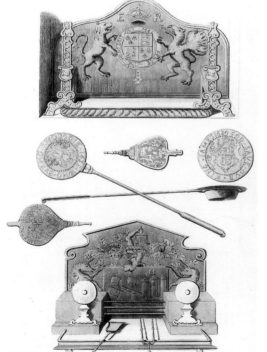

233. Fireplace furniture at Goodrich (Shaw, *Specimens*)

It was indeed published by Willemin, from which Plate 230 comes;[119] when M. Crochard sold the piece is unknown as are the circumstances of Douce's acquisition of it. It is now in the Bargello in Florence and Meyrick's dating was gratifyingly close to that now accepted.[120]

One of the Douce objects kept not in the museum rooms especially created for them, but on a table in the Library was a casket 'made with embossed panels of steel, with its original lining of cloth of gold . . . The panels are elaborately ornamented with Scriptural subjects; the upper one is so contrived, forming a crucifix, as to conceal the key-hole . . . It came from Fonthill.'[121]

This casket (Plate 231) does not appear in the Fonthill sale of 1823, but Meyrick stated that it was 'bought by Mr Douce at Signior Franci's sale'.[122] Franchi, whom we encountered at Fonthill, was Beckford's intimate friend whose collection was sold in 1827, the casket being lot 98 in the sale.[123]

Fortunately Douce kept a 'Diary of Antiquarian Purchases' from 1803 until his death in 1834, and in May 1827 recorded 'Several diptychs, 2 specimens of Limoges enamel etc at Chevalier Franchi's Sale'.[124] It is possible that Franchi acquired objects for himself while searching for objects for Beckford's collection. It is, however, more likely that Beckford gave him objects, especially at the time of the projected Fonthill sale in 1822. If this were the case it would explain Nash's statement — which he presumably heard from Meyrick — that the casket came from Fonthill.

The history of this casket can, like so many of the major objects that entered British collections early in the nineteenth century, be traced back to France. At some time before 1802 Lenoir purchased the casket from a Parisian broker for his celebrated museum. It was No. 560 in his published catalogue, which includes four plates that depict the sides, the ends and the top. Lenoir described 'la beauté et la richesse des cinq bas-reliefs qui le composent, la difficulté vaincue pour leur execution sur une matière aussi ingrate, m'ont déterminé à les faire graver. J'ai achete ce coffre au citoyen Scellier, marchand, rue de Seine.'[125] Lenoir thought that it was French and dated from the 1502s; it is in fact an important example of Augsburg embossed work of 1570–1600.[126] Beckford himself was haunting the Left Bank brokers of St Germain in the 1790s, just when Lenoir must have bought this casket.

But Beckford — or Franchi on his behalf — like any dedicated collector played a waiting game, was still in the market when Lenoir's museum was dispersed after 1815 and when this interesting casket must have been brought to England. The casket was sold along with the rest of the Meyrick collection, but eventually was acquired by Sir Richard Wallace in 1873 and is on display in the Wallace Collection.

A full analysis of the Douce collection has never been undertaken,[127] but even though the collection is now scattered throughout the world it is possible to gain some idea of its richness from the sources quoted above.

The upper floors at Goodrich included room which, like the Queen Anne room discussed above, were furnished in the styles of several English monarchs. This series of rooms, unique for their date, was fully described by Nash, Fosbroke and Shaw, who illustrates some of their furnishings. These rooms were very much the precursors of the period rooms in twentieth-century museums. They were Sir Gelly's Chamber, the James I Room, the Charles II Gallery, the William III Room, the Prince's Chamber, the Page's Vestibule, the Herald's Chamber, the Leech's Chamber, the Greek Room and Llewelyn's Chamber.

Sir Gelly Meyrick (1556–1601) was a prominent Welsh soldier and son of Rowland Meyrick. Whether Meyrick was actually descended from these two men I have been unable to establish, but he was certainly convinced that he was, and wrote an article about Sir Gelly's exploits during the Cadiz expedition of 1596. Sir Gelly's Chamber was 'decorated according to the fashion in the time of queen Elizabeth, with most exquisite panelling, taken from a house at Malines in which Rubens used to paint . . . The napkin-press and cabinets are beautiful specimens, and the looking-glass frame bears the initials of Dr Rowland Meyrick.'[128] The room was thus furnished in a style appropriate to the period in which Sir Gelly lived. The mirror (Plate 232) was illustrated by Shaw and the caption states: 'It has on it in gilt characters the letters *RM* and the date 1559 the year in which Dr Rowland Meyrick was elected Bishop of Bangor. It exhibits in a very satisfactory manner the peculiarity of transition pieces, which so decidedly mark the frame work of the time of Elizabeth.' What the date of the mirror actually was, it is impossible to deduce from the engraving. Shaw also illustrated the Napkin Press as Plate XXXIV, and the fireplace is here Plate 233.

The James I Room naturally included objects of appropriate date. These included the singular bed of an exotic oriental wood inlaid with mother-of-pearl (Plate 234). This had belonged to Douce and could well be early seventeenth century and was probably Portuguese. Where Douce obtained it is unknown.

The Charles I Room contained a bed, this was also illustrated in Shaw, where the caption reads: 'This bedstead has upon it the date 1628 and stands in what is termed from the period of its furniture the Charles First's room.' The William III Room was furnished in a late seventeenth-century style and filled the stylistic gap between the Charles II Gallery and the Queen Anne Drawing Room. In the William III Room, 'The carved folding doors are of oak, purchased from Louvain'.[129] These doors came appropriately from William's own Low Countries, which was presumably what Meyrick had in mind. The bedstead (Plate 235) was of great elaboration, being assembled from Dutch seventeenth-century carved woodwork that included the arms of William and Mary. The tester was made from Mortlake tapestry of the late seventeenth century.

The Prince's Chamber was 'designated in honour of his late Royal Highness the Duke of Sussex, whose intimacy Sir Samuel enjoyed uninterruptedly down to his lamented death ... Here are carefully stored three curious illuminated MSS. that belonged to the Duke. His favourite Highland broad-sword ...'[130] The Duke's page naturally used the Page's Chamber and his doctor slept in the aptly named Leech's Chamber.

The Herald's Chamber was 'named after an old friend of the family, Francis Martin, esq., Norroy king of arms, whose crown, collar of S.S., sword, emblazoned shield, and tabard are therein suspended. This room is fitted up in the modern French style, with original drawings by Sir Thomas Lawrence.'[131] Martin had been present when the foundation-stone of the house was laid.

The Greek Room had a 'frieze formed with Henning's excellent imitations of the Elgin marbles, and contains many Greek and Etruscan vases'.[132] Llewelyn's Chamber was the bedroom of Meyrick's son who died in 1837. It is thus clear that the interiors at Goodrich represented almost every style of interior decoration ranging from the Middle Ages to 'modern French'. I have not met any other sequence of Romantic Interiors within one building in this country at this early date that encompasses such a diverse range of styles. Indeed they point the way to the sequences of 'period rooms' that were to become such a feature of public museums fifty years later.

This completes the discussion of the Goodrich interiors themselves, but a few remarks need to be made concerning Meyrick's collecting activities. The antiquities broker John Coleman Isaac sold antiquities to Meyrick. For instance, '1827 Jan. Recd. of Dr Meyrick £56 for ancient armour ... 1830, 21 July Two cases containing a commode ... by Betts & Drew fly Barque to Bristol and from there to Goodrich Court ... 1832 17 Sept sent a case containing a piece of stained glass to Sir Saml Meyrick.'[133] The glass was presumably ancient, but I have been unable to discover where it was displayed at Goodrich. It is evident that Meyrick's antiquities for Goodrich were sent much of the way by sea from London, as were Scott's for Abbotsford.

As late as 1844 Isaac was still selling objects to Meyrick: '17 July 1844 Sent a case

234. The Douce bed (H.C. Moffatt, *Illustrated Description of some of the furniture at Goodrich ...*, 1928)

235. The William and Mary Bed (Moffatt, *Illustrated Description*)

directed to Sir Saml R Meyrick Goodrich Court'.[134] Meyrick's correspondence with Isaac throws a revealing light upon the antiquities trade and the activities of other dealers. Meyrick wrote to Isaac on 18 June 1831 while Goodrich was actually being built: 'Two pieces of enamel are alone what may probably suit me, but the sum you ask is just twice what it ought to be as Swaby would tell you. I had a little circular box of him with a moveable cover for a guinea at the same time as I was fortunate to pick up your candlesticks.'[135] Isaac's shop was at 12 Wardour Street, and Swaby's, at 109.

Meyrick wrote to Issac on 15 July 1833: 'I find that the letter of my friend reached him too late to bid at Gwennap's sale for the horse figures I had desired him to give for them and their horses £150 each. I learn that they have been bought by you and Swabey, Bentley and Tuck; and that you ask five hundred guineas for them. Should you find no one to give that sum you may have from me four hundred pounds not a sixpence more.'[136]

The sale referred to was that of Gwennap's armour from the Gothic Hall and Oplotheca on 10 June 1833. It is interesting that Meyrick did not reveal to Isaac that Planche at times bid in the rooms for him. It is not clear from the Isaac papers whether Meyrick bought the armour, but it would appear that he was successful for he wrote to Douce on 21 October 1833:

> I have got the mounted Indian Rajah, brought over by Capt Grindlay in the anti-asiatic Armoury and the two splendid suits of the Dukes of Bavaria their horses and armour which were also at Gwennap's in the grand armoury here. I only regret the loss of the embossed suit falsely called Henry IV's which was purchased by a Lord Amelie (a Scotchman I believe). I had intended to have bought it for the termination of the vista . . . the sudden sale and my ignorance of the matters till it was too late to instruct Planche occasioned it to slip through my fingers.[137]

That Meyrick was in touch with other dealers is demonstrated by a letter about the same sale that Meyrick wrote to the armour dealer Dominique Colnaghi — to whom he did reveal Planche's involvement — on 15 July 1833: 'Dear Dominique, I ought to acknowledge with many thousand thanks your great kindness to me respecting the sale of Gwennap's armour. The money you have so kindly advanced shall be returned by the second week in next month . . . the Rajah Planche has bought. I have offered Isaacs £400 for the two mounted suits but will give no more . . . I wish something would lead you to visit the Wye three or four days absence from London would suffice . . . Do you know Lord Ormelie to be a young or an old man? Has he more armour?'[138]

The Earl of Ormelie — the 'Scotchman' Amelie, referred to in the letter to Douce — was the first Marquess of Breadalbane whose seat was that splendid Gothic pile Taymouth Castle which contained a suite of Romantic Interiors far grander than those at Goodrich. Gwennap, the notorious armour dealer, had been a thorn in Meyrick's flesh for years. On 9 April 1821 Meyrick had written to Walter Scott: 'I am sorry to say that I did not succeed in getting anything for you at the sale . . . Gwennap now declares he has got the cream and will therefore open the exhibition in the Haymarket. I know that some rascally conduct was to be expected.'[139]

Meyrick eventually became friendly with Isaac and wrote to him on 2 February 1835: 'I wish exceedingly something would induce you to visit this place and by seeing what there is here you could judge what is wanting. That however is very little and I think that since the addition of Mr Douce's antiquities, you would be quite astonished at the immense quantity of valuable curiosities.'[140]

There is no evidence that Isaac took up Meyrick's offer, but Meyrick ceased to treat him with the usual scepticism of a collector for a dealer, writing on 20 November 1839: 'the high opinion that I have of you is solely the result of your own honourable conduct, which during the period of twenty years strict observance I have invariably found to be the same. Your dealings have always been grounded on such justifyable principles that I feel more pleasure in making a purchase of you than of anyone else.'[141]

It is obvious from the correspondence between Meyrick and Isaac and Meyrick and Scott that Meyrick was actively buying both armour and other antiquities from every available source, and a study of these letters throws a great deal of light upon the nature of collecting and the character of the market in this period immediately following the Napoleonic Wars. As we have seen elsewhere, large quantities of antiquities were flooding into this country from the Continent. Though the supply even in these halcyon days was variable, Meyrick wrote to Scott on 5 July 1821: 'It had been said that there would be large importations of armour from Germany and Spain, but all these vapourings have ended in a few horse-men's suits of the time of Charles 1st.'[142]

Meyrick thus lived in neo-feudal splendour at Goodrich, taking part, like Scott at Abbotsford or George Hammond Lucy at Charlecote, in local events and social life. All these gentlemen attempted to reintroduce into their seats the pomp and splendour that they imagined had once existed — we have already noticed Meyrick's revival of the ancient 'javelin-men'.

Indeed it would seem that Meyrick was always ready to help turn local events into feudal spectacles, for in September 1841 he commissioned Willement to make 'A banner painted on silk with fringe tassels &c for Goodrich Benefit Society, 4 small shields of arms &c ... £6.7.2'.[143] Few village friendly societies in England can have boasted a processional banner painted by a heraldic artist as celebrated as Willement.

On 2 April 1848 Meyrick died, 'bequeathing his noble collection to his executors, Mr Kirkmann, the Chancery barrister, and Mr King, York Herald, upon trust to transfer the same to his cousin a Captain Augustus William Henry Meyrick, of the Scots Fusilier Guards'.[144] He was vigorously pursuing his several interests right up to his death and was at long last about to clinch the purchase of Flansford Priory, which he had attempted to buy before building the Court.

On 9 February he wrote to King, the York Herald, from Goodrich: 'The priory purchase is not yet completed, which is a great nuisance ... can you tell me whether or not J.G. Nichols has inserted in the Gent's Mag. review a critique of mine on the highland costume published by the Stuarts.'[145] The anonymous review of *The Costume of the Clans by John Sobieski Stolberg and Charles Edward Stuart* had appeared in January[146] and is probably the last thing he wrote. It is packed with the antiquarian and scholarly observations for which Meyrick was justly famous and would along with the subject of the book have fascinated his old friend Walter Scott.

The history of Goodrich Court after Meyrick's death does not concern us here and has been fully covered in print.[147] When the Meyrick family disposed of the house later in the century, though almost all his collection was removed, several pieces of furniture remained in the house. Good photographs of these were published alongside pieces in his own collection by the new owner of the house.[148] The beds in Plates 234 and 235 come from this book as does the elaborate oak cabinet in Plate 236.

The important collection of arms, armour, antiquities and works of art were in part displayed at the Manchester Art Treasures Exhibition in 1857 (Plate 239). Appropriately, the catalogue was written by Meyrick's old friend Planche. Meyrick would have been delighted to see that Planche stressed that educational potential of the collection which had been uppermost in Meyrick's mind in all his collecting: 'the principal objects of interest and value in the south armoury, which, though not comprising the whole of the treasures acquired by Sir Samuel Meyrick ... presents a mass of information to such as are inclined to study it, not to be exceeded, even if it can be equalled, by any private collection existing, to the best of our knowledge, in Europe'.[149]

Planche had also arranged the armour helped by none other than the armour

236. An oak cupboard (Moffat, *Illustrated Description*)

237. Armour from Goodrich (Wallace Collection, London)

broker Pratt. Planche paid tribute to him in the catalogue: 'my thanks to Mr Samuel Pratt of Bond Street, not only for the careful and punctual execution of the work he contracted to do; but also for the energy and loyalty with which he laboured to promote by every means in his power the success of the Exhibition'.[150]

The collection was again displayed at the South Kensington Museum from 1868 to 1871, where it caused a sensation and was seen by large numbers of people. The collection was then offered to the government for £50,000, but they very shortsightedly turned down the offer and the collection was sold piecemeal. In 1872 Planche wrote sadly that 'These irreplaceable antiquities are fast leaving England, one Parisian dealer alone having bought to the extent of £12,000'.[151] The dealer in question was Frederic Spitzer (1815–1890), who fortunately sold a number of the objects and armour to Sir Richard Wallace. Two of the most important (Plates 237 and 238) are now on display in the Wallace Collection, Plate 238 being the famous Buckhurst Armour, a back view of which appears in the sketch by Delacroix (Plate 210).

It must be remembered that Meyrick owned paintings and miniatures both purchased by himself and inherited from Douce. For instance, there were two exquisite miniatures in elaborate ivory cases, depicting Henry VIII and Anne of Cleves, which had belonged to Douce. These were attributed by Douce to Holbein; that of Anne came via the Salting Collection to the Victoria & Albert Museum and is still attributed to Holbein. That of Henry also came eventually to the same museum via the Pierpont Morgan collection, but is now thought to be of eighteenth-century date.

In the way that it has in this study so often been the history of the objects that links one collection with another, these two miniatures belonged in the eighteenth century to Mr Barrett of Lee Priory in Kent. Barrett was a friend of Horace Walpole and modelled his house on Strawberry Hill. The Strawberry Room from Lee Priory is now in the Victoria & Albert Museum. Walpole himself discussed the Anne of Cleves miniature in his *Anecdotes*. The Barrett family sold these miniatures in 1826 to a dealer called Tuck who resold them to Douce for 50 guineas.[152]

The name of Meyrick is well known to armour scholars. But of all the house collections discussed in this book Goodrich is today the least known and studied, even though Meyrick published his collection more fully and in a more scholarly way than any of the other collectors discussed here. The character of the collection and the nature of the interiors were, however, different from most other Romantic houses and their collections in the vigorously didactic nature of the arrangement of the objects.

It must also be remembered that Goodrich was regularly open to the public and was thus known to a wide range of collectors and architects. Also Meyrick's high standing in the scholarly world by the 1840s made Goodrich and his collection known in archaeological and antiquarian circles. He was, for instance, a founder member and vice-president in 1846 of the Cambrian Archaeological Society. In the first number of its proceedings the editors 'offer our warmest thanks to H. Shaw Esq., for his great kindness and care in superintending the execution of the plates . . .

238. The Buckhurst Armour (Wallace Collection, London)

239. (left) The Meyrick armour on display at the Manchester Art Treasures Exhibition of 1857, photographed by C. Thurston Thompson

to Thomas Willement, Esq., for a mark of friendship in presenting us with the drawing of the arms of Wales on our title-page in the style of the thirteenth century, according to the blazon upon which Sir S.R. Meyrick did us the honour to give his valuable opinion'.[153] Here we see Meyrick exploiting the expertise of his friends Thomas Willement and Henry Shaw to help the struggling new society; he may even have arranged the printer who was none other than the celebrated William Pickering.

On 9 September 1847 their first annual meeting was held at Aberystwyth, and 'the public rooms were very generally visited, as some interesting objects had been deposited for inspection, which had not been seen before. These included some splendid specimens of British shields and other weapons brought from the armoury at Goodrich Court by Sir S. Meyrick.'[154]

But a similar event the year before had brought Goodrich to the attention of the leading scholars and collectors of the day. In his capacity as the vice-president of the recently formed British Archaeological Association Meyrick invited them to Goodrich during their annual meeting in Gloucester in August 1846. The Association numbered amongst its members many celebrated antiquaries, and present at the Gloucester meeting were Thomas Crofton Croker, J.O. Halliwell, Charles Roach Smith and Planche himself. Goodrich and Meyrick came into their own, and all were given a suitable feudal and antiquarian welcome:

> The day was devoted to a visit, by invitation, to Sir S.R. Meyrick, Vice-President, at Goodrich Court, to examine his unique collection of ancient armour and general national antiquities. The party amounting to nearly seventy were hospitably received by Sir Samuel, who, in person, assisted by Abraham Kirkmann, Esq., Thomas King, Esq., (Rougedragon), and Augustus Meyrick, Esq., conducted the guests over the entire suite of apartments, pointing out and describing the more remarkable and interesting objects in the extensive and valuable collection. The inspection, which exhausted several hours, was diversified by a collation served in the banquetting hall, and the introduction during the repast, of Welsh minstrels, who, in the Minstrel's gallery, played and sang old welsh airs and songs; the history and peculiarities of which were explained by Sir Samuel successively.[155]

Roach Smith also described the event and tells how the harpers played Gorhofedd Gwyr Harlech (The Delight of the Men of Harlech) when the distinguished company entered the Banquetting Hall.[156]

Goodrich was not just, or even mainly, created to entertain and interest the scholarly world, but to be a feature on the Wye tour. Nash's guide, in a paragraph prophetic of the country house visiting of today, but sadly unfulfilled for Goodrich, predicted:

> What would not the intelligent artizans of our manufacturing districts and commercial towns give for a sight of Goodrich ... Let us before we conclude, hold out to them the certain prospect that a few years only will elapse before the gigantic powers of steam locomotion will enable them from one end of the kingdom to the other to embrace the opportunity of reaching the Court by the lines of Railways.[157]

10

CONCLUSION

An old English family mansion is a fertile subject for study. It abounds with illustrations of former times and traces of the tastes, and humours and manners of successive generations.

Washington Irving

In the preceding chapters the interiors of five houses covering the century 1750–1850 have been analyzed in great detail. These houses were chosen because they fulfilled one at least of three criteria: that the building and collecting activities of the creators themselves should be innovatory in terms of the Romantic Interior; that extensive documentation should survive in the form of illustrations and manuscript and printed material; that they should fall within the date range 1750–1850.

There are still in existence many suites of Romantic Interiors within ancient buildings, some recognized as such and others certainly masquerading as actually of the original date of the building. To recognize these interiors without documentation is difficult, especially as their owners, whether private individuals or public bodies, usually are convinced — and often wish to remain so — that the interiors are original. As research into this subject progresses and more documentation is discovered, the numbers of surviving Romantic Interiors in this category will rise year by year. Many groups of family papers in country house muniment rooms and County Record Offices will when fully examined yield up such documentation.

How many of the interiors of ancient demolished houses fell into the category of Romantic Interiors presents a more difficult problem, for here again documentation is even more crucial, as there is no possibility of a physical examination of the interior and its contents for clues to the date. In so many cases, as was so graphically demonstrated in the exhibition 'The Destruction of the Country House',[1] all that survives to document the interiors are one or two photographs of empty rooms often taken just before demolition. In rare cases, perhaps a Victorian watercolour may exist showing a furnished interior.

When surviving buildings and their furnished interiors were created at the same time, as at Abbotsford, there is of course no confusion if documented. In those cases, however, where no documentation survives to show how the present arrangement of the collection relates to that originally created or how and why the objects came into the house in the first place, no real analysis can be made. When such buildings have been demolished, a very real picture of them can be built up only when there is sufficient documentation, as with Fonthill and Goodrich.

I shall illustrate and briefly discuss a selection of Romantic Interiors from the nineteenth century to supplement the case studies. There were many other candidates, but those I have chosen will I hope demonstrate the variety, richness and complexity of the subject.

As I have stressed before, the least well documented group of Romantic Interiors are those in cities often created in a rented terrace house by antiquaries of relatively modest means. Of those interiors created by Scott in his Edinburgh house, by Stukeley in his Bloomsbury rectory or by Douce in his Gower Street house no

240. John Carter in a Library in 1817 by Sylvester Harding and John Carter (British Museum, London)

241. Joseph Mayer and his collection in 1843 by William Daniels (Walker Art Gallery Liverpool)

contemporary illustrations are known. However, there exists a drawn portrait of John Carter, an antiquary and collector who was a contemporary of Scott and Douce, which may show him in his library in London.

We have met John Carter (1748–1817), the watercolourist, at Strawberry Hill. Though trained as an architect,[2] he built little but made his career as a polemical journalist and scholar.[3] He was one of the most celebrated antiquaries of his day and his knowledge of mediaeval art and architecture probably exceeded that of all his contemporaries. His major contributions to scholarship were three books: *Specimens of Ancient Sculpture and Painting* (1780–94), which he dedicated to Walpole; *The Ancient Architecture of England* (1795–1814); and *Specimens of English Ecclesiastical Costume* (1817).

Though not a wealthy man, he certainly collected widely, as demonstrated by the sale of his collection in 1818 after his death: *A Catalogue of the Valuable Collection of Books of Antiquities, Music, Drawings and Prints of the late John Carter, Esq. F.S.A. ... His interesting Collection of Relics of Ancient Architecture, Tesseras, Busts, Paintings, Painted Glass, curious Carved Chairs, Bronzes, Ancient Armour, &c ... Mr Sotheby ... February 23 and Two following Days*. As usual the dealers and collectors did not miss the opportunity, for Colnaghi bought several lots, including lot 254, 'A Pair of Boots and spurs, belonging to K. William III', and lot 315, 'A Suit of Plain Black Horseman's Armour'. Hume bought several lots, including lot 324, 'A Head of a Laughing Faun, in Bronze, the size of Life'. Meyrick bought lot 321, which was an extra lot of arms or armour and not described, and John Britton bought lot 301, 'Two Teapots'. Once again ebony chairs formed part of the collection: lot 304 was

270

'Two Ebony Chairs, Time of Q. Elizabeth'. There were two further pairs of chairs, though not apparently of ebony: lots 305 and 306 were 'Two Chairs, Time of K. Charles II'.

In the drawing of Carter (Plate 240), the figure is by Sylvester Harding and the background by Carter himself. It must date from 1817 the year of his death or shortly before, for he holds in his hand his book on costume, which was only published in 1817. I have discovered no description of the interiors of Carter's house at Upper Eaton Street, Pimlico, so it is impossible to determine whether the room shown was his own library. No clock is listed in the auction catalogue, but the chair in which Carter is sitting is typical of the ebony chairs we have so often encountered in other Romantic Interiors and of which he owned two. Carter the architect, scholar and antiquary was a confirmed 'Goth', and it is totally in character that he should have designed for himself a Gothic Revival library, indeed one that is very reminiscent of that at Strawberry Hill, which he knew well. Even if this interior existed only in Carter's imagination, it is still of interest.

Many Romantic Interiors certainly existed in cities other than London, but they are generally even less well documented. The interior shown in a painting by William Daniels (Plate 241) was created by Joseph Mayer (1803–1889) at his house in Clarence Terrace, Everton, Liverpool. We see Mayer in 1840 in the midst of his collection; he made his fortune as a jeweller and silversmith and was described by a contemporary as 'a tradesman by choice, a gentleman by nature, a scholar by study, a wealthy man by industry, and a modest philanthropist by instinct'.[4] He amassed an important collection of more than 10,000 objects, including both classical and Egyptian pieces, majolica, Wedgwood ceramics, arms and armour and a major group of mediaeval ivories. Fortunately he gave this collection to Liverpool Museum. A number of the objects shown in Plate 241 are still in Liverpool including the Wedgwood piece in his hand. Sadly, the splendid Gothic chair does not survive; it was made from the wood of the house of William Roscoe, the celebrated Liverpool scholar and collector who had owned several objects later acquired by Mayer. After many years in store and some destruction by bombing in the last war the Mayer collection has recently been discussed in an important new book from which Mayer emerges as a collector of international stature.[5]

By the 1850s the artefacts of the late eighteenth century were becoming grist to the collector's mill and appropriately ancient and curious enough to be mixed in a Romantic Interior with mediaeval and Renaissance objects. In Plate 241 Mayer looks

242. David Laing with his collection in 1862 by William Fettes Douglas (National Galleries of Scotland, Edinburgh)

adoringly at a Wedgwood pot and, whilst by the 1850s the opportunities which collectors of mediaeval objects had had a generation before were a thing of the past, the pioneer collectors of Georgian objects now had similar opportunities. Mayer's friend Joseph Clarke of Saffron Walden bought such ceramics for him. In 1854 Clarke found what he called the Old Crockery Shop. He informed Mayer: 'The owner told me he had not been in the rooms for seven years and only once for fourteen and if you had seen me when I came out you would have laughed, no chimney sweep would be blacker, three washings, I am not clean yet — he says he took the stock fifty years ago and a great deal of it *too old fashioned* to sell then, there are cartloads.'[6] The Wedgwood naturally joined the rest of the collection in the Romantic Interiors Mayer had created.

One interesting example of a Romantic Interior from a Scottish city is represented by the painting of David Laing (1793–1878) in his study in 1867 (Plate 242). Laing was a celebrated bibliographer and Librarian to the Writers of the Signet who had been encouraged in his early years by Scott to edit and publish early Scottish literary and historical texts. He formed a considerable collection, which is seen piled around him in a manner worthy of Oldbuck himself. His collection of more than 1,500 Old Master drawings was bequeathed to the Royal Scottish Academy. Though all the objects depicted were actually in Laing's collection, Douglas, the Scottish painter of this picture who frequently painted scenes from Scott's works (Plate 137), did not, I suspect, intend the picture to represent accurately Laing's *sanctum*.

I have found no Welsh urban examples, but one of the best-documented examples of the early use of old oak carvings to decorate and extend a modest existing house is Welsh. The house is Plas Newydd, home of the celebrated 'Ladies of Llangollen' (Plate 243) from 1780 when Lady Eleanor Butler and Sarah Ponsonby settled there until their respective deaths in 1829 and 1831. Their story and that of their house has often been told.[7] They purchased a small cottage near Llangollen in Wales, renaming it Plas Newydd (New Hall). Their way of life, combined with the fact that Llangollen was on the Welsh tourist trail, made them and their house famous. Besides the everyday tourists, the Duke of Wellington, Sir Walter Scott and William

243. The Ladies of Llangollen with their cat

244. The exterior of Plas Newydd in the 1820s

245. The oak porch at Plas Newydd in the 1820s

246. The interior of Plas Newydd in the 1890s

Wordsworth all visited them. Wordsworth in 1824 even dedicated a poem to them.

During the early nineteenth century the ladies embellished both the interior and the exterior of their modest house (Plate 244). In 1814 Sarah wrote that they were 'Seized by ... the Oak carving mania.'[8] Eventually 'work was finished, and the visitor would gaze upon a transmogrified Plas Newydd; its lower windows strangely lidded by oaken canopies, its porch a rich and appalling riot of carving. Since this last item was the *pièce de résistance* its completion called for a celebration, a "Porch warming", to which a number of their friends were invited.'[9]

The porch was illustrated in 1824 (Plate 245), and the book describes 'the embellishments which have been superadded, particularly an elegant door-way or entrance, composed of turned wood columns, in the style of the furniture of the sixteenth century. The whole is ornamented with highly finished carvings, which have been collected from ancient houses in different parts of the kingdom ... These decorate almost every part of the interior as well as the exterior parts of the house.'[10]

The ladies, as we saw in Chapter 3, also incorporated ancient stained glass into their interiors. The old oak furnishings grew apace, for a tradition was soon established and 'All statesmen and nobles paid tribute and homage at Plas Newydd, and none ventured a second visit without bringing a contribution of carved oak, which was the regular passport.'[11]

Sir Walter Scott visited the house in August 1825, knowing the ladies to be great admirers of his works. One of his party described 'the prints, the dogs, the cats, the miniatures, the cram of the cabinets, clocks, glass-cases, books, bijouterie, dragon-china, nodding mandarins, and whirligigs of every shape and hue — the house outside and in ... covered with carved oak.'[12] The house as the ladies left it (Plates 244 and 246) was enlarged later, but still exists in its altered form, though without most of the furnishings.

One category of Romantic Interiors probably created in far greater numbers than those in towns were those in relatively modest ancient country manor houses inherited or purchased by individuals motivated by an enthusiasm for the Romantic Movement. Whilst more of these certainly survive than urban examples, many

273

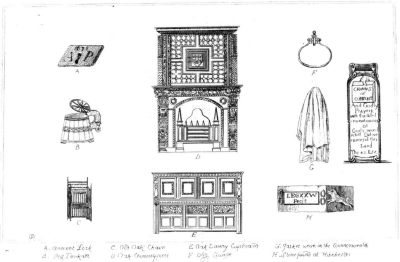

A. *Ancient Lock*   C. *Old Oak Chair*   E. *Oak Livery Cupboard*   G. *Jacket worn in the Commonwealth*
B. *Pot Tankard*   D. *Oak Chimneypiece*   F. *Day Guage*   H. *Stone found at Ribchester*

247. The Hall at Browsholme Hall in 1815 (Thomas Lister Parker, *Description of Browsholme Hall* . . . , 1815)

248. Antiquities at Browsholme in 1815 (Parker, *Description*)

masquerade as genuinely ancient and most are poorly documented by comparison with the grand country houses. Some areas were rich in appropriately sized houses, and we have met Wyresdale in the Lake District already; indeed Lancashire and Cheshire were also richly endowed with these houses.

One important documented early example is Browsholme Hall near Clitheroe in Lancashire, a house of the early sixteenth century. Soon after 1800 the owner, Thomas Lister Parker (1779–1858), began to rearrange the ancient objects already in the house and to collect appropriate pieces of armour, stained glass, furniture and other antiquities to help create a whole range of Romantic Interiors. By 1815, when Parker published his own guide to the house entitled *Description of Browsholme Hall*, the interiors had reached very much their final form. The illustrations were drawn by J.C. Buckler, and in Plates 247 and 248 we see the whole range of objects with which we have become so familiar in the creation of these interiors, arms and armour, old oak furniture and panelling, antlers and two elaborate turned chairs. Parker was at the same time interested in making the house convenient, in common with so many other owners of such houses. To this end he employed Jeffry Wyatt to add a new neo-classical dining room to the house in 1807.

Parker was a celebrated antiquary who rejoiced in the titles of Bowbearer to the Forest of Bowland and Serjeant Trumpeter to the King. He knew Meyrick and Shaw, who dedicated their *Specimens of Ancient Furniture* to 'Thomas Lister Parker Esq. a gentleman whose devotion to the arts of the middle ages and kindness to those engaged in their illustration is universally acknowledged'. Several of the objects at Browsholme were also illustrated in the book. Browsholme fortunately is still in the Parker family and is open to the public; it survives much as Lister Parker left it.[13]

Near to Browsholme in Parker's day was another ancient house, which had been re-edified at much the same date but which does not survive with its collections. This is Bolton Hall at Bolton-by-Bowland in Yorkshire, which was celebrated because of its connection with King Henry VI. By 1785 several of his relics preserved there were published and illustrated: 'the spoon, glove, and boot of Henry VI. Which I delineated from the real ones, as preserved in a chest at Bolton-hall . . . where that prince was some time screened from the unhappy troubles of his reign.'[14] The unfortunate King seems to have left relics all over northern England; he was also sheltered by Sir John Pennington of Muncaster Castle in Cumbria to whom he presented a glass bowl still treasured there as 'The Luck of Muncaster'.

In King Henry's day Bolton Hall was the seat of Sir Ralph Pudsey, but by the time the family sold it in 1804 it was in bad condition. It was purchased as an appropriate ancestral home by Colonel John Bolton (1756–1837), a rich Liverpool merchant who employed J.M. Gandy for several years from 1806 to re-edify the house. It is likely that George Bullock, with whom Gandy was associated at this time, furnished the interiors.[15] The house was described shortly after Bolton's death:

> it has been designed to represent the architecture of the fifteenth century. Under all the circumstances, the effect is perhaps as good as can be expected at the time. The revival of the English styles, at first under the auspices of Horace Walpole and many years after encouraged and promoted by King George the Third, continued for a length of time to languish, and to exhibit little more than awkward imitations . . . It is the prevailing fashion of our days for the possessors of old mansions, that have been more or less mutilated, according to the tasteless habits of the last century to restore tham as nearly as possible to their original state . . . the memorable even [Henry's stay] . . . stamps the manor house of Bolton with a lustre and an interest of which it can never be divested, so long as any portions of its genuine framework shall be held together.[16]

The Pudsey family had retained the Henry relics and they, 'For the better preservation of the relics of King Henry the Sixth . . . caused an ark to be made, in which they were deposited in the year 1822. Its material is oak beautifully designed and executed under the direction of Mr Thomas Rickman, in the style of the fifteenth century. Within it is a handsome plate of brass, bearing a statement of the circumstances under which the relics were left.'[17] In 1832 the family purchased back the Hall from John Bolton and the relics were once again united with the house.

The only illustration of an interior that I can discover (Plate 249) dates from 1839 and is from the particulars of a proposed sale of the estate by Winstanley, the Liverpool firm of auctioneers. Here again are all the elements of the Romantic Interior. The house is now ruined and I can find no trace of Henry's relics and their splendid Gothic Revival ark.

As suggested, there are many surviving groups of papers relating to antiquaries

249. The Hall at Bolton Hall in 1839 (Society of Antiquaries of London)

275

250. The Library at Broomwell House, Bristol, *c*.1825, by W.H. Bartlett (Museum and Art Gallery, Bristol)

251. The Library at Broomwell House, *c*.1825, by W.H. Bartlett (Museum and Art Gallery, Bristol)

and collectors which could yield up sufficient documentation to give a clear impression of the appearance and character of the Romantic Interiors they created for themselves and their collections. A scholarly and pioneering study of the Bristol antiquary George Weare Braikenridge (1775–1856) has recently produced just such results,[18] and therefore I need deal only briefly with Braikenridge.

Braikenridge purchased from London dealers like Rodd and Swaby and also utilized in his house and his estate buildings ancient carved woodwork and stonework which he obtained from demolished buildings in Bristol. He lived at Broomwell House on the edge of Bristol and it was there that he created the splendid library shown in minute detail as it was in about 1825 in Plates 250 and 251. One of his friends described it:

> . . . this rare treasury of ancient art,
> With many a curious monument enrich'd
> Of times long past, helmet and sword and shield,
> And quaint devices of heraldic lore
> And bright emblazonry, varied boast
> Of Broomwell's gothic Hall.[19]

His collection contained several important objects and was not dispersed until 1908.[20] One was the twelfth-century enamelled Malmesbury Ciborium purchased by J.P. Morgan and now in the Pierpont Morgan Library in New York. Another was the cradle Walpole knew as Edward II's, but by the time Shaw illustrated it in *Specimens* it had become that of Henry V. This provenance was accepted by Braikenridge, as it was by the King, when he purchased it at the sale. It is now on display in the Museum of London.

Fortunately, the room in Plates 250 and 251 survives — sadly without its contents — having been moved by his son to Braikenridge's summer residence, Claremont Villa at Clevedon near Bristol. It does include part of the remarkable heraldic ceiling referred to in the poem above, which was painted in 1830 to the designs of the herald and antiquary James Dallaway.

252. A German mediaeval ivory from Pugin's collection (Victoria & Albert Museum, London)

A.W.N. Pugin was a collector and, as we have seen, the catalogues of the sales of his collection after his death include the usual mix of stained glass, armour and other antiquities, many of which he had brought back in his own ship from the Continent. Of the Romantic Interiors which he certainly created for his collections in his several houses of the 1830s and 1840s, no illustrations survive. When Pugin's collection was auctioned,[21] John Webb was on hand to pay £12 for lot 103, 'An ivory tablet in four compartments', for the Museum of Ornamental Art. It is still on display at its successor, the Victoria & Albert Museum (Plate 252). The other half of this French fourteenth-century diptych was in the Cluny Museum by the time Du Sommerard's son wrote the catalogue of 1881.[22] Where Pugin purchased his ivory and when the other half came to the Cluny, I do not know. Pugin was often in Paris, but whether he ever visited the Cluny or met Du Sommerard is also unknown.

Pugin also encouraged several of his clients for whom he worked as an architect to purchase ancient objects and architectural fragments for him to incorporate into their houses. We encountered Charles Scarisbrick purchasing carved woodwork from Pugin's friend Hull, the broker, for his house, Scarisbrick Hall. Indeed one of the great features of Scarisbrick today is the large assemblage of built-in continental carvings.[23] Scarisbrick was a sixteenth-century house which had been radically altered to the designs of Rickman from 1813 to 1816. Then Pugin worked there from the mid-1830s until his death in 1852, by which time all trace of the original house had disappeared. I had considered taking Scarisbrick as one of my case-studies, but, although there is some manuscript material concerning Scarisbrick's collecting activities, only one contemporary illustration for an interior exists. Pugin's own atmospheric watercolour (Plate 253) shows how it was to be rather than as eventually executed, though the interior as executed is in fact very similar.

So much has been published of Pugin the celebrated Gothic Revival architect that his crucial role as a collector, antiquary, and mediaevalist has perhaps been forgotten. This aspect of his career brought him into contact with many of those creating Romantic Interiors, and upon the generation that followed Scott and Meyrick he had a considerable influence. Thanks to his early grounding in mediaeval architecture and design gained while working as a topographical artist for his father, he was from the very outset of his career able to visualize the mediaeval interior with its appropriate furnishings. This can be seen from the frontispiece (Plate 254) of *Examples of Gothic Architecture*, the last book on which he and his father collaborated and which was published in 1834 after his father's death.

In 1834 Pugin was actually involved in a project relating to Scott: he illustrated the essay on ancient furniture in a publication on Scott's poems. Plate 255 was described thus:

The subject of the annexed engraving is calculated to please from its novelty; although most of the articles of ancient furniture present interesting objects of curiosity, these are rarely or never introduced as subordinate parts, even of a picture. Furniture of this early period is yet abundant; but with the almost solitary exception of Hardwick Hall in Derbyshire, the magnificent interiors of the Tudor period have never been made the painter's study ... Two or three very splendid compositions for interiors, of this precise period were painted by Mr Pugin for the interesting ballet Kenilworth.[24]

253. The project for the Great Hall of Scarisbrick painted in 1835 by A.W.N. Pugin (RIBA Drawings Collection, London)

254. A.W.N. Pugin, the frontispiece to *Examples of Gothic Architecture* published in 1834

255. *Ancient Furniture* by A.W.N. Pugin from *Illustrations ... to the poetical works of Sir Walter Scott, Bart*, 1834

256. The Cromwell Hall at Chirk Castle in the 1880s

The book had several authors, but this essay was written by Thomas Moule, the antiquary and author of *The Heraldry of Fish* and *Bibliotheca Heraldica*, who later in the essay relates that 'The very handsome ebony chairs from Esher Palace, and which formerly belonged to Cardinal Wolsey, were amongst the curious furniture collected by William Beckford at Fonthill Abbey'.[25] The part issue of Shaw's *Specimens* illustrating Walpole's ebony chair (Plate 36) had appeared in April 1833, but Walpole's ebony furniture is not mentioned by Moule.

From the late 1840s until his death in 1852 Pugin designed and carried out alterations and additions to the mediaeval Chirk Castle in the Welsh Marches, the seat of the Myddleton family. The Cromwell Hall (Plate 256) has a splendid Pugin fireplace, and the genealogical chart has a Pugin oak frame, but the character of the interior is created by the weapons, armour and old oak furniture with which Pugin had furnished the room. The room derived its name from the Cromwellian arms and armour: 'These items had originally been set up here in 1680 to commemorate the family's exploits in the Civil War; but with a change of fashion the whole collection had been relegated to the Servants Hall in 1768.'[26] Then in the 1770s this room had been Georgianized with classical columns and a black and white marble floor.

So, just as at Charlecote, the neo-classical interiors at Chirk — and Oxburgh, as we shall see — were re-edified after only two generations. The billiard table dates from after Pugin's death. The series of Romantic Interiors created at Chirk included ancient family objects mixed with Pugin furniture and decorations. Sadly, most of the Pugin work was destroyed before the house was recently taken over by the National Trust. The Cromwell Hall fortunately survives much as in Plate 256, though Pugin's proper heraldic colours on the family arms carved on the chimney-piece have been painted out.

A further house that falls into the same category as Charlecote, Browsholme, Bolton and Chirk is Oxburgh Hall in Norfolk. This highly romantic moated house (Plate 257), the seat of the Bedingfeld family since it was built, dates largely from the late fifteenth century, but was, like Charlecote, classicized internally in the eighteenth century, and sash windows replaced the Tudor ones. In 1830 the young Sir Henry Paston-Bedingfeld, Bart. (1830–1862,) inherited the house; 'Oxburgh was

257. Oxburgh Hall in the 1870s
258. The Drawing Room at Oxburgh Hall in the 1870s

once again in bad shape, and Sir Henry, writing to his brother Felix in 1830, puts "The Ruin" as his address; cattle were drinking from the moat. In fact the house was not completely ruinous and was certainly habitable, but many alterations and improvements were now begun.'[27]

The work went on over the next thirty years. Sir Henry was an enthusiastic Goth who had spent part of his childhood on the Continent when his family in 1816 settled in Ghent for several years. The family was an ancient Catholic one, and one of Sir Henry's first acts was to build a splendid private chapel at Oxburgh. It is possible that Pugin was involved in its design, but there is no documentary proof. The chapel, however, contains imported ancient continental woodwork and one of Willement's most important heraldic windows. For much of the work in the house, Sir Henry employed J.C. Buckler (1793–1894), another Catholic architect who was also a celebrated topographical artist who had worked as an artist for Thomas Lister Parker (Plates 247 and 248). Buckler was an obvious choice, for he specialized in re-edifying mediaeval and Tudor houses, but he was, as we shall see, also working for Sir Henry's relations at nearby Costessey. This was the seat of the Jerningham family, and Sir Henry's mother was the daughter of Sir William Jerningham, Bart., of Costessey.

For three decades from the early 1830s work went on at Oxburgh. The Georgian sashes and chimney-stacks were replaced by ones in the Tudor style and many subtle external alterations took place. A garden in the French Renaissance style was created beyond the moat. Inside the house Romantic Interiors were created by mixing ancient continental woodcarvings and leather hangings with modern Tudor or Gothic-style stencilled ceilings, painted tiles and polychromatic carved stone chimney-pieces. The Drawing Room (Plate 258) has an overmantel of late mediaeval continental carved woodwork. The octagonal table was modern and was probably made, like a number of pieces of the furniture, for Sir Henry in Brussels.

The celebrated sixteenth-century needlework hangings which survived in the house were even pressed into service as bed curtains. In an attempt to modernize it and convert it into a dining room, the Georgian picture gallery was painted in rich dark colours and hung with curtains and wallpaper to Pugin's design, though the neo-classical fireplace was retained. A sideboard made up from ancient carvings was acquired bearing the date 1687 and the arms of the family. This was very similar to the sideboard acquired for Charlecote at much the same time (Plates 185 and 186). The dining chairs, which at first sight look like the familiar ebony model and are obviously closely based upon their design, are of walnut and were made in Brussels along with the dining table. Oxburgh now belongs to the National Trust.

Costessey Hall in Norfolk was rebuilt in 1564 by the Jerninghams, an ancient Catholic family like their neighbours the Bedingfelds. In about 1809 the Gothic Revival chapel (seen on the right in Plate 259) was built to the designs of Edward Jerningham, an amateur architect who was the youngest son of Sir William the owner. He was a minor poet, but more relevant here was his close friendship with Horace Walpole. The windows of the chapel were filled with a rich and varied assemblage of stained glass mainly collected on the Continent,[28] but removed from the house and sold early this century.[29]

In the late 1820s J.C. Buckler was employed to enlarge Costessey. The impetus for this came from the success of the Jerninghams in their claim to the barony of Stafford, when Sir George William Stafford Jerningham, 7th Bart., on 5 October 1826 became by Royal Licence the 8th Baron Stafford. As we saw with the case of the Devon claim engineered by Sir Nicholas Harris Nicolas, such claims were expensive and complicated. The Jerningham claim was far stronger than the Devon, for they were clearly descendants of the celebrated Stafford who was attainted and executed in 1680 for his supposed involvement with Titus Oates and the Popish Plot. Even so, the claim was expensive and took many years to achieve, for as early as 1808 Sir George's father had published *The case of Sir William Jerningham, Baronet,*

259. Costessey Hall in the 1890s

260. An interior at Costessey in 1913

on his Petition to the King, claiming the Two baronies of Stafford. As can be imagined an appropriately feudal reception was arranged:

> Lord and Lady Stafford returned to Costessey after officially obtaining the barony ... their horses were replaced by 30 men dressed with sashes and other decorations. They were headed by as many as 150 horsemen riding in pairs, with a band and 100 children carrying banners and flags, &c Church bells and more cannon volleys greeted their arrival ... Lord and Lady Stafford gave each parishioner as well as children: 1 lb. of meat, a twopenny loaf and a pint of beer. For general consumption, there was in addition a fat bullock and a half, 3 sheep, 800 twopenny loaves and as many pints of beer as they could accommodate.[30]

Thus Buckler was employed to create a house suitable for the newly enobled family, and in 1833 a design was shown at the Royal Academy. 'This design of our friend Mr J.C. Buckler, is a loftly Tower with attached staircase turret, capped with machicolations ... the complete revival of ancient English architecture which may be witnessed in this fine seat. The entire design shews a mansion which even Sir Reginald Bray of Cardinal Wolsey might have acknowledged.'[31] Buckler worked at the house until the mid-1860s and eventually the tower rose to 150 feet, but some of the interiors were never completed. One of the interesting characteristics of Buckler's work is his sensitivity to local materials, and at Costessey, Oxburgh and nearby Hengrave he followed the East Anglian vernacular use of moulded red brick in, for instance, the chimneys at Costessey (Plate 259) and Oxburgh (Plate 257). To provide these bricks Buckler and Stafford greatly expanded an existing brickworks owned by the latter, and bricks and terracotta to Buckler's design were manufactured and also sold commercially throughout the area.[32]

In 1866 a considerable quantity of furniture to Buckler's design was ordered from the London cabinet-makers Holland & Son for the three-day visit of the Prince of Wales. The chair on the left beneath the weapons next to the ancient oak cabinet in Plate 260 is one of these pieces. It had the crests of Stafford emblazoned in gold on the red leather back and the 'Stafford Knot' carved on the front rail. One of these chairs can now be seen in the Victoria & Albert Museum. The importance of the collections housed in the Romantic Interiors at Costessey is obvious from the catalogue of the five-day sale of the contents which took place in 1913, with 1,279 lots.[33] The house was later demolished.

One other group of houses that need brief mention are those literary shrines similar to Abbotsford. One example, which still survives and which existed as a house before Abbotsford, is Newstead Abbey, Byron's home near Nottingham (Plates 261 through 263). The house had been created in 1540 by the Byron family

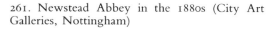
261. Newstead Abbey in the 1880s (City Art Galleries, Nottingham)

262. Relics of Byron at Newstead in the 1880s (City Art Galleries, Nottingham)
263. An interior at Newstead in the 1880s (City Art Galleries, Nottingham)

264. John Sainsbury with his collection (J. Sainsbury, *The Napoleon Museum* ..., 1845)

from the Abbey of Newstead. Curiously, the few alterations made by Byron the Romantic poet were in the modern style, and only after he sold it in 1817 were any Romantic Interiors of interest created in the house. These were created for the new owner, Colonel Thomas Wildman, who was a friend of Henry Shaw and Thomas Willement and whose family made their money as Beckford's agents in the West Indies. Willement supplied stained glass and wallpaper; the wallpaper in the Saloon (Plate 263) is by Willement and is of the same design as that in the library at Charlecote (Plate 195 and 196).

Perhaps predictably, it has been the connection with Byron the poet that has ensured the continuing fame of the house, and Plate 262 shows a group of his relics already revered by the later nineteenth century. The house and contents survive in the hands of the local authority who are carrying out a sensitive restoration programme at the moment which is also doing justice to Wildman's contribution to the house.

Another ancient house celebrated for its connection with a literary figure is Knebworth House in Hertfordshire, the seat of the Lytton family. When Scott died, his place as Britain's most famous historical novelist was soon taken by Edward Bulwer-Lytton, who extended his ancient family house in the Tudor style, creating within it a whole group of Romantic Interiors. He even wrote and published his own guidebook.[34] Its importance has recently been recognized, and it has been fully illustrated and discussed in print.[35] The house survives in the hands of the Lytton family and is open to the public.

I have carried my story through to the middle of the nineteenth century, by which time many more people were collecting, and they were purchasing a far wider range of objects than ever before. Indeed, as we have seen with Mayer, by the 1840s eighteenth-century ceramics were becoming fashionable for collectors and by the 1860s whole interiors were being created using Georgian furniture.[36] William Morris and his generation of Goths fought a rearguard action against the rising tide of neo-Georgianism. In a lecture in Birmingham in 1884 he castigated 'the worthy people who started with regenerating the arts by imitating the 13th century [and who] have grown older and have more or less sunk their ideals and are prepared to put up with the quaint trimness of a Queen Anne house as good enough to make us in this age of ugliness forget the poetry and beauty of a 14th century grange'.[37]

Walpole had been a century out when he perceptively predicted in a letter to his friend Conway of 28 May 1763, shortly after George III had come to the throne, that 'two hundred years hence some man of taste will build a hamlet in the style of George the Third and beg his cousin Tom Hearne to get him some chairs for it of mahogany gilt, and covered with blue damask'.[38]

Also by the 1840s specialization by collecting just one type or class of objects was far more prevalent. In Plate 264 we see the monomaniac collector John Sainsbury in his Napoleonic museum in 1845. He collected only material concerning Napoleon, including sculpture, decorations, prints, drawings, paintings, coins, medals, books and manuscripts. By 1845 he could write that the 'formation of the Museum described in this volume was commenced about twenty seven years ago, when the illustrious individual, whose actions and the events in connection with them form the predominant feature of it, was the all-absorbing topic of public attention'.[39] Though Meyrick, Scott and Beckford had each collected some Napoleonic relics to furnish their houses, these items formed only a small part of their large and varied collections. Scott also wrote one of the important early biographies of Napoleon.

Monomaniac collectors became much more common in the second half of the nineteenth century. For instance, Lady Charlotte Schrieber collected almost exclusively ceramics and left her vast collection to the South Kensington Museum. Whilst such collectors had perforce to co-exist in their houses with their collections, they often did not use their objects to create interesting Romantic Interiors of the type I have been discussing.

By the second half of the nineteenth century so fashionable had small-scale domestic Romantic Interiors become that most of the new genre of manuals on how to furnish one's house were aimed at the wives of middle-class and professional men and included instructions on creating them. Eastlake in his influential treatise on the subject explains:

> The smallest example of rare old porcelain, of ivory carving, of ancient metal-work, of enamels, of Venetian glass, of anything which illustrates good design and skilful workmanship should be acquired whenever possible, and treasured with the greatest care. It is impossible to overrate the influence which such objects may have in educating the eye to appreciate what constitutes good art. An Indian ginger-jar, a Flemish beer-jug, a Japanese fan . . . group them together as much as possible. A set of narrow shelves ranged at the back, and forming part of a dining-room sideboard would be admirable.[40]

By the 1880s everyone was being encouraged to incorporate a few curiosities into their houses, and that other celebrated pundit Colonel Edis, who was involved in the creation of Sandringham, in his treatise for the artistic urban middle classes illustrated 'an arrangement of cupboards and shelves which I have designed for guns, fishing-rods, swords and china, cigars tobacco, and pipes in my own library. This work was done in deal painted, at a moderate cost, the tiles and figure plaques after Teniers being from an old German stove and utterly unseen until placed as I have shown. The whole work was executed for me by an ordinary builder.'[41]

But as early as 1876 another author of a more downmarket treatise was sounding a warning note: 'it may be as well to draw a sharp line between a man who gathers objects in which he alone is interested and the man who desires to beautify his house with what he buys . . . I do not want to see everyone collecting. I do not admire private museums. I think houses which are ugly and badly furnished and uncomfortable, are none the better for being filled with curiosities. But short of this something may be done.'[42]

Even the young Beatrix Potter was caught up with this movement while visiting Oxford with her parents in 1884:

> June 10th — Tuesday, went to a most interesting shop of furniture, china and every kind of curiosity. The house itself was worth seeing, such stairs and

265. The interior of Ellen Terry's country cottage at Smallhythe in Kent in the 1890s

passages, and crammed from basement to roof. Mama ended in buying a Chippendale clock, fourteen guineas. Cheap I think ... If ever I have a house I would have old furniture, oak in the dining room, and Chippendale in the drawing room. It is not as expensive as modern furniture, and incomparably handsomer and better made.[43]

Later in her life she was to create antiquarian interiors in several of her old cottages and houses in the Lake District, furnishing them with ancient local furniture. One of these she imaginatively bequeathed to the National Trust.

Such Arts and Crafts versions of the Romantic Interior were created when country cottages or farmhouses were furnished with ancient objects of a deliberately rustic or simple character, and are a whole study in themselves. Good examples are those interiors created in an ancient farmhouse at Smallhythe in Kent by the actress Ellen Terry following her purchase of the house in 1899. The Dining Room (Plate 265) has some of the appropriate furnishings of simple country life, such as rustic furniture and pewter, but the copper coal scuttle in a hearth where only wood was burnt is as patently impractical as Walpole's curfeu and basket grate (Plates 68 and 71). It is also unlikely that a simple Kentish yeoman farmer would cover his crude brick floor with an expensive Persian rug, especially so close to the fire! The house now belongs to the National Trust and is open to the public.

Such nostalgia for the country and its artefacts stretched back to the eighteenth century, but the desire by the middle and upper classes actually to emulate cottage life was very much a later nineteenth-century movement. The Arts and Crafts movement was to be fuelled by this nostalgia admixed with Christian socialism. With so many of the objects I have described, it was the associations they brought with them that justified their place in a Romantic Interior. As early as 1825 William Cobbett, though rather in advance of his contemporaries, was motivated by just such thoughts. On 25 October 1825 at Reigate in Surrey he

went to a sale at a farm ... Everything about this farmhouse was formerly the scene of plain manners and plentiful living. Oak clothes-chests, oak bed-steads, oak chests of drawers, and oak tables to eat on, long and strong, and well supplied with joint stools ... I could not quit this farmhouse without reflecting on the thousands of scores of bacon and thousands of bushels of bread that had been eaten from the long oak-table which I said to myself, is now perhaps, going at last, to the bottom of a bridge that some stock-jobber will stick up over an artificial river in his cockney garden. '*By — it shant*,' said I, almost in a real passion: so I requested a friend to buy it for me; and if he do so, I will take it to Kensington, or to Fleet-street, and keep it for the good it has done the world.[44]

William Morris had helped to pioneer this move away from the use of grand ancient country houses and their furnishings as exemplars by the creators of Romantic Interiors to a reappraisal of simple country examples. By founding the Society for the Protection of Ancient Buildings he also in a very practical way brought about the preservation of many such houses. At Kelmscott Manor in Oxfordshire, which Morris rented from 1871, he created a series of Romantic Interiors of a very simple kind; these have been fully discussed recently.[45]

Morris's sentiments about the house were very similar to those voiced by so many of the house owners I have discussed: he shared their love of history, tangible signs of age and character, except that Morris was drawn to the simple and rustic examples, which he described in a highly romantic manner. In his celebrated 'Utopian Romance' of 1890 he described Kelmscott as 'this many gabled old house built by the simple country-folk of the long-past times, regardless of all the turmoil that was going on in the cities and courts ... Everywhere there was but little furniture, and that only the most necessary, and of the simplest forms.'[46] Then, writing in October 1895 at the very end of his life:

great parlour (the house is not great at all remember) and is now panelled with pleasing George 1st panelling painted white: the chimney-piece is no doubt of the date of the building, and is of rude but rather amusing country work ... the tapestry [room] is over the big panelled parlour. The walls of it are hung with tapestry of about 1600, representing the story of Samson; they were never great works of art, and now when all the bright colours are faded out, and nothing is left but the inigo blues, the greys and the warm yellowy browns, they look better, I think, than they were meant to look: at any rate they make the walls a

266. *The Bric-à-Brac Hunter at Home* (Byng Hall, *The Bric-à-Brac Hunter ...*, 1875)

very pleasant background for the living people who haunt the room . . . they give an air of romance to the room which nothing else would quite do . . . so much has the old house grown out of the soil and the lives of those that lived on it; needing no grand office-architect.[47]

In the cities by the mid-1870s the whole matter of furnishing with antiques became so widespread that fashionable gentlemen aesthetes had moved into the field. In *The Bric-à-Brac Hunter at Home* (Plate 266), we see the world-weary Major Herbert Byng Hall in his smoking jacket with his hookah close at hand on its Cairene table surrounded with his collection. He summed the matter up thus in the preface to his book: 'My object is simply to give a slight sketch of the various hunting grounds over which I have ranged in search of bric-à-brac — a very agreeable pursuit — which has caused me untiring interest and delight; and thus, by offering the slight practical experience I have gained during foreign travel, I may cause amusement, if not instruction, to the many thousands who have similar tastes.'[48]

Byng Hall seems to have lived the life of the wealthy amateur depicted in Plate 266, also publishing a number of books on sporting and military subjects, including *Soldiers & Sailors in Peace as in War* (1837) and *Highland Sports and Highland Quarters* (1847). There is no doubt that the interiors Byng Hall created to house his collection were Romantic ones, but they and others of their period belong in spirit rather to the fashionable world of later nineteenth-century collecting, the world of Duveen, Berenson, Lord Leverhulme and J.P. Morgan, than to that of the Romantic movement of the years immediately following 1800.

One should not dismiss collections as mere bric-à-brac until they have been fully investigated. The photograph of Lord Llangattock clad in his smoking jacket asleep in his ancient turned 'Welch Chair' in his Oak Parlour (Plate 267) gives much the same impression of mere fashionable collecting as that of Byng Hall. In fact John Rolls (1837–1912), before he became a baron in 1892, had created a series of Romantic Interiors at his house The Hendre near Monmouth to house his important collection.[49] The decoration of these interiors had been carried out by the celebrated firm of Crace.

267. Lord Llangattock asleep in the Oak Parlour at The Hendre in the 1890s

269. The Soulages collection in his house in Toulouse photographed in 1856 by C. Thurston Thompson (Victoria & Albert Museum, London)

The Hendre collection, like so many similar collections I have described, included, due to the energy of collectors like Rolls, a wide range of objects acquired in this country and abroad. These collection as are still disgorging their treasures, and in 1988 the Victoria & Albert Museum, acquired from Rolls's descendants the remarkable twelfth-century enamels (Plate 268) that Rolls acquired as early as the 1850s. His son Charles did not follow his father as a collector, but instead went into making motor cars.

By the 1850s in Britain the collectors and creators of Romantic Interiors were having to compete with the newly awakened interest by the British Museum in mediaeval and Renaissance objects. The extensive purchases by them — through the agency of John Webb — at the Bernal sale, where they bought Lothair's crystal, is a good instance of this. Then in the early 1850s the new Museum of Ornamental Art was set up at Marlborough House in London and began at once to buy antiquities at, for instance, the Pugin and Bernal sales. In 1857 it moved to South Kensington where it was eventually to grow into the Victoria & Albert Museum.

The Museum of Ornamental Art was at first mainly concerned with the acquisition of modern manufactures, but in 1855 Henry Cole, who was shortly to be its celebrated director, and J.C. Robinson, the Curator of the Museum, decided to start acquiring ancient objects as models for British designers. Cole knew that they would be competing both in Britain and on the Continent with well-established collectors who had been buying mediaeval and Renaissance objects for several decades.

In consultation with his friend John Webb, Cole decided to purchase a ready-made collection, which had been formed when there were greater opportunities to acquire such pieces. The collector was Jules Soulages, a lawyer from Toulouse in the south of France who, though an antiquary and a founder member of the Société Archéologique du Midi, lived in Paris for most of his life. He had started to collect

at a time highly favourable in Italy to the acquisition of remnants of ancient wealth and grandeur, that is, some ten years after the tranquilization of Europe, distracted by the long war of the French revolution. Furniture, gems, plate, jewels, lace, porcelain, enamels, bronzes, pictures and tapestries, every *genre* of Art-treasure had been dispersed, and gradually fell into the hands of dealers, who found their market amongst those who had a taste for these rarities and could indulge it. Thus it is that all those collections are formed. Mr Bernal did not perhaps, go very far from home for the majority of his catalogue; but the name of Soulage is probably still remembered in some of the least promising of these dark *botteghe*, in the narrowest and most retired streets of Florence and Rome.[50]

How and where the collection was housed in Paris I have been unable to discover, but in the late 1840s Soulages moved it to Toulouse. It was in Soulages house in Toulouse that Henry Cole and Charles Thurston Thompson, the museum photographer, examined the collection in 1855.[51] Fortunately, Thompson took a number of photographs of objects in the collection but only two of the Romantic Interiors they had been used to create (Plates 269 and 270). These are fascinating and important images, being not only very early photographs of a major Romantic Interior in Europe, but also early examples of the use of photography to promote a museum acquisition.

John Webb was sent by Cole to Toulouse to negotiate a price with Soulages for the whole collection, but the story of its transport to London and the eventual purchase by the South Kensington Museum is a long and complicated one.[52] The collection consisted of more than 700 pieces of late mediaeval and Renaissance continental furniture, glass, majolica, bronzes, glass sculpture and enamels. These were exhibited at Marlborough House in 1856 and a catalogue was published,[53] and in 1857 the collection was also exhibited at the Manchester Art Treasures Exhibition.

Here we see the stripping of a series of important Romantic Interiors to help build up the collections of a major museum. This process of acquiring whole collections or important pieces from them was to accelerate throughout Europe as the century went on and more public museums were created. In 1857 the South Kensington Museum had helped the British Museum dismember the Bernal collection, though at open auction. In 1862 these two museums, following the Soulages example by operating on the Continent, employed John Webb to bid for them at the Soltikoff sale in Paris. The Soltikoff collection had been housed in a splendid Gothic Revival house especially built around the collection. Amongst the objects Webb purchased for South Kensington were the Eltenburgh Reliquary and the Gloucester Candlestick, still two of the museum's most famous objects.

Then in 1882 the South Kensington Museum was bequeathed the whole Jones collection which was then stripped from his house in Piccadilly. In 1910 they acquired the Salting collection, again housed in the West End of London, and removed it to South Kensington. Some Romantic Interiors were preserved by the initiative of their owners who organized for their dwelling houses to become public museums. The Cluny, the Wallace Collection and the Sir John Soane Museum are three well-known examples.

Once a collection is broken up the museums may, of course, immediately acquire object from it, or in some cases the object may pass through several more private collections before eventually ending up in a museum. A considerable number of objects that I have illustrated and discussed in the context of a specific British Romantic Interior have found their way into the British museums. Indeed the museums have the imagination and energy of the creators of these interiors to thank for scouring the Continent for objects and bringing them to Britain in the first place.

The Victoria & Albert Museum has been greatly enriched in this way — for instance, the Mazarin Chest (Plate 101) was bought by Beckford in Paris as were Walpole's bronze angel (Plate 89) and stained glass (Plates 61 and 62). Pugin's ivories

270. A cabinet in Soulages's house in Toulouse photographed in 1856 by C. Thurston Thompson (Victoria & Albert Museum, London)

(Plate 252) were almost certainly acquired abroad. Pugin is likely to have had a hand in the acquisition abroad of the Alton Towers Triptych, which is now one of the museum's most important Romanesque enamels, and which was part of the collection furnishing the Romantic Interiors that Willement and Pugin created for Lord Shrewsbury at Alton Towers. It was purchased at auction by the museum in 1858, when the collections were dispersed following the death of Lord Shrewsbury in 1856.

Even when these objects were acquired by a public museum they were displayed in a manner more akin to the private museums of Tradescant and Mr Green (Plate 11) than to the approved late 1980s manner. A British visitor to the newly opened public museum just over the Channel in Boulogne in 1864 found:

> The Museum ... contains a very respectable collection of antiquities, chiefly donations —
>
>> Every clime and age
>> Jumbled together; celts and calumnets
>> Claymore and snowshoe, toys in lava, fans
>> Of sandal, amber, ancient rosaries,
>> Laborious orient ivory sphere in sphere
>> The cursed Malayan crease, and battle clubs
>> From the isles of palm.
>
> Tennyson's words describe their arrangement, or rather want of management, admirably, and the effect upon the mind, upon looking over the miscellaneous curiosities, is something very short of a nightmare.[54]

At this date the British Museum and the South Kensington Museum were hardly more logically arranged.

When in 1869 the South Kensington Museum acquired its first 'period room' it actually began to compete with the private collectors by creating its own Romantic Interiors by furnishing such rooms with what at the time seemed appropriate furnishings. This first room at South Kensington was eighteenth-century French; the first English period room was acquired in 1891. This was the Inlaid Chamber from Sizergh Castle in Westmorland (Plate 271). It is interesting to see Nash's *Mansions* casting the same spell over museum curators that it had over private collectors of the previous generation.

Nash described it thus: 'Sizergh has been for some centuries the seat of the Strickland family. It is a venerable building ... various portions having undergone modern alterations. The bed-room given here is the most curious feature of the interior, the panelling of which is inlaid with a profuse expenditure of labour quite peculiar to the decoration of former days.'[55] Only the panelling came to South Kensington, the ceiling remains at Sizergh to this day. The museum photographer made the negative of Plate 271, and the celebrated furniture historian John Hungerford Pollen was sent to deepest Westmorland to negotiate the purchase of the panelling and to arrange to have the ceiling copied.

Eventually the celebrated bed shown in Nash was also purchased and the room arranged, as in Plate 272, in a manner that would have delighted Meyrick. Sadly the museum was no less immune to acquiring spurious pieces than had been private collectors and in 1913 under the headline 'Old furniture: Spurious Antiques "Ripening" in London Cellars' it was reported 'that the carved bedstead from Sizergh castle Westmorland, now in the Victoria & Albert Museum, South Kensington, is not the genuine piece of furniture hitherto believed ... it is claimed that, though it was originally a walnut bedstead, only two posts can lay any claim to genuineness, the rest being made in oak.'[56]

Not to be thwarted in its attempt to create a Tudor Romantic Interior, the museum put the Sizergh bed into store and resurrected another bed and suitable

271. The Inlaid Room at Sizergh Castle (J. Nash, *The Mansions of England . . .*, 1839–49)

272. The Inlaid Room from Sizergh Castle as displayed in the South Kensington Museum in 1891 (Victoria & Albert Museum, London)

furnishings for the room. In the early 1980s in a fit of Post-Romantic museum display the room was stripped of its furnishings and remains so today. Sizergh Castle now belongs to the National Trust and recently the bed was lent back to the house. One day the panelling might perhaps rejoin it.

The idea of building an ancient room into a later building had been pioneered by the private creators of Romantic Interiors: indeed Meyrick had created a sequence of such rooms of differing dates, an idea only taken up by public museums in Europe and America later in the nineteenth century.

I have frequently stressed the importance of the motives of the collectors who were the impresarios who created these Romantic Interiors. Their individual views of the past and the character of the interiors they created to house its artefacts were very diverse. The analysis of the theoretical basis for the furnishing of such interiors and the motivation of the collectors who created them have never been thoroughly investigated. Recently, however, some analysis of this type has been undertaken using the modern theoretical tools such as Michel Foucault's theories of 'epistemological totality'. Stephen Bann discusses

> the intriguing paradox of Du Sommerard's achievement. A passionate collector, he was none the less able to transmute his fascination with the objects of the past into an orderly and accessible vision of period and place . . . He showed that an original historical setting, amply furnished with authentic objects, would evoke a potent and sustaining image of the past. Even when the 'Antiquary' was no longer there to weave his story around each object, the internal consistency of the milieu would continue its recreative effect.[57]

The attitude of collectors to the interiors they inhabit and to their collections has also recently been put in a wider context:

> What is acquired in daily contact with ancient objects, by regular visits to antique-dealers and galleries, or more simply by moving in a universe of familiar, intimate objects 'which are there', as Rilke says, 'guileless, good, simple certain' is of course a certain 'taste', which is nothing other than a relation of immediate familiarity with the things of taste. But it is also the sense of belonging to a more polished more polite, better policed world, a world which is justified in existing by its perfection, its harmony and beauty.'[58]

Walpole, Beckford, Scott, Lucy and Meyrick were one and all well aware of the importance of inhabiting interiors 'in daily contact with ancient objects'.

I do not intend to undertake any psychological or sociological analysis into why these singular interiors were created. I am an antiquary by inclination and a museum curator by profession and I will leave such analysis to those more skilled than I in the deployment of the semiotic tools of the 'new art history'. I have attempted in this book to cover a wide enough range of Romantic Interiors in date and type to demonstrate what a rich and complex contribution they have made to our domestic environment and to the history of collecting in Britain.

These interiors were inseparable from and vital to the wider Romantic Movement, and for me the appropriate first response to them is thus a romantic rather than an intellectual or theoretical one. I therefore end with the observations of that perceptive American observer of our national life — Washington Irving:

> An old English family mansion is a fertile subject for study. It abounds with illustrations of former times, and traces of the tastes, and humours, and manners of successive generations. The alterations and additions, in different styles of architecture; the furniture, plate pictures, hangings; the warlike and sporting implements of different ages and fancies; all furnish food for curious and amusing speculation.[59]

NOTES TO THE TEXT

Notes to Chapter 1

1. Joan Evans, *A History of the Society of Antiquaries* (1956), 60.
2. A.S. Bell, ed., *The Scottish Antiquarian Tradition: Essays to Mark the Bicentenary of the Society of Antiquaries of Scotland, 1780–1980* (1981).
3. Horace Walpole, *The Yale Edition of Horace Walpole's Correspondence*, ed. W.S. Lewis (XV)(1951), 179.
4. John Earle, *Microcosmography; or, a Piece of the World Discovered* (1811), 20–1. The first edition appeared in 1628. See also Walter E. Houghton, 'The English Virtuoso in the Seventeenth Century', *Journal of the History of Ideas* (1942), III, 51–73 & 190–219.
5. Thomas Fuller, *The Holy State* (1652), 65.
6. John Nichols, *Literary Anecdotes of the Eighteenth Century . . .* (1812), VI, 208–9.
7. J.G. Jenkins, *The Dragon of Whaddon: Being an Account of the Life and Work of Browne Willis (1682–1760), Antiquary and Historian* (1953).
8. Henry Peacham, *The Compleat Gentleman Fashioning Him absolute in the most Necessary and Commendable Qualities . . .* (1634), 111.
9. This appears as a plate facing p. 262 in vol. III of the 1751 edition of Pope's works, but not in earlier editions. For a fascinating and scholarly discussion of this plate, see R.W. Lightbown's entry, pp. 60–1, in *Rococo Art and Design in Hogarth's England* (1984). It is worth noting that, though inscribed 'N. Blakey inv and del', this plate may have been lifted from a French source. The same plate exists in a scrapbook at the Bibliothèque Nationale in Paris labelled as French and as showing the celebrated French collector Count Caylus (1692–1765), but the source of the plate is not noted.
10. Alexander Pope, *The Works* (1751), III, 262–3.
11. For a full examination of the Gothic Revival in Europe before 1840, see Hôtel de Sully, Paris, *Le Gothique Retrouvé avant Viollet-le-Duc*, exh. cat. (1980).
12. Erwin Panofsky, *Abbot Suger on the Abbey Church of St Denis and its Art Treasures* (1946), 77.
13. Sumner McKnight Crosby et al., *The Royal Abbey of St Denis in the Time of Abbot Suger . . .* (1981), 102–3, shows two early eighteenth-century illustrations.
14. Barbara Jean Balsiger, 'Kunst und Wunderkammern: A Catalogue Raisonné of Collecting in Germany, France and England, 1565–1750', Ph.D. thesis, University of Pittsburgh (1970). The key published works are: Julius von Schlosser, *Die Kunst und Wunderkammern der Spätrenaissance* (1978); Adalgisa Lugli, *Naturalia et mirabilia: Il collezionismo enciclopedico nelle Wunderkammern d'Europa* (1983); Krzysztof Pomian, *Collectionneurs, amateurs et curieux Paris, Venise: XVI–XVIII siècle* (1987); David Murray, *Museums: Their History and their Use* (1904).
15. Brian Cook, 'The Townley Marbles at Westminster and Bloomsbury', *British Museum Yearbook* (1977), II, 34–78.
16. Laurentius Beger, *Thesaurus Brandenburgicus Selectus, Sive Gemmarum et Numismatum Graecorum in Cimeliarchio Electorali Brandenburgico . . .* (1696).
17. *Die Brandenburgisch-Preussiche Kunstkammer: Eine Auswahl aus den alten Bestanden* (1981), 31, pl. 12.
18. *ibid.*, 83–4. Other surviving objects are also illustrated.
19. 'The Electoral Kunstkammer', in *The Splendour of Dresden: Five Centuries of Art Collecting*, exh. cat. State Art-Collections of Dresden, National Gallery of Art, Washington (1978), 74–109.
20. Ole Worm, *Museum Wormianum seu Historia Rariorum . . .* (1655). This plate is the frontispiece.
21. The objects that survive are illustrated in H.D. Schepelern, *Museum Wormianum* (1971), and Bente Dam-Mikkelsen & Torben Lundbaek, *Ethnographic Objects in the Royal Danish Kunstkammer, 1650–1800* (1980).
22. Germain Bazin, *The Museum Age* (1967), 54.
23. Schlosser, *Die Kunst*, pl. 148.
24. *ibid.*, pl. 149.
25. Claude du Molinet, *Le Cabinet de la Bibliothèque de Sainte Geneviève . . .* (1692).
26. William Cole, *A Journal of My Journey to Paris in the year 1765 . . .* (1931), 261.
27. Hôtel de Sully, *Le Gothique*, 75–84. This section includes several illustrations.
28. J. Griffiths, *Museum of French Monuments . . .* (1803). For Lenoir, see B. Deneke & R. Kahsnitz, eds., *Das Kunst- und Kulturgeschlichtliche Museum im 19 Jahrhundert* (1977), 49–59.
29. William Shepherd, *Paris in Eighteen Hundred and Two and Eighteen Hundred and Fourteen* (1814), 83–5.
30. Hôtel de Sully, *Le Gothique*, 99–104. Lenoir and Du Sommerard are discussed in Stephen Bann, *The Clothing of Clio . . .* (1984).
31. Francis Salet & Geneviève Souchal, *The Cluny Museum* (1972), 18. See also Alain Erlande-Brandenburg, 'Evolution du Musée de Cluny', *Monuments Historiques* (1979), No. 104, 21–6.
32. Thomas Raikes, *A Portion of the Journal Kept by T. Raikes, Esq., from 1831 to 1847* (1856), I, 249.
33. Honoré de Balzac, *Cousin Pons* (1886), 11–12. The novel was first published in 1848.
34. Murray, *Museums*, is still the best work available.
35. Arthur Macgregor, ed., *Tradescant's Rarities: Essays on the Foundation of the Ashmolean Museum, 1683,* with a catalogue of the surviving early collections (1983). This scholarly work includes a fascinating essay on continental and British collections of the seventeenth century.
36. *ibid.*, the surviving descriptions are quoted here.
37. John Tradescant, *Musaeum Tradescantianum; or, A collection of rarities preserved at South Lambeth neer London* (1656).
38. Horace Walpole, *The Works of Horatio Walpole* (1798), III, 206.
39. Peacham, *Compleat Gentleman*, 107.
40. John Martin Robinson, *The Dukes of Norfolk: A Quincentennial History* (1982), 98. The portraits are now at Arundel Castle. See also M.F.S. Hervey, *The Life, Correspondence and Collections of Thomas Howard, Earl of Arundel* (1921).
41. David Howarth, *Lord Arundel and his Circle* (1985), and Ashmolean Museum, Oxford, *Thomas Howard, Earl of Arundel*, exh. cat. (1985).
42. Stuart Piggot, *William Stukeley: An Eighteenth Century Antiquary* (1985).
43. H.B. Walters, *The English Antiquaries of the Sixteenth, Seventeenth and Eighteenth Centuries* (1934), 33–4.
44. Bodleian Library MS Eng. Misc. c.538. f.7.
45. *Publications of the Surtees Society* (1885), LXXX, 14.
46. *Catalogue of the genuine and Curious Collection of Mathematical Instruments, Gems, Pictures, Bronzes, Busts, Urns, Cabinets, curious Clocks, Book-cases, &c. of Martin Folkes, Esq; Late of Queen Square, Holborn . . . By Mr Langford . . . 7th and Thursday the 8th, of this instant may 1755 . . .*
47. Louise Lippincott, *Selling Art in Georgian London: The Rise of Arthur Pond* (1983). The author makes no mention of Pond's friendship with Stukeley nor of his presence at the dedication of his Library.
48. *A Catalogue of the Genuine Collection of Coins and Medals, Various Antiquities, Fossils and other Curiosities . . . Manuscripts, Prints and Drawings of the late Rev.d and Learned William Stukeley . . . Auction by Samuel Paterson at Essex House in Essex Street, in the Strand . . . 15th and 16th of May 1766 . . .*
49. Simone Caudron, 'Connoisseurs of Champlève Limoges Enamels in Eighteenth Century England', *British Museum Yearbook* (1977), II, 9–33.
50. Hayward Gallery, London, *English Romanesque Art, 1066–1200*, exh. cat. (1984), 277.
51. *Catalogue of the Genuine Library . . . William Stukeley . . . By Samuel Paterson . . . April 28 1766 and five following evenings . . .*
52. Nichols, *Literary Anecdotes*, V, 248–528.
53. *ibid.*, 252.
54. John Nichols, *Illustrations of the Literary History of the Eighteenth Century . . .* (1822), IV, 432.
55. James Peller Malcolm, *Views Within Twelve Miles*

Round London . . . (1800), pl. XXIV.

56. Nichols, *Illustrations,* VI, 320.

57. Stebbing Shaw, *The History and Antiquities of Staffordshire . . .* (1798), I, 331.

58. *A Descriptive Catalogue of the Rarities in Mr Greene's Museum at Lichfield* (1773), 1.

59. Nichols, *Illustrations,* VI, 318–19.

60. *Gentleman's Magazine* (1788), LVIII, pt. II, 847–8.

61. Sir John Soane, *Description of the House and Museum . . .* (1835); John Britton, *The Union of Architecture and Painting: . . . The House and Galleries of John Soane* (1827); Susan Gail Feinberg, 'Sir John Soane's "Museum" . . .', Ph.D. thesis, University of Michigan (1979).

62. Pope, *Works,* III, 269.

63. *Christmas with the Poets . . .* (1872), 20.

64. John Selden, *Table Talk . . .* (1689), 22.

65. Thomas Shadwell, *The Lancashire Witches and Teague O'Divelly the Irish Priest: A Comedy* (1689), 36.

66. 'Common Sense No. 150', *Gentleman's Magazine* (1739), IX, 641.

67. *Gentleman's Magazine* (1755), XXV, 100.

68. Walpole, *Correspondence* (1960), XX, 16.

69. Charles L. Eastlake, *A History of the Gothic Revival* (1872), 356–7.

70. Nicholas Condy, *Cothele on the banks of the Tamar the ancient Seat of the Rt Honble The Earl of Mount Edgcumbe* [*c.* 1840], 12.

71. C.S. Gilbert, *A Historical Survey of the County of Cornwall . . .* (1820), 450.

72. A.W.N. Pugin, *Contrasts; or, A parallel between the noble edifices of the fourteenth and fifteenth centuries and corresponding buildings of the present day; shewing the present decay of taste* (1836). The relevant plate is captioned 'Contrasted Residences of the Poor'.

73. *Publications of the Surtees Society* (1877), LXVII, 214.

74. *ibid.,* CLXVIII, 16.

75. Thomas Hardy, *The Return of the Native* (1890), 123.

76. J.G. Lockhart, *Memoirs of Sir Walter Scott* (1900), III, 219–20.

77. *The Dictionary of Welsh Biography . . .* (1959), 735.

78. Thomas Gray, *Correspondence of Thomas Gray,* ed. Paget Toynbee & Leonard Whibley (1935), II, 501–2.

79. John Byng, *The Torrington Diaries, containing the Tours through England and Wales of the Hon. John Byng . . .,* ed. C.B. Andrews (1934), I, 162–3.

80. *ibid.,* III, 244–5.

81. *Welsh Biography,* 456–7.

82. Francis Douce, *Illustrations of Shakespeare . . . with dissertations on clowns and fools . . .* (1839). The first edition was published in 1807.

83. Hervey, *Life of Howard,* 175–81, pl. XII illustrates the painting. See also Francis Heumer, *Corpus Rubenianum Ludwig Burchart* (1977), XIX, 85–8 and fig. 35.

84. J.A. Brooks, *Muncaster Castle: A Guide to its Treasures and History* (1978), illustrates the painting.

85. Douce, *Illustrations,* 503.

86. The epitaph was published in *The Works of the Rev. Jonathan Swift . . .* (1824), XV, 212. Appropriately, the editor was Sir Walter Scott.

87. Walter Scott, *The Letters of Sir Walter Scott, 1808–1811,* ed. H.J.C. Grierson (1932), II, 16.

88. Ian Anstruther, *The Knight and the Umbrella: An Account of the Eglinton Tournament, 1839* (1963).

89. Brighton Museum, *Treasures from Sussex Houses: An Exhibition . . .,* exh. cat. (1985), 68.

90. Sam Mullins, *Dr Brookes & the Olympics,* Shropshire County Museum Service Information Sheet No. 9 (1982), 4.

91. Joseph Nash, *Descriptions of the Plates of the Mansions of England in the Olden Time* (1849), 1st ser., 1–2. This is a separate publication from the four elephant folios of plates which came out from 1839 to 1849.

92. John Martin Robinson, *The Dukes of Norfolk: A Quincentenial History* (1982), 176.

93. *The Howard Papers,* ed. H.K.S. Causton (1862), 486–7.

94. Charles Milner Atkinson, *Jeremy Bentham: His Life and Work* (1905), 166. As Professor J.M. Crook has kindly pointed out to me, Bentham had been an undergraduate at Queen's College, Oxford, which was famous for its Christmas feasts.

95. John Stuart Mill, *Autobiography of John Stuart Mill* (1964), 58–9.

96. Richard Hurd, *Letters on Chivalry and Romance* (1762), letter i, lines 1–5.

Notes to Chapter 2

1. Frank Herrmann, *Sotheby's: Portrait of an Auction House* (1980).

2. W. Roberts, *Memorials of Christie's: A Record of Art Sales, 1766–1896* (1897). See also Denys Sutton, 'The King of Epithets: A Study of James Christie', *Apollo* (1966), LXXIV, 364–75.

3. A.N.L. Munby & L. Coral, *British Book Sale Catalogues, 1676–1800* (1977), ix–x.

4. Ronald Parkinson, 'The First Kings of Epithets: Early Picture Auctioneers and their Auctions', *Connoisseur* (1978), CXCVII, No. 794, 269.

5. Francis Henry Cripps-Day, *A Record of Armour Sales, 1881–1924* (1925). This reference is from the unique copy of this book in the Victoria & Albert Museum Library which was grangerized by Day himself with a list of further armour sales and his notes concerning them.

6. Horace Walpole, *A Description of the Villa . . . at Strawberry Hill . . .* (1784), ii.

7. *A Catalogue of the Pictures, Prints, Drawings, Jewels, antique Cristals, Vases, Plate, Medals, and Variety of Curiosities; being Part of the Old Arundel Collection, and belonging to the Late Earl of Stafford Together with fine Japan and China: As Also Household Furniture . . . April, at Stafford-House, in Petty France Westminster . . .*

8. It was shown recently in two exhibitions. Orleans House Gallery, Twickenham, *Horace Walpole and Strawberry Hill . . .,* exh. cat. (1980), 16 & 41; Hayward Gallery, London, *English Romanesque Art, 1066–1200,* exh. cat. (1984), 366. See also the *Proceedings of the Society of Antiquaries of London* (1916), XXVIII, 168–71.

9. Humphrey Wanley, *The Diary of Humphrey Wanley, 1715–1726,* ed. C.E. Wright & R.C. Wright (1966), I, 46.

10. Horace Walpole, *The Duchess of Portland's Museum,* intro. W.S. Lewis (1936), 10.

11. A. Ivanov, 'A Group of Iranian Daggers of the Period from the Fifteenth Century to the Beginning of the Seventeenth', in *Islamic Arms and Armour,* ed. Robert Elgood (1979). I am indebted to Sue Stronge, Claude Blair and Anthony North for help with this dagger.

12. Edward Edwards, *Lives of the Founders of the British Museum . . .* (1870), I, 242.

13. *ibid.*

14. *A Catalogue of . . . coins . . . of Edward Harley Earl of Oxford . . . by Auction by Mr Cock . . . March 18 1741–2 . . .*

15. Lady Mary Coke, *The Letters & Journals of Lady Mary Coke,* ed. J.A. Home (1889–96), III, 56.

16. Bodleian Library, Oxford, *The Douce Legacy: An Exhibition to Commemorate the 150th Anniversary of the Bequest of Francis Douce (1757–1834),* exh. cat. (1984).

17. *Gentleman's Magazine* (1834), CLVI, pt. II, 213.

18. A.N.L. Munby, *Connoisseurs and Mediaeval Miniatures, 1750–1850* (1972), 36–7.

19. Thomas Frognall Dibdin, *Reminiscences of a Literary Life . . .* (1836), II, 638.

20. Bodleian, *Douce Legacy,* 20.

21. Robert H. Cunnington, *From Antiquary to Archaeologist: A Biography of William Cunnington (1754–1810)* (1975), 37–8.

22. *Holden's Triennial Directory . . .* (1808).

23. Roberts, *Memorials of Christie's,* 80.

24. Samuel Johnson, *A Dictionary of the English Language . . . (1807).*

25. Ben Johnson, *Every Man in his Humour* (1616), act 3, scene 5, 60.

26. Geoffrey Wills, 'On Nicknackitarianism', *Apollo* (1978), CVIII, No. 201, 327.

27. Walter Scott, *The Letters of Sir Walter Scott, 1821–23,* ed. H.J.C. Grierson (1934), VII, 280.

28. *ibid.,* VIII, 18.

29. *London in 1710: From the Travels of Zacharias Conrad von Uffenbach,* ed. W.H. Quarrell & Margaret Mare (1934), 36–7.

30. *ibid.,* 70–1.

31. Ralph Thoresby, *The Diary of Ralph Thoresby . . .,* ed. Joseph Hunter (1830) II, 33.

32. *ibid.,* 97.

33. *London and its Environs Described* (1761), V, 9–10.

34. Coke, *Letters,* II, 242.

35. The Sun Insurance records are in the Guildhall Library, Swain's policy is in vol. 240, 285, ref. 356650.

36. *ibid.,* vol. 287, 190, ref. 433585.

37. *ibid.,* vol. 236, 119, ref. 392819.

38. Aleph, *London Scenes and London People* (1864), 35.

39. Aleph, *The Old City and its Highways and Byways* (1865), 39. This is quoted in Geoffrey de Bellaigue, 'Edward Holmes Baldock', *Connoisseur* (1975), pt. I, CLXXXIX, No. 762, 292; pt. II, CXC, No. 763, 18–25.

40. J.C. Loudon, *An Encyclopaedia of Cottage, Farm and Villa Architecture* (1835), 1101.

41. J.D. Burn, *Commercial Enterprise and Social Progress; or, Gleanings in London* (1858), 12.

42. *The Survey of London: The Parish of St Anne Soho,* ed. F.H.W. Sheppard (1966), XXXIII, 291.

43. John Nichols, *Literary Anecdotes of the Eighteenth Century . . .* (1814), VIII, 462–3.

44. Sir Walter Scott, *Chronicles of The Canongate* (1827) I, 99.

45. Charles Knight, *London* (1843), V, 399.

46. Robert Allbut, 'The Old Curiosity Shop', *Dickensian* (1910), VI, 44–5.

47. E. Beresford Chancellor, *The London of Charles Dickens* (1924), 139–43.

48. Charles Dickens, *Master Humphrey's Clock* (1840), 40.

49. Charles Dickens, *The Letters of Charles Dickens,* Pilgrim ed., ed. M. House & G. Storey (1969), II, 8.

50. *ibid.,* III, 397.

51. F.G. Kitton, *Charles Dickens by Pen and Pencil . . .* (1890), III, 179–80.

52. The transcript of Cooke's diary is lodged at the National Maritime Museum and I am indebted to John Munday for bringing it to my attention.

53. Clergy of St Anne's Soho, *Two Centuries of Soho* (1898), 189–90. For Edwards and Roberts, see Clive Wainwright, 'The Dark Ages of Art Revived . . .', *Connoisseur* (1978), CXCVIII, No. 796, 95–105.

54. *The Historical Manuscripts Commission Report on the Manuscripts of his Grace the Duke of Portland ...* (1901), VI, 50.
55. T.F. Dibdin, *The Bibliographical Decameron ...* (1817), III, 283.
56. *ibid.*, I, 173.
57. Wanley, *Diary*, 103, 205, 271.
58. Horace Walpole, *The Yale Edition of Horace Walpole's Correspondence*, ed. W.S. Lewis (1951), XVI, 49-50.
59. *Gentleman's Magazine* (1785), LV, pt. II, 887.
60. *Remarks and Collections of Thomas Hearne*, ed. C.E. Doble (1915), X, 168.
61. *ibid.*, XI, 208.
62. J.G. Nichols, *Illustrations of the Literary History of the Eighteenth Century* (1817-58), VIII, 544.
63. *Publications of the Surtees Society* (1880), LXXIII, 82.
64. Nichols, *Anecdotes* (1814), VIII, 509.
65. Nichols, *Illustrations*, III, 544.
66. The 1762 Minute Book of the Society of Antiquaries of London.
67. Bellaigue, 'Baldock'.
68. Frederick Litchfield, *Antiques Genuine and Spurious* (1921), 239.
69. Benjamin Disraeli, *Letters, 1815-1834*, ed. J.A.W. Gunn et al. (1982), I, 253.
70. Clergy of St Anne's, *Two Centuries*, 195.
71. John Culme, 'Kensington Lewis: A Nineteenth-Century Businessman', *Connoisseur* (1975), CXC, No. 763, 26-41.
72. Hugh Brigstocke, *William Buchanan and the 19th Century Art Trade: 100 Letters to his Agents in London and Italy* (1982).
73. E.T. Joys, 'John Coleman Isaac: An Early Nineteenth Century Antique Dealer', *Connoisseur* (1962), CLI, 241-2. This article is largely based upon Isaac's 'Waste Books, 1815-1845' which along with letters and other papers survive in a private collection.
74. *ibid.*, 241.
75. *ibid.*, 242.
76. Clive Wainwright, 'A.W.N. Pugin's Early Furniture', *Connoisseur* (1976), CXCI, No. 767, 3-11.
77. Benjamin Ferrey, *Recollections of A.N. Welby Pugin and his father Augustus Pugin* (1861), 117.
78. Phoebe Stanton, *Pugin* (1971), 17.
79. Henry Shaw, *Specimens of Ancient Furniture drawn from existing authorities ... with descriptions by Sir Samuel Rush Meyrick ...* (1836), 43, pl. XLV.
80. Lancashire Record Office D.D.Sc. 78/4/10.
81. Royal Archives, Windsor, MSS 36821-5.c.1819.
82. Shaw, *Specimens*, pl. XIX.
83. *Catalogue of the Specimens of Cabinet Work Exhibited at Gore House Kensington ...* (1853).
84. M.H. Port, *The Houses of Parliament* (1976), 283-7.
85. Clive Wainwright, 'Curiosities to Fine Art: Bond Street's First Dealers', *Country Life* (1986), CLXXIX, No. 4632, 1528-9.
86. *Journal of Design* (1849), I, 7.
87. Celia Brunel Noble, *The Brunels, Father and Son* (1938), 187.
88. The Diary of John Evelyn (1955), I, 65-6.
89. *A Catalogue of the Pictures, Drawings, Painted Glass &c, &c ... sold by private contract at the European Museum, King Street, St James's Square 1791*, 3.
90. Gustav Waagen, *Works of Art and Artists in England* (1838), I, 55.
91. *Journal of a Party of Pleasure to Paris in the Month of August 1802 ...* (1802), 47.
92. Brigstocke, *Buchanan*, 12.
93. *ibid.*, 70.
94. *ibid.*, 77.

95. Michael Jaffé, 'Pesaro Family Portraits: Pordone, Lotto, and Titian', *Burlington Magazine* (1971), CXIII, No. 825, 701.
96. A.N.L. Munby, *The Formation of the Phillips Library up to the Year 1840*, Phillips Studies No. 3 (1954), 50.
97. *ibid.*, 51 lists at least 55.
98. National Library of Scotland Ms 3887.f.72.
99. W. Partington, *Sir Walter's Post-Bag* (1932), 187.
100. Ferrey, *Recollections of Pugin*, 62.
101. There were two sales of Pugin's collection at Sotheby's: *Catalogue of the valuable Collection of mediaeval carvings in oak ... 12 February 1853* followed by *Original drawings and sketches ... 7 April 1853*.
102. Henry Rumsey Forster, *The Stowe Catalogue Priced and Annotated* (1848), 33.
103. *ibid.*
104. *ibid.*, xxxiv.
105. Thomas Winstanley, *Observations on the Arts* (1828), 5-6.
106. Munby, *Phillips Library*, 26.
107. *ibid.*, 34.
108. Miklos Rajnai & Marjorie Allthorpe-Guyton, *John Sell Cotman: Drawings of Normandy in Norwich Castle Museum* (1975), 45.
109. Arts Council of Great Britain, *John Sell Cotman, 1782-1842: A Touring Exhibition*, exh. cat. (1982), 122.
110. Rajnai & Allthorpe-Guyton, *Cotman*, 45.
111. *The extensive and valuable collection of rare and fine engravings ... a collection of ancient armour foreign & miscellaneous curiosities, carvings ... auction by William Spelman ... 10th, 11th & 12th Sept 1834 at the residence of John Sell Cotman Esq, St Martin's Plain Norwich ...*
112. *Catalogue des collections Laissees Par Feu Madame Mertens-Schaaffhausen ... les objets d'art et de curiosité du moyen-âge ... 12 Juillet 1859 ... J.M. Heberlé & H. Lempertz ...*, iii.
113. *Catalogue de la collection des antiquités et d'objets de haute curiosité qui composent le cabinet ... Pierre Leven à Cologne ... 4 Octobre 1853 ... J.M. Heberlé à Cologne ...*
114. *Dr Sulpiz Boisserée's Bibliothek, welche am 3 Novbr 1854 bei M. Lempertz in Bonn ...*
115. William Vaughan, *German Romanticism and English Art* (1979), 22.
116. Gisela Goldberg, 'The History of the Boisserée Collection', *Apollo* (1977) CVI, No. 248, 210-13.
117. Philip Henry Bagenal, *The Life of Ralph Bernal Osborne, M.P.* (1884), 5-6.
118. O.M. Dalton, *Catalogue of the Engraved Gems ... British Museum* (1915), 78.
119. *Catalogue of the celebrated collection of works of art ... of the distinguished collector Ralph Bernal ... Christie ... March 5th 1855 ...*, lot 1295.
120. National Library of Scotland MS 3893.f.129.
121. Essex Record Office, 'The Journal of the 3rd Lord Braybrook', Acc. 6767.
122. Anglo-Jewish Archives, Mocatta Library, University of London, AJ 53/136.

Notes to Chapter 3

1. *Publications of the Surtees Society* (1883), LXXVI, 43.
2. Bodleian Library MS Eng. Misc. c.538.f.45.
3. John Byng, *The Torrington Diaries, containing the Tours through England and Wales of the Hon. John Byng ...*, ed. C.B. Andrews (1935), II, 220.
4. Horace Walpole, *The Yale Edition of Horace Walpole's Correspondence*, ed. W.S. Lewis (1937), I, 142.

5. *ibid.*, 343.
6. *London Magazine* (March 1774), 133-6.
7. Sir Richard Colt Hoare, *The History of Modern Wiltshire: Hundreds of Everly, Ambresbury and Underditch* (1826), 43.
8. *Lonsdale Magazine* (June 1821), No. XVIII, 201-5.
9. *ibid.*
10. *Handbook to Chatsworth & Hardwick* (1844), 20.
11. J.C. Loudon, *An Encyclopaedia of Cottage, Farm and Villa Architecture* (1835), 1101.
12. Clergy of St Anne's Soho, *Two Centuries of Soho* (1898), 195-6.
13. The Ratebooks for Wardour Street are in the Westminster Public Library.
14. *Archaeological Magazine of Bristol, Bath, South Wales ...* (1843), No. II, 80.
15. Margaret B. Freeman, 'Late Gothic Woodcarvings from Normandy', *Metropolitan Museum of Art Bulletin* (1951), IX, No. 10, 260-9.
16. C. Nodier & J. Taylor, *Voyages pittoresques et romantiques dans l'ancienne France* (1825), 127-33.
17. I would like to thank Nina James for giving me access to her 1987 B.A. thesis on Highcliffe, a copy of which is in the Department of Furniture and Interior Design at the Victoria & Albert Museum.
18. Victor Hugo, *Oeuvres complètes* (1882), I, 320.
19. This quotation is from the very rare one page prospectus for Shaw's book; the only copy known to me is in the library of the Society of Antiquaries of London.
20. Henry Shaw, *Specimens of Ancient Furniture drawn from exisiting authorities ... with descriptions by Sir Samuel Rush Meyrick ...* (1836), 26.
21. Loudon, *Encyclopaedia*, 1102.
22. *Gentleman's Magazine* (1842), CLXXI, 19.
23. Bristol Record Office MS 14182/HB/X/4, 64. I am indebted to Sheena Stoddard for this reference.
24. *A Catalogue of Authentic Portraits ... also a few carvings in wood ... By Horatio Rodd, 9 Great Newport Street, Long Acre* (1824).
25. Walpole, *Correspondence*, I, 90.
26. Richard Warner, *An History of the Abbey of Glaston ...* (1826), pl. XVI.
27. Loudon, *Encyclopaedia*, 1101.
28. Clive Wainwright, 'The True Black Blood', *Furniture History* (1985), XXI, 250-5.
29. James Macaulay, *The Gothic Revival, 1745-1845* (1975), 330-2.
30. Scottish Record Office MS GD 152/58/2/6.
31. *A Select Collection of English Songs ...* (1783), II, 140-2.
32. Francis Henry Cripps-Day, *A Record of Armour Sales, 1881-1924* (1925).
33. *A Catalogue of the Genuine and curious collection of ... Ebenezer Mussell ... Auction by Mr Langford ... 5th and 6th of this instant June 1765 ...*
34. *Gentleman's Magazine* (1789), LIX, pt. II, 1057.
35. Francis Grose, *The Olio: being a collection of essays ...* (1792), 16-17.
36. Harriet Arbuthnot, *The Journal of Mrs Arbuthnot, 1820-1832*, ed. Francis Bamford & the Duke of Wellington (1950), II, 175.
37. Nicholas Condy, *Cothele on the banks of the Tamar: the ancient seat of the Rt Honble The Earl of Mount Edgcumbe* [c.1840], 12.
38. Ian H.C. Fraser, *The Heir of Parham, Robert Curzon, 14th Baron Zouche* (1986).
39. A.N.L. Munby, *Connoisseurs and Mediaeval Miniatures, 1750-1850* (1972), 85.
40. *ibid.*, 87.
41. The story was told by C.A. De Cosson in his introduction to the *Catalogue of ... Armour and Weapons formed by Robert Curzon ... Sotheby ... 10th November 1920 ...*

42. Ian Anstruther, *The Knight and the Umbrella: An Account of the Eglinton Tournament, 1839* (1963).

43. Henry Goddard, *Memoirs of a Bow Street Runner* (1956), 167.

44. *Gentleman's Magazine* (1838), CLXIII, 532.

45. *The Times* (16 April 1838), 3.

46. Cripps-Day, *Armour Sales*, xlviii–liii.

47. Claude Blair, 'A Cuirassier Armour in the Scott Collection ...', *Scottish Art Review* (1969), XII, No. 2, 22.

48. *Ackerman's Repository of the Arts* (1811), VI, 29–30.

49. Nathaniel Whittock, *The Decorative Painters and Glaziers Guide* (1827), 192.

50. The discovery was made by Lucy Wood who describes the work at Cholmondeley in her essay in *George Bullock, Cabinet-Maker*, intro. Clive Wainwright (1988).

51. Malcolm Baker, 'A Victorian Collector of Armour: Sir Joseph Noel Paton', *Country Life* (1973), CLIII, No. 3944, 232–6.

52. Two important articles deal with this subject: Jean Lafond, 'The Traffic in Old Stained Glass from Abroad during the 18th and 19th Centuries in England', *Journal of the British Society of Master Glass Painters* (1964), XIV, No. 1, 58–71; Bernard Rackham, 'English Importations of Foreign Stained Glass in the early Nineteenth Century', *ibid.* (1927), II, 86–94.

53. *Publications of the Surtees Society* (1883), LXXVI, 324–5.

54. *ibid.*, 325–6.

55. *ibid.*, 328.

56. Thomas Gray, *Correspondence of Thomas Gray*, ed. Paget Toynbee & Leonard Whibley (1971), II, 736.

57. Byng, *Torrington Diaries*, II, 318–19.

58. *ibid.*, 374.

59. Philip Nelson, *Ancient Painted Glass in England, 1170–1500* (1913), 48.

60. Horace Walpole, *Anecdotes of Painting ...* (1786), 120–1.

61. *A Catalogue of the Pictures, Drawings, Painted Glass &c, &c ... sold by private contract at the European Museum, King Street, St James's Square 1791.*

62. Ernest A. Kent, 'John Christopher Hampp of Norwich', *Journal of the British Society of Master Glass Painters* (1937), VI, No. 4, 191–6.

63. Rackham, 'English Importations'.

64. 'Catalogue of a Sale of Stained Glass in 1804', *Journal of the British Society of Master Glass Painters* (1955), XII, No. 1, 22–9.

65. Christopher Woodforde, 'Foreign Stained and Painted Glass in Norfolk', *Norfolk Archaeology* (1936), XXIV, 73–84.

66. Rackham, 'English Importations', 87.

67. Françoise Perrot, 'Vitraux heraldiques venant du Château d'Ecouen ...', *Revue du Louvre et des Musées de France* (1973), XXIII, 77.

68. Lafonde, 'Traffic in Old Stained Glass', 58.

69. *ibid.*, 61.

70. Derek Linstrum, *Sir Jeffry Wyatville ...* (1972), 98–105.

71. Bernard Rackham, 'The Ashridge Stained Glass', *Journal of the British Archaeological Association* (1945–7), X, 1–22; idem, 'The Mariawald-Ashridge Glass', *Burlington Magazine* (1944), LXXXV, 266–73, & LXXXVII, 90–4.

72. Rackham, 'Ashridge Stained Glass', 1

73. *ibid.*

74. John Nichols, *Illustrations of the Literary History of the Eighteenth Century* (1817–58), II, 299.

75. *ibid.*, 300.

76. *ibid.*, 289.

77. Mostyn Lewis, *Stained Glass in North Wales up to 1850* (1970), 119–22.

78. *ibid.*

79. H.L. Thrale, *Thraliana: The Diary of Mrs Hester Lynch Thrale, later Mrs Piozzi, 1776–1809*, ed. Katherine C. Balderstone (1942), II, 957.

80. Henry Rumsey Forster, *The Stowe Catalogue, Priced and Annotated* (1848), 102.

81. William Makepeace Thackeray, *The History of Pendennis ...* (1885), 361–2. The first edition was published in 1850.

Notes to Chapter 4

1. Horace Walpole, *The Yale Edition of Horace Walpole's Correspondence*, ed. W.S. Lewis, (1937–84); hereafter referred to as *Corr.*, followed by volume and page number.

2. Horace Walpole, *A Description of the Villa of Mr Horace Walpole Youngest son of Sir Robert Walpole Earl of Orford at Strawberry Hill near Twickenham Middlesex with an inventory of the Furniture, Pictures, Curiosities &c* (1784); referred to throughout these notes as *Desc.*

3. *Strawberry Hill the renowned seat of Horace Walpole Mr George Robins is Honoured by having been selected by the Earl of Waldegrave to sell by public competition the valuable contents of Strawberry Hill and it may fearlessly be proclaimed as the most distinguished gem that has ever adorned the annals of auctions it is definitely fixed for Monday the 25th day of April 1842 and the twenty three following days.* For the full bibliographical details, see Perceval Merritt, 'Strawberry Hill Catalogues', *Notes and Queries* (25 January 1947), 33–5. This sale is referred to throughout as *Sale*, followed by day of sale and lot number.

4. W.S. Lewis, 'The Genesis of Strawberry Hill', *Metropolitan Museum Studies* (1934), V, 57–92.

5. H. Avray Tipping, 'Strawberry Hill Middlesex ...', *Country Life* (1924), LVI, Nos. 1435–6, 18–25 & 56–64.

6. J. Mordaunt Crook, 'Strawberry Hill Revisited', *Country Life* (1973), CLIII, Nos. 3963–5, 1598–1602, 1726–30 & 1794–7.

7. Orleans House Gallery, Twickenham, *Horace Walpole and Strawberry Hill*, exh. cat. (1980). This exhibition catalogue includes three essays: 'Horace Walpole, Builder and Designer' by Michael Snodin; 'Horace Walpole and his Collection' by Clive Wainwright; and 'Horace Walpole, Writer and Printer' by Stephen Calloway.

8. *Corr.*, XVII, 41.

9. *ibid.*, 73.

10. *ibid.*, XV, 11–12.

11. *ibid.*

12. *Wateringbury Place Maidstone Kent ... Messrs Christies ... May 31 1978 ...*, lot 61.

13. *Corr.*, XV, 15–17.

14. *ibid.*, 19.

15. Conyers Middleton, *Germana quaedam antiquitatis eruditae monumenta ...* (1745).

16. *ibid.*, viii. This passage can be translated 'But of these riches of the Roman soil I believe none of our travellers has brought thence a more valuable hoarde of objects both choice and precious than my noble friend Horace Walpole'.

17. *Corr.*, XVIII, 465. This was 'Consul Smith', the celebrated collector, connoisseur and dealer. See K.A. Piacenti, 'Consul Smith's Gems', *Connoisseur* (1977), CXCV, No. 784, 79–83.

18. *Desc.*, 62.

19. *Corr.*, XXII, 528.

20. *ibid.*, XXIII, 285.

21. *ibid.*, 285 quotes from the *St James's Chronicle* (21–3 March 1771).

22. *ibid.*, XVIII, 277.

23. *Desc.*, 56–61.

24. Horace Walpole, *The Works of Horatio Walpole* (1798), III, 481. For a full description of the figures, see William King, 'A Relic of Horace Walpole', *Burlington Magazine* (1926), XLVIII, 98–103.

25. *A Catalogue of the Collection of the Right Honourable Edward Earl of Oxford ... Auction by Mr Cock at his house in the Great Piazza Covent-Garden on Monday the 8th of March 1741–2 and the five following days.*

26. *ibid.*, 15, lot 28.

27. *A Catalogue of the Greek, Roman and English Coins ... of Edward Harley & ... Auction by Mr Cock March 18 1741–2 and five following days.* Lot 109 in the section devoted to Elizabethan coins. He also bought lots 101 and 108 in this section.

28. *The Museum or the Literary and Historical Register* (1746), I, 46–7.

29 *Corr.*, XX, 359.

30. E. St. John Brooks, *Sir Hans Sloane: The Great Collector and his Circle* (1954), 194–6.

31. *Corr.*, XXIII, 285.

32. *ibid.*, 432.

33. *ibid.*, 459–60.

34. *ibid.*, XXV, 165–6.

35. *ibid.*, XXXIII, 450. Mathew Duane (1707–1785) was a celebrated coin and medal collector and a Trustee of the British Museum. See John Nichols, *Literary Anecdotes of the Eighteenth Century ...* (1812), III, 497–9.

36. *Corr.*, XXXIII, 484.

37. *ibid.*, XV, 192.

38. *ibid.*, XXXIII, 518. *Catalogue of the Portland Museum Lately the Property of The Duchess Dowager of Portland Deceased: Which will be sold by Auction by Mr Skinner and Co. On Monday the 24th of April, 1786, and the Thirty Seven Following Days ... At her late Dwelling House, In Privy-Garden Whitehall ...*

39. *Corr.*, II, 284.

40. *ibid.*, XXXII, 216.

41. *ibid.*, II, 254.

42. *ibid.*, XXXIII, 575–6.

43. *ibid.*, I, 166.

44. A.T. Hazen, *A Bibliography of the Strawberry Hill Press ...* (1973), 210. He also illustrates a ticket of admission.

45. *ibid.*, 225. The rules are illustrated, 226–7.

46. *ibid.*, 123–9. Given is a full analysis. See also Merritt, 'Strawberry Hill Catalogues'.

47. Hazen, *Strawberry Hill Press*, 125.

48. *ibid.* See also *Gentleman's Magazine* (1789), LIX, pt. I, 271, for an account of the exhumation of Edward IV.

49. Hazen, *Strawberry Hill Press*, 125.

50. A.T. Hazen, *A Bibliography of Horace Walpole* (1948), 26. The manuscript is now in the Pierpont Morgan Library in New York.

51. *ibid.*, 30.

52. Hieronymous Tetius, *Aedes Barberinae ad Quirinalem ... descriptae* (1642). Published in Rome. Walpole had a copy, item 3725 in A.T. Hazen, *A Catalogue of Horace Walpole's Library* (1969).

53. *Galleria Giustinianae del Marchese Vincenza Giustiniani* (1631). This catalogue has 322 plates and is in two folio volumes; it was published in Rome. Walpole did not have a copy.

54. Walpole, *Works*, II, 225–6.

55. *Desc.*, i–iv.

56. *Corr.*, XXVIII, 28.

57. *ibid.*, XXXII, 241–2.

58. *ibid.*, I, 325–6.

59. Orleans House, *Walpole*.

60. Lewis, 'Genesis'.

61. *Desc.*, 3.

62. *Sale*, XIX/39.
63. Paget Toynbee, ed., *Strawberry Hill Accounts: A Record of Expenditure in Building, Furnishing &c kept by Mr Horace Walpole from 1747 to 1795* (1927), 39–40; hereafter called *Accounts*.
64. Thomas Gray, *Correspondence of Thomas Gray*, ed. Paget Toynbee & Leonard Whibley (1971), II, 750.
65. *ibid.*, 640.
66. *Corr.*, XXXV, 80.
67. *Desc.*, 4.
68. *Accounts*, 15.
69. Michael Wynne, *Irish Stained Glass* (1977), 4.
70. *Corr.*, I, 201.
71. *Sale*, XXIV/62–5.
72. *Corr.*, XX, 111.
73. *ibid.*, 371.
74. Walpole, *Works*, III, 159.
75. *Sale*, XIX/41.
76. G. de Bellaigue, *The James A. Rothschild Collection at Waddesdon Manor: Furniture Clocks and Gilt Bronzes* (1974), 104–7.
77. *Accounts*, 6.
78. Anthony Coleridge, 'A Reappraisal of William Hallett', *Furniture History* (1965), I, 11–13.
79. *Sale*, XIX/45.
80. *Accounts*, 7.
81. See 'Walpole's Account of Richard Bentley', in *Corr.*, XXXV, 643–5.
82. *Accounts*, 6.
83. One chair is in the Victoria & Albert Museum and four are in the Lewis Collection at Farmington, Connecticut. One mirror also exists and was shown at Orleans House, *Walpole*.
84. *Corr.*, XXXV, 181–2. The original letter is not extant; it included Walpole's drawing for the chair. The source quoted is taken from another printed source which did not include the drawing.
85. *ibid.*, 233.
86. Batty Langley, *Gothic Architecture Improved by Rules . . .* (1747).
87. *Sale*, XVI/115.
88. *Desc.*, 4.
89. *Sale*, XIX/48.
90. *Accounts*, 5.
91. Walpole, *Works*, III, 449. For Clermont, see also Edward Croft Murray, *Decorative Painting in England* (1970), II, 192.
92. *Corr.*, XXXV, 171–2.
93. *Desc.*, 33–4.
94. *ibid.*
95. Lewis, 'Genesis', fig. 10.
96. *Corr.*, XXXV, 157.
97. *ibid.*, 164.
98. Hazen, *Catalogue*, I, [l].
99. *ibid.*, [lxxiv].
100. *ibid.*, 173.
101. *ibid.*, 167.
102. *ibid.*, 129.
103. *Accounts*, 6.
104. *ibid.*
105. *Desc.*, 34.
106. *Sale*, XXIV/22–6.
107. Crook, 'Strawberry Hill Revisited', fig. 4 shows the coloured version of this plate, and the desk seems to be mahogany.
108. *Sale*, XVII.
109. Gray, *Correspondence*, I, 363–4. See also Clive Wainwright, 'Only the True Black Blood', *Furniture History* (1985), XXI, 250–5, and Jan Veenendaal, *Furniture from Indonesia, Sri Lanka and India during the Dutch Period* (1986), 53–60.
110. *Corr.*, IX, 71.
111. Gray, *Correspondence*, I, 404.
112. Esher Place was enlarged and altered by Kent in

1729–33. See John Harris, 'A William Kent Discovery: Designs for Esher Place, Surrey', *Country Life* (1959), CXXV, No. 3252, 1076–8; *idem*, 'Esher Place, Surrey', *Country Life* (1987), CLXXXI, 94–7. Also J.W. Lindus Forge, 'Kentissime', *Architectural Review* (1949), CVI, No. 633, 186–8.
113. Gray, *Correspondence*, II, 641.
114. *Corr.*, X, 76–7.
115. Gray, *Correspondence*, II, 805.
116. *Accounts*, 10.
117. J. & J.B. Burke, *A Genealogical and Heraldic History of the Extinct and Dormant Baronetcies of England . . .* (1844), 127–9.
118. 'The Parish, The Rectory, Vicarage, Staughton House', *Cambridgeshire & Huntingdonshire Archaeological Society Proceedings* (1904–14), III, 36–9.
119. *Desc.*, 33.
120. The part of the collection devoted to *Medals, Antiquities and Curiosities* was sold at Langford's Rooms in London on 7 June 1777.
121. Hazen, *Catalogue*, III, 212, item 3785.
122. *Desc.*, 36.
123. *ibid.*, 35. For the bracket, see Orleans House, *Walpole*, 33.
124. *Corr.*, IX, 304.
125. *A Catalogue of the noble collection of Pictures, Miniatures, Bronzes, Gems . . . of the Right Honourable Lady Elizabeth Germaine Lately Deceased Being the Collection of the Old Earls of Peterborough and also part of the Arundelian Collection . . . By Mr Langford . . . the 7th instant March 1770 and three following days.*
126. *ibid.*, 3rd day, lot 63.
127. *ibid.*, 3rd day, lot 72.
128. *Desc.*, 63.
129. *ibid.*, 39–40. All 25 are described.
130. *Corr.*, IX, 304.
131. *ibid.*, XXXIV, 12.
132. *Desc.*, 94.
133. *Accounts*, 7.
134. *ibid.*, 8.
135. *Desc.*, 42–3.
136. Gray, *Correspondence*, II, 641.
137. J.F. Pommeraye, *Histoire de l'Abbaye de S. Ouen de Rouen* (1662), pl. on 192.
138. W.H. St John Hope, *Windsor Castle: An Architectural History* (1913), I, 340.
139. *ibid.*, 351.
140. For the alterations to this part of the Castle, see Clive Wainwright, 'The Furnishing of the Royal Library Windsor', *Connoisseur* (1977), CXCV, No. 784, 104–9.
141. Gray, *Correspondence*, II, 641.
142. *Desc.*, 44.
143. *ibid.*, 46.
144. A wax after this figure was shown at Orleans House, *Walpole*, 36. See also *Sale*, XX/52.
145. *Desc.*, 43.
146. Orleans House, *Walpole*, 36.
147. Gray, *Correspondence*, II, 641–2.
148. Eric Till, 'Georgian Cabinet Makers at Burghley', *Country Life* (1974), CLVI, No. 4026, 562–4.
149. *Accounts*, 8.
150. *Desc.*, 43.
151. Lewis, 'Genesis', 88, fig. 37.
152. *Desc.*, 43.
153. Gray, *Correspondence*, II, 650–1.
154. *Sale*, XXIV/41–3.
155. Walpole, *Works*, III, 159.
156. *Desc.*, 43.
157. Lewis, 'Genesis', 86, fig. 35.
158. *Desc.*, 43.
159. *ibid.*
160. *ibid.*

161. *Corr.*, XXXV, 106.
162. Hazen, *Catalogue*, 190, item 658 is Thomas Hearne, *The History and Antiquities of Glastonbury* (1722).
163. Horace Walpole, *A Catalogue of the pictures and drawings in the Holbein-Chamber, at Strawberry-Hill* (1760). This rare eight page pamphlet is located in the British Library, Pressmark 688.c.28(2).
164. *Corr.*, XXXIII, 208.
165. *ibid.*, XXXII, 156.
166. Hazen, *Catalogue*, pl. XI facing lxxx.
167. *Desc.*, 47.
168. *ibid.*, 3.
169. *Accounts*, 5.
170. E.A. Entwhistle, 'Eighteenth-Century London Paperstainers: Thomas Bromwich *at the Golden Lion, Ludgate Hill*', *Connoisseur* (October 1952), CXXX, 106–10.
171. *Corr.*, XXXV, 191.
172. Gray, *Correspondence*, II, 761.
173. *Corr.*, XXXV, 150.
174. *ibid.*
175. *ibid.*, XX, 372.
176. *ibid.*, 381.
177. *ibid.*
178. *Desc.*, 32.
179. *ibid.*, 33. For Pownall (1722–1805), author, diplomat and antiquary, see *Antiquity*, XLVIII, 116–25. See also Nichols, *Anecdotes*, VIII, 81–6.
180. *Desc.*, 31–2.
181. *Corr.*, XXXV, 420–1.
182. A.R.E. North, 'Arms and Armour from Arundel Castle', *Connoisseur* (1978), CXCVII, No. 793, 188, pl. A.
183. Helen Adamson, 'Armour and Weapons from the Tower of London', *Scottish Arts Review* (1982), XV, No. 2, 23–4. I am indebted to Mr Woosnam Savage for help with the provenance of this shield.
184. *Desc.*, 31.
185. *Corr.*, I, 243.
186. Francis Henry Cripps-Day, *A Record of Armour Sales, 1881–1924* (1925), xxxv. Claude Blair, formerly of the Metalwork Department, Victoria & Albert Museum, informs me that this armour exists in a private collection.
187. *ibid.*, xxxiv.
188. William Cole, *A Journal of My Journey to Paris in the year 1765* (1931), 244–5. For Walpole's French ceramics, see the essay by F.J.B. Watson, 'Walpole and the Taste for French Porcelain', in *Horace Walpole Writer, Politician, and Connoisseur*, ed. Warren Hunting Smith (1967). For one of the pieces of Sèvres from the Vyne, see Orleans House, *Walpole*, 35.
189. *Corr.*, XVI, 192–3.
190. *ibid.*, II, 275.
191. Peter Thornton & William Reider, 'Pierre Langlois Ebeniste', *Connoisseur* (1971), CLXXVIII, No. 718, 285. This is the first of a series of articles concerning Langlois.
192. William Rieder, 'A Golden Age of English Furniture', *Apollo* (1980), CXI, No. 216, 114–15.
193. *Corr.*, X, 53.
194. *Accounts*, 9.
195. *Corr.*, XXXVI, 38–9.
196. John Henniker, *Two letters on the origin, antiquity and history of Norman tiles, tained with armorial bearings* (1794), 87, fig. 17.
197. *Corr.*, X, 43.
198. *ibid.*, XXXII, 245–6.
199. *Desc.*, 42.
200. *Mediaeval Works of Art . . . Sotheby . . . 14 July 1977 . . .*, lot 188.
201. Michael McCarthy, *The Origins of the Gothic Revival* (1987).

Notes to Chapter 5

1. The relevant books and articles are quoted in my footnotes, several of the most important being those by the late Boyd Alexander.

2. *The Unique and Splendid Effects of Fonthill Abbey ... Which will be Sold by Auction by Mr Phillips at the Abbey on Tuesday, the 23rd of September 1823 and Seven following Days, And on Thursday, 16th of October, and Four following Days ...*

3. Clive Wainwright, 'Some Objects from William Beckford's Collection now in the Victoria & Albert Museum', *Burlington Magazine* (1971), CXIII, No. 818, 254–64.

4. John Wilton Ely, 'The Genesis and Evolution of Fonthill Abbey', *Architectural History* (1980), XXIII, 40–51; idem, 'Beckford the Builder', *William Beckford* exh. cat., Salisbury Public Library (1976) 34–57.

5. Wilton Ely, 'Genesis', 51.

6. John Harris, 'Fonthill Wiltshire — I. Alderman Beckford's Houses', *Country Life* (1966), CXL, 1374.

7. John Britton, *The Beauties of Wiltshire* (1801), I, 212–13.

8. The Beckford Papers acquired by the Bodleian Library in 1985, but as yet not fully catalogued, will from my limited examination of them illuminate many aspects of Beckford's life, including his collecting activities.

9. Guy Chapman, *Beckford* (1937), 225. The account of Beckford's foreign travels is particularly good. See also Palacio de Queluz, Lisbon, *William Beckford & Portugal: An Impassioned Journey, 1787, 1794, 1798*, exh. cat. (1987).

10. Boyd Alexander, *England's Wealthiest Son: A Study of William Beckford* (1962), 142.

11. Musée Rodin, Paris, *La Rue de Varenne*, exh. cat. (1981), 71.

12. Alexander, *England's Wealthiest*, 141.

13. ibid., 139–41, tells the story of the arrest.

14. Musée Rodin, Paris, *Le Fauborg Saint-Germain, La rue Saint-Dominique: Hôtels et amateurs*, exh. cat. (1984), 126.

15. Chapman, *Beckford*, 172.

16. Horace Walpole, *The Yale Edition of Horace Walpole's Correspondence*, ed. W.S. Lewis (1973), XXXVI, 216.

17. Lewis Melville, *The Life and Letters of William Beckford of Fonthill* (1910), 248–9.

18. F.J.B. Watson, 'Beckford, Mme de Pompadour, the duc de Bouillon and the Taste for Japanese Lacquer in Eighteenth Century France', *Gazette des Beaux-Arts* (1963), LXI, 101–27.

19. Wainwright, 'Some Objects', 262. See also Joe Earle, 'Genji Meets Yang Guifei: A Group of Japanese Export Lacquers', *Transactions of the Oriental Ceramic Society* (1982–3), 45–75.

20. Boyd Alexander, *From Lisbon to Baker Street* (1977).

21. Boyd Alexander, *Life at Fonthill* (1957), 136.

22. Michael Snodin & Malcolm Baker, 'William Beckford's Silver', *Burlington Magazine* (1980), CXXII, Nos. 932–3, 735–48 & 820–34.

23. *Magnificent Effects at Fonthill Abbey Wilts to be sold by Auction by Mr Christie ... October 1, 1822 ...*

24. John Rutter, *A Description of Fonthill Abbey and Demesne ... Including a list of paintings, cabinets &c*, 3rd. ed. (1822), 59. This is not to be confused with Rutter's *Delineations of Fonthill and its Abbey* of 1823.

25. Rutter, *Delineations*, 37.

26. Wendy Greenhouse, 'Benjamin West and Edward III: A Neoclassical Painter and Medieval History', *Art History* (1985), VIII, No. 2, 178–91.

27. Rutter, *Delineations*, 113.

28. John Britton, *Illustrations Graphical and Literary of Fonthill Abbey ...* (1823), 45.

29. Rutter, *Description*, 54.

30. 'Glass Painters, 1750–1850', *Journal of the British Society of Master Glass Painters* (1959–63), XIII, 406.

31. Joseph Farington, *The Diary of Joseph Farington*, ed. Kenneth Garlick & Angus Macintyre (1979), III, 912.

32. Rutter, *Delineations*, 31.

33. Millard F. Rogers Jr., 'Benjamin West and the Caliph: Two Paintings for Fonthill Abbey', *Apollo* (1966), LXXXIII, No. 52, 420. See also John Dillenberger, *Benjamin West: The Context of his Life's Work with Particular Attention to Paintings with Religious Subject Matter* (1977), 106–10.

34. G. McN. Rushforth, 'The Painted Glass in the Lord Mayor's Chapel, Bristol', *Transactions of the Bristol and Gloucestershire Archaeological Society* (1927), XLIX, 301–31.

35. Rutter, *Delineations*, 55.

36. W.C. Aitken, 'Francis Eginton', *Birmingham and Midland Institute Archaeological Section Transactions and Reports* (1872), 27–43.

37. *Short Account of some of the works executed in stained glass by William Raphael Eginton ...* (1818).

38. Alexander, *England's Wealthiest*, 284.

39. Melville, *Life of Beckford*, 155.

40. Rushforth, 'Painted Glass'.

41. Michael Archer, '"Monmorency's Sword" from Ecouen', *Burlington Magazine* (1987), CXXIX, No. 1010, 298–303.

42. Rutter, *Description*, 55.

43. Mary Elizabeth Lucy, *Mistress of Charlecote: The Memoirs of Mary Elizabeth Lucy*, ed. Alice Fairfax-Lucy (1983), 57.

44. Melville, *Life of Beckford*, 91.

45. Wilton Ely, 'Beckford the Builder', 48.

46. John Martin Robinson, *The Wyatts: An Architectural Dynasty* (1979).

47. Simon S. Jervis, 'Cottage, Farm and Villa Furniture', *Burlington Magazine* (1975), CXVII, No. 873, 848–59.

48. Britton, *Beauties of Wiltshire*, 45.

49. William Clarke, *Repertorium bibliographicum; or, Some account of the most celebrated British libraries* (1819), 204.

50. William Beckford, *The Journal of William Beckford in Portugal and Spain, 1787–1788*, ed. Boyd Alexander (1954), 123–4.

51. Alexander, *Life at Fonthill*, 47.

52. ibid., 74.

53. ibid., 187.

54. ibid., 191.

55. ibid., 302.

56. Alexander, *England's Wealthiest*, 230–1.

57. A.A. Tait, 'The Duke of Hamilton's Palace', *Burlington Magazine* (1983), CXXV, No. 964, 395.

58. *Catalogue of the Pictures, Works of Art and Decorative Objects the Property of His Grace the Duke of Hamilton ... Christie ... June 17 ... 1882 ...*

59. Wainwright, 'Some Objects'; Watson, 'Beckford and Japanese Lacquer'; Earle, 'Genji'.

60. Hugh Roberts, 'Beckford, Vuillamy and Old Japan', *Apollo* (1986), CXXIV, No. 296, 338–41.

61. Melville, *Life of Beckford*, 105.

62. J.W. Oliver, *The Life of William Beckford* (1937), 162.

63. Snodin & Baker, 'Beckford's Silver'.

64. Wainwright, 'Some Objects', 263–4. It was thought in 1974 that the cup bore the mark of the silversmith Joseph Angell, but Snodin & Baker have proved that the mark is in fact that of James Aldridge, the maker of a number of the pieces of Beckford's plate which they have discovered.

65. Snodin & Baker, 'Beckford's Silver', illustrate several examples.

66. ibid. illustrates several.

67. Hugh Tait, 'Huguenot Silver made in London, c.1690–1723', *Connoisseur* (1972), CLXXX, No. 726, 267–77.

68. ibid., 272.

69. Rutter, *Description*, 55–6.

70. Tait, 'Hamilton's Palace', describes their whole history.

71. Rutter, *Description*, 56–7.

72. Rutter, *Delineations*, 35.

73. ibid., 34–5.

74. ibid., 39.

75. Rutter, *Description*, 58.

76. James Storer, *A Description of Fonthill* (1812), 24.

77. Snodin & Baker, 'Beckford's Silver', 740.

78. Rutter, *Description*, 59.

79. Rutter, *Delineations*, xix.

80. Rutter, *Description*, 59.

81. Britton, *Illustrations*, 28.

82. Cyrus Redding, *Memoirs of William Beckford* (1859), II, 123–4.

83. Britton, *Illustrations*, 30.

84. *Gentleman's Magazine* (1801), LXXI, pt. I, 297.

85. Melville, *Life of Beckford*, 238.

86. Britton, *Illustrations*, 53.

87. Rutter, *Delineations*, 52.

88. Britton, *Illustrations*, 53–4.

89. ibid., 54–5.

90. Alexander, *England's Wealthiest*, 171.

91. Rutter, *Delineations*, 53–4. For the Holbein Cabinet, see Wainwright, 'Some Objects', 54.

92. Rutter, *Description*, 60.

93. Wainwright, 'Some Objects'.

94. Rutter, *Delineations*, 54.

95. Britton, *Illustrations*, 55.

96. Storer, *Description of Fonthill*, 15.

97. Redding, *Memoirs of Beckford*, 122.

98. Clive Wainwright, 'William Beckford's Furniture', *Connoisseur* (1976), CXCI, No. 770, 290–7. pls. 11 & 16.

99. Pierre Verlet, 'Les Deux Armoires de Boulle d'Hamilton Palace', *La Revue des Arts* (1951), I, 246–7.

100. *Catalogue des Vases, Colonnes, Tables de Marbres rares, Figures de bronze, Porcelaines de choix, Laques, Meubles precieux ... De feu M. Le Duc d'Aumont ... 12 Decembre 1782 ... en son Hôtel, Place Louis XV ...*

101. Snodin & Baker, 'Beckford's Silver', 740.

102. William Beckford, *Italy, with sketches of Spain and Portugal* (1834), I, 327.

103. Rutter, *Description*, 60.

104. Christie's, 15 April 1982, lot 2. The price was £13,500.

105. Rutter, *Description*, 63.

106. Storer, *Description of Fonthill*, 15.

107. Britton, *Illustrations*, 55.

108. See Simon Caudron, 'Connoisseurs of Champlève Limoges Enamels in Eighteenth Century England', *British Museum Yearbook* (1977), II, 9–33.

109. Britton, *Illustrations*, 30.

110. John Evelyn, *The Diary of John Evelyn*, ed. E.S. De Beer (1955), I, 58.

111. *Abbot Suger on the Abbey Church of St-Denis and its Art Treasures*, ed. & trans. E. Panofsky (1946).

112. *A History and a Description of the Royal Abbaye of Saint Denis ...* (1795), iii–iv.

113. Comte Blaise de Montesquiou-Fezensac, 'A Carolingian Rock Crystal from the Abbey of Saint-

Denis at the British Museum', *Antiquaries Journal* (1954), XXXIV, 42.

114. *ibid.*

115. Melville, *Life of Beckford*, 190.

116. Comte Blaise de Montesquiou-Fezensac, *Le Tresor de Saint-Denis*, 3 vols. (1973–7).

117. Cass Canfield, *The Incredible Pierpont Morgan, Financier and Art Collector* (1974), 70, where it is illustrated in colour.

118. Marie-Madeleine Gauthier, *Emaux meridioneaux: Catalogue international de l'oeuvre de Limoges* (1987), I, 181–2. The whole history of the Beckford chasse is given here.

119. Arthur Lane, 'The Gagnières-Fonthill Vase: A Chinese Porcelain of about 1300', *Burlington Magazine* (1961), CIII, No. 697, 124–32.

120. *ibid.*, 127, illustrates this watercolour.

121. Marvin Chauncey Ross, 'The Rubens Vase: Its History and Date', *Journal of the Walters Art Gallery* (1943), VI, 8–39.

122. *The Times* (19 January 1882), 5.

123. *Sotheby ... The Beckford Library Removed from Hamilton Palace ... 20 June 1882 et seq. ...*

124. Clarke, *Reptorium Bibliographicum*, 203–4.

125. Britton, *Illustrations*, 53.

126. Wainwright, 'Some Objects', 263.

127. A.R.A. Hobson, 'William Beckford's Binders', *Festschrift Ernst Kyriss* (1961), 378–9.

128. Alexander, *Life at Fonthill*, 218.

129. Storer, *Description of Fonthill*, 11.

130. Rutter, *Delineations*, 14

131. John Britton, *The Auto-Biography* (1850), I, 179.

132. William Gibbs Rogers, *A List of Carvings and other Works of Art ...* (1854), 26. For Aldegraver, see Snodin & Baker, 'Beckford's Silver'.

133. Rutter, *Delineations*, 31.

134. Alexander, *Life at Fonthill*, 166–7.

135. Wainwright, 'Some Objects', 257.

136. F.J.B. Watson, *Wallace Collection Catalogues: Furniture* (1956), 69–76.

137. Musée Rodin, *Le Rue de Varenne*, 67; for d'Orsay, see also Svend Eriksen, *Early Neo-Classicism in France* (1974), 210.

138. Musée Rodin, *La Rue de Varenne*, 71.

139. For instance, Joseph Alsop, 'The Fakers Art', *New York Review of Books* (23 October 1986), 25–31. I intend to discuss this matter in print in the near future.

140. Snodin & Baker, 'Beckford's Silver', 744. The Hazlitt quote is from *Criticisms of Art* (1843), 285. For a fascinating discussion of Hazlitt and Fonthill, see Stanley Jones, 'The Fonthill Abbey Picture: Two Additions to the Hazlitt Canon', *Journal of the Warburg and Courtauld Institutes* (1978), XLI, 278–96.

141. *Salisbury Journal* (23 December 1825).

142. Thomas Hope, *Observations of the Plans and Elevations designed by James Wyatt architect for Downing College Cambridge ...* (1804), 15.

143. Farington, *Diary*, VI, 2283.

144. Clive Wainwright, 'William Beckford e la sua collezione', *Arte Illustrata* (1971), IV, Nos. 39–40, 52–60. See also Phillipa Bishop, 'Beckford in Bath', *Bath History* (1988), II, 85–112.

145. [Cyrus Redding], 'Memoirs of William Beckford of Fonthill', *Gentleman's Magazine* (1859), VI, 255–60.

Notes to Chapter 6

1. Walter Scott, *The Miscellaneous Prose Works* (1841), I, 306.

2. *ibid.*

3. John Ruskin, *The Works of John Ruskin*, Library ed., ed. E.T. Cook & A. Wedderburn (1909), XXXVI, 16–17.

4. Kata Phusin, 'Whether Works of Art may, with Propriety be combined with the Sublimity of Nature; and what would be the most appropriate Situation for the proposed Monument to the Memory of Sir Walter Scott, in Edinburgh', *Architectural Magazine* (1839), V, 625–36.

5. John Henry Raleigh, 'What Scott Meant to the Victorians', *Victorian Studies* (1963), VII, 7–34. This essay goes some way to describe why Scott's popularity lasted out the nineteenth century.

6. J.P. Neale, *Views of the Seats of Noblemen and Gentlemen ...*, 2nd ser. (1829), V.

7. *Edinburgh Review* (1808), XII, 32.

8. Martin Kemp, 'Scott and Delacroix, with Some Assistance from Hugo and Bonnington', *Scott Bicentenary Essays*, ed. Alan Bell (1973), 213–17.

9. Beth Segal Wright, 'Scott's Historical Novels and French History Painting, 1815–1855', *Art Bulletin* (1981), XLIII, No. 2, 268–87.

10. Mr Titmarsh [William Thackeray], *The Paris Sketch Book* (1885), 67–8. The first edition was published in 1840.

11. J.G. Lockhart, *Memoirs of Sir Walter Scott* (1900), III, 228–9. The first edition was published in 1838 and Lockhart produced an enlarged one in 1839 which is often cited as the standard one, but in 1848 in his abridged edition Lockhart incorporated new material not in the earlier editions. The 5 vol. 1900 English Classics edition used here is a reprint of the 1839 edition to which is added the 1848 material; it is therefore, I suggest, the best edition for my purposes. See James C. Corson, *A Bibliography of Sir Walter Scott ...* (1943), 45–6.

12. Lockhart, *Memories*, III 230.

13. *ibid.*, IV, 206.

14. Maryland Historical Society, Baltimore, Robert Gilmor Jr Papers MS 387. I am indebted to Stiles T. Colwill for this reference.

15. Lockhart, *Memoirs*, I, 71.

16. Three important exhibitions chart this world. Stuart Piggot & Marjorie Robertson, *3 Centuries of Scottish Archaeology ...*, exh. cat., Edinburgh University Library (1977); James Holloway & Lindsay Errington, *The Discovery of Scotland ...*, exh. cat., National Gallery of Scotland, Edinburgh (1978); I. Gordon Brown, *The Hobby Horsical Antiquary ...*, exh. cat., National Library of Scotland, Edinburgh (1980).

17. E.L. Cloyd, *James Burnett Lord Monboddo* (1972).

18. Lockhart, *Memoirs*, I, 29–30. Thomas Percy's *Reliques of Ancient English Poetry* was published in 1770.

19. W.E. Wilson, 'The Making of the "Minstrelsey": Scott and Shortreed in Liddesdale', *Cornhill Magazine* (1932), n.s., LXXIII, 271–4.

20. *ibid.*, 276.

21. *ibid.*, 277.

22. Fortunately Scott as a folklorist has been well covered in Richard M. Dorson, *The British Folklorists: A History* (1968), and more recently Charles G. Zug III, 'The Ballad Editor as Antiquary: Scott and the Minstrelsey', *Journal of the Folklore Institute* (1976), XIII, 57–73.

23. Walter Scott, *The Letters of Sir Walter Scott*, ed. Herbert J.C. Grierson, 12 vols. (1932–7), I, 38. Hereafter I shall refer to these as *Letters*. An invaluable supplementary volume has recently been published: James C. Corson, *Notes and Index to Sir Herbert Grierson's Edition of the Letters of Sir Walter Scott* (1979).

24. Lockhart, *Memoirs*, I, 151–2.

25. *ibid.*, 152–3. The whole story of Broughton's visits to Scott's father is told here.

26. *ibid.*, 118–21. See also Scott, who in his anonymous review of his own *Tales of my Landlord* in the *Quarterley Review* (1817), XVI, 433–5, deals with Invernahyle at length.

27. Lord Archibald Campbell, *Highland Dress, Arms and Ornament* (1899), 96.

28. *Letters*, I, 224.

29. *ibid.*, III, 455.

30. Lockhart, *Memoirs*, III, 183–5.

31. *Letters*, II, 343–4.

32. Lockhart, *Memoirs*, II, 119.

33. *Letters*, II, 369.

34. 'Gillows Packing Book, 1809–1814', 110, item 927. This packing book is a manuscript in the Gillow Archive at Westminster Public Library.

35. 'Cabinet Maker's Sketch Book' (1801), 19. Location as 34.

36. Mary Monica Maxwell Scott, *Abbotsford: The Personal Relics and Antiquarian Treasures* (1893), pl. I shows the desk open.

37. *Letters*, II, 508. I have discussed the question of conservatories in relation to houses elsewhere, see my essay 'The Garden Indoors', in Victoria & Albert Museum, London, *The Garden*, exh. cat., ed. John Harris (1979).

38. 'On Landscape Gardening', in Scott, *Miscellaneous Prose Works*, I, 774–92. This essay was originally published in the *Quarterly Review* in March 1828.

39. *Letters*, II, 519.

40. Wilfred Partington, *Sir Walter's Post-Bag: More Stories and Sidelights from his Unpublished Letter-Books* (1932), 67.

41. *Letters*, III, 122.

42. *ibid.*, 128.

43. *ibid.*, 135.

44. *ibid.*, 156.

45. James Macaulay, *The Gothic Revival, 1745–1845* (1975), chap. XII, 'Abbotsford and its Precursors'.

46. *ibid.*, 224.

47. James Skene, *The Skene Papers: Memoires of Sir Walter Scott*, ed. Basil Thomson (1909).

48. Hugh Meller, 'From Engraver to Architect', *Country Life* (1978), CLXIV, 1205–6.

49. For Atkinson's Scottish work, see Macaulay, *Gothic Revival*.

50. *Letters*, 291.

51. Lockhart, *Memoirs*, II, 187–8.

52. *Letters*, XII, 335.

53. *Dictionary of National Biography*, under Terry.

54. National Library of Scotland MS 3889.f.192; hereafter called NLS MS. These hundreds of letters are largely unpublished and are of crucial importance to the study of Scott. They are letters *to* Scott and are the other side of the correspondence published by Grierson.

55. Lockhart, *Memoirs*, II, 194.

56. *Letters*, III, 153–4.

57. *ibid.*, 185.

58. *ibid.*, 514.

59. *ibid.*, 301.

60. Skene, *Papers*, 231–2.

61. *Letters*, IV, 289–90.

62. For Bullock's Scottish work, see Anthony Coleridge, 'The Work of George Bullock, Cabinet-Maker in Scotland', *Connoisseur* (1965), CLVIII, 249–52 & CLIX, 13–17. See also Clive Wainwright, Intro. to *George Bullock, Cabinet-Maker* (1988).

63. John Cornforth, 'Bowhill', *Country Life* (1969), CLVII, No. 4006, 1448–51.

64. For William Bullock, see the numerous references

in Richard B. Altick, *The Shows of London* . . . (1978).

65. *Letters*, IV, 302.

66. ibid., 333–6.

67. NLS MS 3887.f.161.

68. *Letters*, IV, 542.

69. ibid., VI, 323–4. The date in *Letters* is wrong. Corson, *Notes and Index*, gives December 1816.

70. *Letters*, V, 91. 'Pic-nic' here follows the definition given in the *Oxford English Dictionary* under 'Pick-nickery': 'A collection of things contributed from various sources'.

71. Walter Scott, *Waverley; or, 'Tis sixty years since* (1814), I, 107–8.

72. *Waverley* . . ., ed. Claire Lamont (1981), 424.

73. *Scots Magazine* (1927), n.s., VII, 478.

74. ibid.

75. ibid., 479.

76. Samuel Smiles, *A Publisher and his Friends: Memoir and Correspondence of the late John Murray* (1891), 397.

77. Lockhart, *Memoirs*, III, 217.

78. ibid., V, 444–5.

79. This whole question is discussed in an important new book: Francis Russell, *Portraits of Sir Walter Scott: A Study of Romantic Portraiture* (1987), 25–7.

80. *Letters*, V, 3.

81. W.S. Crockett, *The Sir Walter Scott Originals* (1932), 123.

82. [Walter Scott], *The Antiquary* (1816), I, 46–53.

83. Brown, *Hobby Horsical Antiquary*, 17–18.

84. Jane Millgate, 'Guy Mannering in Edinburgh: The Evidence of the Manuscript', *Library* (1977), 5th ser., XXXII, 239.

85. Walter Scott, *Illustre l'Antiquaire*, trans. E. Scheffter (1882).

86. Walter Scott, *The Journal of Sir Walter Scott*, ed. W.E.K. Anderson (1972), 410.

87. *Familiar Letters of Sir Walter Scott*, ed. D. Douglas (1894), I, 245–6.

88. Lockhart, *Memoirs*, V, 275–6.

89. NLS MS 745.f.211.

90. NLS MS 1752.f.387.

91. *Letters*, XI, 292.

92. ibid., 164.

93. Scott, *Journal*, 699.

94. Two parts of the manuscript were published by Mary Monica Maxwell Scott, 'Gabions of Abbotsford . . .', *Harper's Monthly Magazine*, European ed. (1899), XVII, 778–88; 'Sir Walter Scott on his "Gabions"', *The Nineteenth Century* (1905), LVIII, 621–33; hereafter referred to as 'Gabions'.

95. [Scott], *Antiquary*, I, 48.

96. The *Oxford English Dictionary* defines a 'gabion' as 'A wicker basket of cylindrical form usually open both ends . . . for use in fortification and engineering'; the term is derived from 'gabbia' — a cage.

97. 'Gabions', 779. The *Oxford English Dictionary* gives this definition to Scott as his unique alternative to that quoted in note 96.

98. Lockhart, *Memoirs*, III, 183–4.

99. *Letters*, V, 65.

100. ibid., IV, 399.

101. Lockhart, *Memoris*, II, 515–16. Loosely translated this inscription runs 'Weigh it — how many pounds to the mightiest general — Death alone tells what trifles are the puny bodies of men'.

102. ibid.

103. ibid.

104. *Letters*, IV, 289. Grierson takes this letter from Lockhart who dates it to 12 November 1816. Corson, *Notes and Index*, states that the letter is made up of several letters run together, so the date cannot be trusted.

105. Clive Wainwright, 'Walter Scott and the Furnishing of Abbotsford: The Gabions of Jonathan Oldbuck Esq.', *Connoisseur* (1977), CXCIV, No. 779, 10.

106. *The Times* (6 August 1981). This stand returned to Abbotsford in late October 1981.

107. *Letters*, IV, 289.

108. 'Gabions', 787.

109. *Letters*, IV, 295–6.

110. 'Gabions', 624–5.

111. John Britton, *The Autobiography of John Britton, F.S.A.* (1850), pt. III, Appendix, 6–8.

112. Terry Friedman, 'Samuel Joseph Phrenologized', *Leeds Arts Calendar* (1980), No. 86, 20–8. The whole question of Scott's skull is fascinatingly dealt with in an essay by George Combe, 'On the Size of Sir Walter Scott's Brain, and the Phrenological Development indicated by his Bust . . .', *Phrenological Journal* (1838), n.s., LVIII, 44–9.

113. *Gentleman's Magazine* (1815), LXXXV, pt. I, 5.

114. 'Gabions', 786–7.

115. *Letters*, IV, 289. See note 104 for the dates of this letter.

116. NLS MS 3889.f.17.

117. *Letters*, V, 133.

118. NLS MS 3896.f.112.

119. D.R. Hay, *The Laws of Harmonious Colouring adapted to Interior Decorations with observations on the practice of house painting*, 6th ed. (1847), 181–3. This appendix occurs only in the sixth edition. Fortunately Ian Gow is now carrying out research on Hay which is already yielding fascinating material concerning his career.

120. ibid., 185.

121. Mrs Hughes, *Letters and Recollections of Sir Walter Scott* (1910), 73. This account was written after a visit to Abbotsford in May 1824.

122. NLS MS 7976.

123. *Letters*, V, 3.

124. ibid., V, 136–7.

125. NLS MS 3889.f.189.

126. ibid. 3890.f.72.

127. *A catalogue of the superb furniture and sculptured articles of Mona marbles . . . The whole finished stock of that highly ingenious Artist Mr George Bullock . . . by Mr Christie on the premises no. 4 Tenterden Street Hanover Square on Monday the 3d of May 1819 and two following days . . .*

128. NLS MS 3890.f.128.

129. *Letters*, V, 164.

130. NLS MS 3889.ff.189–92.

131. *Letters*, V, 169. Grierson gives a date of 11 or 18; Corson, *Notes and Index*, gives 16.

132. NLS MS 3889.f.192.

133. *Letters*, V, 196. Grierson gives date of after 16 September, as it is a reply to Terry's letter of 16th. It must, as Corson, *Notes and Index*, suggests, date from about the 20th.

134. NLS MS 3889.f.27.

135. *Letters*, V, 393–4. This quotation is a good example of Scott's constant references to Shakespeare. It comes from act 1, scene 1, of *The Merry Wives of Windsor*.

136. NLS MS 3890.f.114.

137. ibid., 1750.f.242.

138. ibid., 3890.f.212.

139. 'Gabions', 787.

140. Virginia Glenn, 'George Bullock, Richard Bridgens and James Watt's Regency Furnishing Schemes', *Furniture History* (1979), XV, 54–68.

141. *George Bullock*, 19.

142. *Letters*, V, 364.

143. NLS MS 3890.f.141.

144. ibid., f.114.

145. Hay, *Laws of Colouring*, 183.

146. *Letters*, V, 63.

147. *George Bullock*, 57.

148. NLS MS 3889.ff.60–3.

149. *Letters*, V, 133.

150. ibid., IV, 338. Mountstuart Elphinstone, *Account of Caubul* (1815), and Sir John Malcolm, *History of Persia* (1815).

151. *Letters*, IV, 338.

152. ibid., V, 171.

153. NLS MS 7976.

154. *Letters*, V, 197. Undated, but Grierson says late September or early October; I agree.

155. NLS MS 3887.f.88.

156. ibid., f.52.

157. *Letters*, IV, 290.

158. ibid., 529.

159. NLS MS 3889.f.192.

160. *Letters*, V, 203.

161. ibid., 501.

162. ibid., IV, 397.

163. ibid., 396–7.

164. John B. Papworth, *Rural Residences* . . . (1818), 85–6.

165. *Letters*, IV, 355. Had Scott or indeed his wife needed instruction concerning how to grow plants in Scotland in a 'green room' an excellent book had been recently published in Edinburgh on that very subject. It was Walter Nicol, *The Villa Garden Directory . . . with hints of the treatment of shrubs and flowers usually kept in the green room the lobby and the drawing room* (1809). Nichol was an Edinburgh landscape gardener.

166. *Letters*, IV, 425.

Notes to Chapter 7

1. Walter Scott, *The Letters of Sir Walter Scott*, ed. Herbert J.C. Grierson, 12 vols. (1932–7), VI, 155; hereafter *Letters*.

2. J.G. Lockhart, *Memoirs of Sir Walter Scott* (1900), III, 500.

3. National Library of Scotland MS 3893.f.155; hereafter NLS.

4. *Letters*, VII, 39.

5. ibid., 56.

6. ibid., 164.

7. James Skene., *The Skene Papers: Memoirs of Sir Walter Scott*, ed. Basil Thomson (1909), 98.

8. J. Collingwood Bruce, 'Inscriptions at Abbotsford . . .', *Archaeologia Aeliana* (1876), VII, 212–16.

9. Lockhart, *Memoirs*, IV, 121 & 127.

10. *Letters*, VII, 182.

11. D.R. Hay, *The Laws of Harmonious Colouring adapted to Interior Decorations with observations on the practice of house painting*, 6th ed. (1847), 190.

12. ibid., 188.

13. *Letters*, VII, 260.

14. NLS MS 3895.f.228.

15. Wilfred Partington, *Sir Walter's Post-Bag: More Stories and Sidelights from his Unpublished Letter-Books* (1932), 187.

16. *Letters*, VII, 330.

17. ibid., footnote by Grierson, 330.

18. ibid., VIII, 129. Dated November or December. Walter Scott, *The Journal of Sir Walter Scott*, ed. W.E.K. Anderson (1972), 716, gives a short account of the Gas Company.

19. James C. Corson, *Notes and Index to Sir Herbert Grierson's Edition of the Letters of Sir Walter Scott* (1979), 214. For Milne, see also *Letters*, VIII, 155.

20. *Letters*, VIII, 90.

21. *ibid.*, 107–8.
22. *ibid.*, VII, 347, gives a March date; Corson, *Notes and Index*, gives October.
23. Lockhart, *Memoirs*, IV, 99. There was no doubt that the form of gas burner used at this date did produce several by-products harmful to health. This problem was not solved until Scott's friend Sir John Robison invented the 'atmospheric burner' in 1840. See *Edinburgh New Philosophical Transactions* (1840), XXVIII, 291.
24. Virginia Woolf, *The Moment and Other Essays* (1949), 50–5.
25. Mark Girouard, *The Victorian Country House* (1971), 17.
26. Scott, *Journal*, 411.
27. William Bewick, *Life and Letters of William Bewick, Artist*, ed. Thomas Landseer (1871), I, 182–93.
28. *Letters*, VII, 279–80.
29. NLS MS 3896.ff.78–92.
30. *Letters*, VIII, 213–14.
31. *ibid.*, 181–2.
32. Geoffrey de Bellaigue, 'Edward Holmes Baldock', *Connoisseur* (1975), CLXXXIX, 290–9, & CXC, 18–25.
33. *Letters*, IX, 115.
34. *ibid.*, X, 450–1. This bust is fully described in National Portrait Gallery, London, *Sir Francis Chantrey (1781–1841): Sculptor of the Great*, exh. cat. (1981).
35. Mary Monica Maxwell Scott, 'Sir Walter Scott on his "Gabions",' *The Nineteenth Century* (1905), LVIII, 785; hereafter referred to as 'Gabions'.
36. *Letters*, IV, 393.
37. NLS MS 3896.ff.25–9.
38. 'Gabions', 782–3.
39. NLS MS 3889.f.17.
40. *ibid.*, 3893.f.33.
41. *Letters*, VIII, 333.
42. J. Mordaunt Crook, *The Greek Revival* (1972), 58.
43. *Letters*, VII, 17.
44. NLS MS 3895.f.262. Dated 1822 but no month or day, very probably relates to Terry's letter of 18 November (see notes 45 & 46).
45. *ibid.*, f.227.
46. *Letters*, VII, 278–9.
47. *ibid.*, 300.
48. Walter Scott, *The Poetical Works* (1883), VI, 206–9.
49. *ibid.*, 208.
50. *Letters*, VII, 301.
51. *ibid.*, 182.
52. Lockhart, *Memoirs*, IV, 147.
53. Corson, *Notes and Index*, 211. Pigot's . . . *Directory* (1823–4) gives 'Potts & Collinson Chenies Street Bedford Square upholsterers'.
54. NLS MS 3895.f.25.
55. *ibid.*, 3896.f.82.
56. *ibid.*, f.79.
57. *Letters*, VIII, 167.
58. Hay, *Laws of Colouring*, 195.
59. *Letters*, VIII, 258.
60. *ibid.*, 277.
61. In the London Library there is a manuscript entitled 'Memorials of the Heath Family'; the section quoted is dated October 1825 and is f.116.
62. *ibid.*
63. [G.K. Mathews], *Abbotsford and Sir Walter Scott . . .* (1854), 27.
64. 'Abbotsford', *The Anniversary* (1829), 95–7. There has been debate over the author of this essay, which is a very well informed and important one. *Letters*, XI, 60, suggests Lockhart, but James C. Corson, *A Bibliography of Sir Walter Scott . . .* (1943), 380, gives it to J.W. Lake; see entry No. 2781.

65. *Letters*, VII, 248–9. The memoir is 343–7, Walter Scott, *The Miscellaneous Prose Works* (1841), I.
66. NLS MS 3897.f.231.
67. *Letters*, VII, 301, 305–6. Lady Wishfort is a character in Congreve's play *The Way of the World*.
68. NLS MS 3896.ff.25–9.
69. *ibid.*, ff.78–82.
70. *ibid.*, f.29.
71. Bellaigue, 'Baldock'.
72. Charles Dickens, *The Life of Charles James Mathews* (1879), I, 234–6.
73. Scott, *Journal*, 114.
74. *Letters*, VII, 389.
75. *ibid.*, 19.
76. NLS MS 3896.ff.152–4.
77. *Proceedings of the Berwickshire Naturalists Club* (1846), XVI, 381.
78. Lockhart, *Memoirs*, IV, 146.
79. Thomas Constable, *Archibald Constable and his Literary Correspondents* (1873), III, 219–20.
80. NLS MS 683.f.4.
81. *ibid.*, f.6.
82. Anthony Coleridge, 'Andrea Brustalon: Some Additions to his Oeuvre', *Apollo* (1963), LXXVII, 209–12. The Abbotsford chairs are discussed and illustrated by Coleridge.
83. [Mathews], *Abbotsford*, 234–6.
84. 'Gabions', 784. Scott's use of printed historical sources is very interestingly discussed in James Anderson, *Sir Walter Scott and History . . .* (1981). Anderson gives lists of the sources used by Scott in his writings.
85. 'Gabions', 623.
86. *Catalogue of the Library at Abbotsford* (1838), iii. This appeared as Vol. XLV in the Maitland Club series. The name J.G. Cochrane appears as 'The Compiler' but G.H. Gordon was probably the main author; see 'Sir Walter Scott and the Catalogue of the Abbotsford Library', *Gentleman's Magazine* (1852), n.s., XXXVIII, 53–4.
87. This is illustrated in the *Connoisseur* (1947), CXIX, 116.
88. 'Gabions', 784–5.
89. Bewick, *Life and Letters*, II, 251.
90. *Letters*, VIII, 18.
91. *ibid.*
92. *ibid.*, VII, 280.
93. *ibid.*, 299.
94. *ibid.*, VIII, 18.
95. NLS MS 856.f.44. This letter would seem to date from late May or June 1823.
96. *ibid.* This note was written in 1837 by Andrew Shortreed.
97. Lockhart, *Memoirs*, II, 374.
98. The inscription is given in *ibid.*, IV, 151. For details of this interesting character, see John Paterson, *Memoir of Joseph Train, F.S.A.: The Antiquarian Correspondent of Sir Walter Scott* (1857), and William Van Antwerp, *A Forgotten Antiquary* (1932).
99. Lockhart, *Memoirs*, IV, 150.
100. *ibid.*, 151. Corson, *Notes and Index*, 203, states that the chair was made by John Stirling of Kirkintilloch.
101. *Letters*, VII, 176.
102. Mary Monica Maxwell Scott, *Catalogue of the Armour & Antiquities of Abbotsford* (1888), 32–45.
103. Gerald Finley, *Landscapes of Memory: Turner as an Illustrator to Scott* (1980), 103–25.
104. 'Gabions', 779–81.
105. Hay, *Laws of Colouring*, 193–4.
106. A.V.B. Norman, 'Arms and Armour at Abbotsford', *Apollo* (1963), LXXVI, 525–9.
107. Scott's memoir of this singular and engaging char-

acter was published in *Poems and Ballads by Dr John Leyden . . .* (1858).
108. R.H. Cholmondeley, *The Heber Letters, 1783–1832* (1950), 205.
109. *Letters*, II, 473–4.
110. Prudence Summerhayes, 'Hetman of the Cossacks Count Platov (1751–1818)', *Country Life* (1982), CLXXI, No. 4423, 1566–7.
111. *Letters*, III, 271.
112. *ibid.*, 378.
113. *ibid.*, XII, 145–6. This letter dates from late August 1815.
114. Lockhart, *Memoirs*, III, 36.
115. Walter Scott, *Paul's Letters to his Kinsfolk* (1816), 207–18.
116. Scott, *Catalogue of the Armour*, 32.
117. Scott, *Paul's Letters*, 159.
118. Karl Pearson, 'King Robert the Bruce, 1274–1329: His Skull and Portraiture', *Biometrika* (1937), XVI, 6–7. An off-print of this is in the Victoria & Albert Museum Library. The whole question of Bruce's skull is dealt with in minute detail. See also *Transactions of the Phrenological Society Edinburgh* (1824), 247–8.
119. *Letters*, III, 45.
120. *ibid.*, 100.
121. [Walter Scott], *The Antiquary* (1816), III, 333–4.
122. Walter Scott, *Waverley; or, 'Tis sixty years since* (1814), III, 31–3.
123. Walter Scott, *The Waverley Novels* (1830), II, 201.
124. Paterson, *Train*, 111–13.
125. Scott, *Journal*, 602.
126. NLS MS 3892.ff 69–70.
127. *ibid.*, 3894.f.112.
128. *ibid.*, 3895.f.131.
129. The best nineteenth-century sources are the two chapters in Lord Archibald Campbell's *Highland Dress and Ornament* (1899) and his pamphlet *Notes on Swords From the Battle-Field of Culloden* (1894).
130. J. Skelton, *Engraved Illustrations of Antient Arms and Armour from the Collection of Llewelyn Meyrick Esq . . .* (1830), caption to pl. LV, fig. 16.
131. Claude Blair, 'New Light on Andrea Ferrara', *Arms and Armour Society Newsletter* (1984), No. 1, 6–7. I am indebted to Claude Blair and Anthony North for help with the strange case of Andrea Ferrara.
132. NLS MS 3893.f.48.
133. *Letters*, VIII, 113.
134. Samuel Rush Meyrick, *A Critical Inquiry into Antient Armour as it existed in Europe but particularly in England from the Norman Conquest to the reign of King Charles II . . .* (1824).
135. *ibid.*, 10.
136. *Letters*, X, 510.
137. Lockhart, *Memoirs*, V, 212.
138. 'Gabions', 780.
139. Paterson, *Memoir of Train*, 134.
140. NLS MS 856.f.44.
141. *Letters*, VIII, 18–19.
142. *ibid.*, X, 120.
143. Constable, *Archibald Constable*, III, 298–9.
144. Scott, *Journal*, 279. Scott is mistaken here; as William Vaughan has kindly pointed out to me, *The Robbers* was written by Schiller, not Goethe. Scott certainly knew *The Robbers* and mentions the story in one his letters.
145. *Letters*, X, 252.
146. Nathaniel Hawthorne, *The English Notebooks*, ed. Randall Stewart (1941), 540.

Notes to Chapter 8

1. The most important manuscript source is the extensive collection of Lucy papers on deposit at the Warwickshire County Record Office in Warwick. I shall refer to these papers as WROL. The best printed sources are Mary Elizabeth Lucy, *Biography of the Lucy Family of Charlecote Park in the County of Warwick* (1862), and Alice Fairfax Lucy's, *Charlecote and the Lucys: The Chronicle of an English Family* (1958), and *Mistress of Charlecote: The Memoirs of Mary Elizabeth Lucy* (1983).

2. John Hardy & Clive Wainwright, 'Elizabethan-Revival Charlecote Revived', *The National Trust Year Book* (1976–7), 12–19. See also *Charlecote Park*, guidebook (1974), and Clive Wainwright, 'Charlecote Park Warwickshire', *Country Life* (1985), CLXXVII, 446–50, and 506–10.

3. Lucy, *Charlecote*, 73.

4. ibid., 74.

5. *The Works of Mr William Shakespeare; in Six Volumes Adorn'd With Cuts Revis'd and Corrected With an Account of The Life and Writings of the Author . . .*, ed. N. Rowe (1709), I, v.

6. ibid., xvii.

7. ibid. (1823 ed.), 2.

8. J.O. Haliwell Philipps, *Observations on the Charlecote Traditions and on the Personification of Sir Thomas Lucy in the Character of Justice Shallow* (1887), 26. There is a presentation copy of this book in the Library at Charlecote with the Haliwell Philipps letter which accompanied it.

9. William Shakespeare, *The Dramatic Works* (1860), 886. These lines occur at the very start of act 1, scene 1, of the play.

10. John Bowyer Nichols, *Collectanea Topographica and Heraldica* (1837), IV, 346. This description of the stained glass at Charlecote was written by Thomas Willement. Thomas Moule in his *Heraldry of Fish* (1842), 13, states: 'old French. Hauriant, a word now obsolete, means fish raised upright, in which manner, with their heads above water, fish refresh themselves by sucking air in the air'.

11. For a full description of this event, see Christine Deelman, *The Great Shakespeare Jubilee* (1964), and Martha Winburn England, *Garrick and Stratford* (1962).

12. WROL 6/1473.

13. WROL 6/1102.

14. Lucy, *Charlecote*, 229.

15. WROL 6/1463.

16. Lucy, *Biography*, 112–13.

17. Samuel Ireland, *Picturesque Views on the Upper or Warwickshire Avon . . .* (1795), 159–60.

18. [Washington Irving], *The Sketch Book of Geoffrey Crayon, Gent.* (1821), II, 149–56.

19. WROL 6/1507.

20. The history of the house is told in Susan Foister, *The National Gallery at Bodelwyddan Castle* (1988).

21. Lucy, *Biography*, 134.

22. John Rutter, *Delineations of Fonthill and its Abbey* (1823).

23. *The Unique and Splendid Effects of Fonthill Abbey . . .* (1823), 146.

24. Lucy, *Biography*, 127.

25. Walter Scott, *The Journal of Sir Walter Scott*, ed. W.E.K. Anderson (1972), 454–5.

26. Lucy, *Biography*, 136.

27. Howard Colvin, *A Biographical Dictionary of British Architects, 1600–1840* (1978), 746.

28. Lucy, *Charlecote*, 278.

29. WROL 6/1117.

30. Lucy, *Charlecote*, 282.

31. Clive Wainwright, 'Davington Priory, Kent', *Country Life* (1971), CL, 1650–3, 1716–19. Clive Wainwright, 'Thomas Willement's Stained Glass Windows in the Choir Aisles', *Report of the Society of the Friends of St Georges and the Descendants of the Knights of the Garter* (1971–2), V, 105–18.

32. Lucy, *Biography*, 164.

33. Thomas Willement, *A Concise Account of the Principal Works in Stained Glass that have been executed by Thomas Willement* (1840).

34. Colvin, *Biographical Dictionary*, 746.

35. Willement, *Concise Account*, 53.

36. Thomas Willement's manuscript list of his works in stained glass survives as British Library Add. MSS 52413. The relevant part here is folio 10.

37. WROL 6/1124.

38. WROL 6/1122.

39. Nichols, *Collectanea Topographica*, 349.

40. WROL 6/1123.

41. Sir Bernard Burke, *A Genealogical History of the Dormant, Abeyant, Forfeited and Extinct Peerages of the British Empire* (1866), 336. Full details of the Lucy barony are given here, 335–6.

42. *Gentleman's Magazine* (1848), CLXXXIV, 426–9.

43. G.E. Cokayne, *The Complete Peerage . . .* (1912), III, 336.

44. Benjamin Disraeli, *Sybil; or, Two Nations* (1954 ed.), 231–6. I can find no mention in the published Disraeli literature of the identity of Baptist Hatton in real life. One possible explanation of Disraeli's choice of name is that in 1845 Nicolas was working on his book *Memoirs of the Life and Times of Sir Christopher Hatton . . .*, which was eventually published in 1847.

45. *Gentleman's Magazine* (1831), CI, pt. I, 290.

46. WROL 6/1129.

47. WROL 6/1142.

48. These can be identified in Nichols, *Collectanea Topographica*, 348.

49. WROL 6/1140.

50. Lucy, *Biography*, 165.

51. WROL 6/1120.

52. ibid. This slab is illustrated in colour in *Country Life* (1985), CLXXVII, No. 4567, 50.

53. Victoria & Albert Museum Prints and Drawings Department, No. Q.13.D.

54. WROL 6/1118. This is an extract from a letter written by William Buchanan; see note 75.

55. John Tallis, *London Street Views* (1847).

56. WROL 6/1120.

57. Lucy, *Biography*, 148.

58. ibid., 153–4. The pedestals arrived at Charlecote in 1845. Letter from George Lucy to Brown & Co., 11 March 1845, WROL 6/1120.

59. WROL 6/1120, letter from Behnes to George Lucy.

60. Lucy, *Biography*, 154.

61. WROL 6/1118.

62. WROL 6/1117.

63. ibid.

64. WROL 6/1128.

65. WROL 6/1114.

66. British Library Add. MSS 52413, f.17.

67. *Sotheby's Chester . . . Woodcarvings . . . 18 June 1983*.

68. Amongst the un-numbered documents at Charlecote.

69. WROL 6/1138.

70. WROL 6/1124.

71. WROL 6/1135.

72. Un-numbered Willement drawing at Charlecote.

73. See note 53.

74. WROL 6/1120. Mr Holford was R.S. Holford (1808–1891), the rich collector and connoisseur who owned Holford House in London and Westonbirt in Gloucestershire.

75. William Buchanan, *Memoirs of painting, with a chronological History of the importation of pictures by the great masters into England since the French Revolution* (1824).

76. Frank Hermann, 'Collecting Classics — 2. William Buchanan's Memoirs of Painting', *Connoisseur* (1966), CLXI, 250. For Buchanan, see also Francis Haskell, *Rediscoveries in Art: Some Aspects of Taste, Fashion and Collecting in England and France* (1976).

77. WROL 6/1118.

78. WROL 6/1117.

79. WROL 6/1118.

80. The whole story of these cabinets has recently been fascinatingly told. Reinier Baarsen, 'Mix and Match Marquetry', *Country Life* (1988), CLXXXII, No. 41, 225.

81. WROL 6/1118.

82. WROL 6/1117.

83. Un-numbered watercolour at Charlecote.

84. WROL 6/1114.

85. WROL 6/1118.

86. Geoffrey de Bellaigue, 'Edward Holmes Baldock', *Connoisseur* (1975), CLXXXIX, 290–9, & CXC, 18–25.

87. ibid., CXC, 19. This table is now at Temple Newsam House in Leeds, another is in the Victoria & Albert Museum, another at Carlton Towers in Yorkshire and a further one at Penrhyn Castle in North Wales.

88. WROL 6/1117.

89. ibid.

90. WROL 6/1120. Hume, as we saw in Chapter 5, worked extensively for William Beckford as an agent and as a cabinet-maker.

91. ibid. For the Italian acquisitions, see Lucy, *Biography*, 153.

92. Henry Summerson, 'The Lucys of Charlecote and their Library', *National Trust Studies* (1979), 149–59.

93. Sir Geoffrey Keynes, *William Pickering Publisher* (1969).

94. 'Antiquarian Bibliography', *Archaeologia Cambrensis* (1848), III, 278.

95. WROL 6/1145.

96. ibid.

97. WROL 6/1138.

98. Henry Shaw, *Details of Elizabethan Architecture* (1839), 46. The plate is dated February 1834 and the book was issued in parts before it appeared as a complete volume in 1839. The first part was reviewed in the *Gentleman's Magazine* (1834), CLV, 419.

99. WROL 6/1118.

100. ibid. Thomas Bott is described as an 'upholsterer' in *Robsons London Directory* (1838).

101. Virginia Glenn, 'George Bullock, Richard Bridgens and James Watt's Regency Furnishing Schemes', *Furniture History* (1979), XV, pls. 102 & 103.

102. Samuel Carter Hall, *The Baronial Halls and Picturesque Edifices of England* (1848), II, 4.

103. This very detailed inventory survives at Charlecote. It was signed 'Ada Christina Lucy Oct 12 1891'.

104. WROL 6/1117.

105. Lucy, *Biography*.

106. WROL 6/1118.

107. ibid. Erlestoke is near Devizes in Wiltshire; the sale lasted from 9 July to 1 August 1832.

108. Mary Elizabeth Lucy, *The Private Journal of a tour on the Continent in the years 1841–43* (1845).

109. Lucy, *Biography*, 136. Hume's bill is WROL 6/1120.
110. Lucy, *Biography*, 157.
111. *ibid.*
112. *ibid.*, 153.
113. *ibid.*, 154.
114. Nathaniel Hawthorne, *The English Notebooks*, ed. Randall Stewart (1941), 135.

Notes to Chapter 9

1. For full details of Meyrick's antecedents, see his obituary, *Gentleman's Magazine* (1848), CLXXXIV, pt. II, 92–5. See also *The Dictionary of Welsh Biography down to 1940* (1959), 629–37.
2. *Archaeologia* (1817), XVIII, 442–3. See also J.J. Marquet De Vasselot, *Les Crosses Limousines du XIIIe siècle* (1941), 262.
3. Obituary, 92.
4. Arts Council of Great Britain, *Delacroix: An Exhibition of Paintings, Drawings and Lithographs*, exh. cat. (1964), 46–7.
5. *ibid.*, 47.
6. Sir James Mann, *Wallace Collection Catalogues: European Arms and Armour* (1962), I, 78–83.
7. J. Stewart, *Eugène Delacroix: Selected Letters, 1813–1863* (1971), 371.
8. Lee Johnson, *The Paintings of Eugène Delacroix: A Critical Catalogue, 1816–31* (1981), I, 131–3.
9. *ibid.* and Marcia Pointon, *The Bonington Circle: English Watercolour and Anglo-French Landscape, 1790–1855* (1985), 97.
10. *Gentleman's Magazine* (1826), XCVI, pt. I, 319.
11. *ibid.*, 65.
12. *ibid.*, 329.
13. *ibid.*
14. *ibid.*, XCVIII, pt. II, 356.
15. Claude Blair, Preface to John Hewitt, *Ancient Armour* ... (1967), iv.
16. J.R. Planche, *The Recollections and Reflections* ... (1872), I, 53–4.
17. *ibid.*, 57.
18. *ibid.*, 223–4.
19. Alan Borg, 'Two Studies in the History of the Tower Armouries', *Archaeologia* (1976), CV, 321.
20. *ibid.*
21. *Gentleman's Magazine* (1827) XCVII, pt. I, 195–6.
22. Thomas Willement, *A Concise Account of the Principal Works in Stained Glass* ... (1840), 14.
23. 'A Letter Concerning the Horse Armoury at the Tower of London From Sir Samuel Rush Meyrick 1827', *Connoisseur* (1939), CIV, 91.
24. *Gentleman's Magazine* (1828), CVIII, pt. I, 463.
25. *ibid.*, (1848), CLXXXIV, pt. II, 93.
26. Samuel Rush Meyrick, *A Critical Inquiry into Antient Armour, as it existed in Europe but particularly in England* ... (1823), III, 137–8.
27. National Library of Scotland MS 3892.ff.85–6.
28. *ibid.*, 3893.f.7.
29. *ibid.*, 3895.ff.131–2.
30. Bodleian Library Douce MS d.24.f.149.
31. F. Grose, *The Antiquities of England and Wales* (1783–97), II, 238–42, pls. 107 & 108.
32. *Gentleman's Magazine* (1848), CLXXXIV, pt. II, 93.
33. Bodleian Library Douce MS d.26.f.100.
34. *Gentleman's Magazine* (1838), XCVIII, pt. I, 463.
35. Charles Nash, *The Goodrich Court Guide* (1845), 5–6. There is no copy of this guide, from which I shall frequently quote, in the Victoria & Albert Museum Library or the British Library. I know of

only one copy, which is in my collection.
36. Hugh Meller, 'The Architectural History of Goodrich Court, Herefordshire', *Transactions of the Woolhope Naturalists' Field Club* (1977), XLII, pt. II, 175–85.
37. I shall quote from three sources: Thomas Dudley Fosbroke, *The Wye Tour* ... [c.1842]; Thomas Roscoe, *Wanderings and Excursions in South Wales* ... (1837); and John Bernard Burke, *A Visitation of the Seats and Arms* ... (1853), II, 226. The Rev. Fosbroke, the author of the well-known *Encyclopaedia of Antiquities* is a very reliable source, for he knew Meyrick and was the vicar of Walford in Herefordshire near to Goodrich.
38. Bodleian Library Douce MS d.28.f.169.
39. *Gentleman's Magazine* (1828), XCVIII, pt. II, 357.
40. Roscoe, *Wanderings*, 107.
41. *ibid.*, 108.
42. Nash, *Guide*, 6.
43. Joseph Skelton, *Engraved Illustrations of Antient Arms and Armour, from the collection of Llewelyn Meyrick, Esq., LL.B. and F.S.A. at Goodrich Court, Herefordshire; after the drawings and with the Descriptions of Dr Meyrick* (1830), I, caption to pl. I.
44. *Gentleman's Magazine* (1827), CVII, pt. I, 56–7.
45. *ibid.* (1828), XCVIII, pt. I, 356–7.
46. Planche, *Recollections*, II, 145–6.
47. Skelton, *Antient Arms*, caption to pl. I.
48. Willement, *Principal Works*, 24.
49. Skelton, *Antient Arms*, caption to pl. I.
50. *ibid.*, iii.
51. Thomas Aymot, 'Letter from Thomas Aymot accompanying a transcript of two Rolls containing an inventory of effects formerly belonging to Sir John Fastolffe', *Archaeologia* (1827), XXI, 236. Though not published until 1827, this paper was read at the Antiquaries Rooms on 19 May 1825.
52. Planche, *Recollections*, II, 269.
53. Skelton, *Antient Arms*, xxix.
54. *ibid.*, ii.
55. F.H. Cripps-Day, 'The Greatest Armour Collector of All Time, Ferdinand Archduke of Austria, 1529–1595', *Connoisseur* (1945), CXV, No. 496, 86–93.
56. Manfred Leithe-Jasper and Rudolf Distelberger, *Vienna: The Kunsthistorische Museum, the Treasury and the Collection of Sculpture and Decorative Arts* (1982), 97.
57. Skelton, *Antient Arms*, ii.
58. Meyrick, *Inquiry*, 142.
59. Iacobo Schrenckhio, *Augustissi morum Imperatorium ... in celebri Ambrasianae arcis Armamentario* ... (1601).
60. *A Catalogue of the very valuable Antiquarian and Historical Library of the late Sir Samuel Rush Meyrick ... Sotheby ... 20 July 1871 ...*, lot 948.
61. Jacob Schrencken, *Ambrasische Helden Rust Kammer* ... (1735).
62. The book was John George Keysler, *Travels Through Germany, Bohemia, Hungary* ... (1760). The first edition was published in Hanover in 1741, but Keysler notes that he was at Ambras on 13 June 1729. This was lot 821 in the sale of the library.
63. *ibid.*, 36–8.
64. Laurin Luchner, *Denkmal eines Renaissancefursten versuch Rekonstruktion des Ambraser Museums von 1583* (1958).
65. Elisabeth Screicher, *Die Kunst und Wunderkammern der Habsburger* (1979).
66. Fosbroke, *Wye Tour*, 61.
67. Nash, *Guide*, 9.
68. Fosbroke, *Wye Tour*, 67.
69. Robert Melville Grindlay, *Scenery, Costumes and*

Architecture chiefly on the Western Side of India (1826).
70. Victoria & Albert Museum Library MS 86 NN. Box II.
71. *Catalogue of the whole of the remaining beautiful works of that great artist William Etty ... Christie ... May 14 1850.*
72. Victoria & Albert Museum Library MS 86 NN. Box II.
73. Nash, *Guide*, 9.
74. 'Tower of London', *Gentleman's Magazine* (1829), XCIX, pt. II, 629.
75. Nash, *Guide*, 9–10.
76. Skelton, *Antient Arms*, caption to pl. CXXXIII.
77. Fosbroke, *Wye Tour*, 68–9.
78. *A Companion to the Museum (Late Sir Aston Lever's)* ... (1790), 9.
79. *Catalogue of the Leverian Museum* ... The actual sale dates are unclear, but the fifty-seventh day was 10 July 1806. The cap was lot 11 on that day, and the sale lasted three further days.
80. *Part fourth: Catalogue of the London Museum of Natural History ... by Mr Bullock ... June 4 1819.*
81. Adrienne L. Kaeppler, 'Cook Voyage Provenance of the "Artificial Curiosities" of Bullock's Museum', *Man* (1974), IX, 68–92.
82. Skelton, *Antient Arms*, xxiii.
83. Nash, *Guide*, 11–13.
84. A Ledger of Willement's works from 1841 to 1865 survives in a private collection; this Goodrich work is described on p. 156.
85. Willement, *Principal Works*, 21.
86. Fosbroke, *Wye Tour*, 71–2.
87. Skelton, *Antient Arms*, caption to pl. III.
88. Nash, *Guide*, 13.
89. *Gentleman's Magazine* (1848), CLXXXIV, pt. II, 93.
90. Fosbroke, *Wye Tour*, 73–9.
91. Roscoe, *Wanderings*, 109–10.
92. Louisa Anne Twamley, *The Annual of British Landscape Scenery: An Autumn Ramble on the Wye* (1839), 109–10.
93. Nash, *Guide*, 14.
94. *ibid.*, 21.
95. *Library Catalogue* (see note 60).
96. Fosbroke, *Wye Tour*, 64.
97. Willement Ledger, 156.
98. Nash, *Guide*, 23.
99. Fosbroke, *Wye Tour*, 64–5.
100. Planche, *Recollections*, I, 232.
101. An obituary appeared in the *Athenaeum* (1844), No. 848, 90–1.
102. Nash, *Guide*, 24.
103. Marie-Madeleine Gauthier, *Emaux Meridionaux: Catalogue international de l'oeuvre de Limoges* ... (1987), 175.
104. Samuel Rush Meyrick, 'Observations upon a Pair of Candlesticks and a Pix, both of the Twelfth Century, preserved at Goodrich Court Herefordshire', *Archaeologia* (1831), XXIII, 317.
105. Fosbroke, *Wye Tour*, 65–6.
106. Bodleian Library Douce MS d.27.f.20.
107. *ibid.*, f.23.
108. Fosbroke, *Wye Tour*, 66.
109. Clive Wainwright, 'Specimens of Ancient Furniture', *Connoisseur* (1973), CLXXXIV, No. 740, 105–13.
110. Henry Shaw, *Specimens of Ancient Furniture* ... (1836), 26.
111. C.J. Richardson, *Studies from Old English Mansions* ... (1848), IV, pl. 22.
112. Nash, *Guide*, 30.
113. Bodleian Library Douce MS d.27.f.75.
114. *ibid.*, f.150.

115. 'Obituary, Francis Douce, Esq., F.S.A.' *Gentleman's Magazine* (1834), CLVI, pt. II, 216.

116. Samuel Rush Meyrick, 'The Doucean Museum', *Gentleman's Magazine* (1836), CVI, pt. I, 245–53, 378–84, 585–90; and pt. II, 158–60, 378–84, 492–4, 598–601.

117. *ibid.*, pt. II, 379.

118. *ibid.*, 158.

119. N.X. Willemin, *Monuments français* . . . (1839), 21, pl. 30. The apparent discrepancy in dates — Douce died in 1834, Meyrick published this piece in 1836, yet Willemin's book is dated 1839 — is explained by the fact that the whole book was only published following its issue in parts over some years.

120. Marian Campbell, ' "Scribe faber lima": A Crozier in Florence Reconsidered', *Burlington Magazine* (1979), CXXI, No. 915, 364–9. See also Hayward Gallery, London, *English Romanesque Art, 1066–1200*, exh. cat. (1984), 282–3. I am indebted to Marian Campbell for her help with the history of this object.

121. Nash, *Guide*, 21–2.

122. *Gentleman's Magazine* (1836), CVI, pt. I, 378.

123. *A Catalogue of a Select and very beautiful assemblage of ancient and modern small sculptures and carvings and chasings . . . collected . . . by the Chevalier Franchi . . . Christie . . . May the 16, 1827 . . .*

124. Bodleian Library Douce MS e.66.

125. Alexandre Lenoir, *Musée des Monuments Français ou Description* . . . (1802), 159.

126. J.F. Hayward, 'The Erlangen Saddle Plate Designs', *Livrustkammaren* (1976–8), XIV, 248.

127. The catalogue of the 1984 exhibition at the Bodleian Library, *The Douce Legacy: An Exhibition to Commemorate the 150th Anniversary of the Bequest of Francis Douce (1757–1834)*, however, goes some way towards this.

128. Fosbroke, *Wye Tour*, 82–3.

129. Nash, *Guide*, 27.

130. *ibid.*, 28.

131. Fosbroke, *Wye Tour*, 87.

132. *ibid.*

133. These quotations are from Isaac's 'Waste Book' which is unpaginated, but starts in 1815. It is in a private collection.

134. *ibid.*

135. Some of Isaac's papers are in the Anglo-Jewish Archives in the Mocatta Library at University College, London. They are numbered 53/. The letter quoted is 53/178.

136. *ibid.*, 53/131.

137. Bodleian Library Douce MS d.28.f.169.

138. This letter is in the archives of Colnaghi, and I would like to thank Donald Garstang of Colnaghi for his kindness in providing me with a copy.

139. National Library of Scotland MS 3893.f.85.

140. Isaac Papers, 53/183.

141. *ibid.*, 53/193.

142. National Library of Scotland MS 3893.ff.7–8.

143. Willement Ledger, 93.

144. Burke, *Visitation*, 229.

145. This letter is in my collection.

146. *Gentleman's Magazine* (1848), CLXXXIII, pt. I, 58–60.

147. Meller, 'Architectural History of Goodrich'.

148. H.C. Moffatt, *Illustrated Description of some of the Furniture at Goodrich Court Herefordshire and Hamptworth Lodge Wiltshire* (1928).

149. J.R. Planche, *Some Account of the Armour and Weapons, Exhibited Amongst the Art Treasure of the United Kingdom at Manchester in 1857* (1857), 17.

150. *ibid.*, 3.

151. Planche, *Recollections*, II, 270.

152. Arthur B. Chamberlain, *Hans Holbein the Younger* (1913), 181–2.

153. *Archaeologia Cambrensis* . . . (1846), I, 1–2.

154. *ibid.*, (1847), II, 359.

155. *Journal of the British Archaeological Association* (1847), II, 391.

156. Charles Roach Smith, *Retrospections Social and Archaeological* (1883), I, 41–3.

157. Nash, *Guide*, 34.

Notes to Chapter 10

1. Roy Strong, Marcus Binney & John Harris, *The Destruction of the Country House, 1875–1975* (1975), This book accompanied the exhibition held at the Victoria & Albert Museum.

2. Howard Colvin, *A Biographical Dictionary of British Architects, 1600–1840* (1978), 198–200.

3. His obituary appeared in the *Gentleman's Magazine* (1817), II, 363–8.

4. Susan Nicholson & Margaret Warhurst, *Joseph Mayer, 1803–1886* (1983), 77.

5. *Joseph Mayer of Liverpool, 1803–1886*, ed. Margaret Gibson & Susan M. Wright (1988).

6. *ibid.*, 199.

7. Elizabeth Mavor, *The Ladies of Llangollen* (1971), is the most thorough account.

8. *ibid.*, 175.

9. *ibid.*, 176.

10. S. & G. Nicholson, *Plas Newydd and Vale Crucis Abbey* (1824), 11.

11. *Plas Newydd as it was and is* . . . (1888), 4.

12. J.G. Lockhart, *Memoirs of the Life of Sir Walter Scott, Bart.* (1837), VI, 77.

13. My colleague at the Victoria & Albert Museum Simon Jervis has written the current guidebook to Browsholme and is working on a full study of Parker and his collections. Were this not the case I would have treated his important series of Romantic Interiors more fully here.

14. *Gentleman's Magazine* (1785) LV, 418.

15. Clive Wainwright, Intro. to *George Bullock, Cabinet-Maker* (1988), 15, 152.

16. *Gentleman's Magazine* (1841), CLXIX, 581–2.

17. *ibid.*, 584.

18. Sheena Stoddard, 'George Weare Braikenridge (1775–1856): A Bristol Antiquarian and his Collections', M.Phil. thesis, Bristol University (1986).

19. Sheena Stoddard, *Mr Braikenridge's Brislington*, exh. cat., Bristol Museum and Art Gallery (1981), 45. This exhibition catalogue includes the best published account of Braikenridge, his house and his collections.

20. *ibid.*, 25.

21. *Catalogue of the valuable collection of mediaeval carvings . . . A.W.N. Pugin . . . S. Leigh Sotheby & John Wilkinson . . . 12 February 1853 . . .*

22. Margaret H. Longhurst, *Victoria & Albert Museum catalogue of Carvings in Ivory* (1929), II, 22.

23. Rachel Hasted, *Scarisbrick Hall: A Guide* (1987).

24. *Illustrations; Landscape, Historical, and Antiquarian, to the Poetical Works of Sir Walter Scott, Bart.* (1834) This work has no printed pagination.

25. *ibid.*

26. *Chirk Castle Clwyd* (1988), 10.

27. Henry Bedingfeld, *Oxburgh Hall: The First 500 Years* (1982), 21.

28. 'Costessey Hall', *Norfolk Archaeology* (1914), XVIII, liv.

29. Maurice Drake, *The Costessey Collection of Stained Glass* . . . (1920).

30. T.B. Norgate, *The History of Costessey* (1972), 32.

31. *Gentleman's Magazine* (1833), CIII, pt. I, 534.

32. Harry E. Gunton, 'Costessey Brickworks', *Transactions of the Newcomen Society* (1968), XL, 165–8.

33. *Costessey Hall . . . Catalogue of the Important and valuable contents of the Mansion . . . George Cubitt . . . Dec 8,9,10,11 & 12, 1913 . . .* Cubitt was a Norwich auctioneer.

34. Edward Bulwer-Lytton, *Guidebook to Visitors of Knebworth* (1850).

35. Sybilla Jane Flower, 'Knebworth House, Hertfordshire, The Home of the Hon. David and Mrs Lytton Cobbold', *Country Life* (1985) CLXXVII, Nos. 4563–5, 244–8; 320–3; 374–7.

36. Clive Wainwright, 'The Dark Ages of English Art Revived: Edwards and Roberts and the Regency Revival', *Connoisseur* (1978), CXCVIII, No. 796, 95–105.

37. William Morris, *The Unpublished Lectures of William Morris*, ed. Eugene D. Lemire (1969), 80.

38. Horace Walpole, *The Yale Edition of Horace Walpole's Correspondence*, ed. W.S. Lewis (1974), XXXVIII, 206–7.

39. John Sainsbury, *The Napoleon Museum* . . . (1845), 2.

40. Charles L. Eastlake, *Hints on Household Taste in Furniture, Upholstery and other details* (1869), 121.

41. Robert W. Edis, *Decoration & Furniture of Town Houses* (1881), 126.

42. W.J. Loftie, *A Plea For Art In The House* . . . (1876), 21–2.

43. Beatrix Potter, *The Journal of Beatrix Potter*, ed. L. Lincler (1966), 90.

44. William Cobbett, *Rural Rides* (1985), 226–9. I am indebted to Paul Harrison for bringing this quote to my attention.

45. *William Morris and Kelmscott* (1981).

46. William Morris, *News from Nowhere* . . . (1924), 236–7.

47. William Morris, 'Gossip about an Old House on the Upper Thames', *Quest* (1895), No. IV, 9–14.

48. H. Byng Hall, *The Bric-à-Brac Hunter; or, Chapters on Chinamania* (1875), ix.

49. Leonard Willoughby, 'Lord Llangattock's Monmouth Seat: The Hendre and its Art Treasures', *Connoisseur* (1907), XVII, 149–58.

50. 'The Soulage Collection', *Art Journal* (1856), 381.

51. I am indebted to Elizabeth Bonython for information on Soulages.

52. Clive Wainwright, 'Models of Inspiration', *Country Life* (1988), CLXXXII, No. 23, 266–7.

53. J.C. Robinson, *Catalogue of the Soulages Collection* . . . (1856).

54. *Builder* (12 November 1864), 830–1. The Tennyson quotation is from *The Princess* (1847), 2.

55. Joseph Nash, *Descriptions of the Plates of the Mansions of England in the Olden Time* (1849), 55.

56. *The Star* (22 May 1913).

57. Stephen Bann, *The Clothing of Clio: A Study of the Representation of History in Nineteenth Century Britain and France* (1984), 92.

58. Pierre Bourdieu, *Distinction: A Social Critique of the Judgement of Taste* (1984), 77.

59. Geoffrey Crayon [Washington Irving], *Bracebridge Hall; or, The Humorists* (1822), I, 57–8.

INDEX

DATE DUE

DEMCO 38-297